This is the Last Page!

It's true: In keeping with the original Japanese comic format, this book reads from right to left—so action, sound effects and word balloons are completely reversed. This preserves the orientation of the original artwork—plus, it's fun! Check out the diagram shown here to get the hang of things, and then turn to the other side of the book to get started!

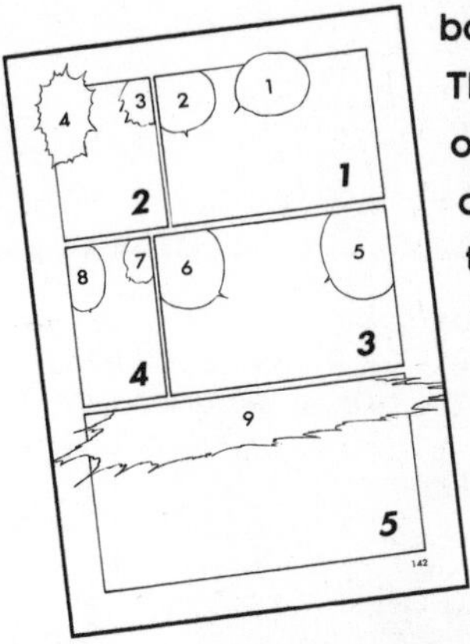
1
2
3
4
1
2
5
6
7
8
3
4
9
5
142

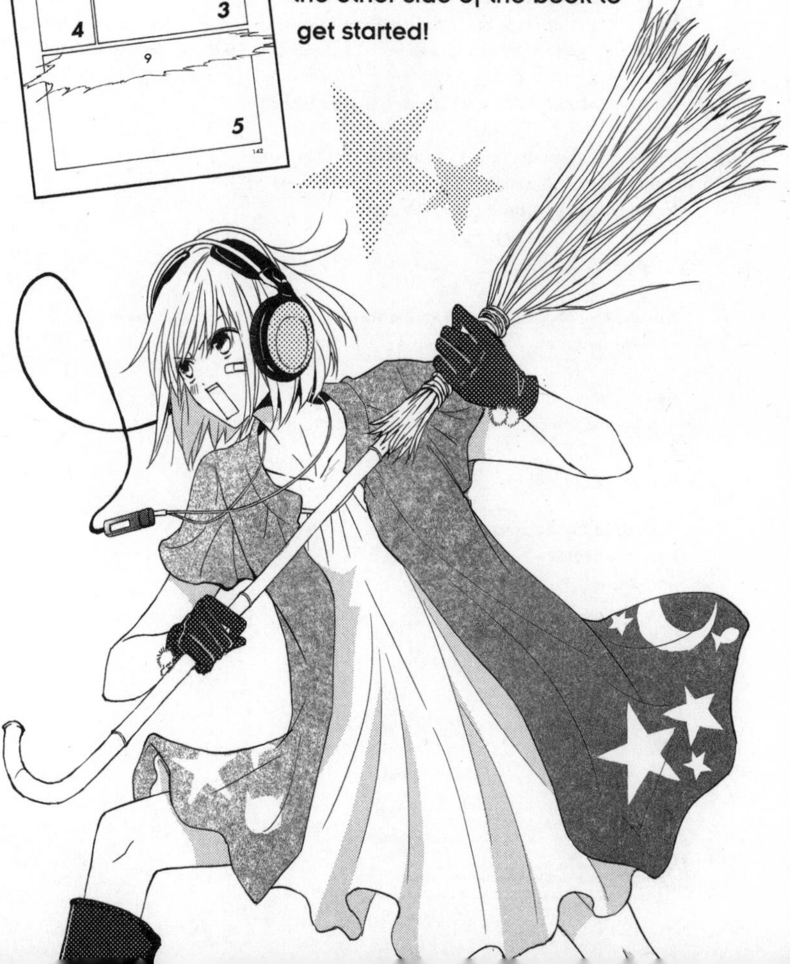

Queen's Quality

Vol. 8
Shojo Beat Edition

STORY AND ART BY
KYOUSUKE MOTOMI

QUEEN'S QUALITY Vol. 8
by Kyousuke MOTOMI
© 2016 Kyousuke MOTOMI
All rights reserved.
Original Japanese edition published by SHOGAKUKAN.
English translation rights in the United States of America, Canada, the United
Kingdom, Ireland, Australia and New Zealand arranged with SHOGAKUKAN.

ORIGINAL DESIGN/Chie SATO+Bay Bridge Studio

English Adaptation/Ysabet Reinhardt MacFarlane
Translation/JN Productions
Touch-Up Art & Lettering/Rina Mapa
Design/Julian [JR] Robinson
Editor/Amy Yu

Printed in the U.S.A.

Published by VIZ Media, LLC
P.O. Box 77010
San Francisco, CA 94107

10 9 8 7 6 5 4 3 2 1
First printing, December 2019

viz.com   shojobeat.com

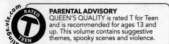

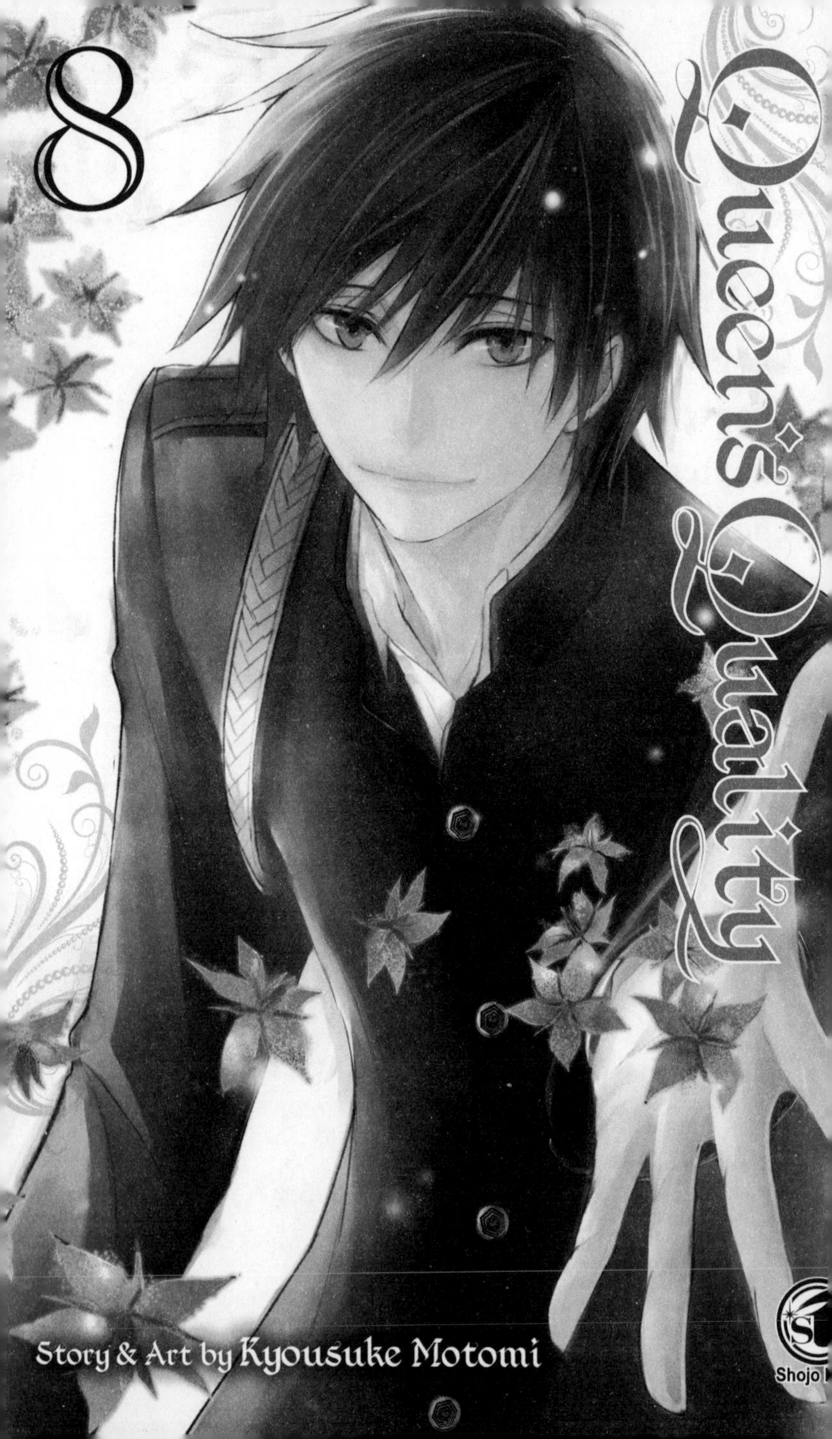
8
Queen's Quality
Story & Art by Kyousuke Motomi
Shojo

Queen's Quality

CONTENTS

Chapter 36 5

Chapter 37 43

Chapter 38 81

Chapter 39 119

Chapter 40 155

8

◇ Cast of ◆
  Characters

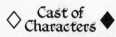

Fumi Nishioka

An apprentice
Sweeper with the
powers of a Queen,
this second-year high
school student dreams
of finding her very own
Prince Charming.

Kyutaro Horikita

A mind Sweeper who
cleanses people's
minds of dangerous
impurities. He's
incredibly awkward
with people, but he
has feelings for Fumi.

Ataru Shikata

A former bug handler
who uses bugs to
manipulate people.
Saved by Fumi and
Kyutaro, he has joined
the Genbu Clan.

Miyako Horikita

The prior head of the
Genbu Gate Sweepers.
She can be both strict
and kind, and she
watches over and
advises Fumi.

Koichi Kitagawa

The chairman of the
school Fumi and
Kyutaro attend. He's
a Sweeper as well
as being Kyutaro's
brother-in-law.

Takaya Kitahara

A psychiatrist who's
related to the Genbu
Gate Sweepers. He's
an expert with suggestive
therapy, and he
counsels Fumi.

◇   Story Thus Far   ◆

The Horikitas are a family of Sweepers—people who cleanse
impurities from human hearts. After seeing Fumi's potential, they
take her on as an assistant and trainee. Within Fumi dwells the
power of both the White and the Dark-Gray queens, both of
whom have the ability to give people immense power.

Ten years ago, during the Great Sickness of the Byakko Gate,
Takaya witnesses Kyutaro's father Yataro killing his wife Toko.
Yataro also put a spell on Kyutaro that would kill him if the
spell is lifted before the appropriate time. Yataro then leaves
with a young Fumi to teach her all she needs to know in order
to survive. Now Toko, who is inside Yataro's Corpse Vault, reveals
another truth...!

MONTHLY BETSUCOMI SALE DATE NOTICE ON TWITTER

CHAPTER 36

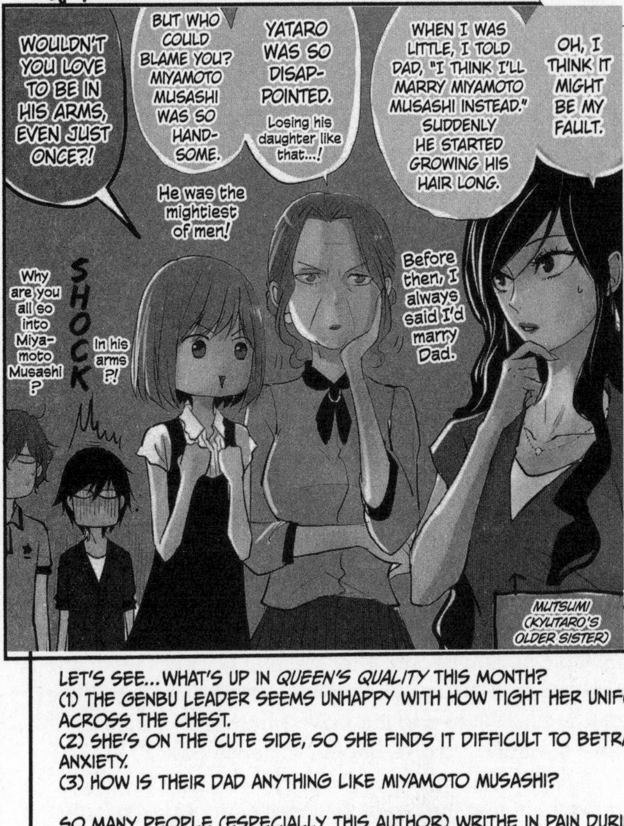
OH, I THINK IT MIGHT BE MY FAULT.
WHEN I WAS LITTLE, I TOLD DAD, "I THINK I'LL MARRY MIYAMOTO MUSASHI INSTEAD." SUDDENLY HE STARTED GROWING HIS HAIR LONG.
Before then, I always said I'd marry Dad.
YATARO WAS SO DISAPPOINTED.
Losing his daughter like that...!
BUT WHO COULD BLAME YOU? MIYAMOTO MUSASHI WAS SO HANDSOME.
He was the mightiest of men!
WOULDN'T YOU LOVE TO BE IN HIS ARMS, EVEN JUST ONCE?!
In his arms?!
SHOCK
Why are you all so into Miyamoto Musashi?
MUTSUMI (KYUTARO'S OLDER SISTER)

EVERYONE GOES THROUGH A PHASE OF FALLING IN LOVE WITH SOME HISTORICAL FIGURE, RIGHT? NO...? THIS AUTHOR'S FIRST LOVE WAS MINAMOTO NO YOSHITSUNE.

LET'S SEE...WHAT'S UP IN *QUEEN'S QUALITY* THIS MONTH?
(1) THE GENBU LEADER SEEMS UNHAPPY WITH HOW TIGHT HER UNIFORM IS ACROSS THE CHEST.
(2) SHE'S ON THE CUTE SIDE, SO SHE FINDS IT DIFFICULT TO BETRAY ANY ANXIETY.
(3) HOW IS THEIR DAD ANYTHING LIKE MIYAMOTO MUSASHI?

SO MANY PEOPLE (ESPECIALLY THIS AUTHOR) WRITHE IN PAIN DURING THE COURSE OF THIS CHAPTER OF REMINISCENCES.

I POST TWEETS LIKE THIS EVERY MONTH. YOU'LL FIND ME MUTTERING ABOUT OTHER SILLY STUFF TOO.

@motomikyosuke

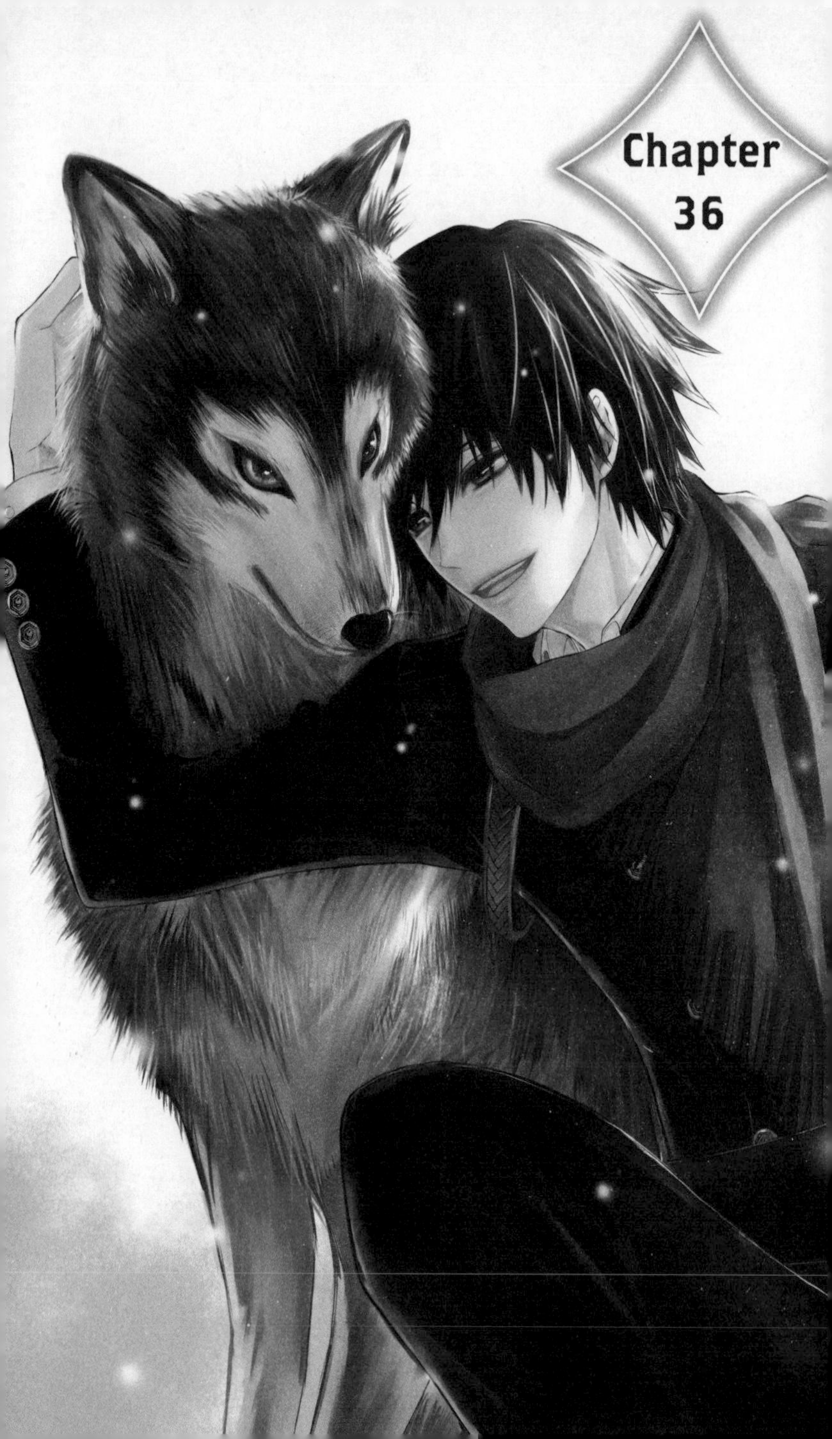
Chapter
36

Queen's Quality

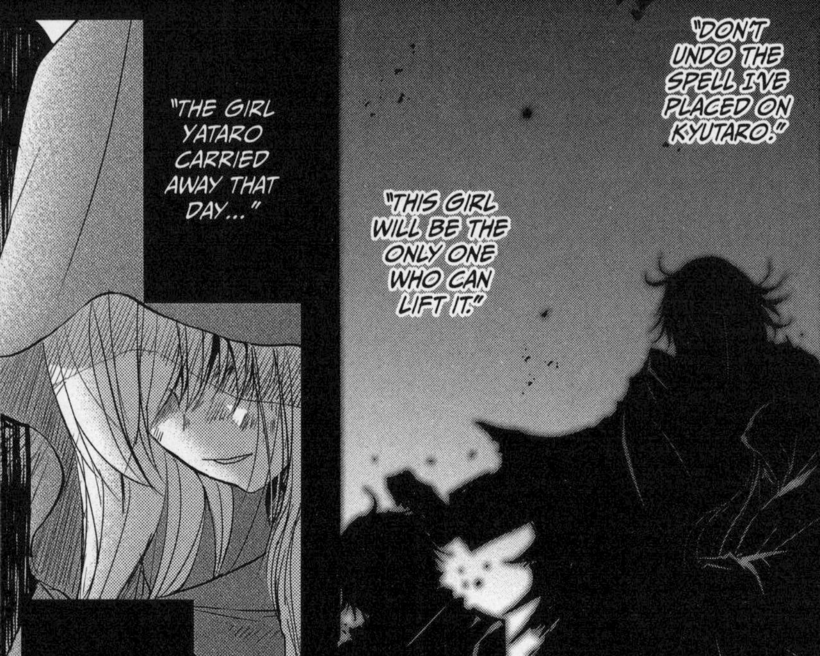
"DON'T UNDO THE SPELL I'VE PLACED ON KYUTARO."
"THIS GIRL WILL BE THE ONLY ONE WHO CAN LIFT IT."
"THE GIRL YATARO CARRIED AWAY THAT DAY..."
"...WAS YOU, FUMI."

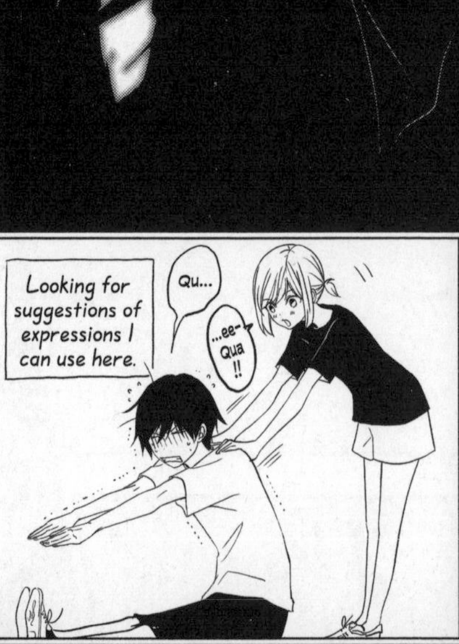
Looking for suggestions of expressions I can use here.
Qu...
...ee-Qua !!

Hello, everyone! Kyousuke Motomi here. Thank you for picking up volume 8 of *Queen's Quality*. I think you'll find many revelations and unbelievable twists in this volume. I hope you enjoy it!

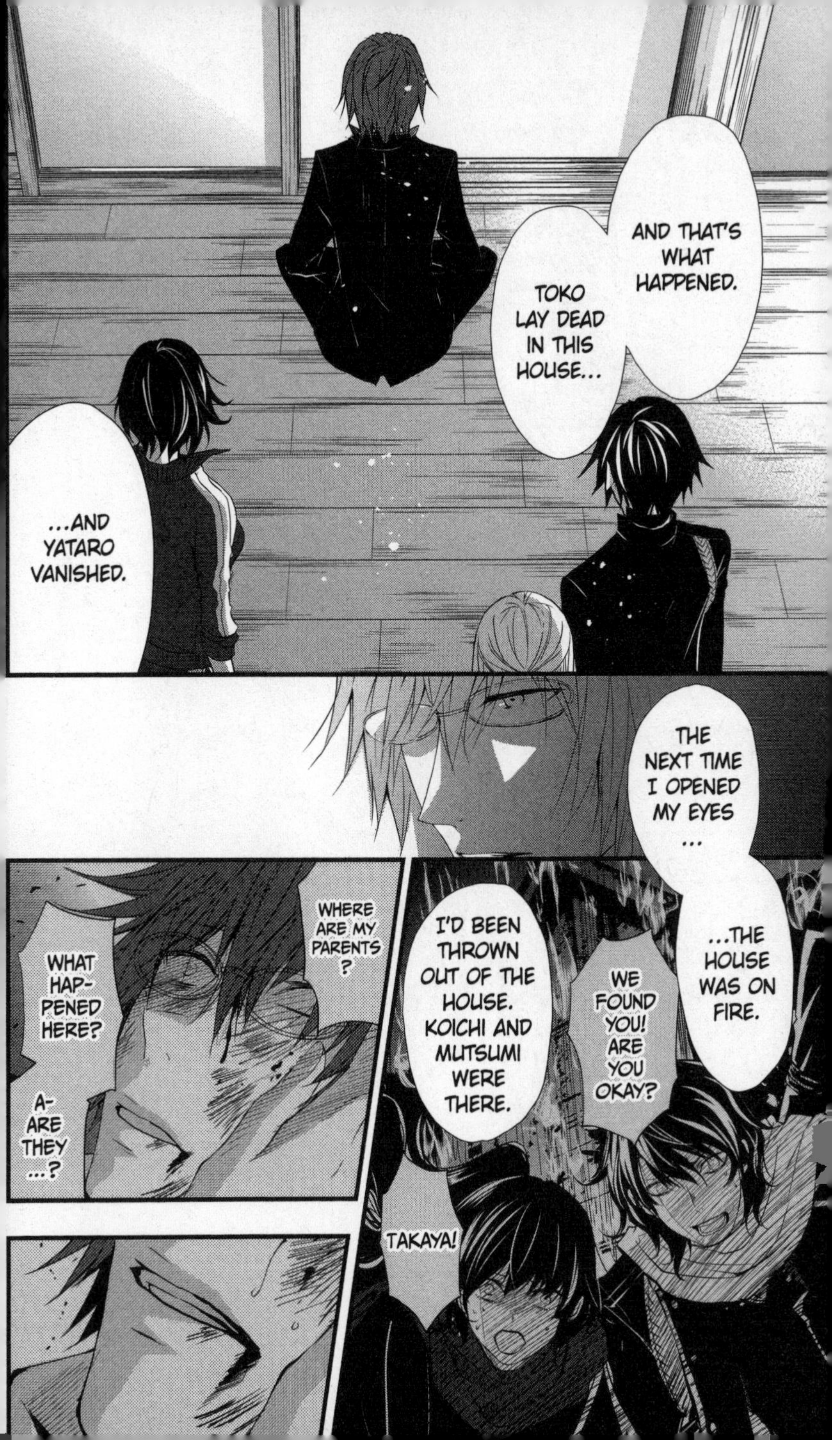
AND THAT'S WHAT HAPPENED.
TOKO LAY DEAD IN THIS HOUSE...
...AND YATARO VANISHED.
THE NEXT TIME I OPENED MY EYES ...
...THE HOUSE WAS ON FIRE.
WE FOUND YOU! ARE YOU OKAY?
I'D BEEN THROWN OUT OF THE HOUSE. KOICHI AND MUTSUMI WERE THERE.
TAKAYA!
WHERE ARE MY PARENTS?
WHAT HAP-PENED HERE?
A-ARE THEY ...?

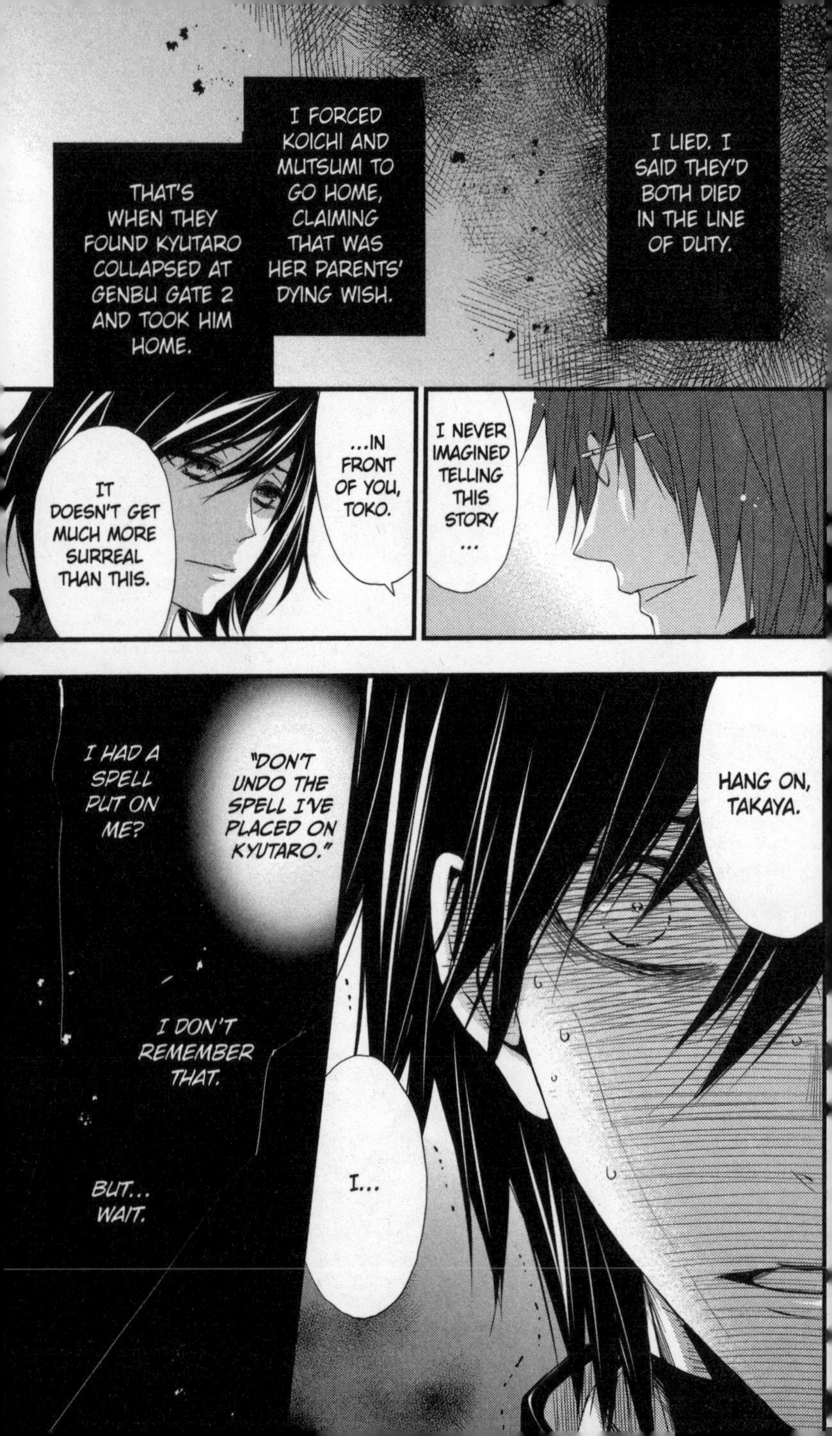
I LIED. I SAID THEY'D BOTH DIED IN THE LINE OF DUTY.
I FORCED KOICHI AND MUTSUMI TO GO HOME, CLAIMING THAT WAS HER PARENTS' DYING WISH.
THAT'S WHEN THEY FOUND KYUTARO COLLAPSED AT GENBU GATE 2 AND TOOK HIM HOME.
I NEVER IMAGINED TELLING THIS STORY ...
...IN FRONT OF YOU, TOKO.
IT DOESN'T GET MUCH MORE SURREAL THAN THIS.
HANG ON, TAKAYA.
"DON'T UNDO THE SPELL I'VE PLACED ON KYUTARO."
I HAD A SPELL PUT ON ME?
I DON'T REMEMBER THAT.
I...
BUT... WAIT.

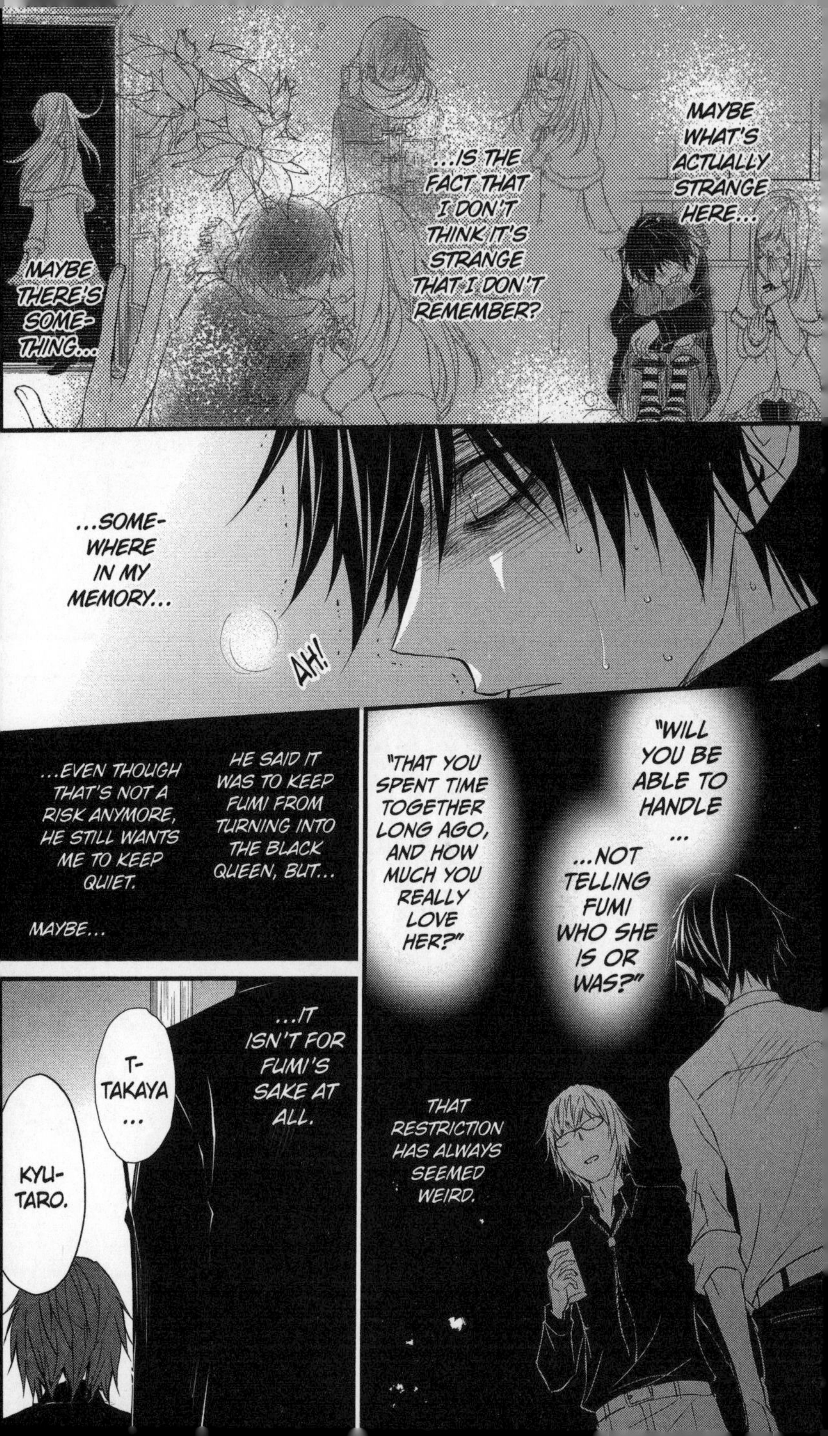
MAYBE WHAT'S ACTUALLY STRANGE HERE...
...IS THE FACT THAT I DON'T THINK IT'S STRANGE THAT I DON'T REMEMBER?
MAYBE THERE'S SOME-THING...
...SOME-WHERE IN MY MEMORY...
AH!
"WILL YOU BE ABLE TO HANDLE ...
...NOT TELLING FUMI WHO SHE IS OR WAS?"
"THAT YOU SPENT TIME TOGETHER LONG AGO, AND HOW MUCH YOU REALLY LOVE HER?"
THAT RESTRICTION HAS ALWAYS SEEMED WEIRD.
HE SAID IT WAS TO KEEP FUMI FROM TURNING INTO THE BLACK QUEEN, BUT...
...EVEN THOUGH THAT'S NOT A RISK ANYMORE, HE STILL WANTS ME TO KEEP QUIET.
MAYBE...
...IT ISN'T FOR FUMI'S SAKE AT ALL.
T-TAKAYA ...
KYU-TARO.

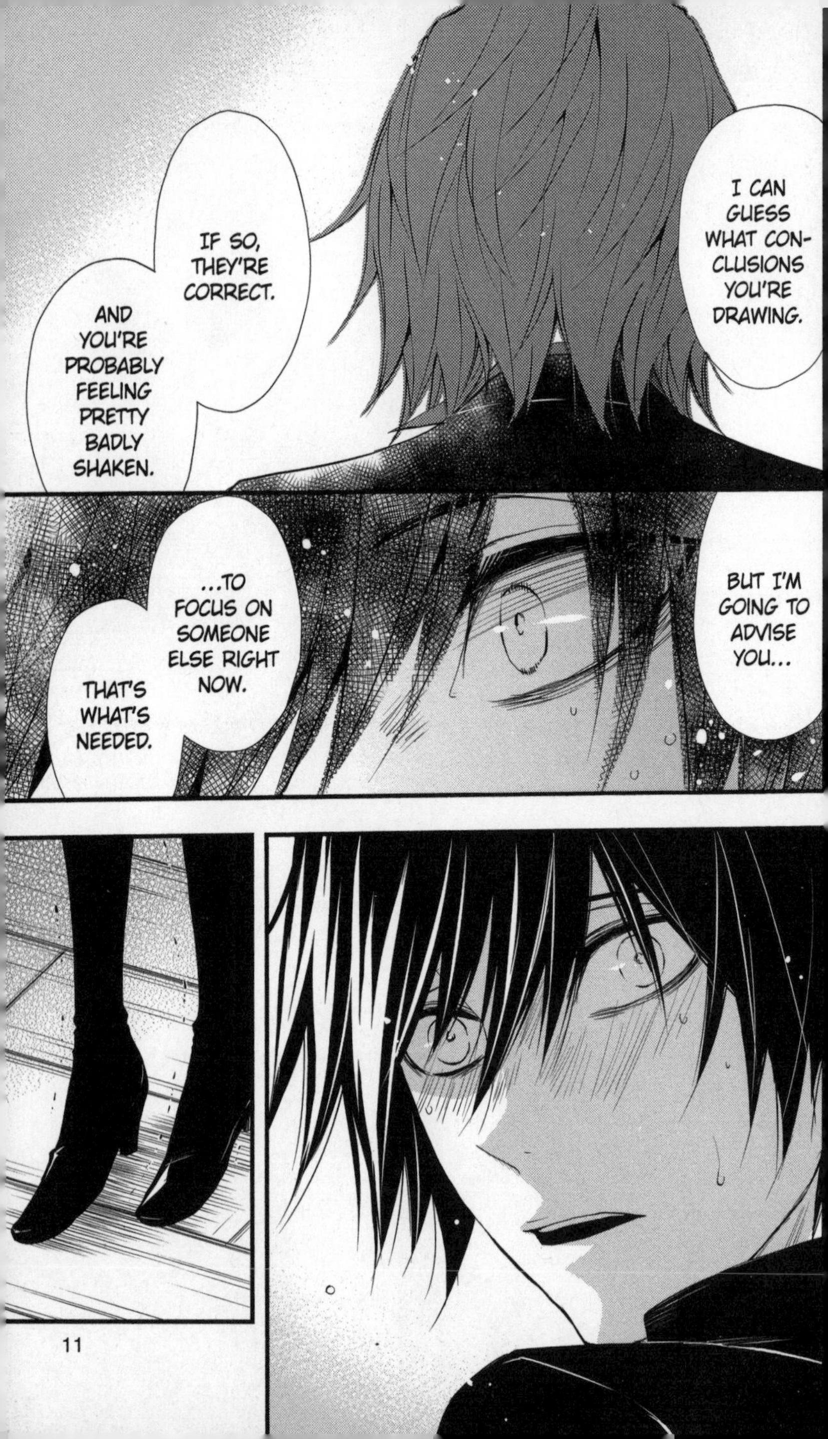
I CAN GUESS WHAT CON- CLUSIONS YOU'RE DRAWING.
IF SO, THEY'RE CORRECT.
AND YOU'RE PROBABLY FEELING PRETTY BADLY SHAKEN.
BUT I'M GOING TO ADVISE YOU...
...TO FOCUS ON SOMEONE ELSE RIGHT NOW.
THAT'S WHAT'S NEEDED.

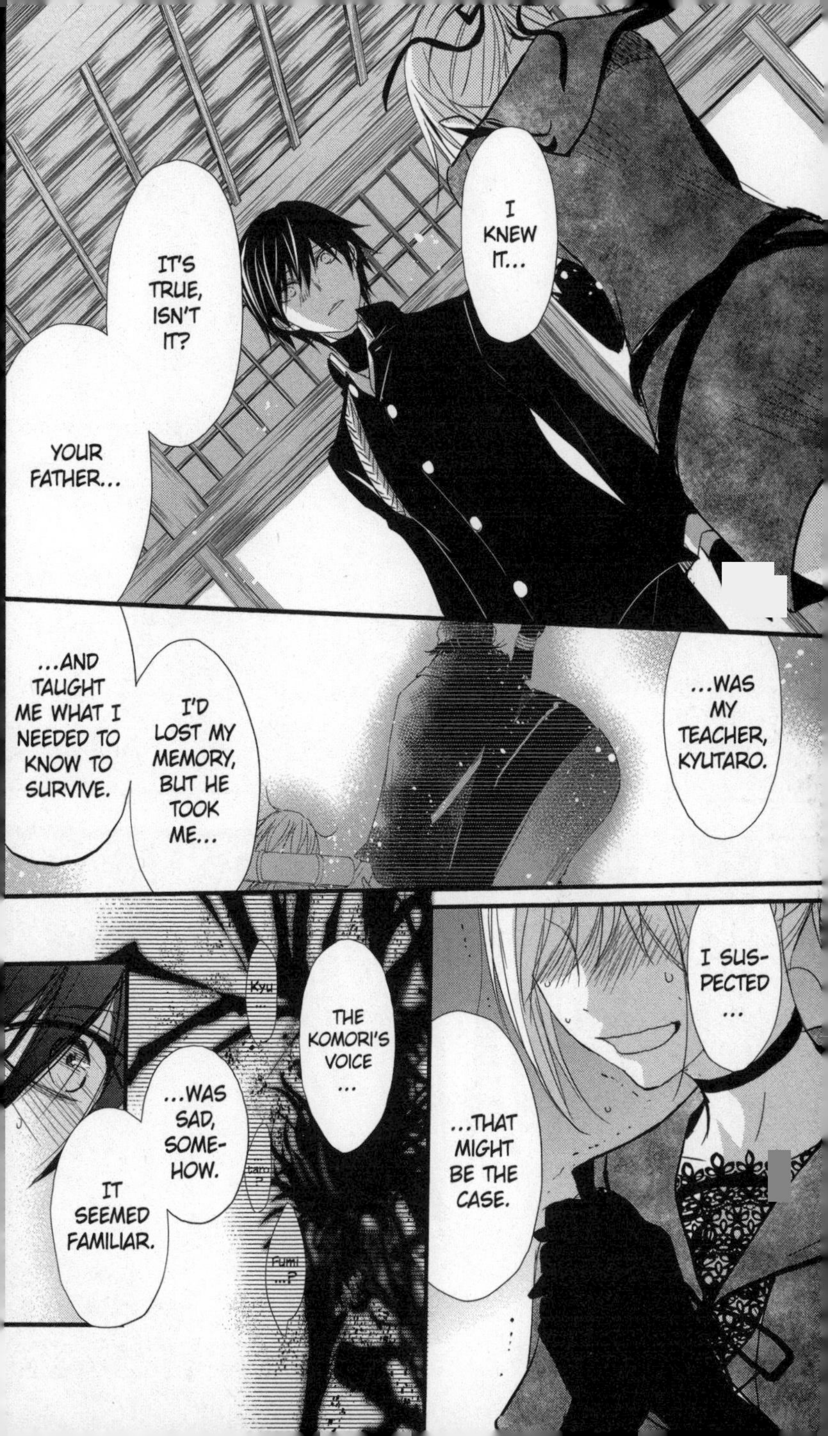
I KNEW IT...
IT'S TRUE, ISN'T IT?
YOUR FATHER...
...WAS MY TEACHER, KYUTARO.
I'D LOST MY MEMORY, BUT HE TOOK ME...
...AND TAUGHT ME WHAT I NEEDED TO KNOW TO SURVIVE.
I SUS-PECTED...
...THAT MIGHT BE THE CASE.
...
THE KOMORI'S VOICE...
Kyu...
...WAS SAD, SOMEHOW.
...taro?
IT SEEMED FAMILIAR.
Fumi...?

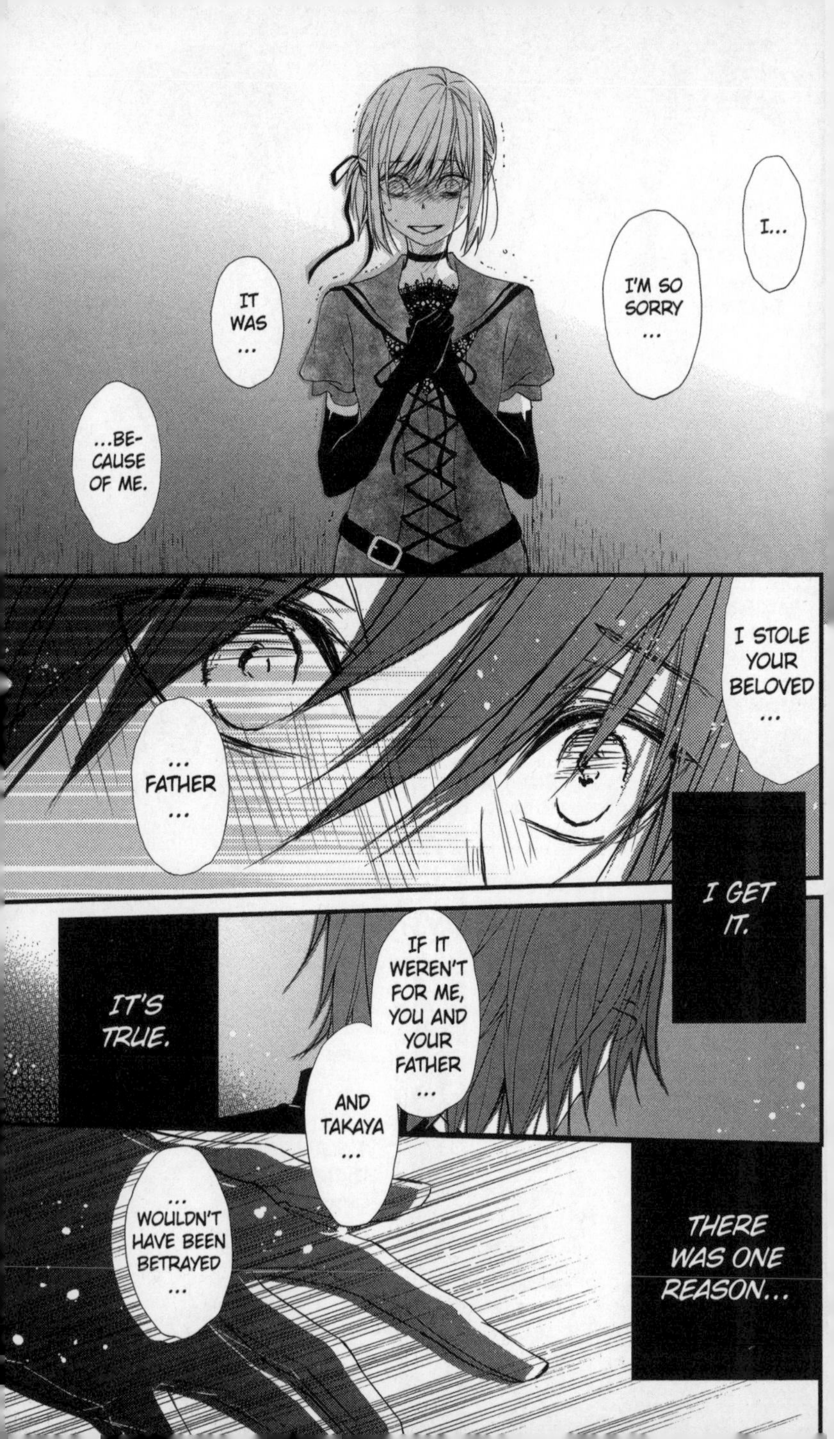
I...
I'M SO SORRY ...
IT WAS ...
...BE-CAUSE OF ME.
I STOLE YOUR BELOVED ...
... FATHER ...
I GET IT.
IF IT WEREN'T FOR ME, YOU AND YOUR FATHER ...
AND TAKAYA ...
IT'S TRUE.
THERE WAS ONE REASON...
... WOULDN'T HAVE BEEN BETRAYED ...

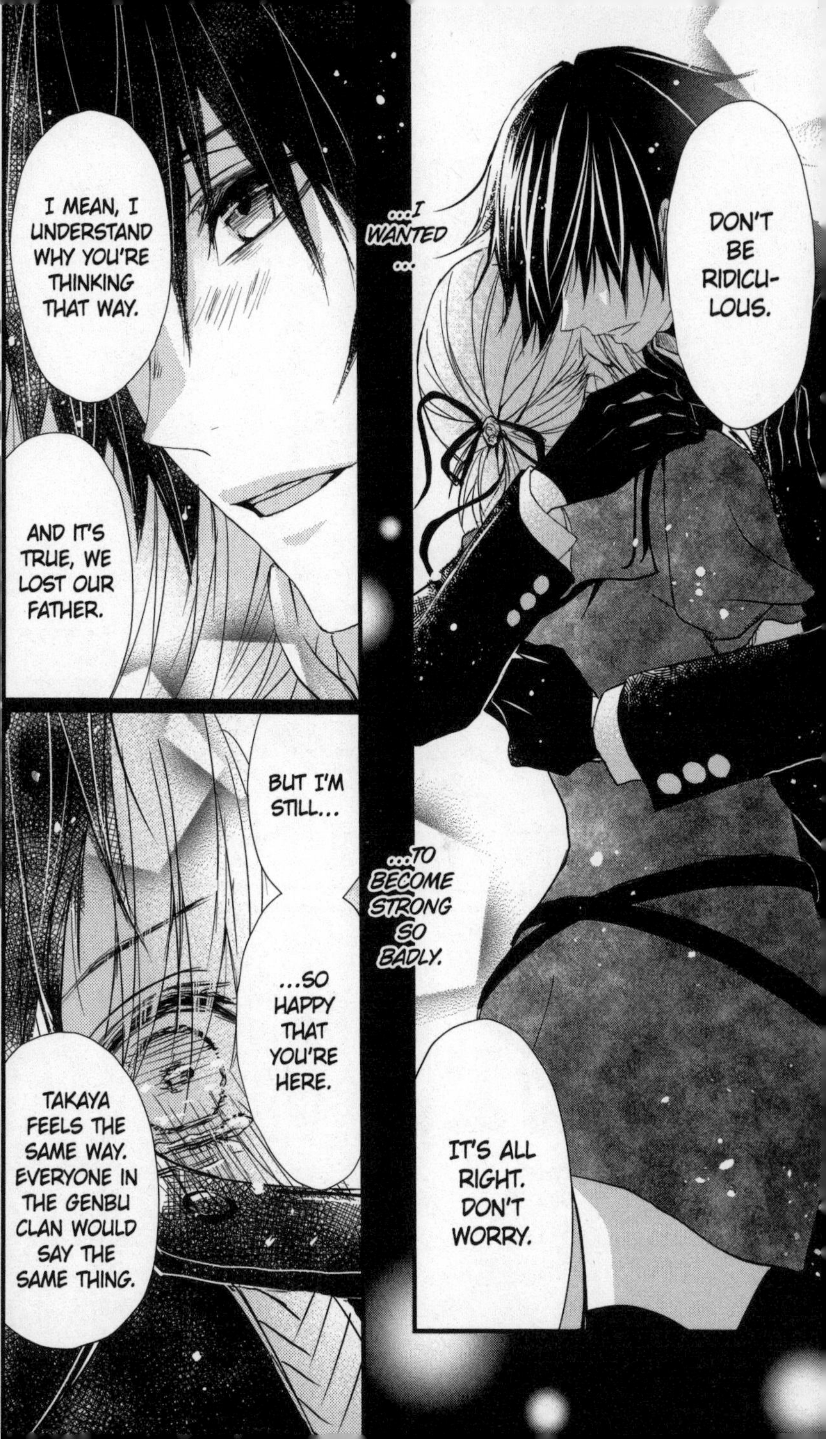
DON'T BE RIDICULOUS.
...I WANTED...
...TO BECOME STRONG SO BADLY.
IT'S ALL RIGHT. DON'T WORRY.
I MEAN, I UNDERSTAND WHY YOU'RE THINKING THAT WAY.
AND IT'S TRUE, WE LOST OUR FATHER.
BUT I'M STILL...
...SO HAPPY THAT YOU'RE HERE.
TAKAYA FEELS THE SAME WAY. EVERYONE IN THE GENBU CLAN WOULD SAY THE SAME THING.

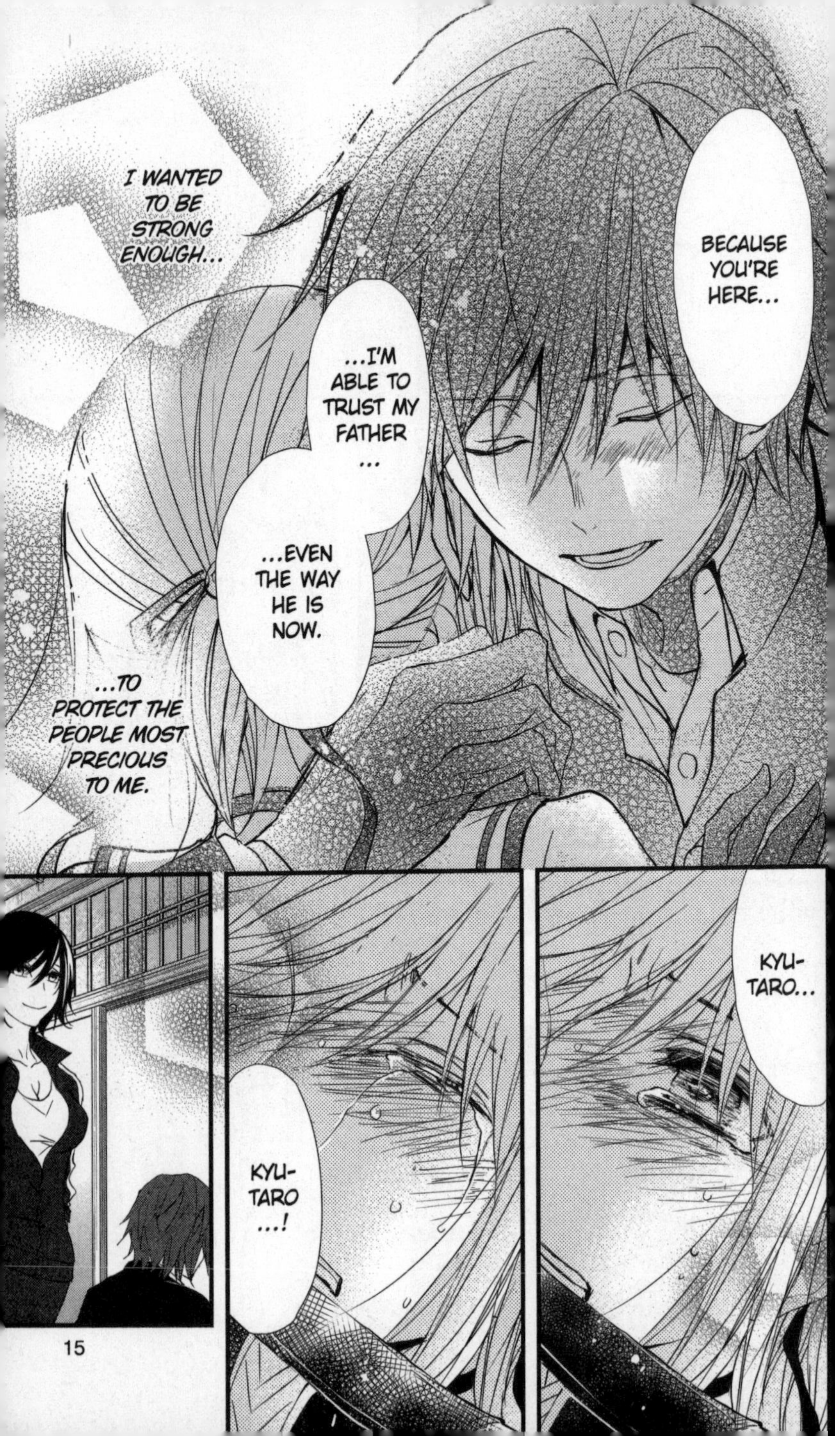
BECAUSE YOU'RE HERE...
...I'M ABLE TO TRUST MY FATHER ...
...EVEN THE WAY HE IS NOW.
I WANTED TO BE STRONG ENOUGH...
...TO PROTECT THE PEOPLE MOST PRECIOUS TO ME.
KYU-TARO...
KYU-TARO ...!

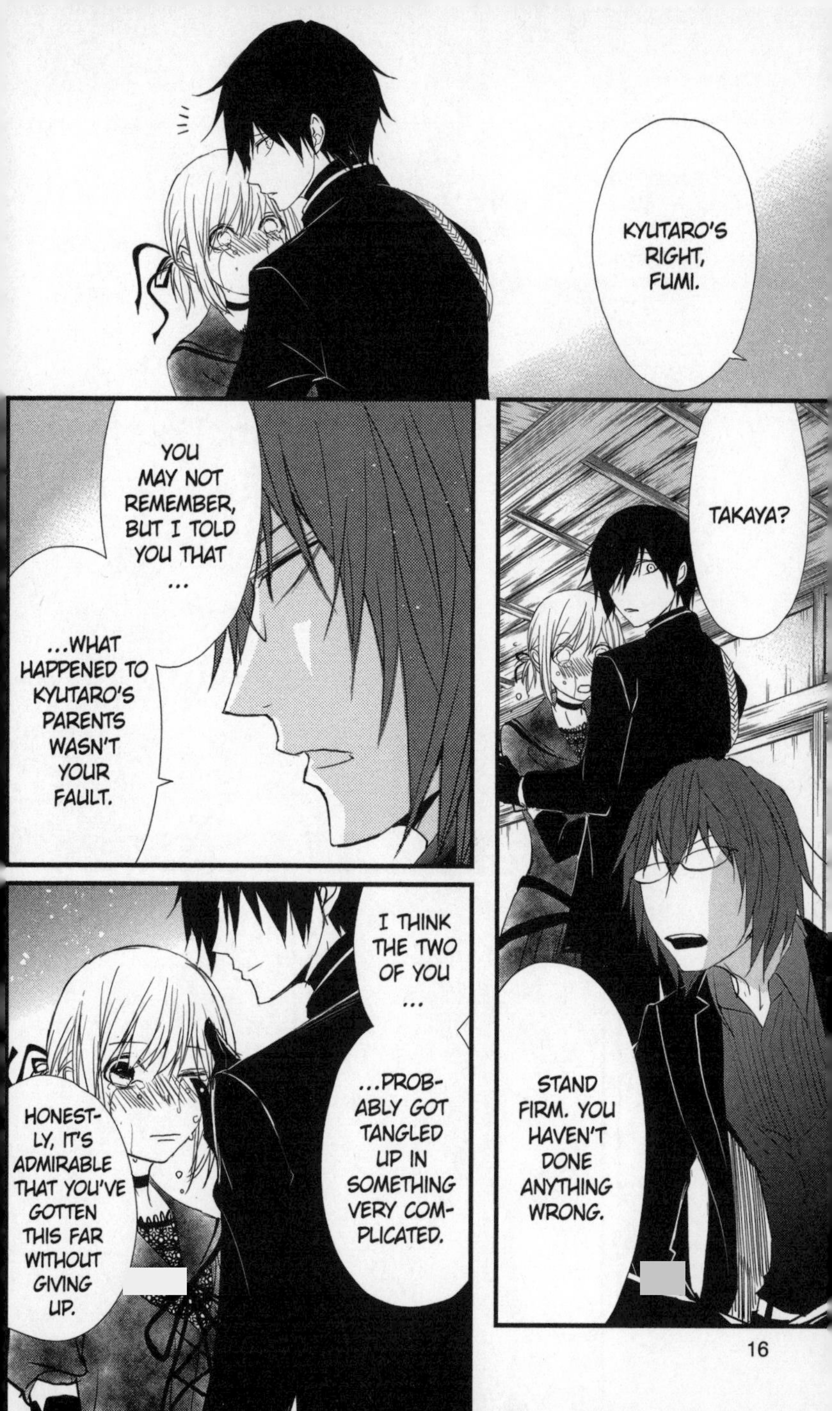
KYUTARO'S RIGHT, FUMI.
TAKAYA?
STAND FIRM. YOU HAVEN'T DONE ANYTHING WRONG.
YOU MAY NOT REMEMBER, BUT I TOLD YOU THAT ...
...WHAT HAPPENED TO KYUTARO'S PARENTS WASN'T YOUR FAULT.
I THINK THE TWO OF YOU ...
...PROBABLY GOT TANGLED UP IN SOMETHING VERY COMPLICATED.
HONESTLY, IT'S ADMIRABLE THAT YOU'VE GOTTEN THIS FAR WITHOUT GIVING UP.

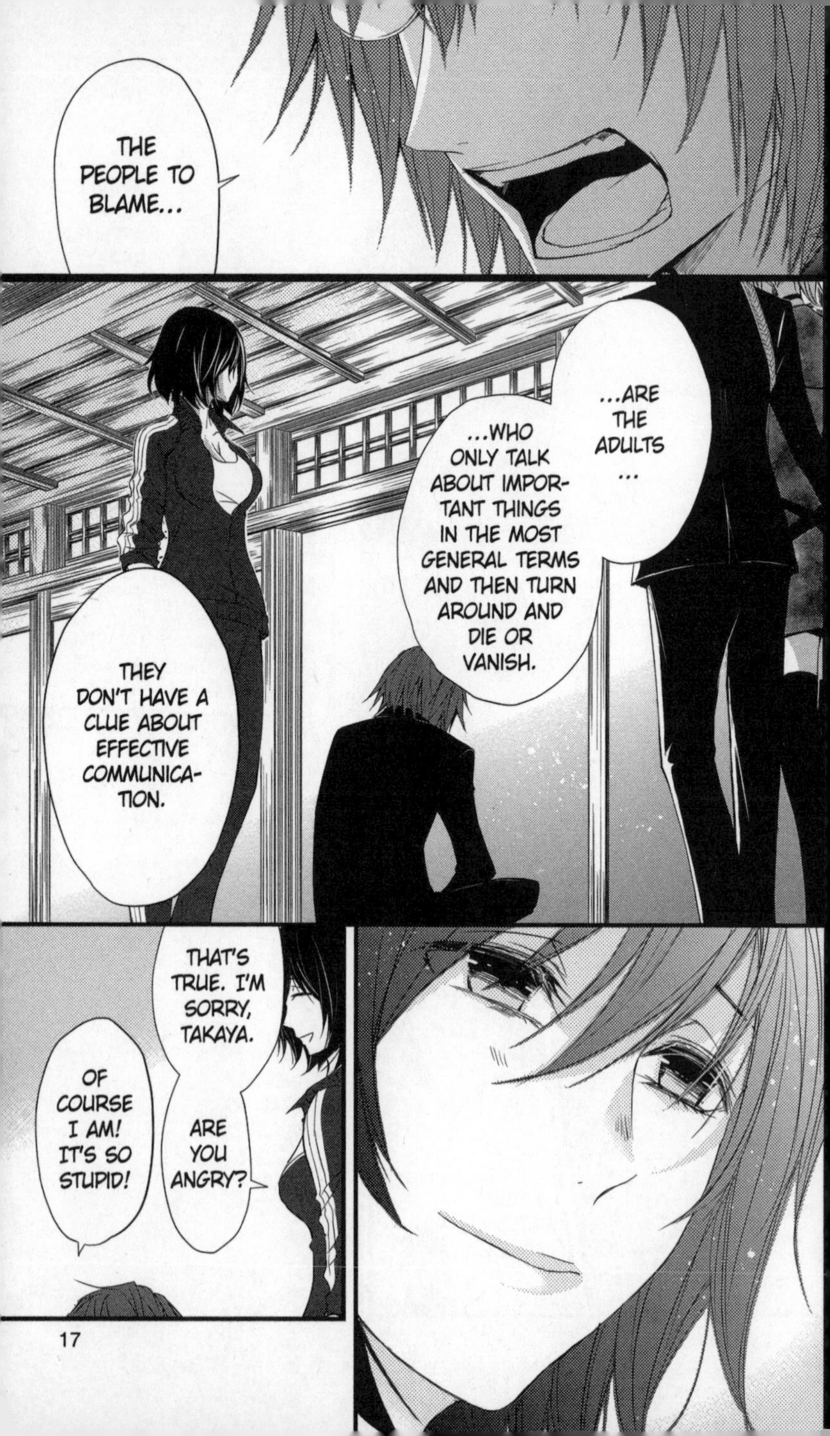
THE PEOPLE TO BLAME...
...ARE THE ADULTS ...
...WHO ONLY TALK ABOUT IMPORTANT THINGS IN THE MOST GENERAL TERMS AND THEN TURN AROUND AND DIE OR VANISH.
THEY DON'T HAVE A CLUE ABOUT EFFECTIVE COMMUNICATION.
THAT'S TRUE. I'M SORRY, TAKAYA.
ARE YOU ANGRY?
OF COURSE I AM! IT'S SO STUPID!

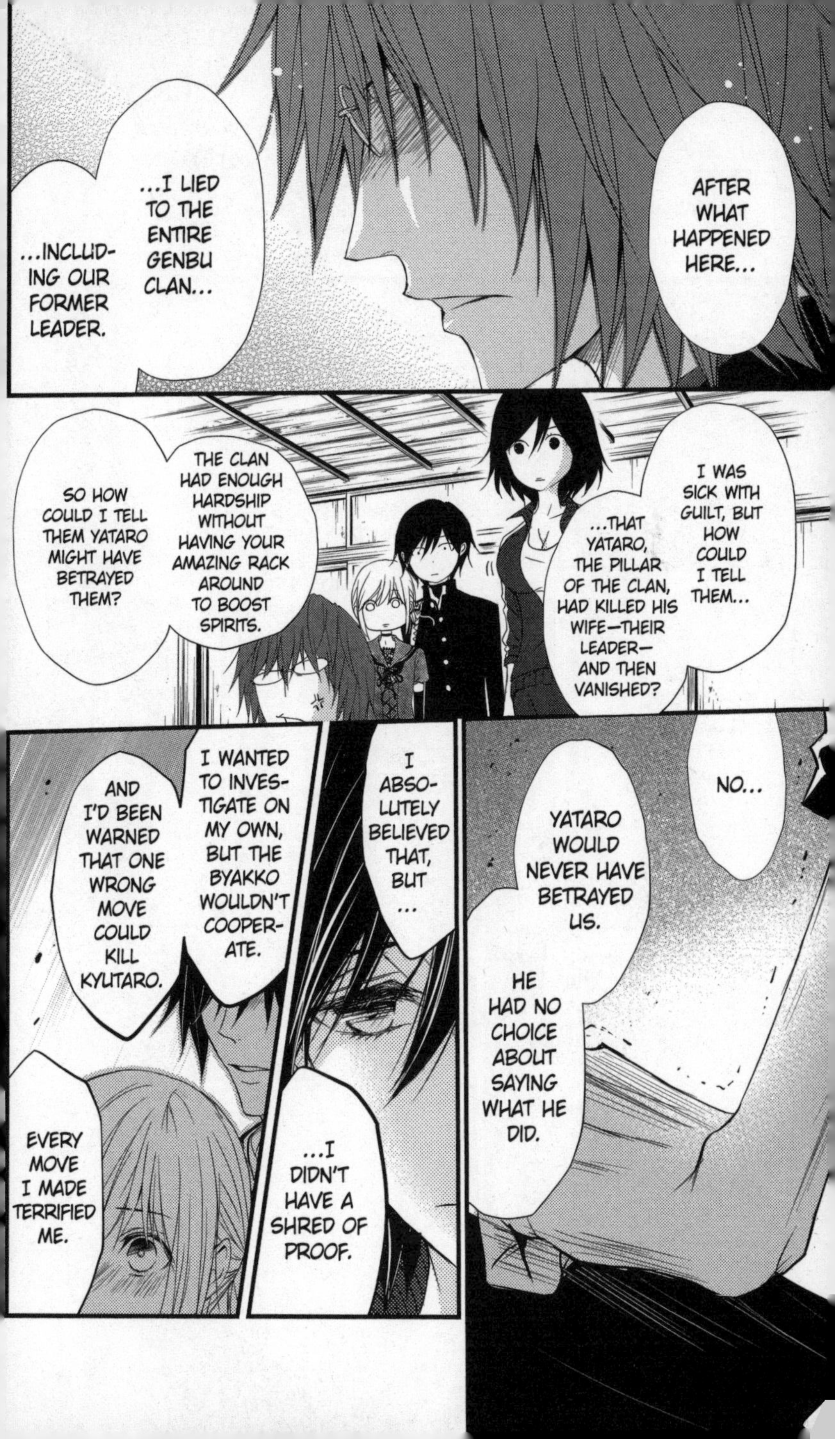
AFTER WHAT HAPPENED HERE...
...I LIED TO THE ENTIRE GENBU CLAN...
...INCLUDING OUR FORMER LEADER.
I WAS SICK WITH GUILT, BUT HOW COULD I TELL THEM...
...THAT YATARO, THE PILLAR OF THE CLAN, HAD KILLED HIS WIFE—THEIR LEADER—AND THEN VANISHED?
THE CLAN HAD ENOUGH HARDSHIP WITHOUT HAVING YOUR AMAZING RACK AROUND TO BOOST SPIRITS.
SO HOW COULD I TELL THEM YATARO MIGHT HAVE BETRAYED THEM?
NO...
YATARO WOULD NEVER HAVE BETRAYED US.
HE HAD NO CHOICE ABOUT SAYING WHAT HE DID.
I ABSOLUTELY BELIEVED THAT, BUT...
...I DIDN'T HAVE A SHRED OF PROOF.
I WANTED TO INVESTIGATE ON MY OWN, BUT THE BYAKKO WOULDN'T COOPERATE.
AND I'D BEEN WARNED THAT ONE WRONG MOVE COULD KILL KYUTARO.
EVERY MOVE I MADE TERRIFIED ME.

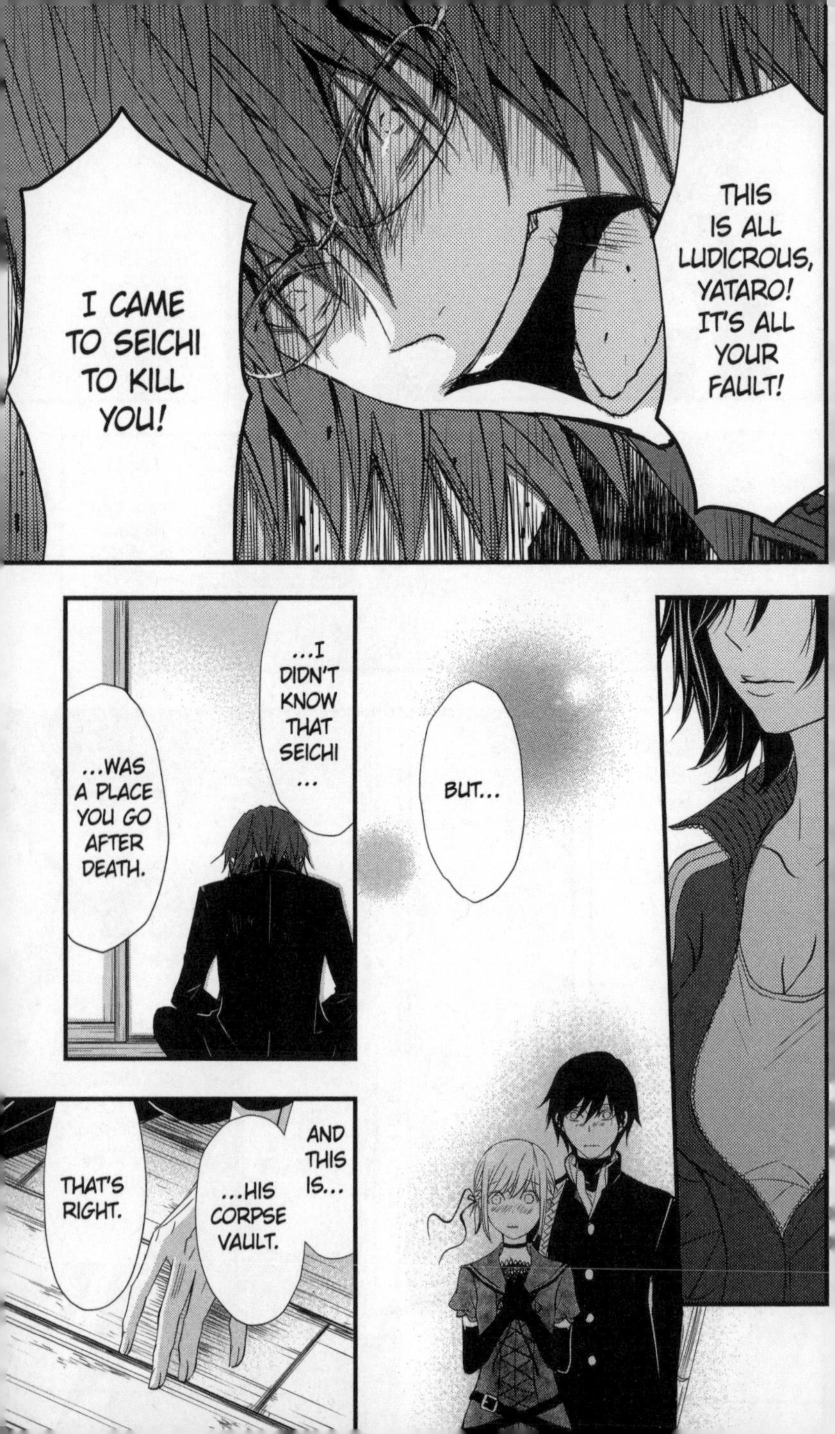
THIS IS ALL LUDICROUS, YATARO! IT'S ALL YOUR FAULT!
I CAME TO SEICHI TO KILL YOU!
BUT...
...I DIDN'T KNOW THAT SEICHI...
...WAS A PLACE YOU GO AFTER DEATH.
AND THIS IS...
...HIS CORPSE VAULT.
THAT'S RIGHT.

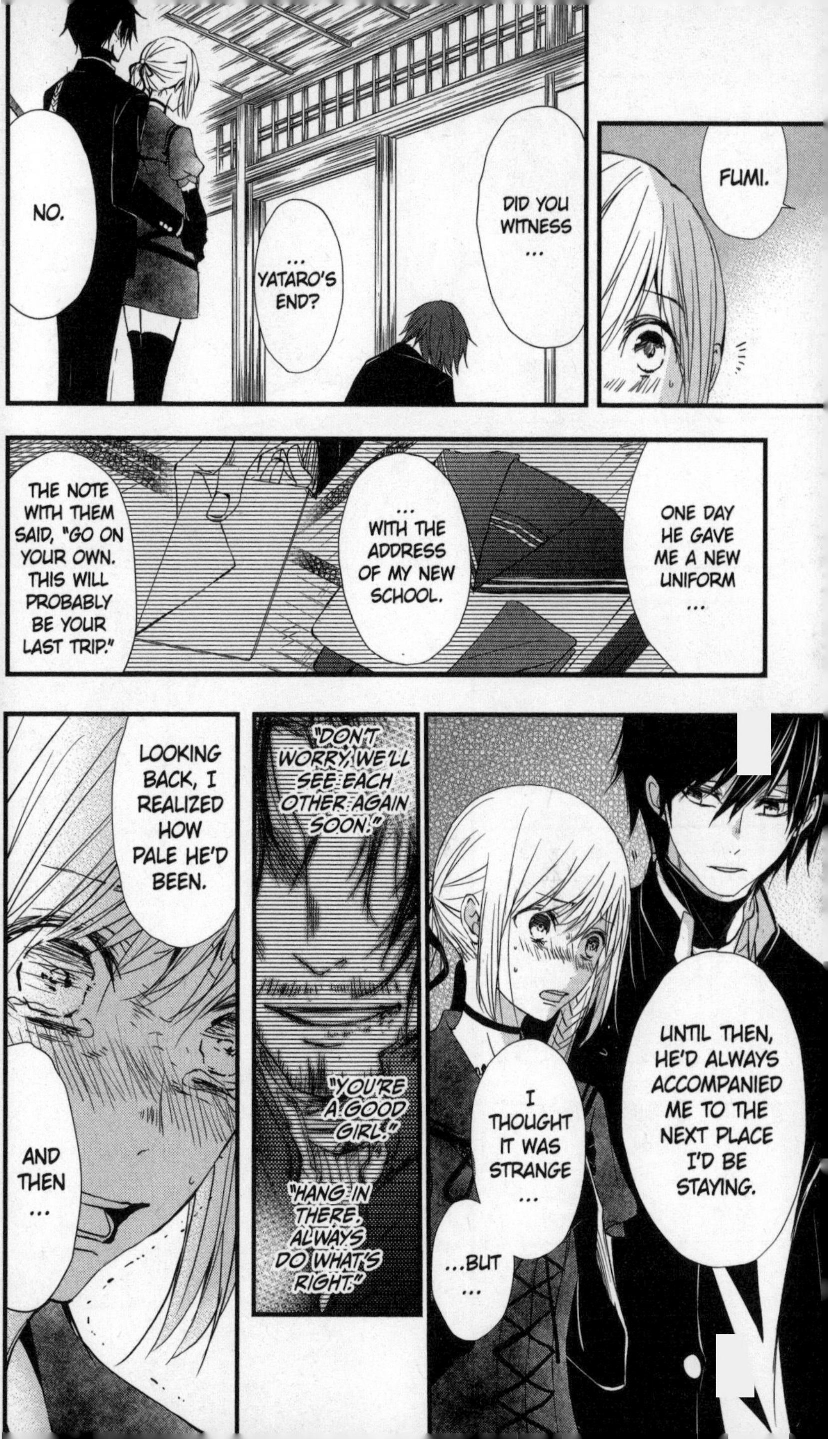
FUMI.
DID YOU WITNESS ...
... YATARO'S END?
NO.
ONE DAY HE GAVE ME A NEW UNIFORM ...
... WITH THE ADDRESS OF MY NEW SCHOOL.
THE NOTE WITH THEM SAID, "GO ON YOUR OWN. THIS WILL PROBABLY BE YOUR LAST TRIP."
UNTIL THEN, HE'D ALWAYS ACCOMPANIED ME TO THE NEXT PLACE I'D BE STAYING.
I THOUGHT IT WAS STRANGE ...
...BUT ...
"DON'T WORRY, WE'LL SEE EACH OTHER AGAIN SOON."
"YOU'RE A GOOD GIRL."
"HANG IN THERE. ALWAYS DO WHAT'S RIGHT."
LOOKING BACK, I REALIZED HOW PALE HE'D BEEN.
AND THEN ...

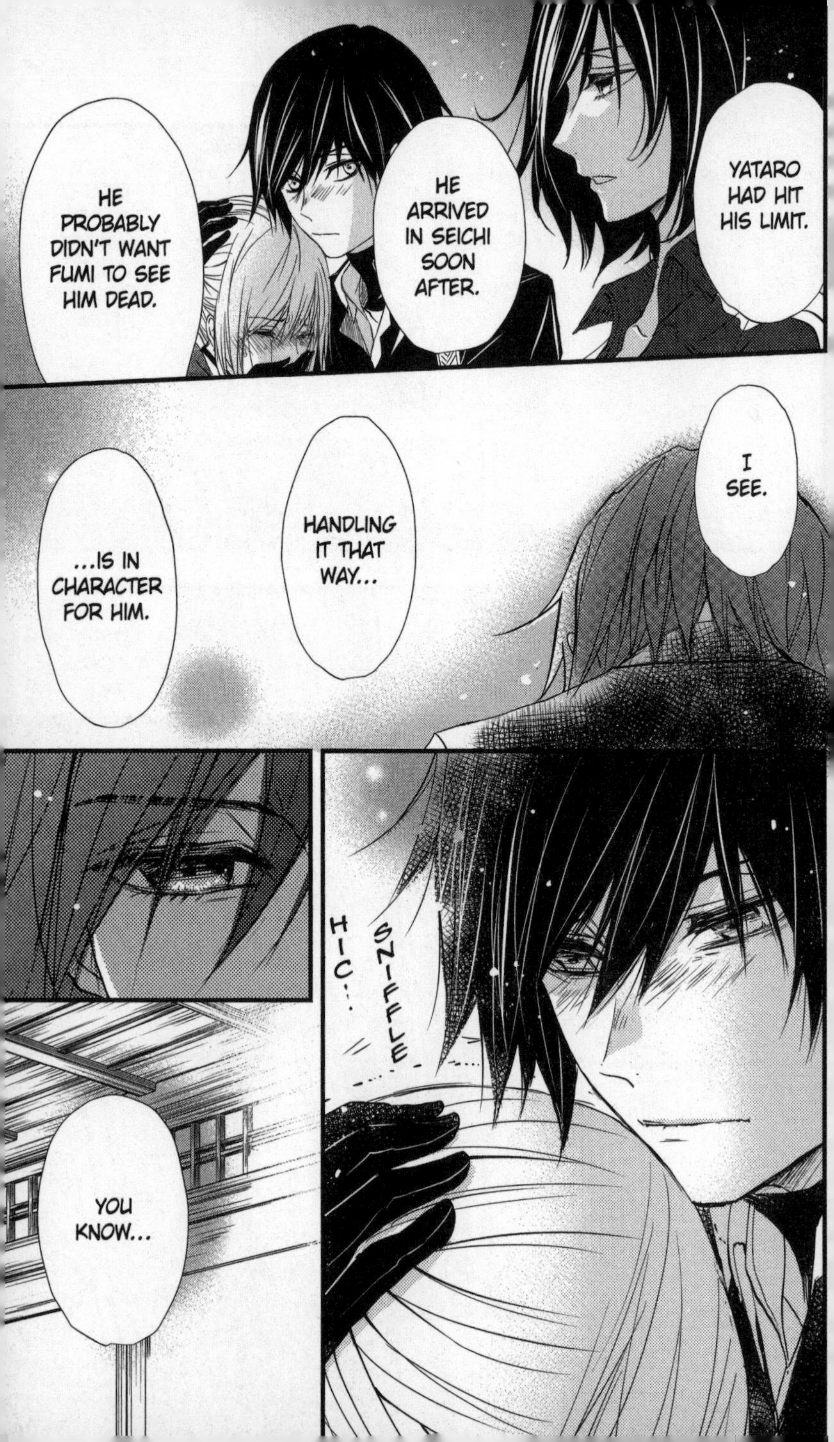
YATARO HAD HIT HIS LIMIT.
HE ARRIVED IN SEICHI SOON AFTER.
HE PROBABLY DIDN'T WANT FUMI TO SEE HIM DEAD.
I SEE.
HANDLING IT THAT WAY...
...IS IN CHARACTER FOR HIM.
SNIFFLE
HIC...
YOU KNOW...

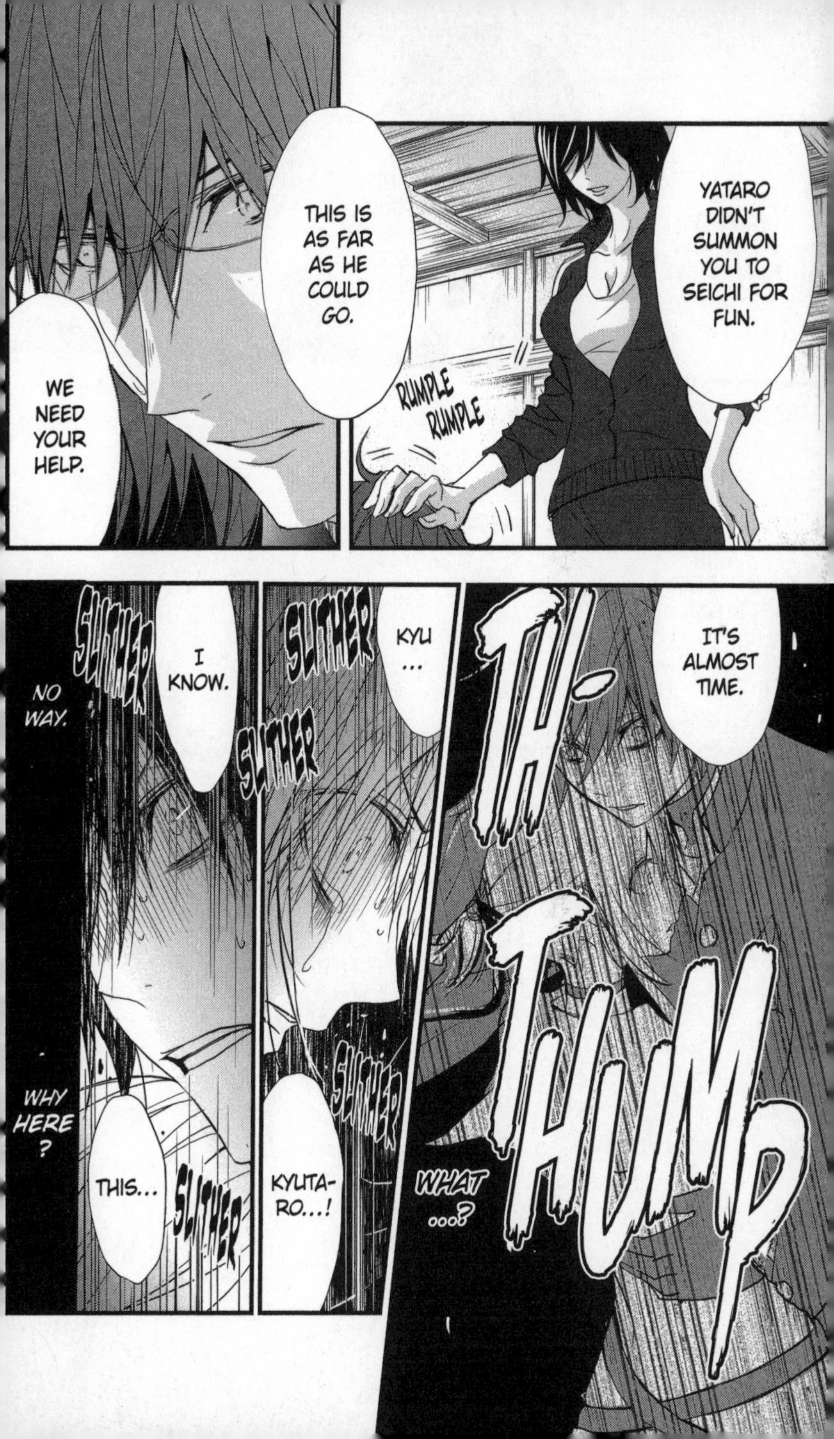
YATARO DIDN'T SUMMON YOU TO SEICHI FOR FUN.
RUMPLE RUMPLE
THIS IS AS FAR AS HE COULD GO.
WE NEED YOUR HELP.
IT'S ALMOST TIME.
TH-THUMP
WHAT...?
KYU...
SLITHER
SLITHER
SLITHER
KYUTA-RO...!
SLITHER
I KNOW.
NO WAY.
WHY HERE?
THIS...
SLITHER

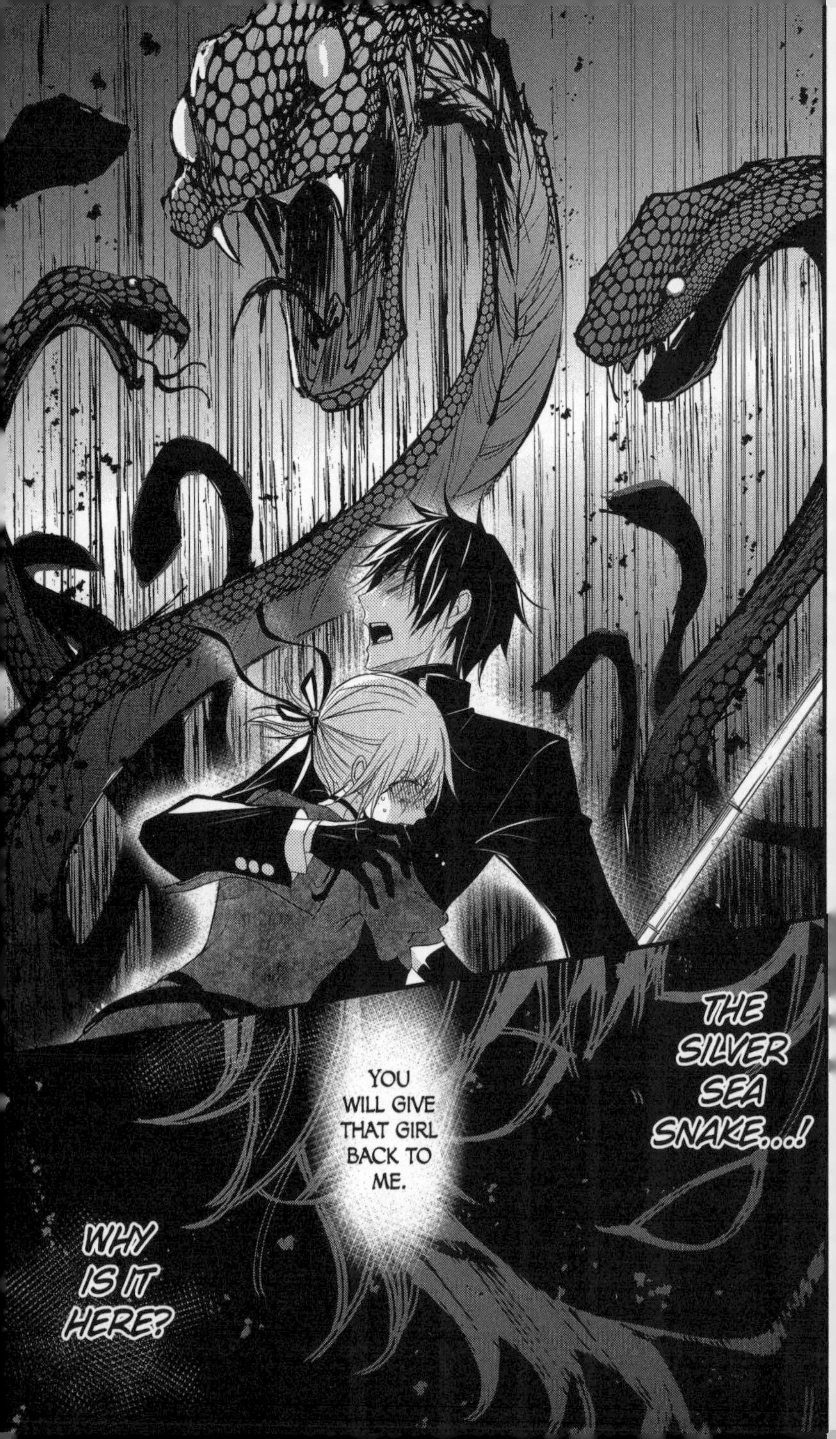
THE SILVER SEA SNAKE...!
YOU WILL GIVE THAT GIRL BACK TO ME.
WHY IS IT HERE?

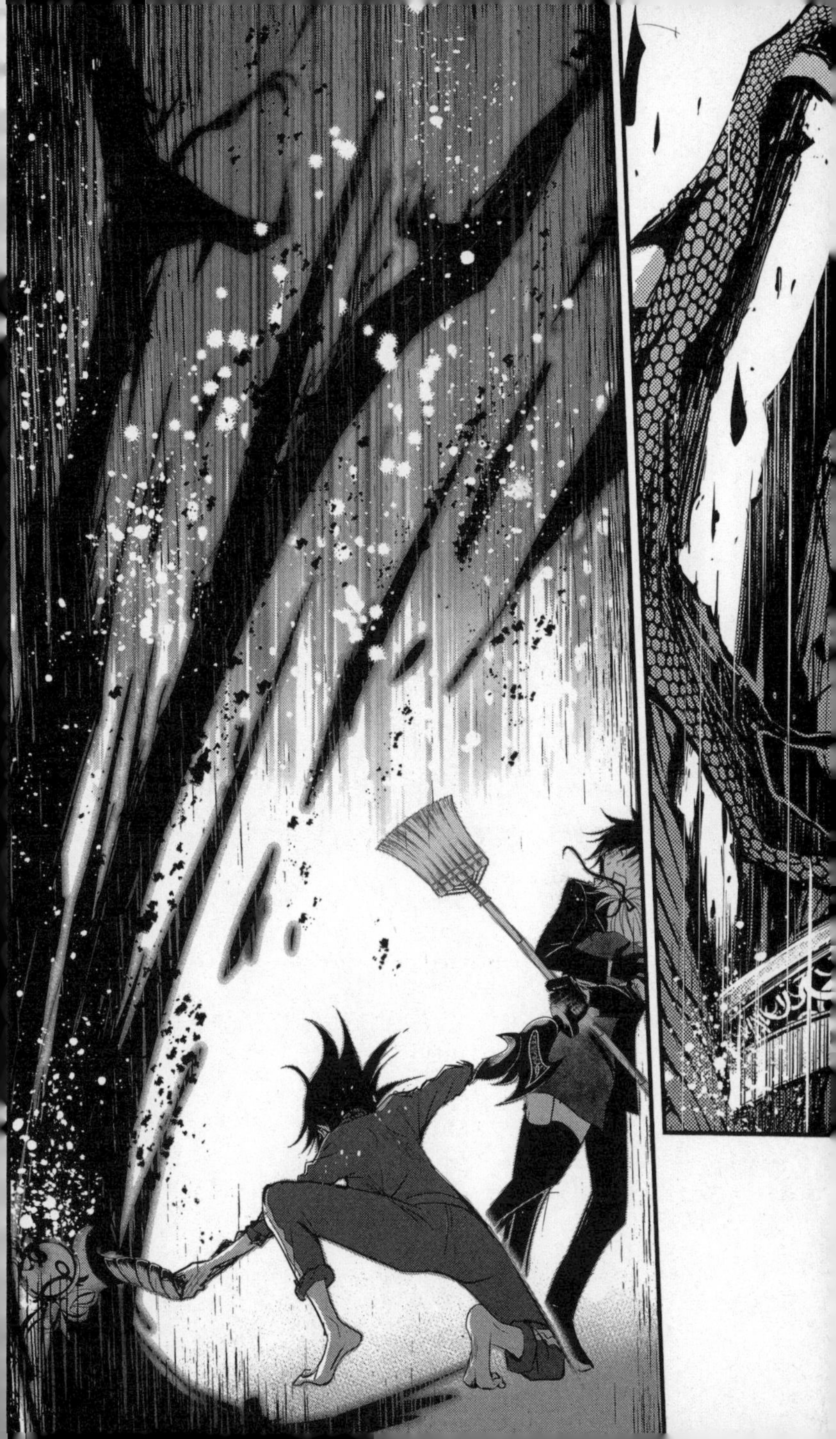

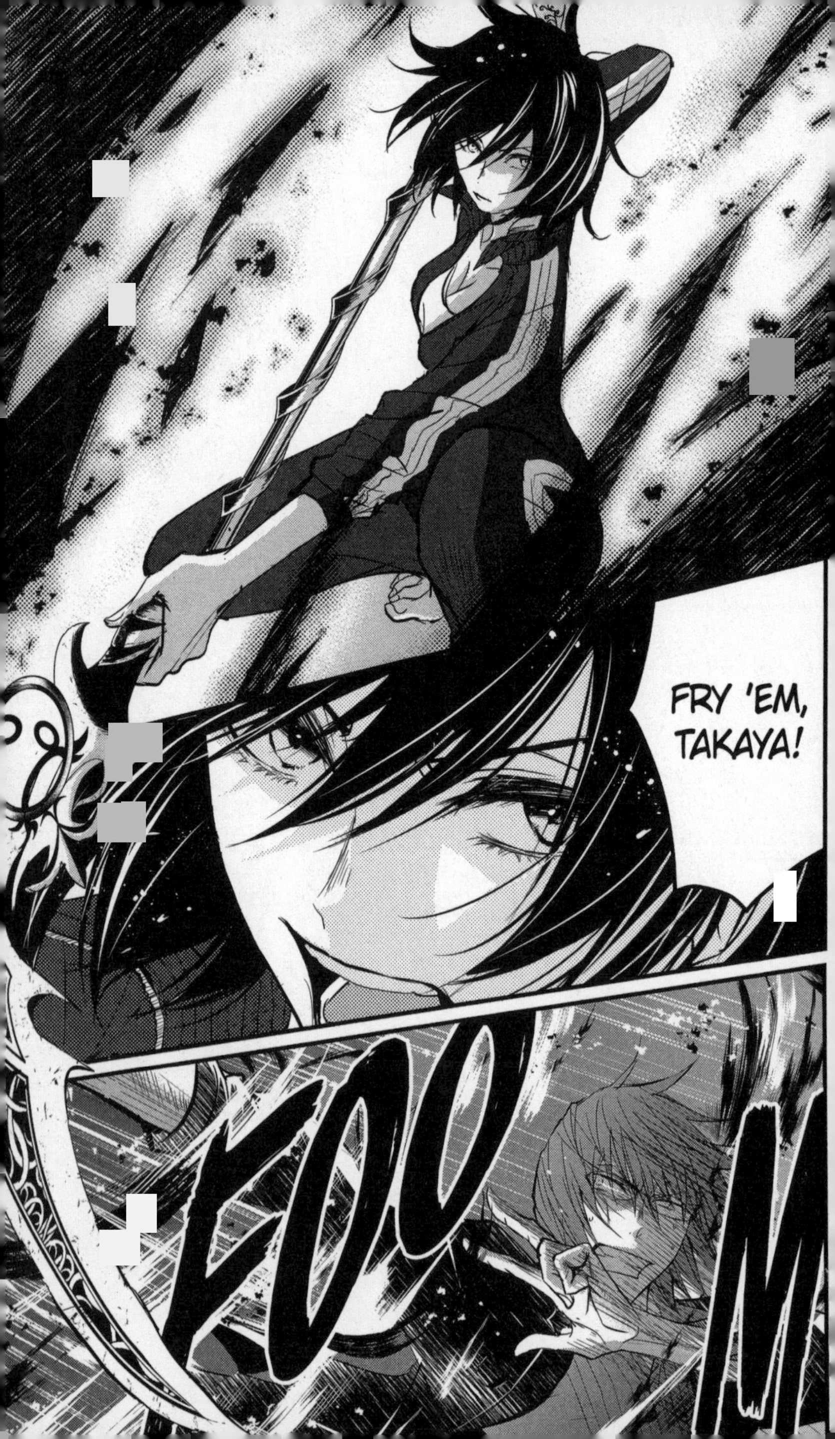
FRY 'EM, TAKAYA!
ZOOM

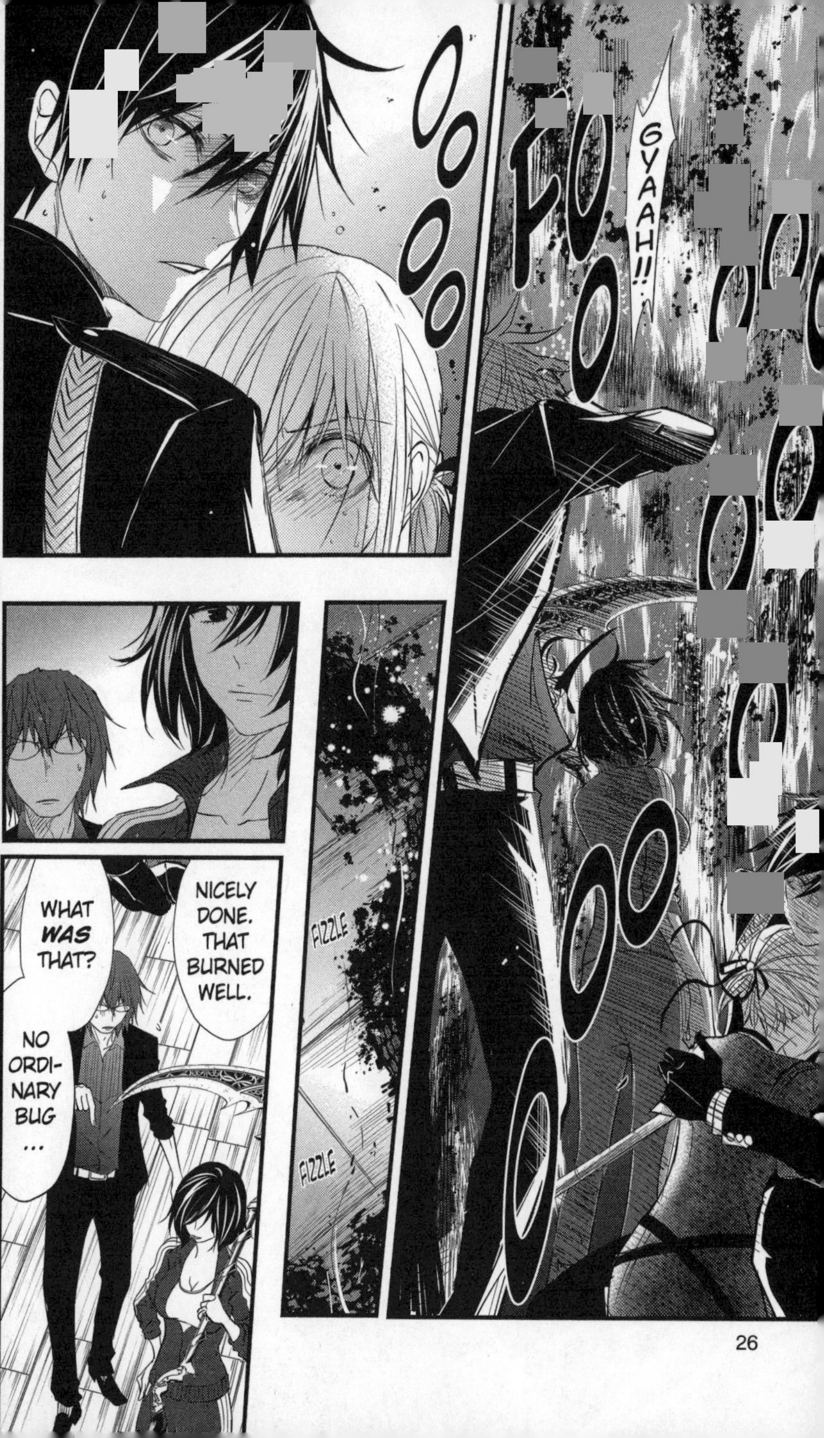

FOOOO
GYAAH!!
OOOOO
FIZZLE
FIZZLE
NICELY DONE. THAT BURNED WELL.
WHAT *WAS* THAT?
NO ORDI-NARY BUG ...

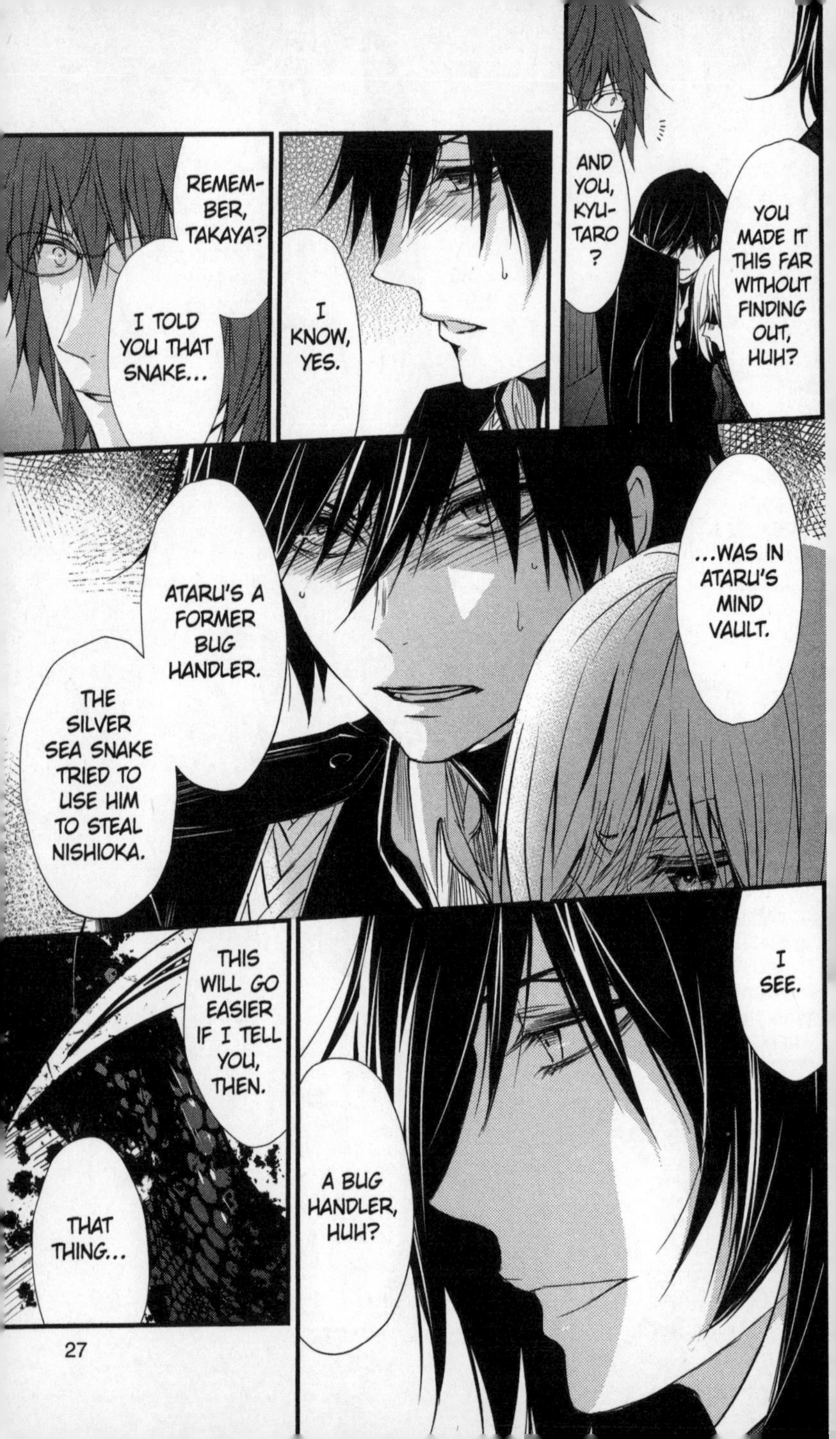
YOU MADE IT THIS FAR WITHOUT FINDING OUT, HUH?
AND YOU, KYU-TARO?
I KNOW, YES.
REMEM-BER, TAKAYA?
I TOLD YOU THAT SNAKE...
...WAS IN ATARU'S MIND VAULT.
ATARU'S A FORMER BUG HANDLER.
THE SILVER SEA SNAKE TRIED TO USE HIM TO STEAL NISHIOKA.
I SEE.
A BUG HANDLER, HUH?
THIS WILL GO EASIER IF I TELL YOU, THEN.
THAT THING...

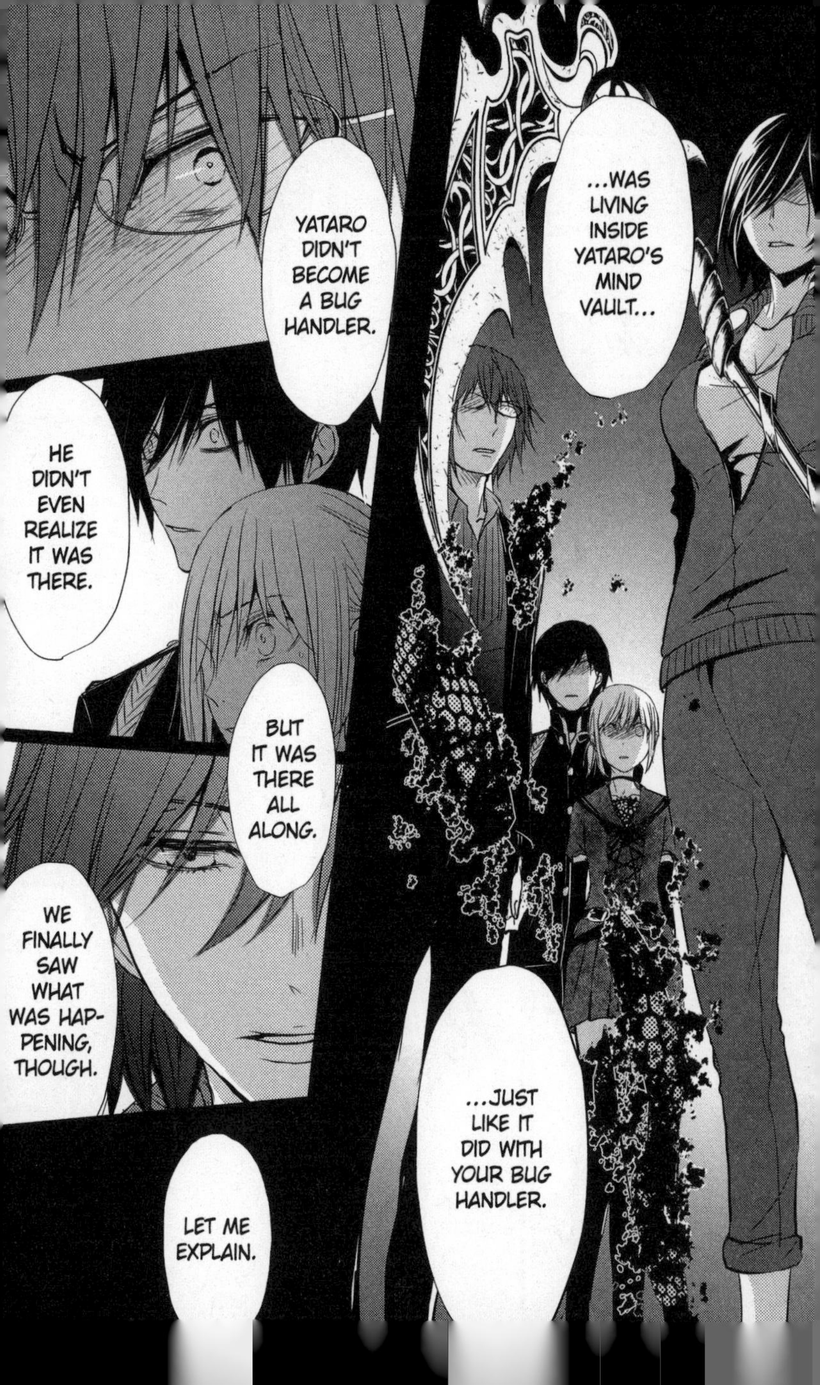
...WAS LIVING INSIDE YATARO'S MIND VAULT...
...JUST LIKE IT DID WITH YOUR BUG HANDLER.
YATARO DIDN'T BECOME A BUG HANDLER.
HE DIDN'T EVEN REALIZE IT WAS THERE.
BUT IT WAS THERE ALL ALONG.
WE FINALLY SAW WHAT WAS HAP-PENING, THOUGH.
LET ME EXPLAIN.

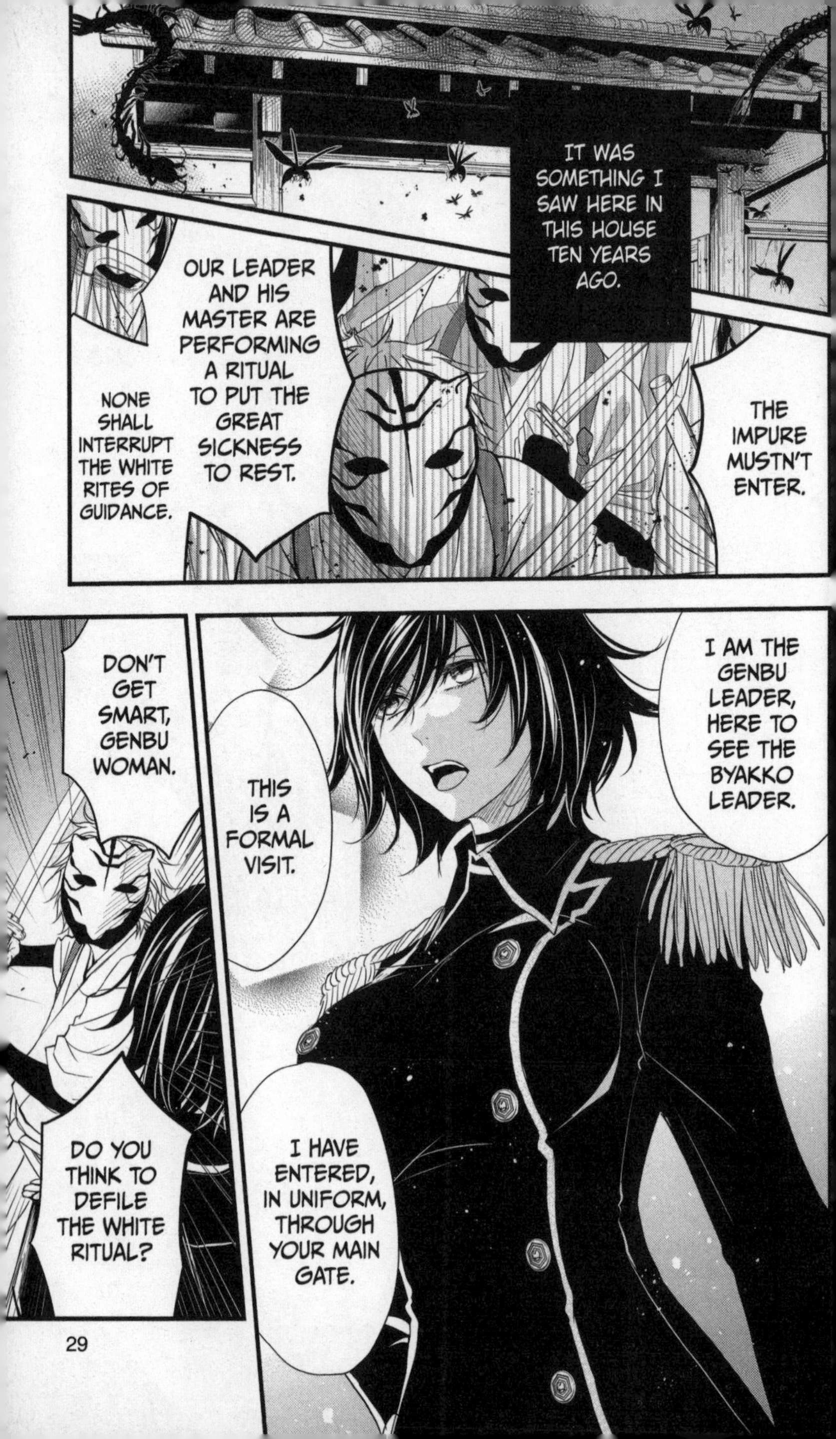

IT WAS SOMETHING I SAW HERE IN THIS HOUSE TEN YEARS AGO.
THE IMPURE MUSTN'T ENTER.
OUR LEADER AND HIS MASTER ARE PERFORMING A RITUAL TO PUT THE GREAT SICKNESS TO REST.
NONE SHALL INTERRUPT THE WHITE RITES OF GUIDANCE.
I AM THE GENBU LEADER, HERE TO SEE THE BYAKKO LEADER.
THIS IS A FORMAL VISIT.
I HAVE ENTERED, IN UNIFORM, THROUGH YOUR MAIN GATE.
DON'T GET SMART, GENBU WOMAN.
DO YOU THINK TO DEFILE THE WHITE RITUAL?

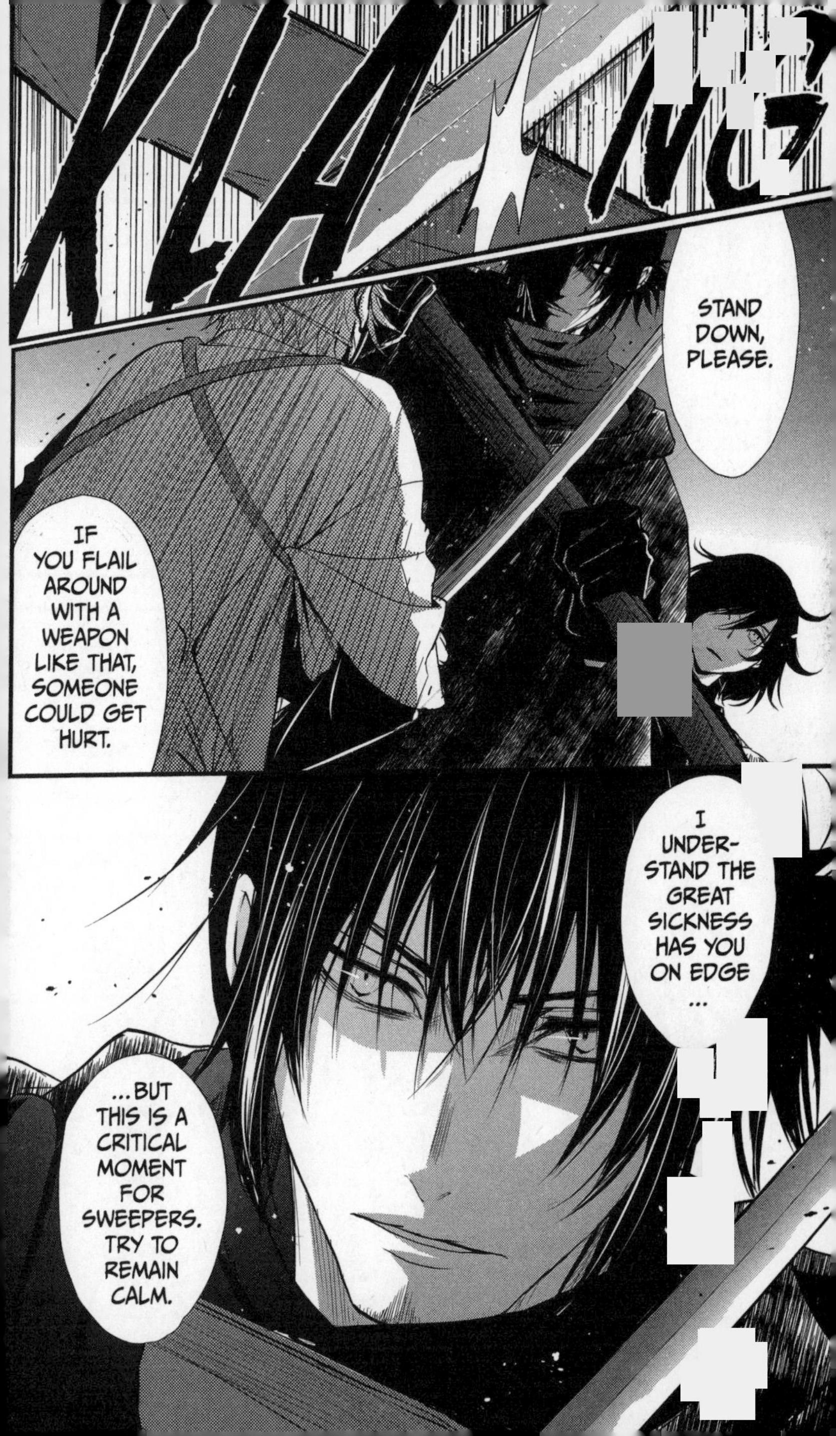
STAND DOWN, PLEASE.
IF YOU FLAIL AROUND WITH A WEAPON LIKE THAT, SOMEONE COULD GET HURT.
I UNDER-STAND THE GREAT SICKNESS HAS YOU ON EDGE...
...BUT THIS IS A CRITICAL MOMENT FOR SWEEPERS. TRY TO REMAIN CALM.

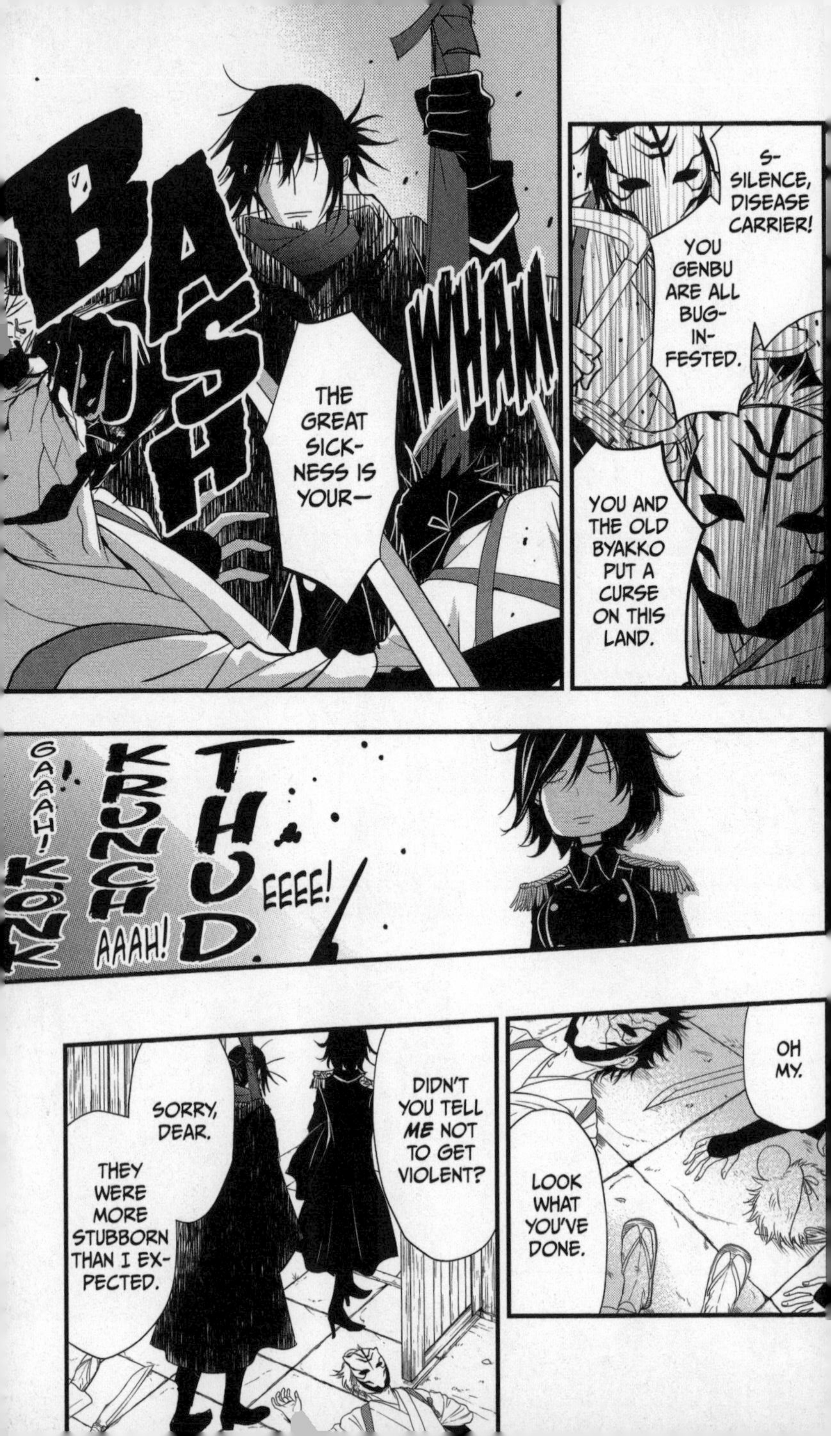
S-SILENCE, DISEASE CARRIER!
YOU GENBU ARE ALL BUG-INFESTED.
YOU AND THE OLD BYAKKO PUT A CURSE ON THIS LAND.
WHAM
THE GREAT SICKNESS IS YOUR—
BASH
EEEE!
THUD
AAAH!
KRUNCH
GAAAAH!
KONK
OH MY.
LOOK WHAT YOU'VE DONE.
DIDN'T YOU TELL *ME* NOT TO GET VIOLENT?
SORRY, DEAR.
THEY WERE MORE STUBBORN THAN I EXPECTED.

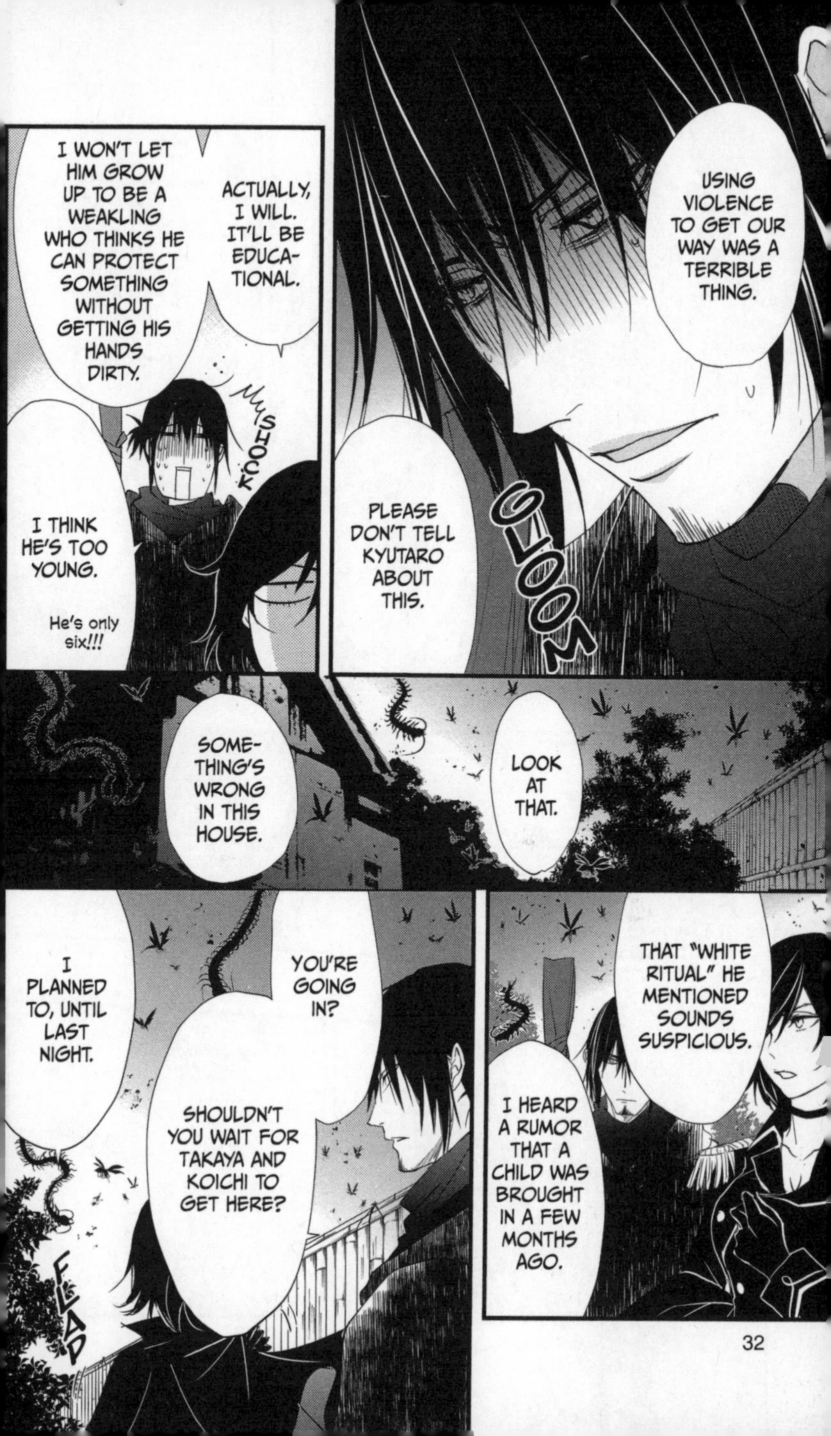
USING VIOLENCE TO GET OUR WAY WAS A TERRIBLE THING.
PLEASE DON'T TELL KYUTARO ABOUT THIS.
GLOOOM
ACTUALLY, I WILL. IT'LL BE EDUCATIONAL.
I WON'T LET HIM GROW UP TO BE A WEAKLING WHO THINKS HE CAN PROTECT SOMETHING WITHOUT GETTING HIS HANDS DIRTY.
MY SHOCK
I THINK HE'S TOO YOUNG.
He's only six!!!
LOOK AT THAT.
SOMETHING'S WRONG IN THIS HOUSE.
THAT "WHITE RITUAL" HE MENTIONED SOUNDS SUSPICIOUS.
I HEARD A RUMOR THAT A CHILD WAS BROUGHT IN A FEW MONTHS AGO.
YOU'RE GOING IN?
I PLANNED TO, UNTIL LAST NIGHT.
SHOULDN'T YOU WAIT FOR TAKAYA AND KOICHI TO GET HERE?
FLAP

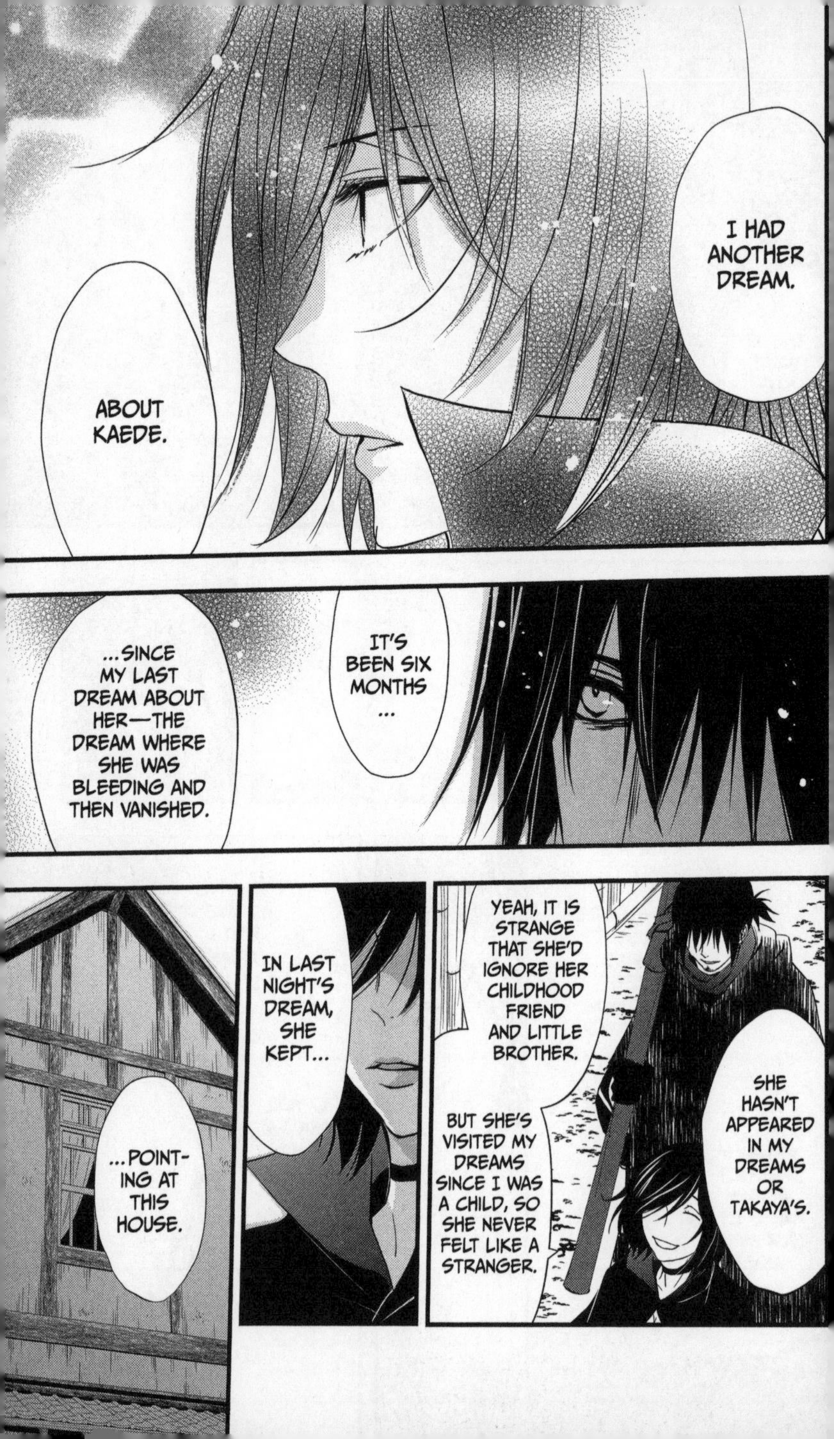
I HAD ANOTHER DREAM.
ABOUT KAEDE.
IT'S BEEN SIX MONTHS ...
...SINCE MY LAST DREAM ABOUT HER—THE DREAM WHERE SHE WAS BLEEDING AND THEN VANISHED.
SHE HASN'T APPEARED IN MY DREAMS OR TAKAYA'S.
YEAH, IT IS STRANGE THAT SHE'D IGNORE HER CHILDHOOD FRIEND AND LITTLE BROTHER.
BUT SHE'S VISITED MY DREAMS SINCE I WAS A CHILD, SO SHE NEVER FELT LIKE A STRANGER.
IN LAST NIGHT'S DREAM, SHE KEPT...
...POINT-ING AT THIS HOUSE.

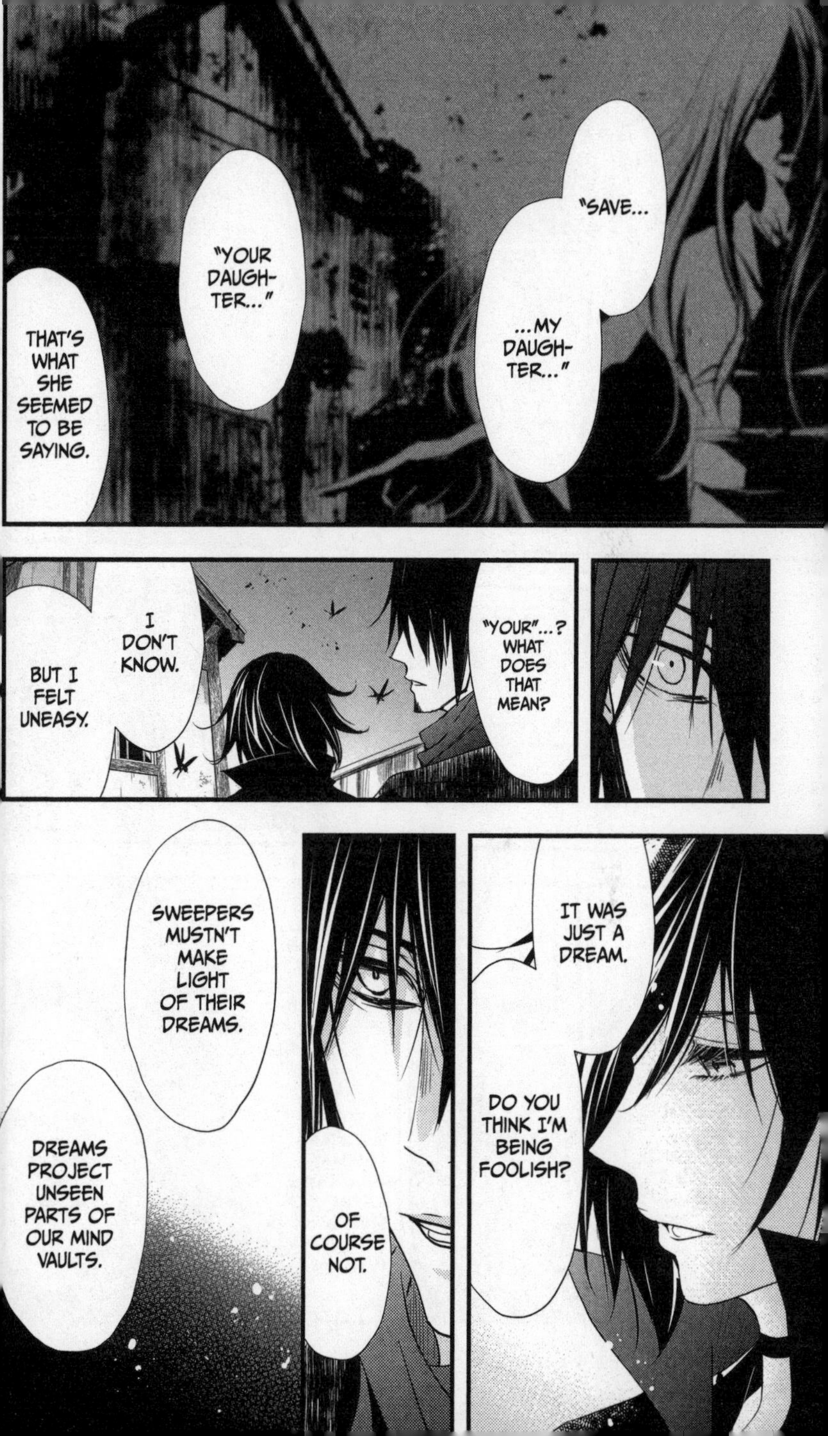
"SAVE...
...MY DAUGHTER..."
"YOUR DAUGHTER..."
THAT'S WHAT SHE SEEMED TO BE SAYING.
"YOUR"...? WHAT DOES THAT MEAN?
I DON'T KNOW.
BUT I FELT UNEASY.
IT WAS JUST A DREAM.
DO YOU THINK I'M BEING FOOLISH?
OF COURSE NOT.
SWEEPERS MUSTN'T MAKE LIGHT OF THEIR DREAMS.
DREAMS PROJECT UNSEEN PARTS OF OUR MIND VAULTS.

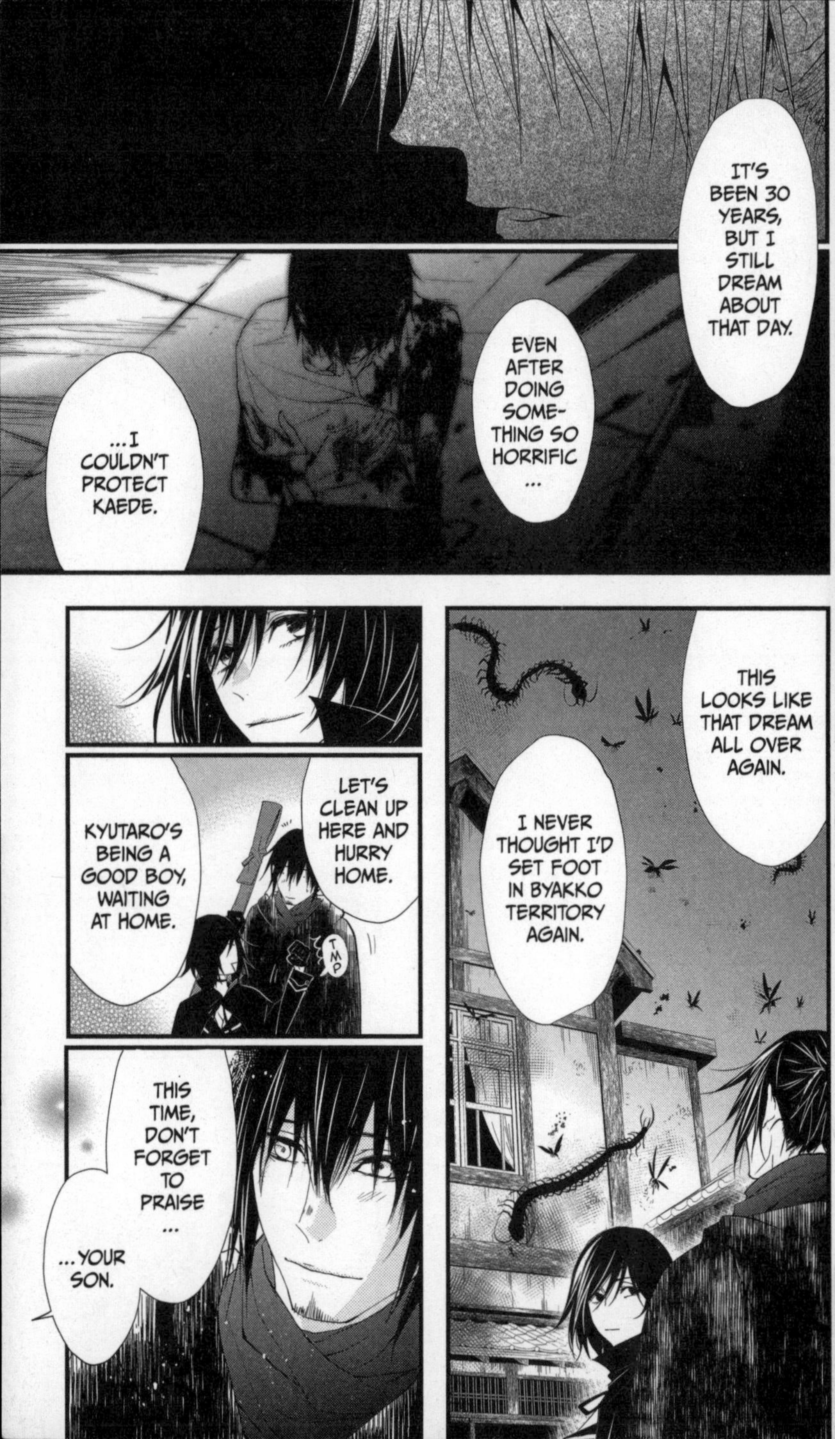
IT'S BEEN 30 YEARS, BUT I STILL DREAM ABOUT THAT DAY.
EVEN AFTER DOING SOMETHING SO HORRIFIC...
...I COULDN'T PROTECT KAEDE.
THIS LOOKS LIKE THAT DREAM ALL OVER AGAIN.
I NEVER THOUGHT I'D SET FOOT IN BYAKKO TERRITORY AGAIN.
LET'S CLEAN UP HERE AND HURRY HOME.
TMP
KYUTARO'S BEING A GOOD BOY, WAITING AT HOME.
THIS TIME, DON'T FORGET TO PRAISE...
...YOUR SON.

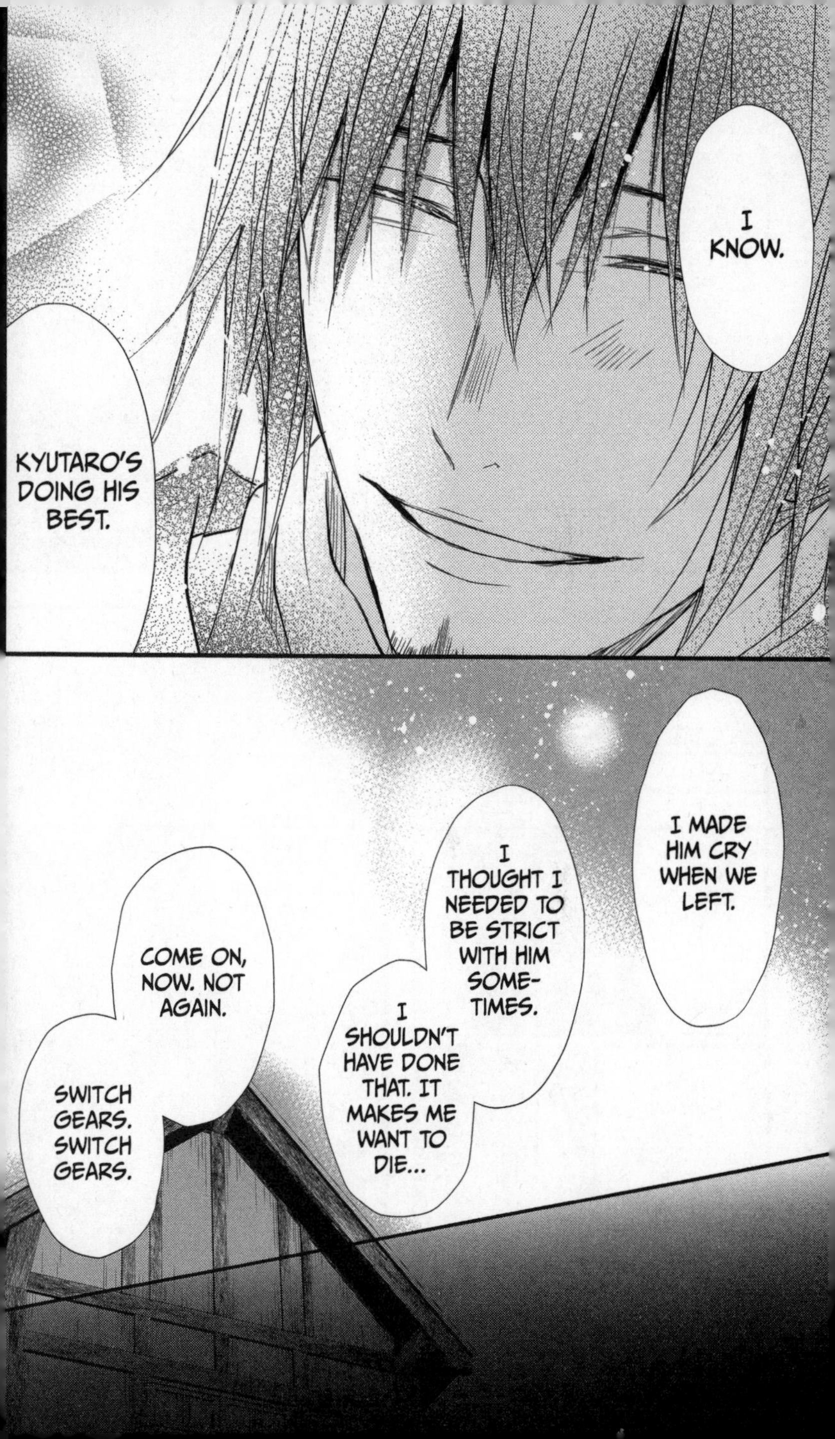
I KNOW.
KYUTARO'S DOING HIS BEST.
I MADE HIM CRY WHEN WE LEFT.
I THOUGHT I NEEDED TO BE STRICT WITH HIM SOME-TIMES.
I SHOULDN'T HAVE DONE THAT. IT MAKES ME WANT TO DIE...
COME ON, NOW. NOT AGAIN.
SWITCH GEARS. SWITCH GEARS.

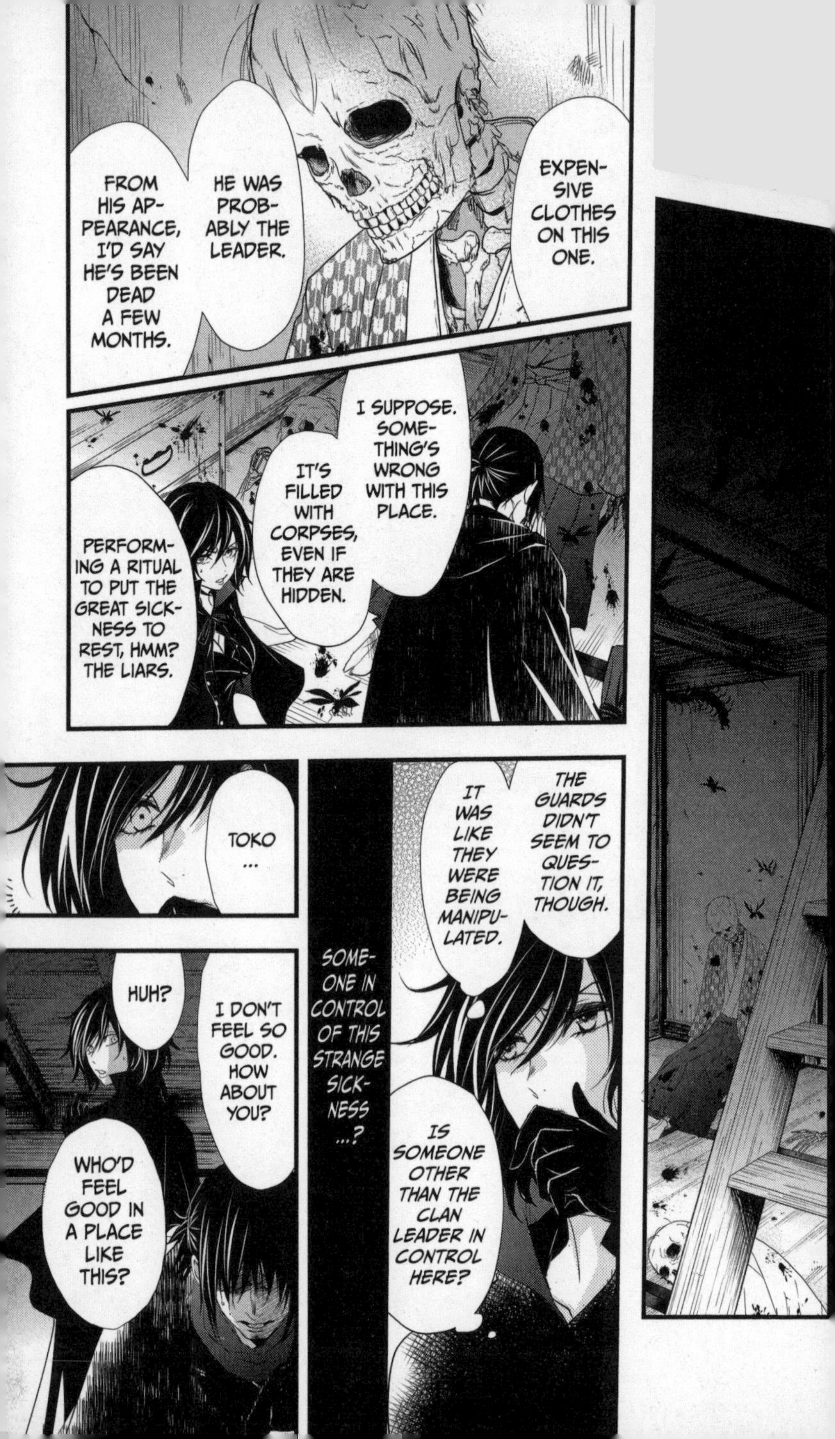
EXPENSIVE CLOTHES ON THIS ONE.
HE WAS PROBABLY THE LEADER.
FROM HIS APPEARANCE, I'D SAY HE'S BEEN DEAD A FEW MONTHS.
I SUPPOSE. SOMETHING'S WRONG WITH THIS PLACE.
IT'S FILLED WITH CORPSES, EVEN IF THEY ARE HIDDEN.
PERFORMING A RITUAL TO PUT THE GREAT SICKNESS TO REST, HMM? THE LIARS.
THE GUARDS DIDN'T SEEM TO QUESTION IT, THOUGH.
IT WAS LIKE THEY WERE BEING MANIPULATED.
SOMEONE IN CONTROL OF THIS STRANGE SICKNESS ...?
IS SOMEONE OTHER THAN THE CLAN LEADER IN CONTROL HERE?
TOKO ...
HUH?
I DON'T FEEL SO GOOD. HOW ABOUT YOU?
WHO'D FEEL GOOD IN A PLACE LIKE THIS?

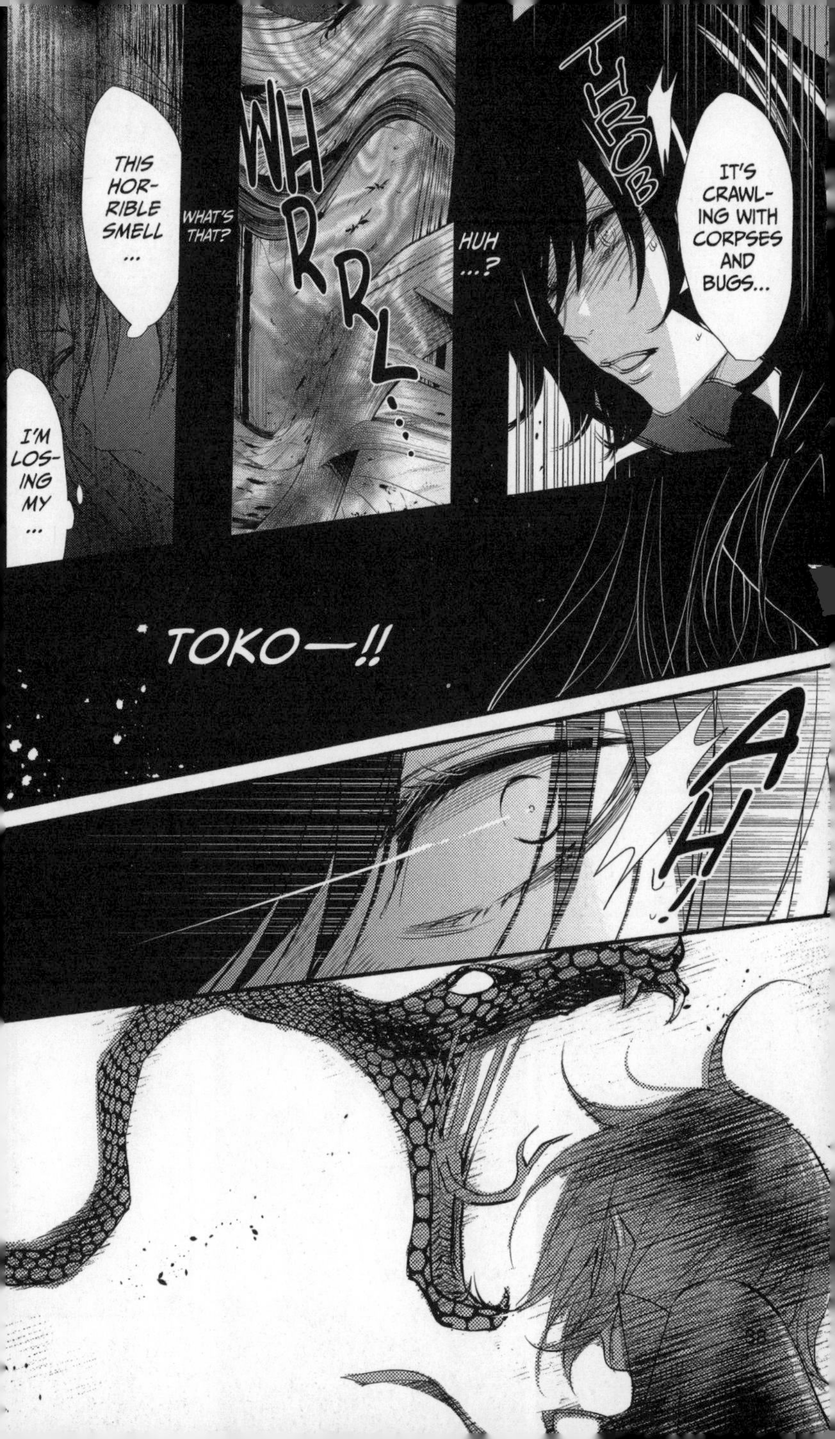
THROB
IT'S CRAWLING WITH CORPSES AND BUGS...
HUH ...?
WHRRL...
WHAT'S THAT?
THIS HORRIBLE SMELL ...
I'M LOSING MY ...
TOKO—!!
AH!

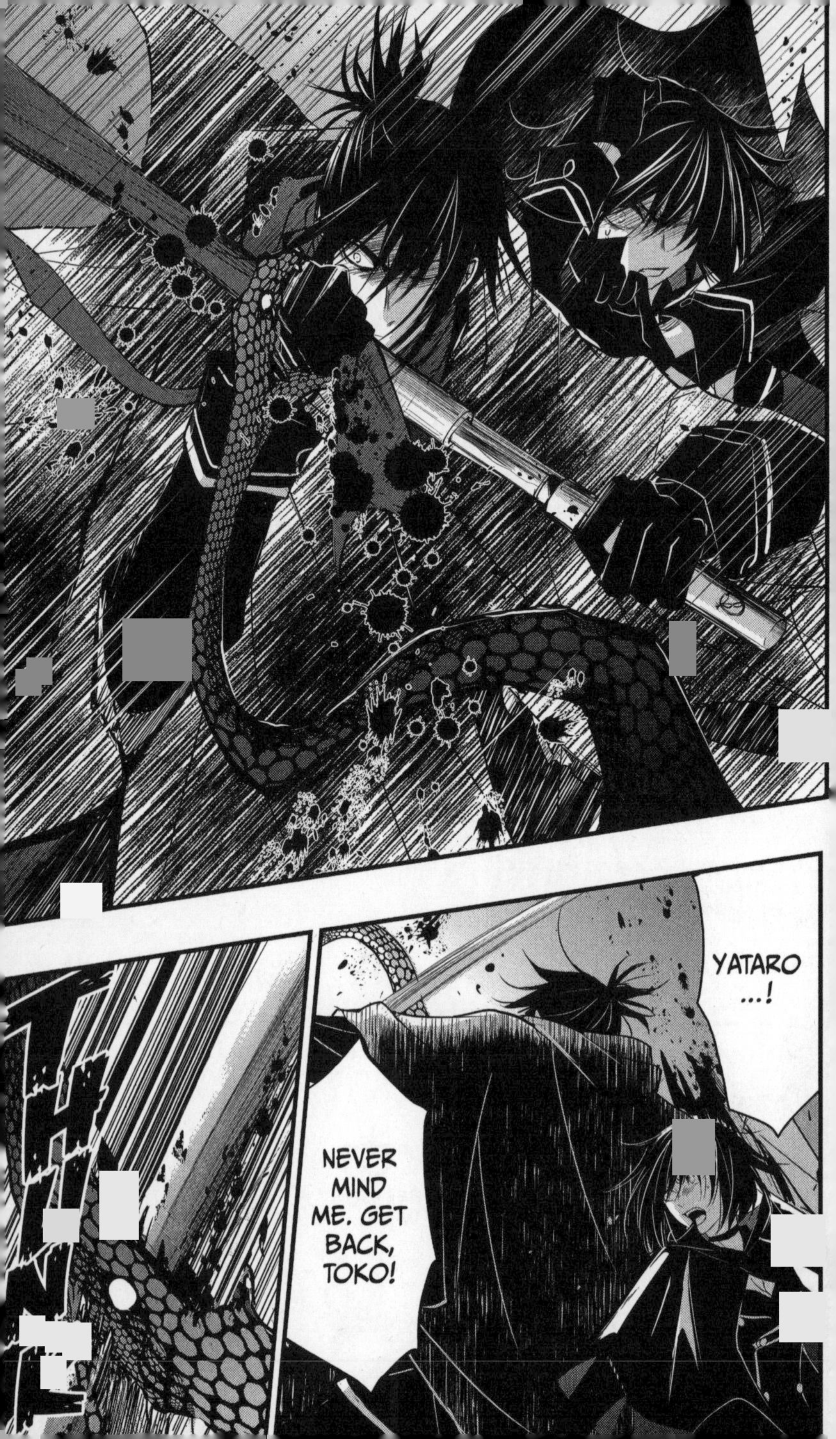
YATARO ...!
NEVER MIND ME. GET BACK, TOKO!

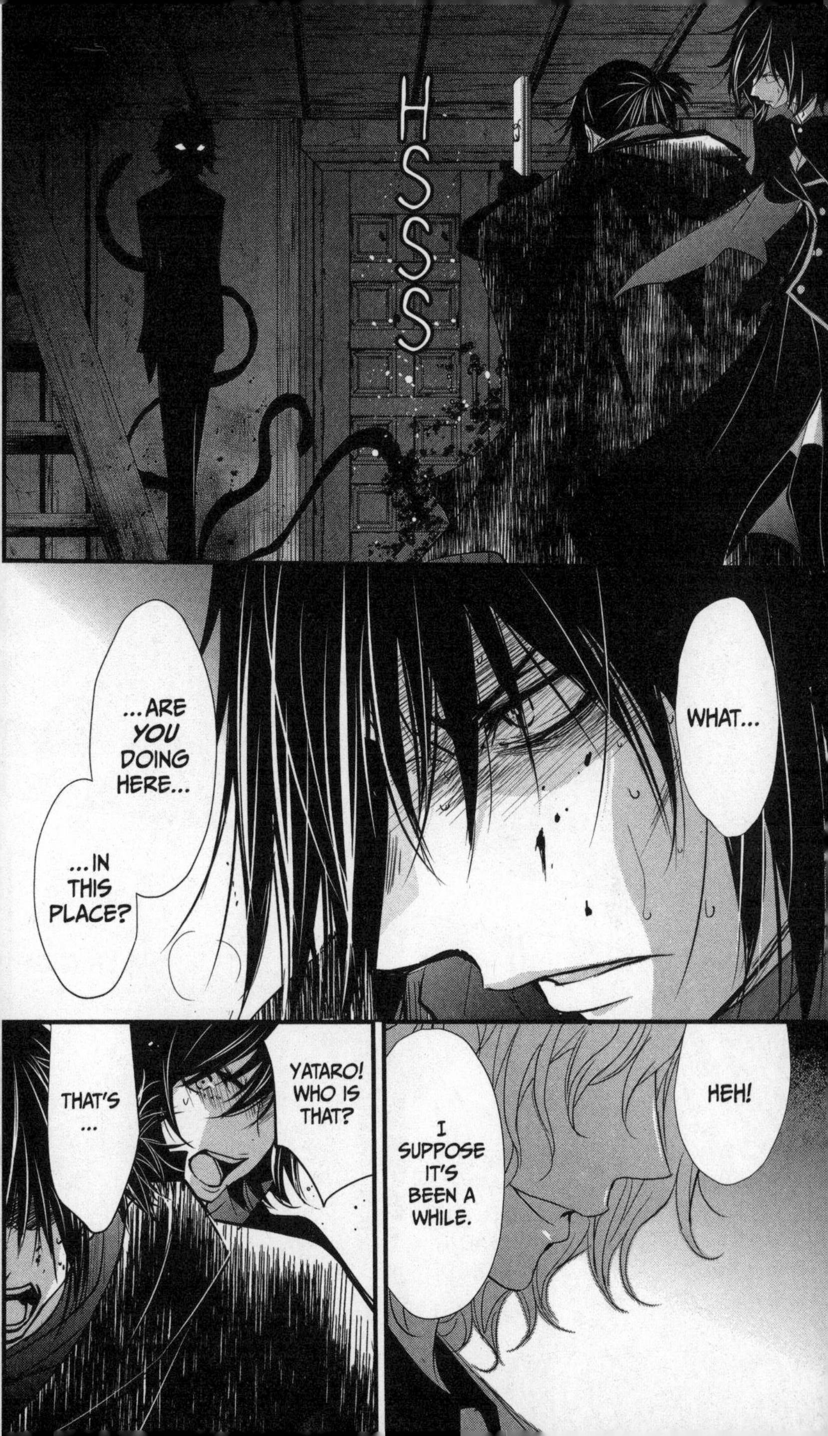
HSSS
WHAT...
...ARE YOU DOING HERE...
...IN THIS PLACE?
HEH!
I SUPPOSE IT'S BEEN A WHILE.
YATARO! WHO IS THAT?
THAT'S ...

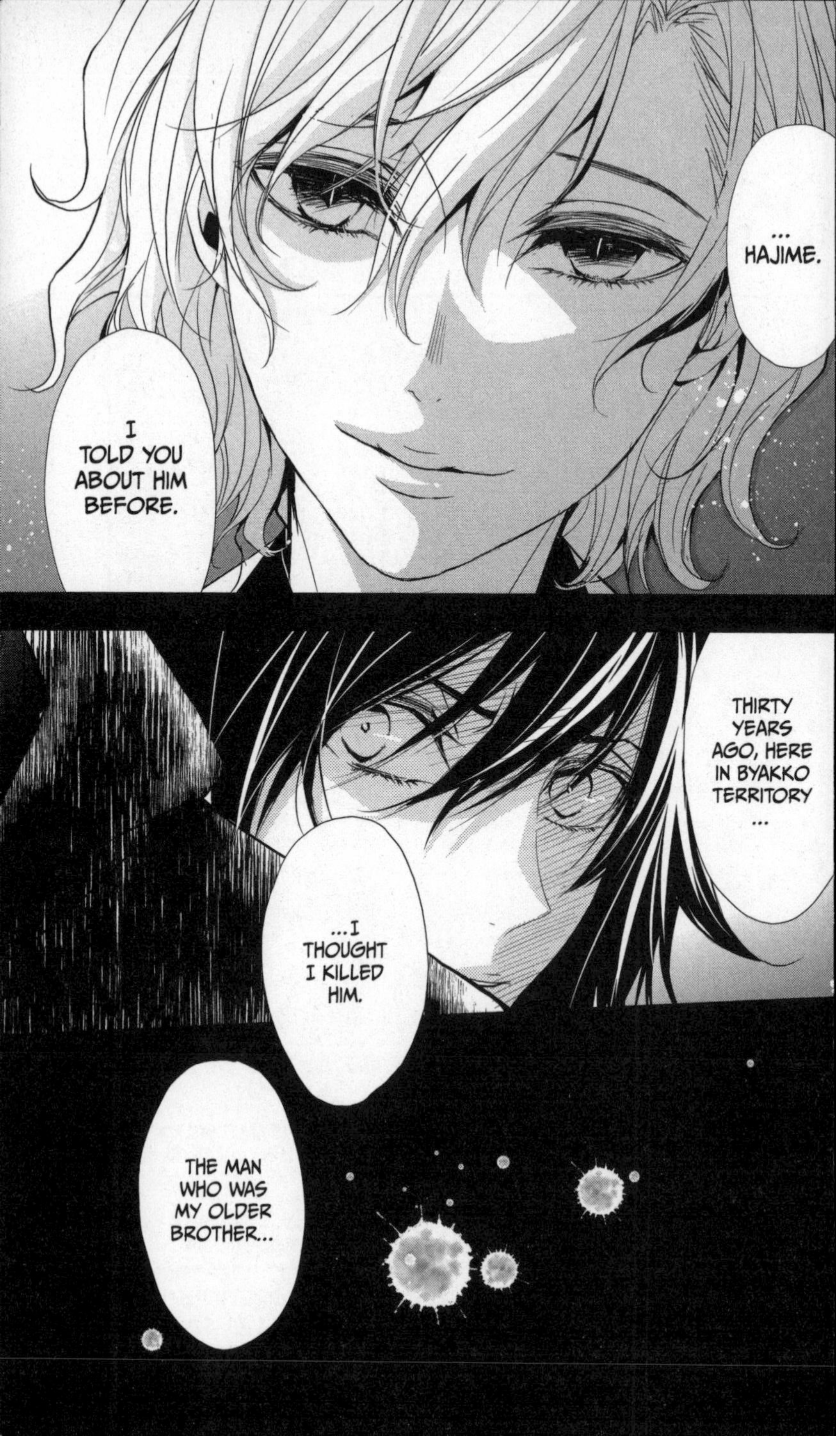
...HAJIME.
I TOLD YOU ABOUT HIM BEFORE.
THIRTY YEARS AGO, HERE IN BYAKKO TERRITORY...
...I THOUGHT I KILLED HIM.
THE MAN WHO WAS MY OLDER BROTHER...

MONTHLY BETSUCOMI SALE DATE NOTICE ON TWITTER

CHAPTER 37

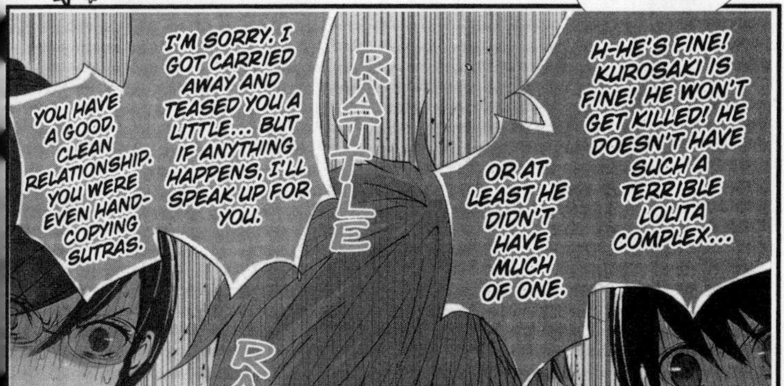
H-HE'S FINE! KUROSAKI IS FINE! HE WON'T GET KILLED! HE DOESN'T HAVE SUCH A TERRIBLE LOLITA COMPLEX...
OR AT LEAST HE DIDN'T HAVE MUCH OF ONE.
RATTLE
I'M SORRY. I GOT CARRIED AWAY AND TEASED YOU A LITTLE... BUT IF ANYTHING HAPPENS, I'LL SPEAK UP FOR YOU.
YOU HAVE A GOOD, CLEAN RELATIONSHIP. YOU WERE EVEN HAND-COPYING SUTRAS.
RATTLE
RATTLE
RATTLE
BETSUCOMI

LET'S SEE... WHAT'S UP IN *QUEEN'S QUALITY* THIS MONTH?

(1) THE BYAKKO LEADER ISN'T USED TO HAVING FRIENDS.
(2) I PUT A FACE ON THAT THING FOR FUN AND IT GOT REALLY SPOOKY.
(3) THAT COUPLE WOULD NEVER ALLOW SOMEONE TO HAVE A LOLITA COMPLEX. THEY'D PROBABLY KILL ANYONE WHO DID.

THIS CHAPTER COMES TO YOU FROM SOMEONE WHO WOULD NEVER FORGIVE A LOLITA COMPLEX AND WOULD GLADLY KILL ANYONE WHO HAS ONE.

THE CHARACTERS HERE ARE FROM MY PREVIOUS SERIES *DENGEKI DAISY*—KUROSAKI, WITH A SLIGHT LOLITA COMPLEX, AND TERU AND RIKO. I DRAW MY *DAISY* CHARACTERS FOR MY TWEETS SOMETIMES AND TALK ABOUT THEM.

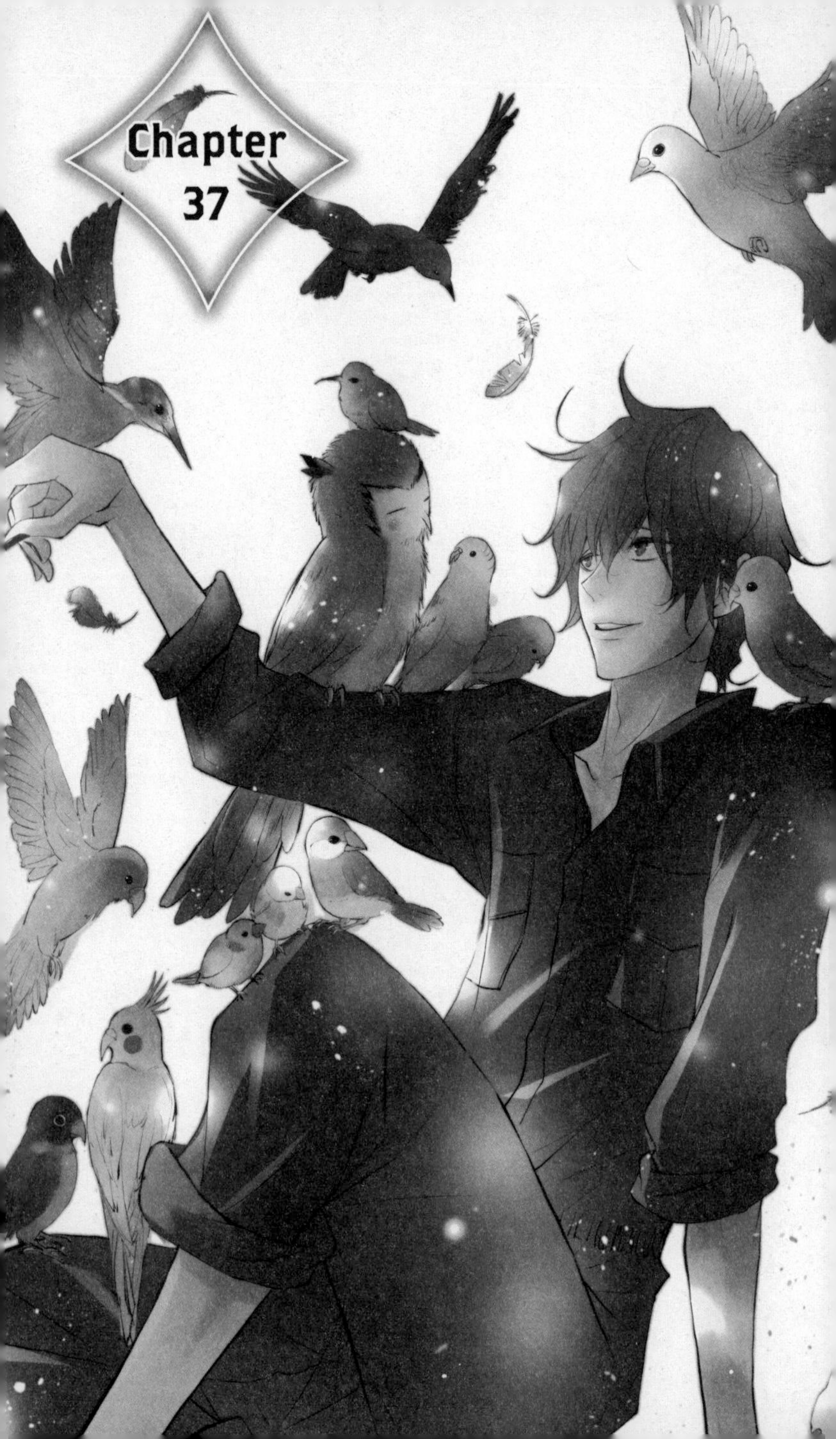
Chapter
37

Queen's Quality

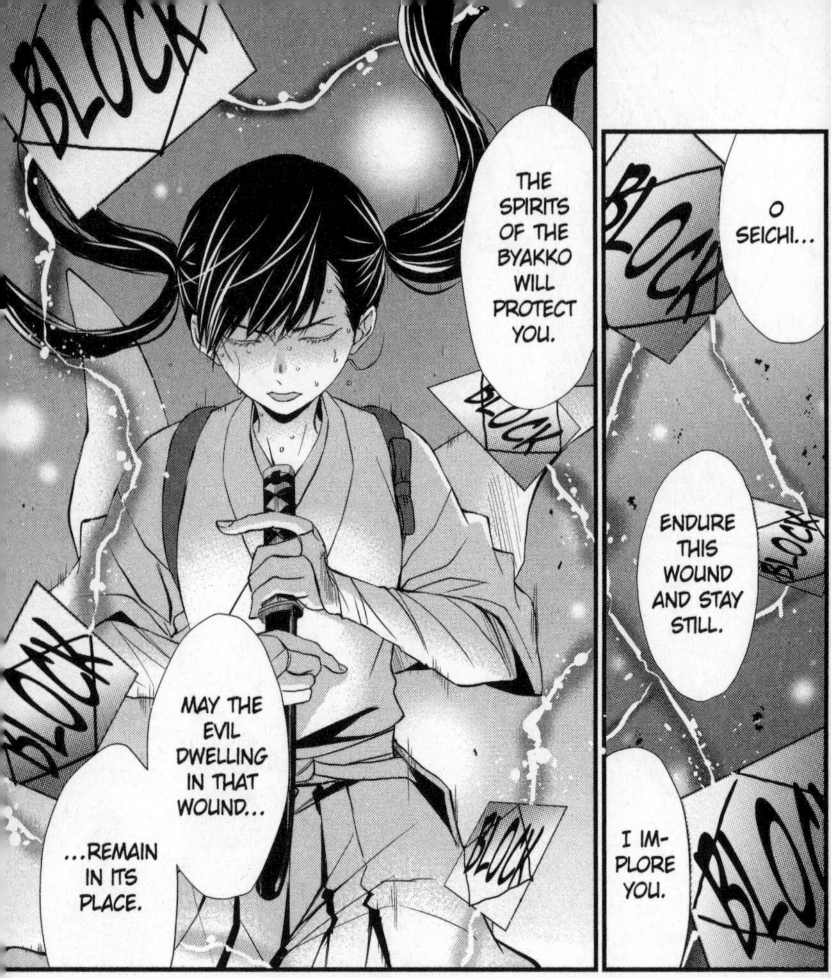
BLOCK
O SEICHI...
BLOCK
ENDURE THIS WOUND AND STAY STILL.
BLOCK
I IMPLORE YOU.
BLOCK
BLOCK
THE SPIRITS OF THE BYAKKO WILL PROTECT YOU.
BLOCK
BLOCK
MAY THE EVIL DWELLING IN THAT WOUND...
BLOCK
...REMAIN IN ITS PLACE.

I haven't played any games recently. (Oh, except once, when I had some time off, I played Steins; Gate Elite and cleared it in about two days...and I bawled over it.)

As for Pokemon GO, when I got a new smartphone, I couldn't find my account. It was such a shock! I didn't feel like starting over. If I'm going to play, I'd rather play on a game console than my smartphone. I want a game that I can play in spurts during my breaks. I need to not get so caught up in it that I'd lose work time, but it also has to be fun.

Of the Horikita household, Granny is the best gamer. Her *Monster Hunter* weapon of choice is the Flame Lance.

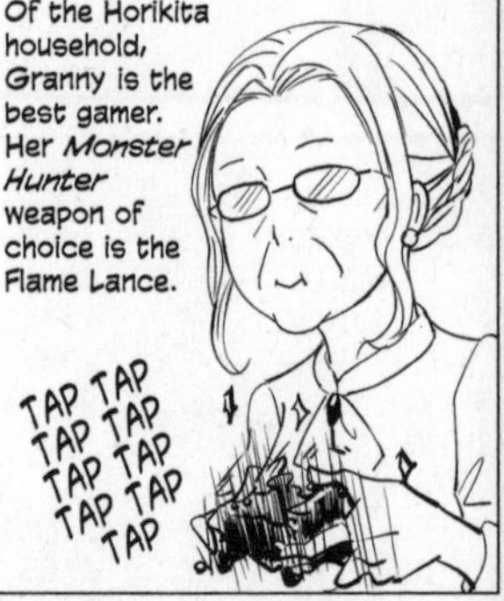
TAP TAP TAP TAP TAP TAP TAP TAP TAP

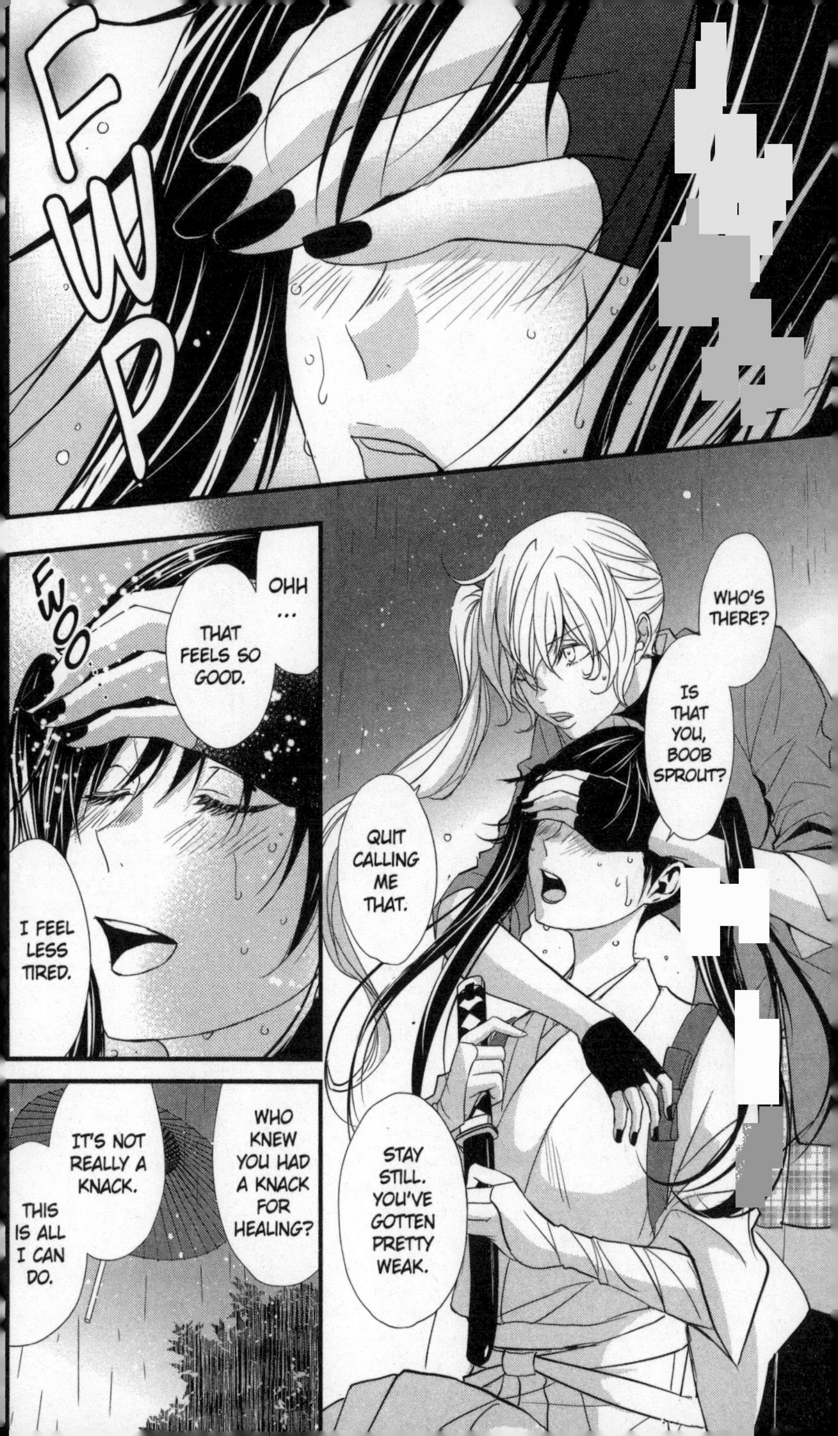
FWP
WHO'S THERE?
IS THAT YOU, BOOB SPROUT?
QUIT CALLING ME THAT.
STAY STILL. YOU'VE GOTTEN PRETTY WEAK.
OHH ... THAT FEELS SO GOOD.
FWOO
I FEEL LESS TIRED.
WHO KNEW YOU HAD A KNACK FOR HEALING?
IT'S NOT REALLY A KNACK.
THIS IS ALL I CAN DO.

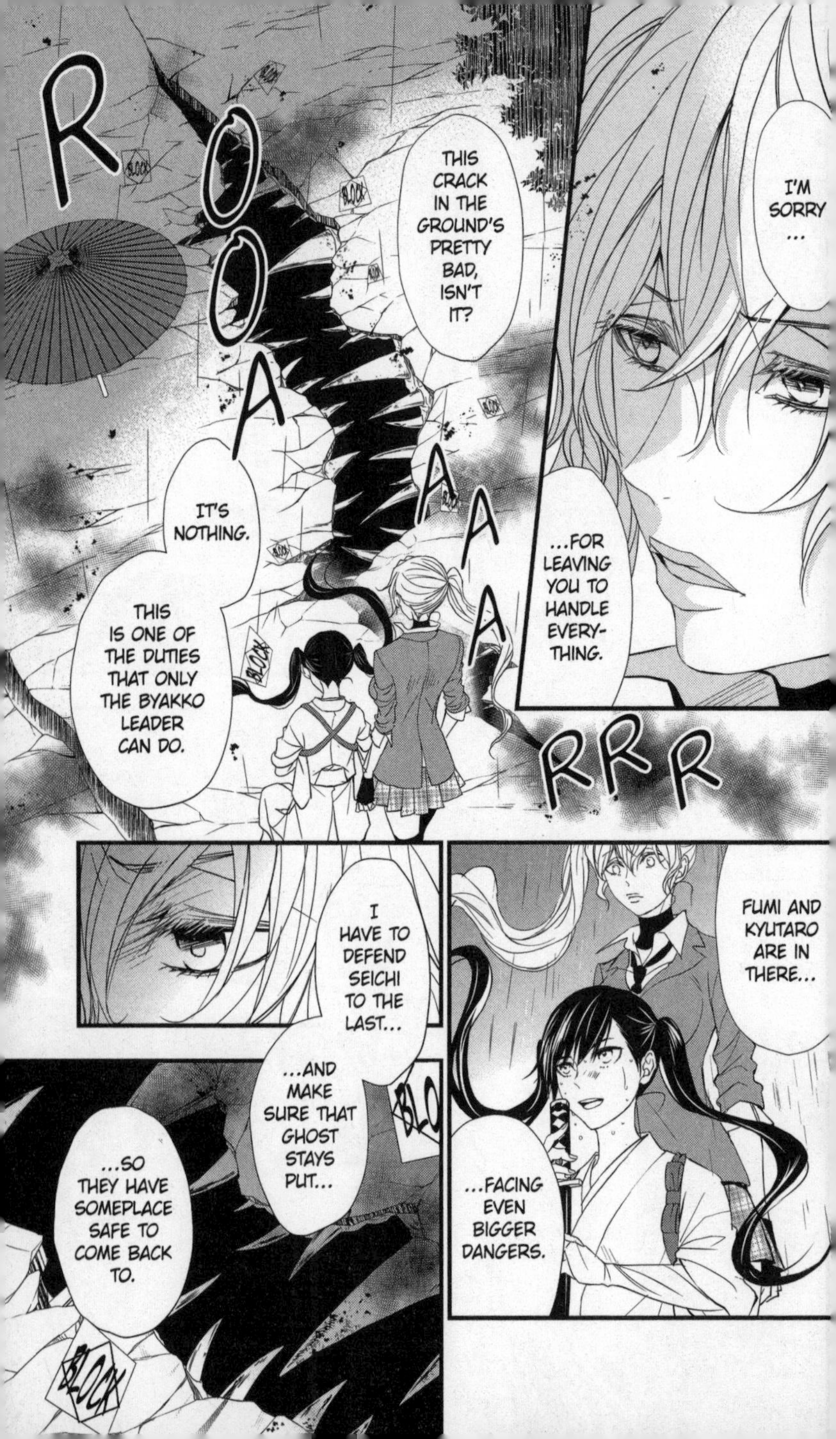
I'M SORRY...
...FOR LEAVING YOU TO HANDLE EVERYTHING.
ROOAAAA
THIS CRACK IN THE GROUND'S PRETTY BAD, ISN'T IT?
IT'S NOTHING.
THIS IS ONE OF THE DUTIES THAT ONLY THE BYAKKO LEADER CAN DO.
RRR
BLOCK
FUMI AND KYUTARO ARE IN THERE...
...FACING EVEN BIGGER DANGERS.
I HAVE TO DEFEND SEICHI TO THE LAST...
...AND MAKE SURE THAT GHOST STAYS PUT...
...SO THEY HAVE SOMEPLACE SAFE TO COME BACK TO.
BLOCK

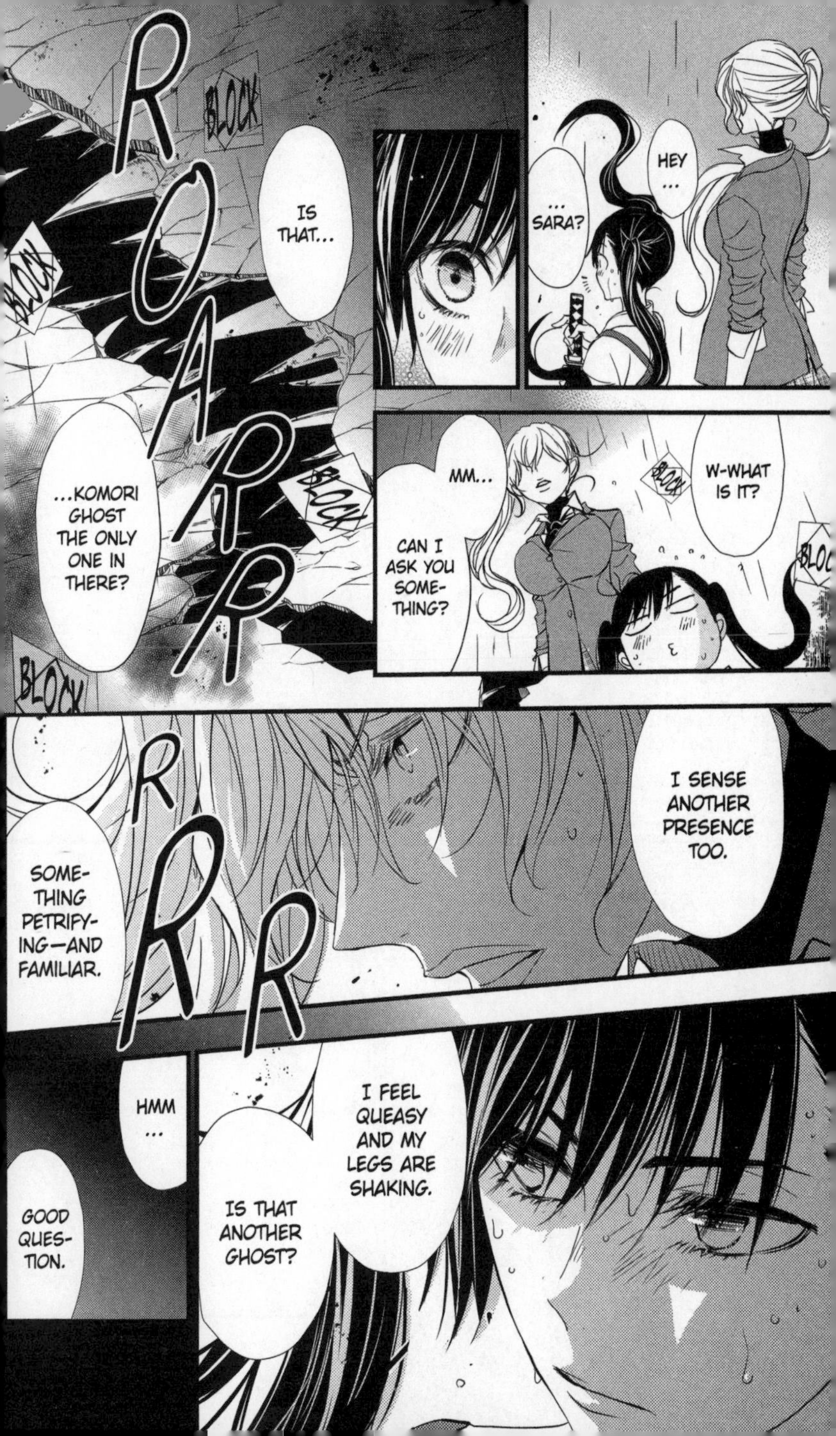
HEY ...
... SARA?
W-WHAT IS IT?
BLOCK
MM...
CAN I ASK YOU SOME-THING?
BLOCK
ROARRR
BLOCK
BLOCK
BLOCK
IS THAT...
...KOMORI GHOST THE ONLY ONE IN THERE?
I SENSE ANOTHER PRESENCE TOO.
SOME-THING PETRIFY-ING—AND FAMILIAR.
RRR
I FEEL QUEASY AND MY LEGS ARE SHAKING.
IS THAT ANOTHER GHOST?
HMM ...
GOOD QUES-TION.

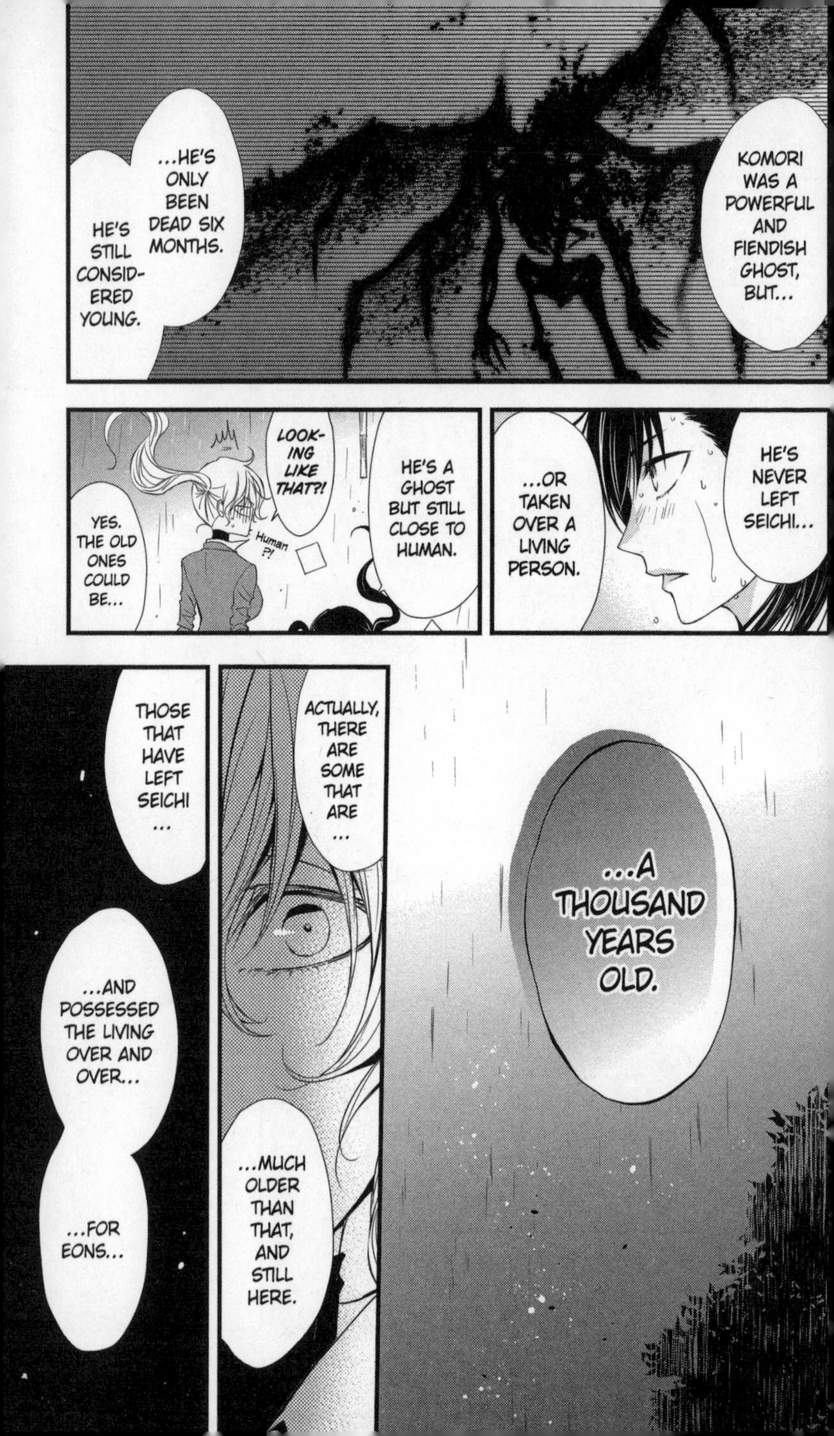
KOMORI WAS A POWERFUL AND FIENDISH GHOST, BUT...
...HE'S ONLY BEEN DEAD SIX MONTHS.
HE'S STILL CONSID-ERED YOUNG.
HE'S NEVER LEFT SEICHI...
...OR TAKEN OVER A LIVING PERSON.
HE'S A GHOST BUT STILL CLOSE TO HUMAN.
LOOK-ING LIKE THAT?!
Human ?!
YES. THE OLD ONES COULD BE...
...A THOUSAND YEARS OLD.
ACTUALLY, THERE ARE SOME THAT ARE...
...MUCH OLDER THAN THAT, AND STILL HERE.
THOSE THAT HAVE LEFT SEICHI...
...AND POSSESSED THE LIVING OVER AND OVER...
...FOR EONS...

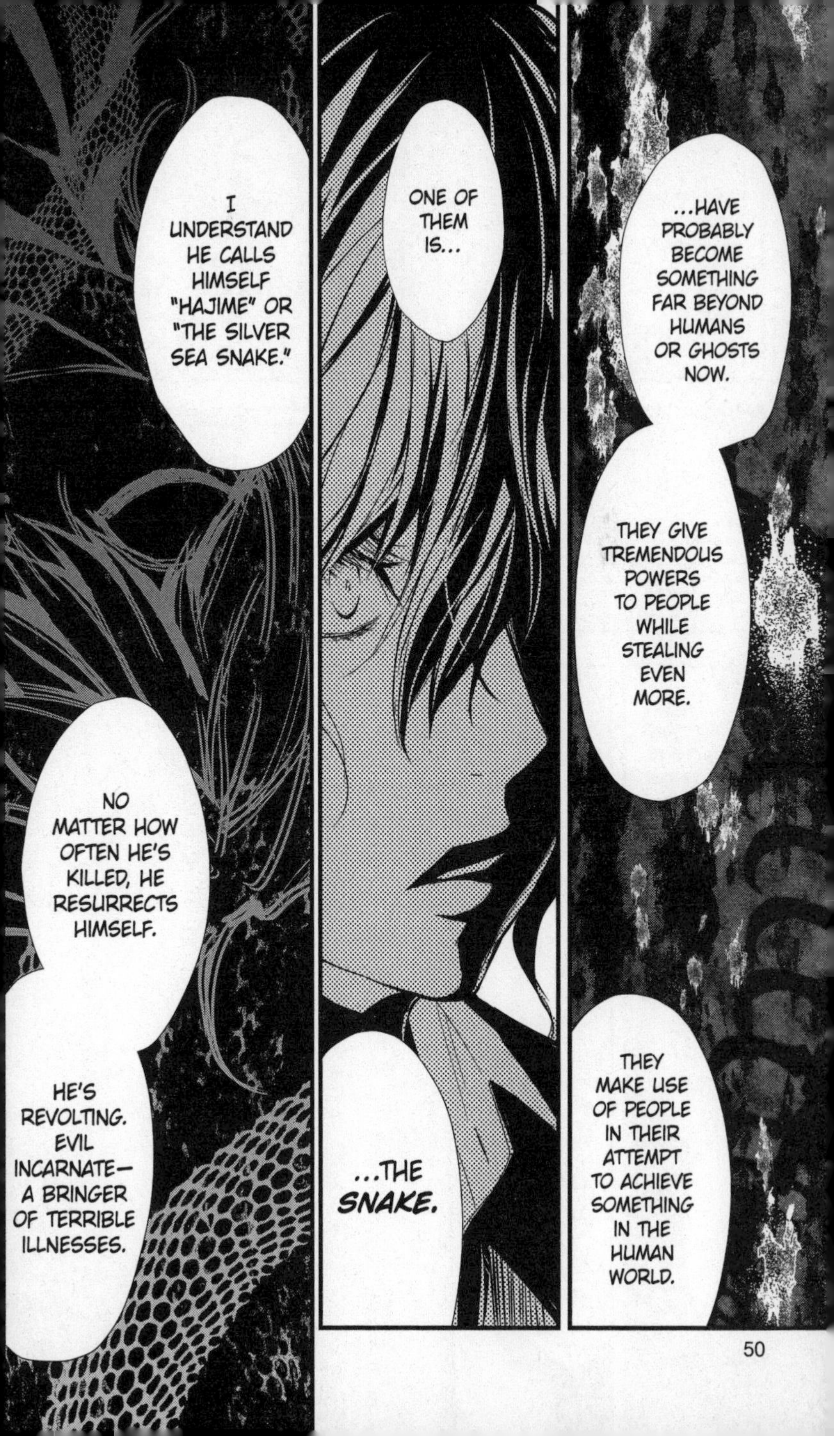
...HAVE PROBABLY BECOME SOMETHING FAR BEYOND HUMANS OR GHOSTS NOW.
THEY GIVE TREMENDOUS POWERS TO PEOPLE WHILE STEALING EVEN MORE.
THEY MAKE USE OF PEOPLE IN THEIR ATTEMPT TO ACHIEVE SOMETHING IN THE HUMAN WORLD.
ONE OF THEM IS...
...THE *SNAKE.*
I UNDERSTAND HE CALLS HIMSELF "HAJIME" OR "THE SILVER SEA SNAKE."
NO MATTER HOW OFTEN HE'S KILLED, HE RESURRECTS HIMSELF.
HE'S REVOLTING. EVIL INCARNATE—A BRINGER OF TERRIBLE ILLNESSES.

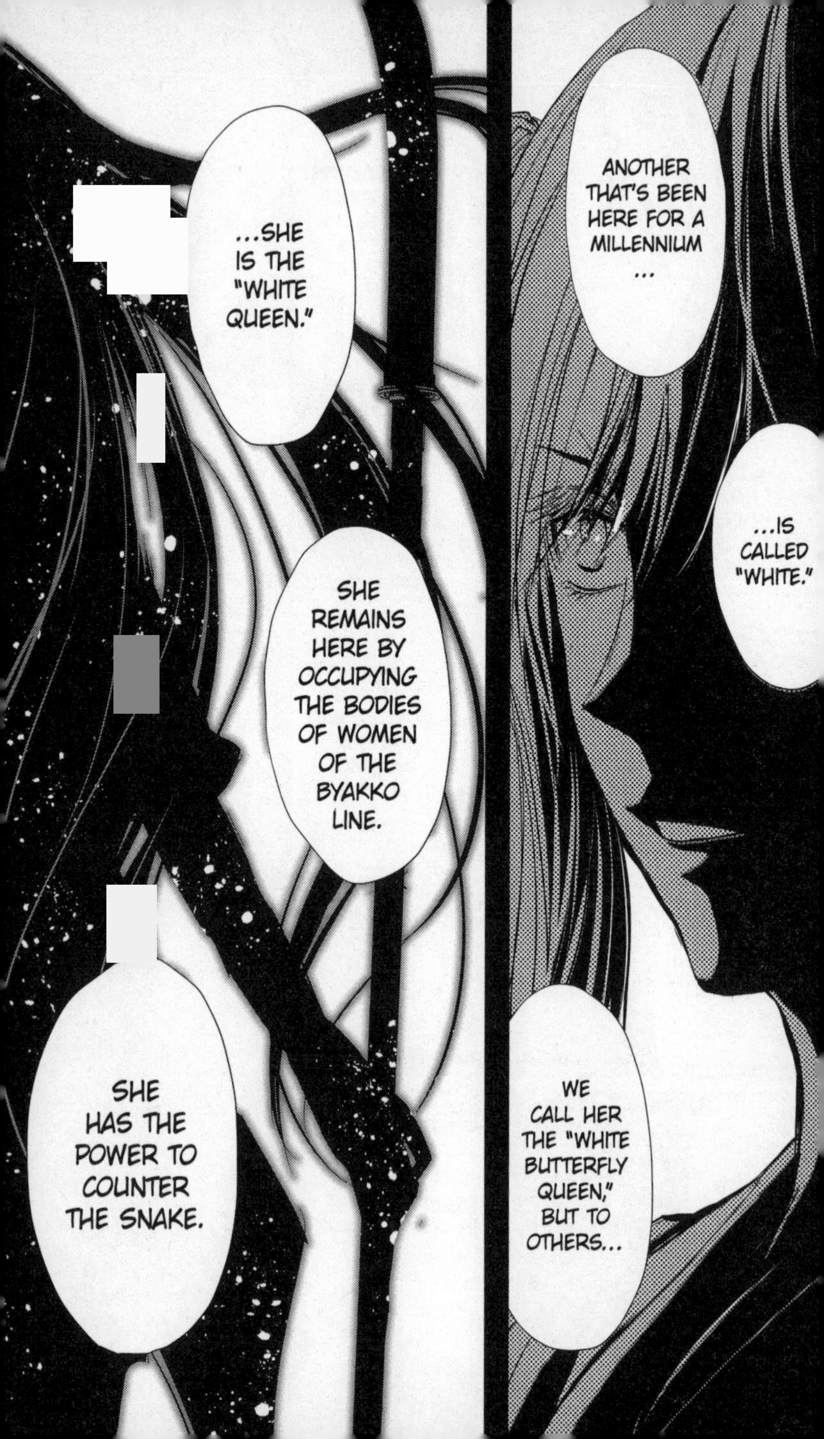
ANOTHER THAT'S BEEN HERE FOR A MILLENNIUM ...
...IS CALLED "WHITE."
WE CALL HER THE "WHITE BUTTERFLY QUEEN," BUT TO OTHERS...
...SHE IS THE "WHITE QUEEN."
SHE REMAINS HERE BY OCCUPYING THE BODIES OF WOMEN OF THE BYAKKO LINE.
SHE HAS THE POWER TO COUNTER THE SNAKE.

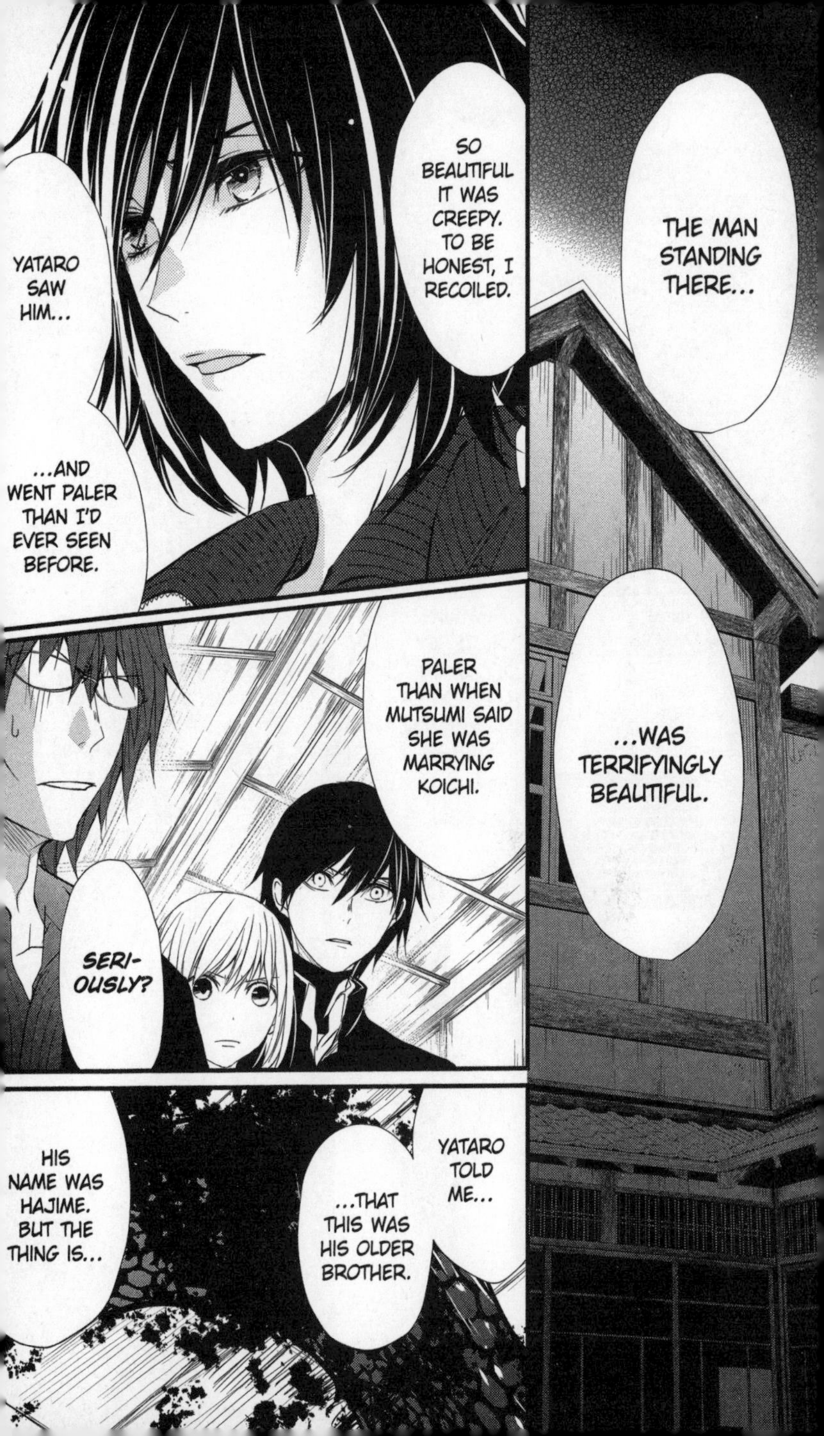
THE MAN STANDING THERE...
...WAS TERRIFYINGLY BEAUTIFUL.
SO BEAUTIFUL IT WAS CREEPY. TO BE HONEST, I RECOILED.
YATARO SAW HIM...
...AND WENT PALER THAN I'D EVER SEEN BEFORE.
PALER THAN WHEN MUTSUMI SAID SHE WAS MARRYING KOICHI.
SERI-OUSLY?
YATARO TOLD ME...
...THAT THIS WAS HIS OLDER BROTHER.
HIS NAME WAS HAJIME. BUT THE THING IS...

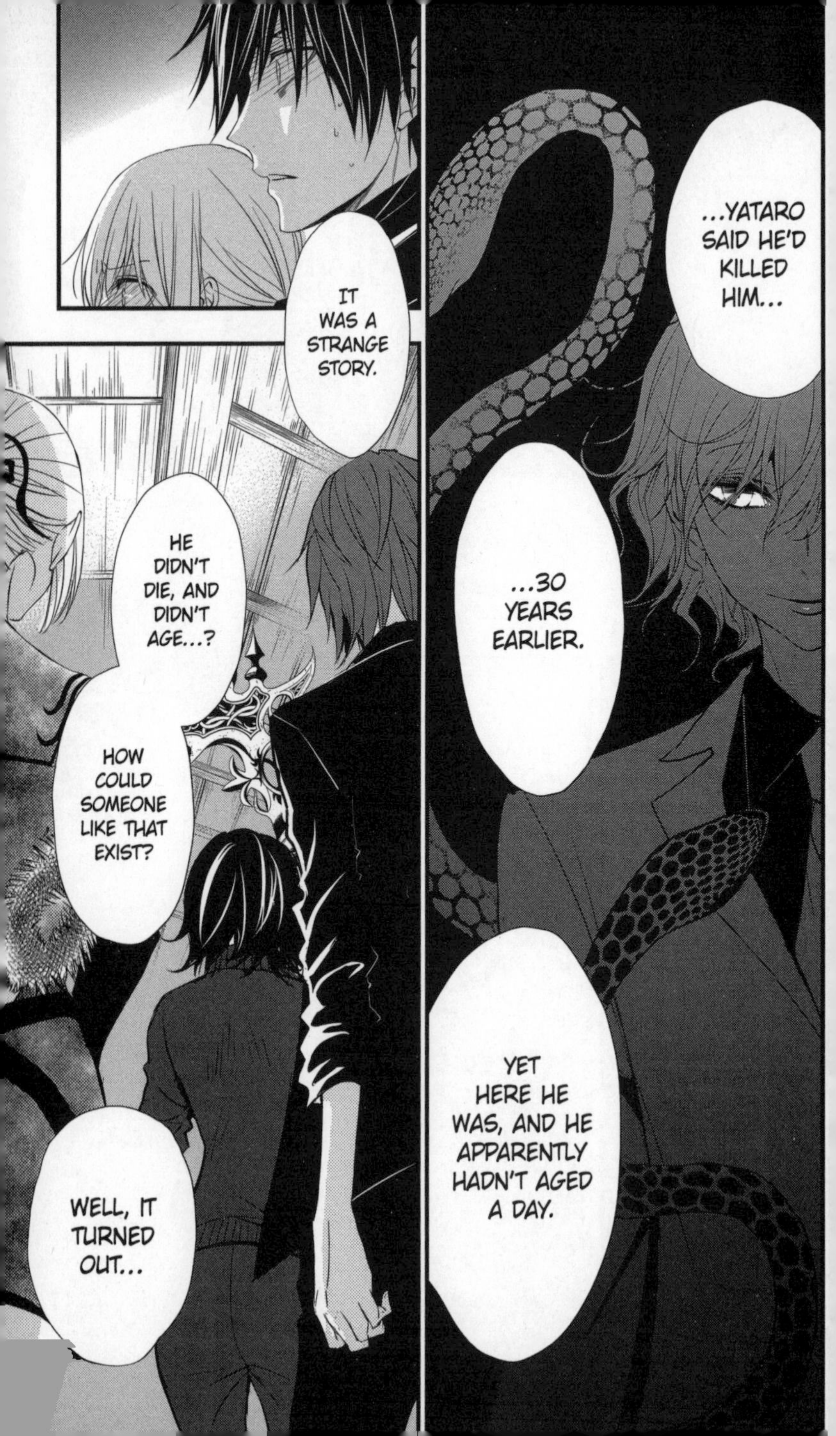
...YATARO SAID HE'D KILLED HIM...
...30 YEARS EARLIER.
YET HERE HE WAS, AND HE APPARENTLY HADN'T AGED A DAY.
IT WAS A STRANGE STORY.
HE DIDN'T DIE, AND DIDN'T AGE...?
HOW COULD SOMEONE LIKE THAT EXIST?
WELL, IT TURNED OUT...

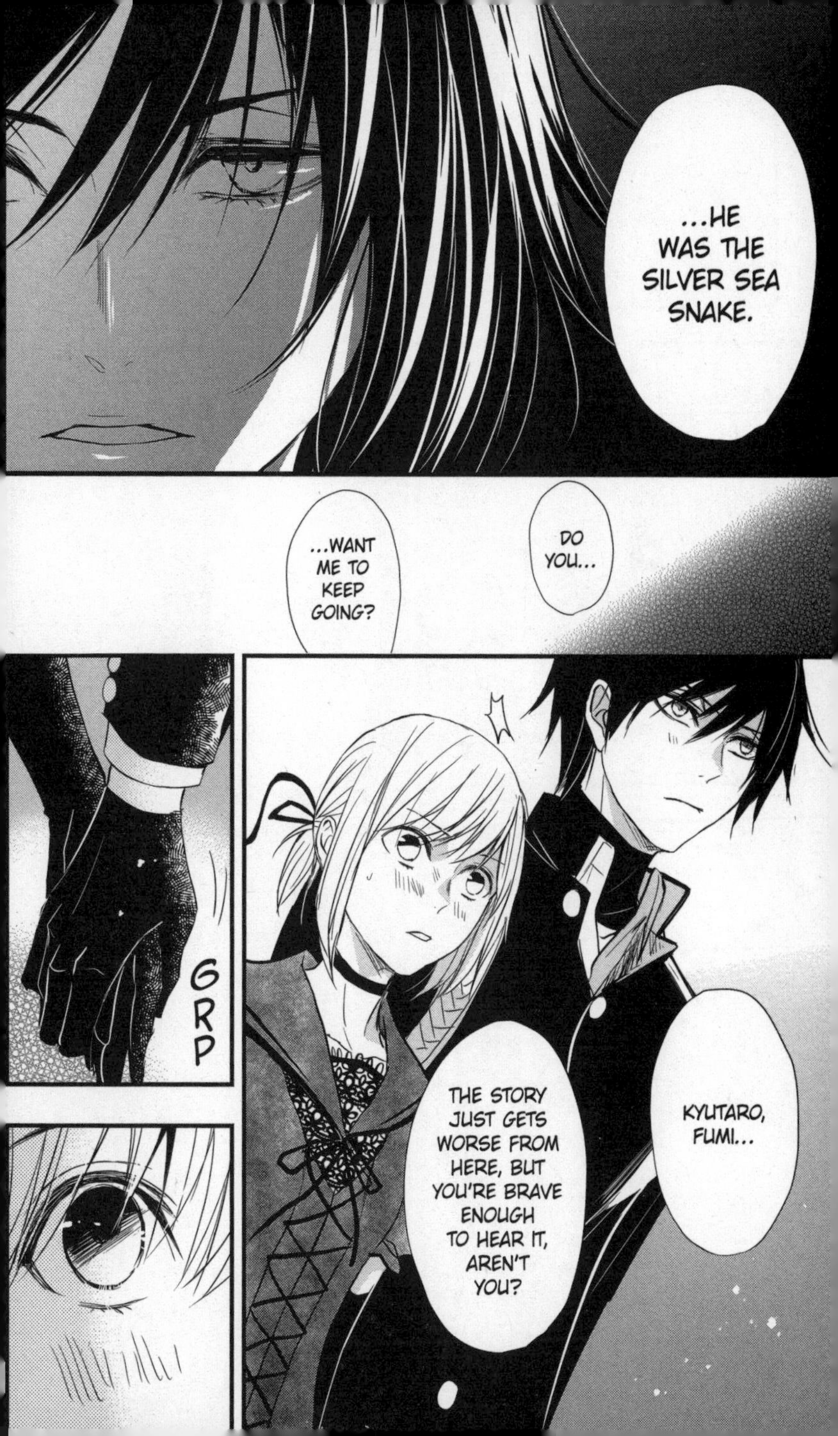
...HE WAS THE SILVER SEA SNAKE.
DO YOU...
...WANT ME TO KEEP GOING?
KYUTARO, FUMI...
THE STORY JUST GETS WORSE FROM HERE, BUT YOU'RE BRAVE ENOUGH TO HEAR IT, AREN'T YOU?
GRP

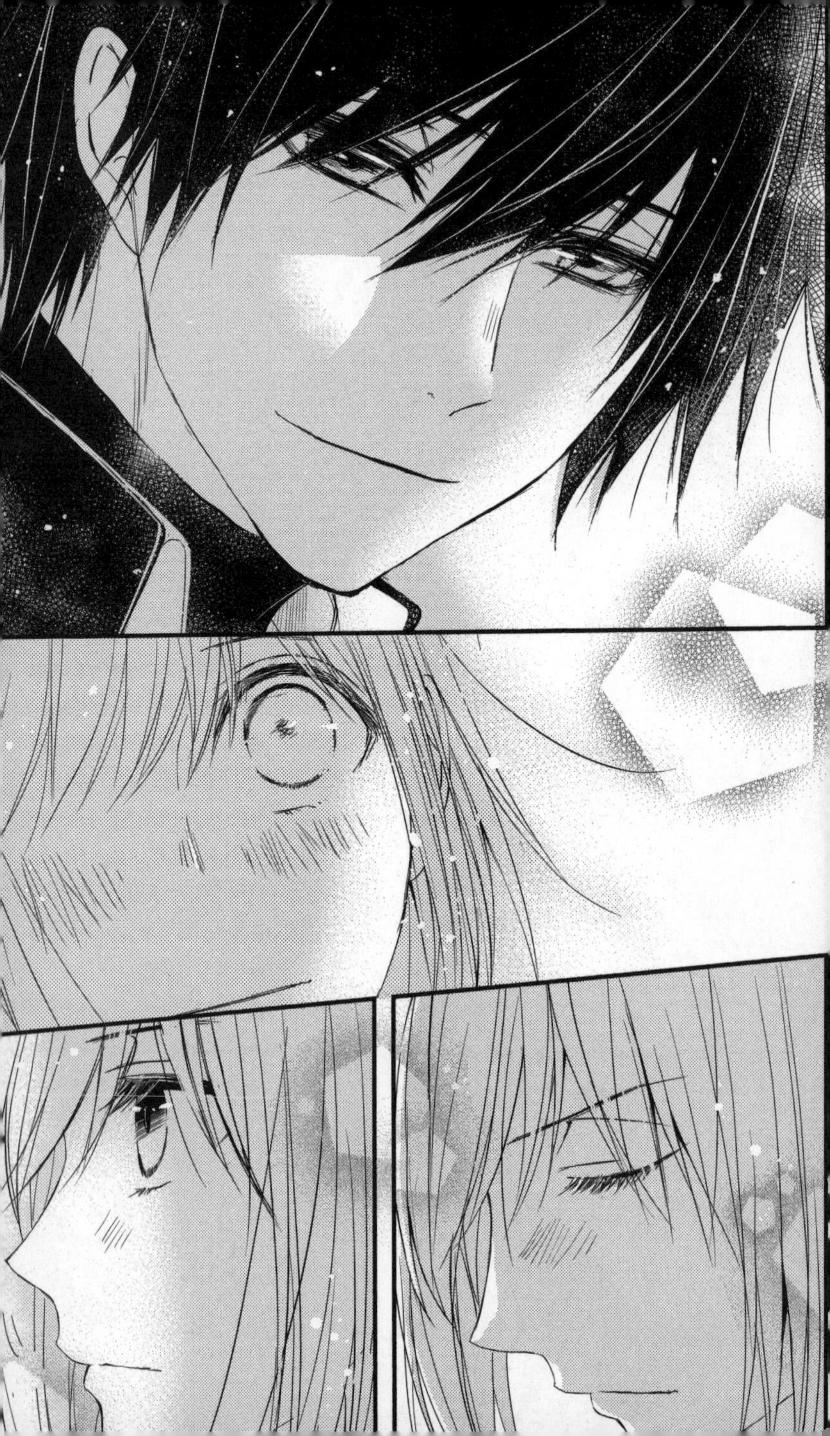

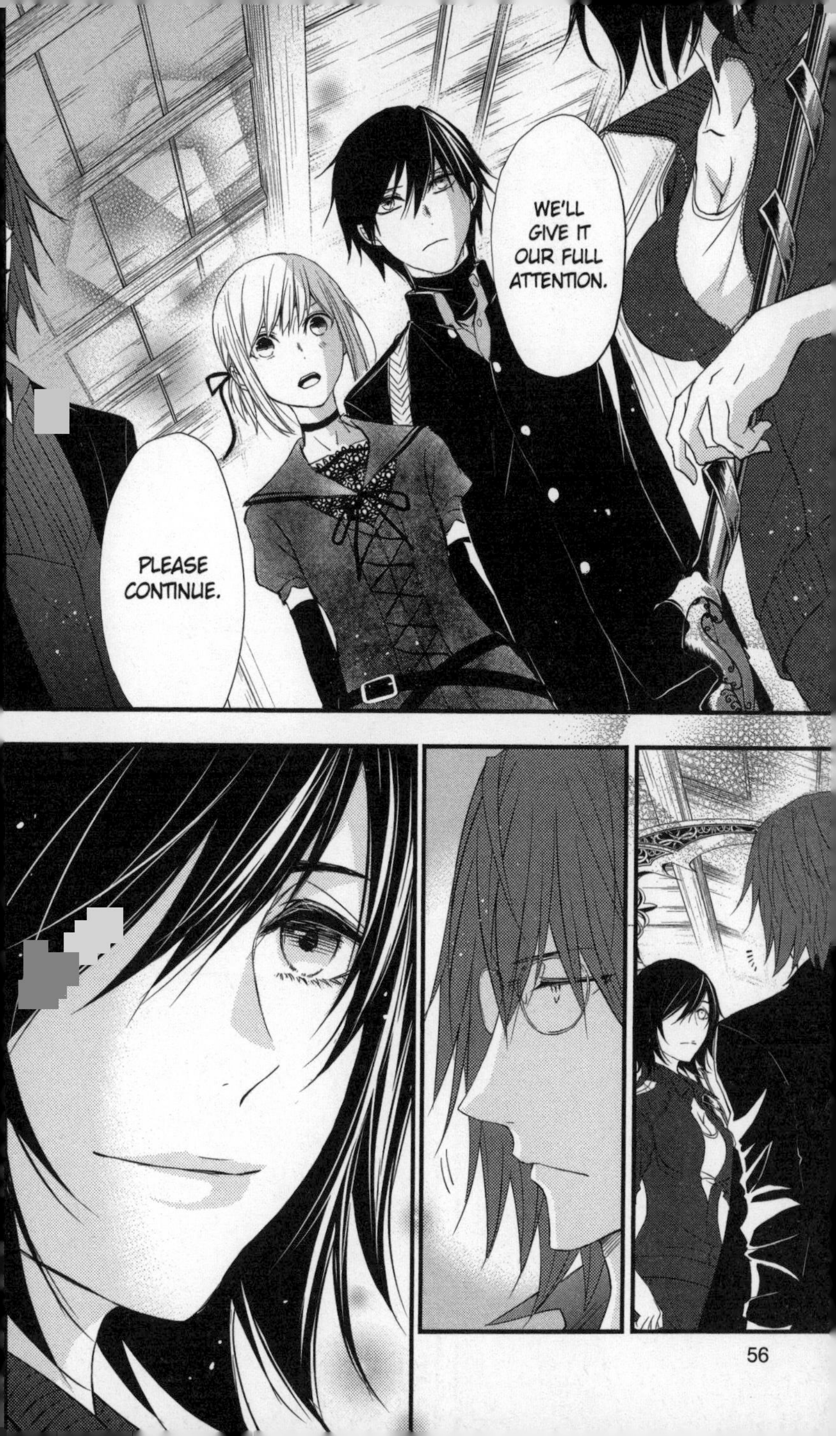
WE'LL GIVE IT OUR FULL ATTENTION.
PLEASE CONTINUE.

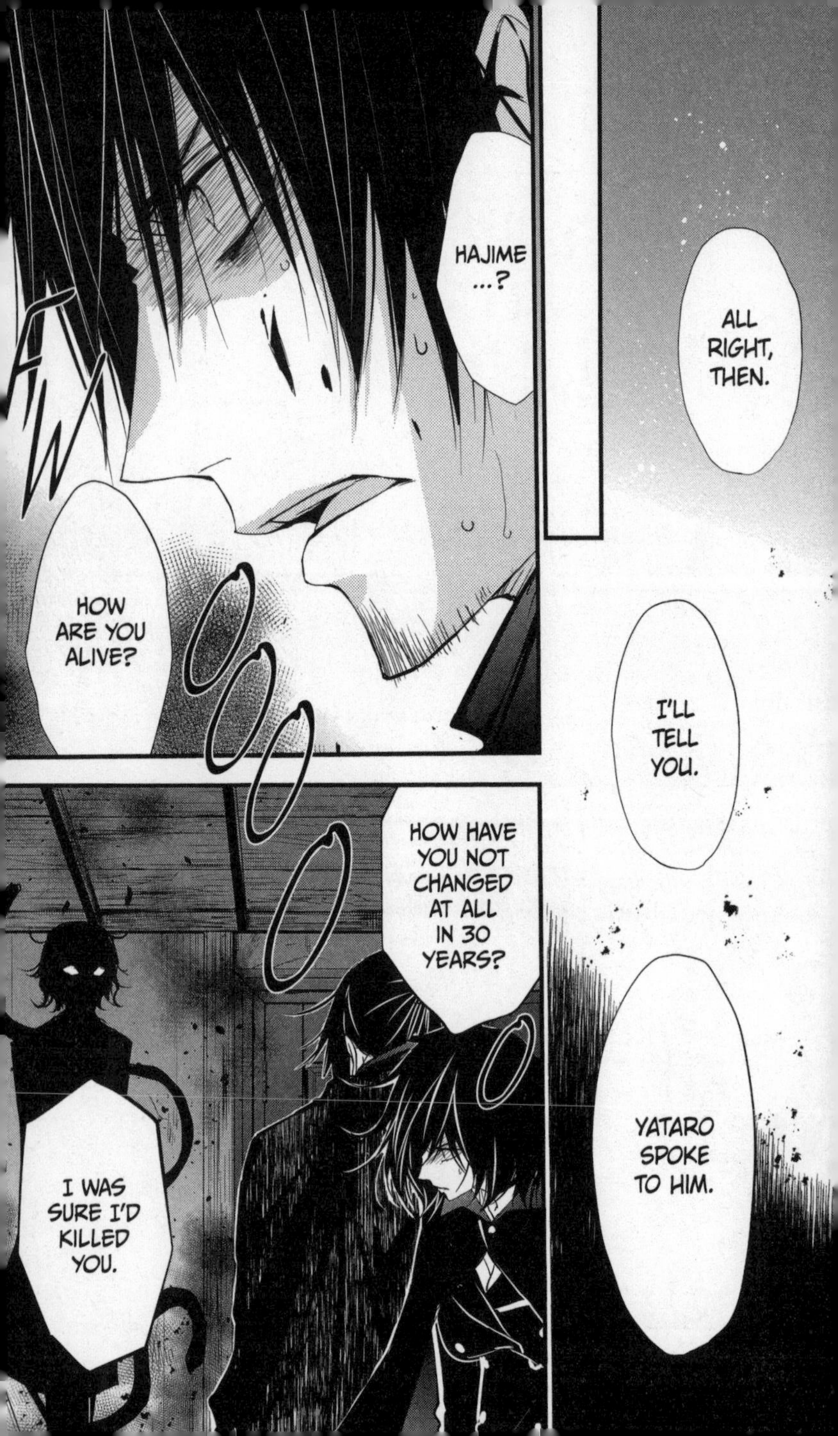
ALL RIGHT, THEN.
I'LL TELL YOU.
YATARO SPOKE TO HIM.
HAJIME ...?
HOW ARE YOU ALIVE?
HOW HAVE YOU NOT CHANGED AT ALL IN 30 YEARS?
I WAS SURE I'D KILLED YOU.

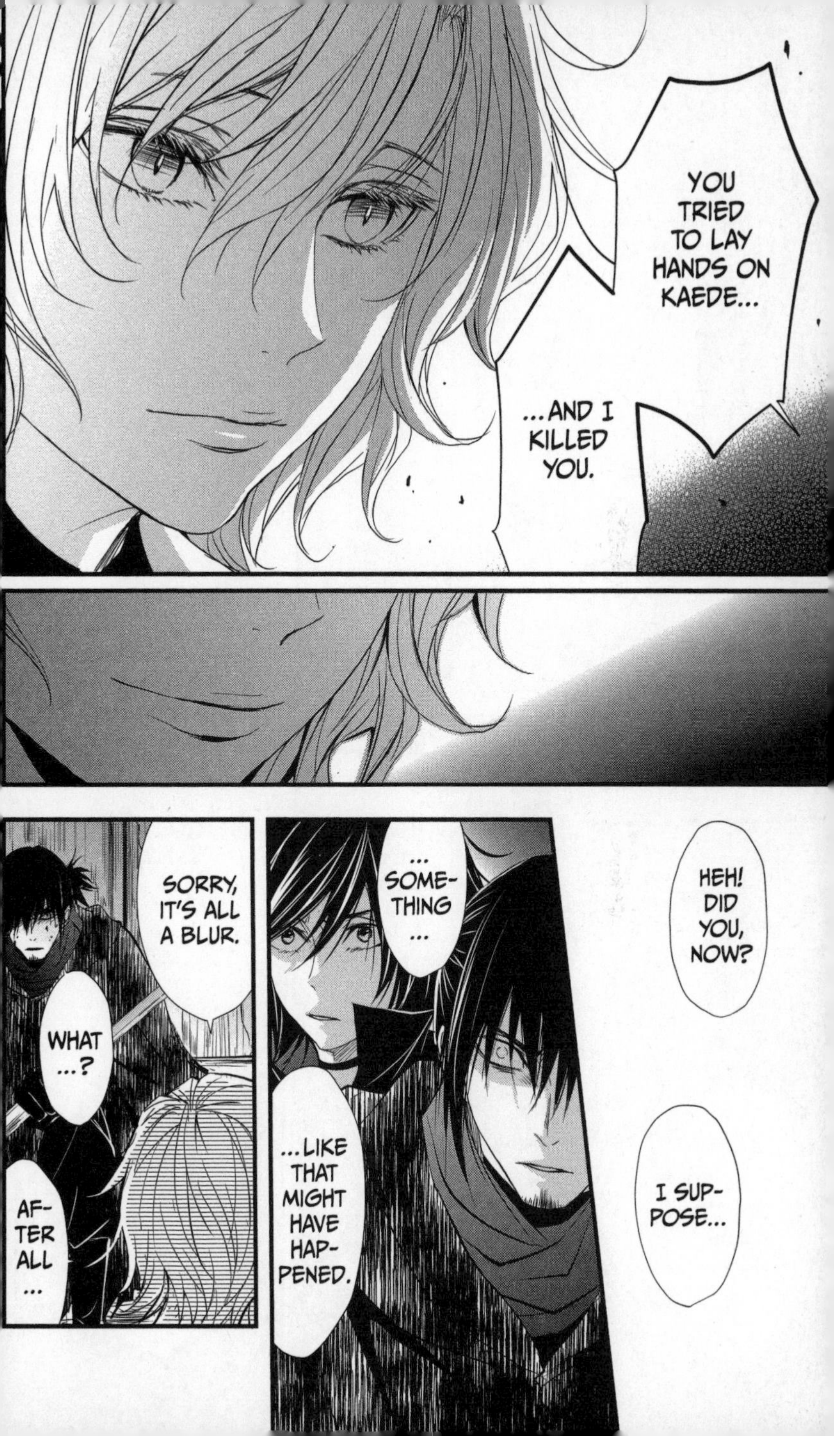
YOU TRIED TO LAY HANDS ON KAEDE...
...AND I KILLED YOU.
HEH! DID YOU, NOW?
... SOME-THING ...
I SUP-POSE...
...LIKE THAT MIGHT HAVE HAP-PENED.
SORRY, IT'S ALL A BLUR.
WHAT ...?
AF-TER ALL ...

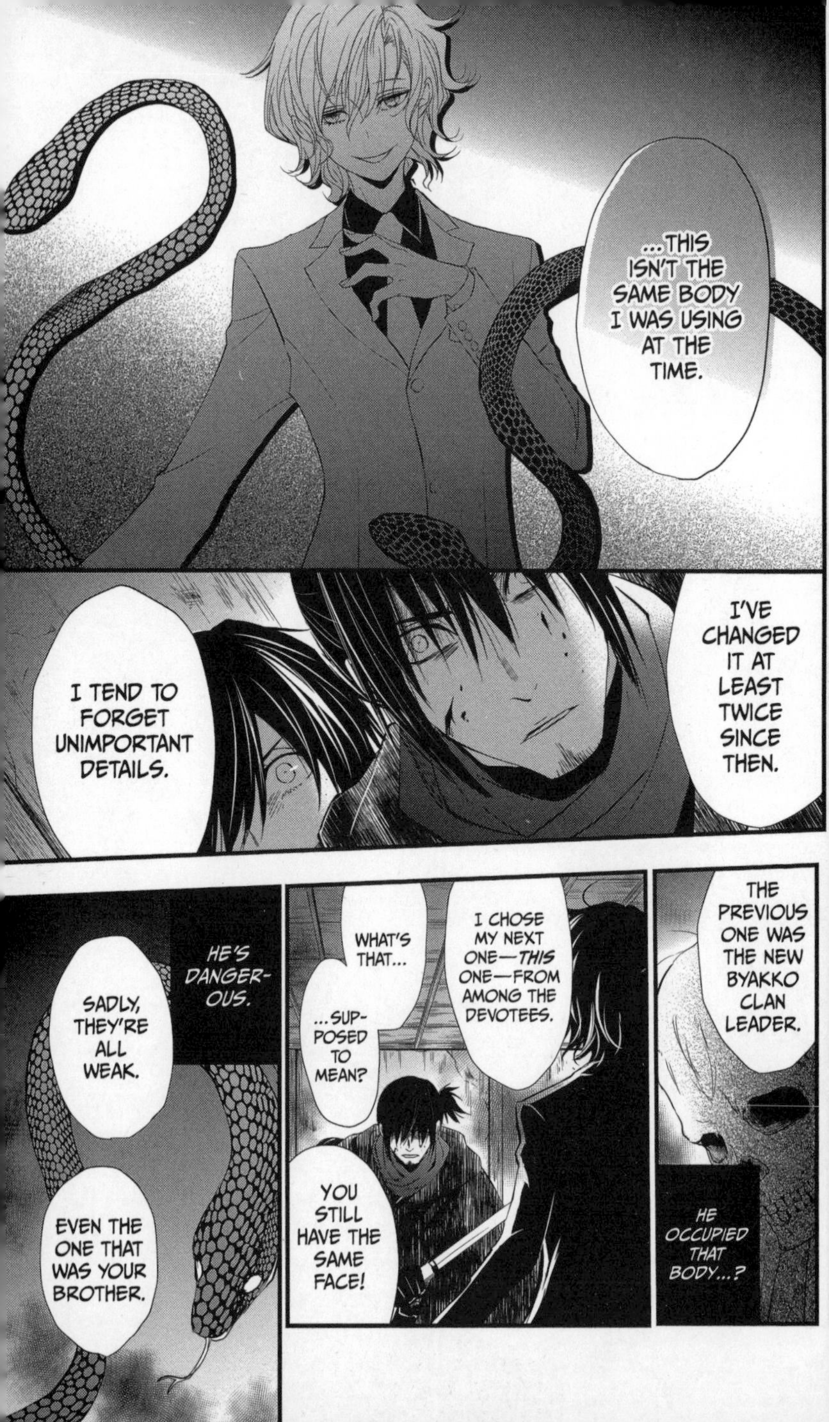
...THIS ISN'T THE SAME BODY I WAS USING AT THE TIME.
I'VE CHANGED IT AT LEAST TWICE SINCE THEN.
I TEND TO FORGET UNIMPORTANT DETAILS.
THE PREVIOUS ONE WAS THE NEW BYAKKO CLAN LEADER.
HE OCCUPIED THAT BODY...?
I CHOSE MY NEXT ONE—*THIS* ONE—FROM AMONG THE DEVOTEES.
WHAT'S THAT...
...SUP-POSED TO MEAN?
YOU STILL HAVE THE SAME FACE!
HE'S DANGER-OUS.
SADLY, THEY'RE ALL WEAK.
EVEN THE ONE THAT WAS YOUR BROTHER.

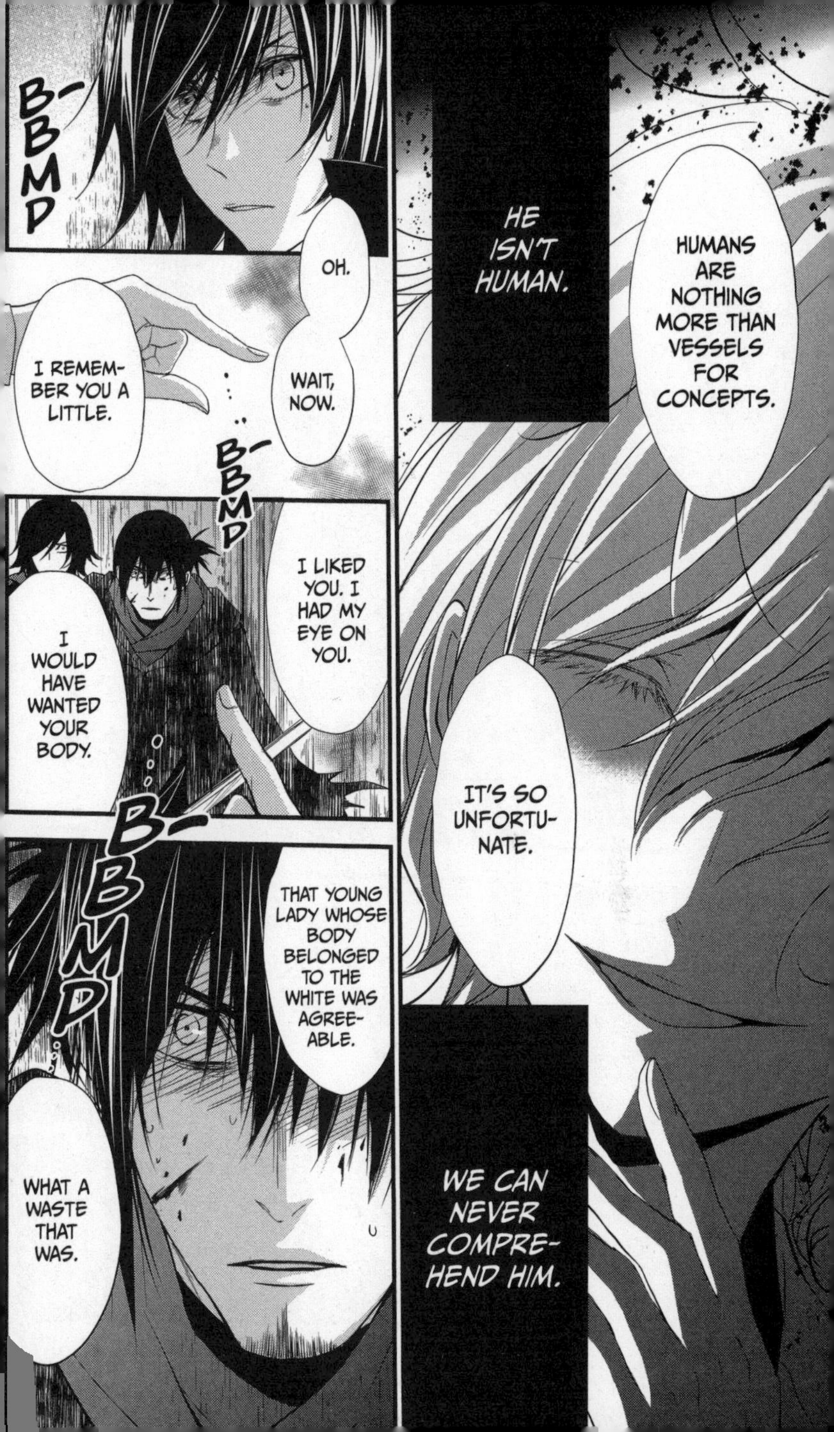
HUMANS ARE NOTHING MORE THAN VESSELS FOR CONCEPTS.
HE ISN'T HUMAN.
IT'S SO UNFORTUNATE.
WE CAN NEVER COMPREHEND HIM.
B-BBMP
OH.
WAIT, NOW.
I REMEMBER YOU A LITTLE.
B-BBMP
I LIKED YOU. I HAD MY EYE ON YOU.
I WOULD HAVE WANTED YOUR BODY.
B-BBMP
THAT YOUNG LADY WHOSE BODY BELONGED TO THE WHITE WAS AGREEABLE.
WHAT A WASTE THAT WAS.

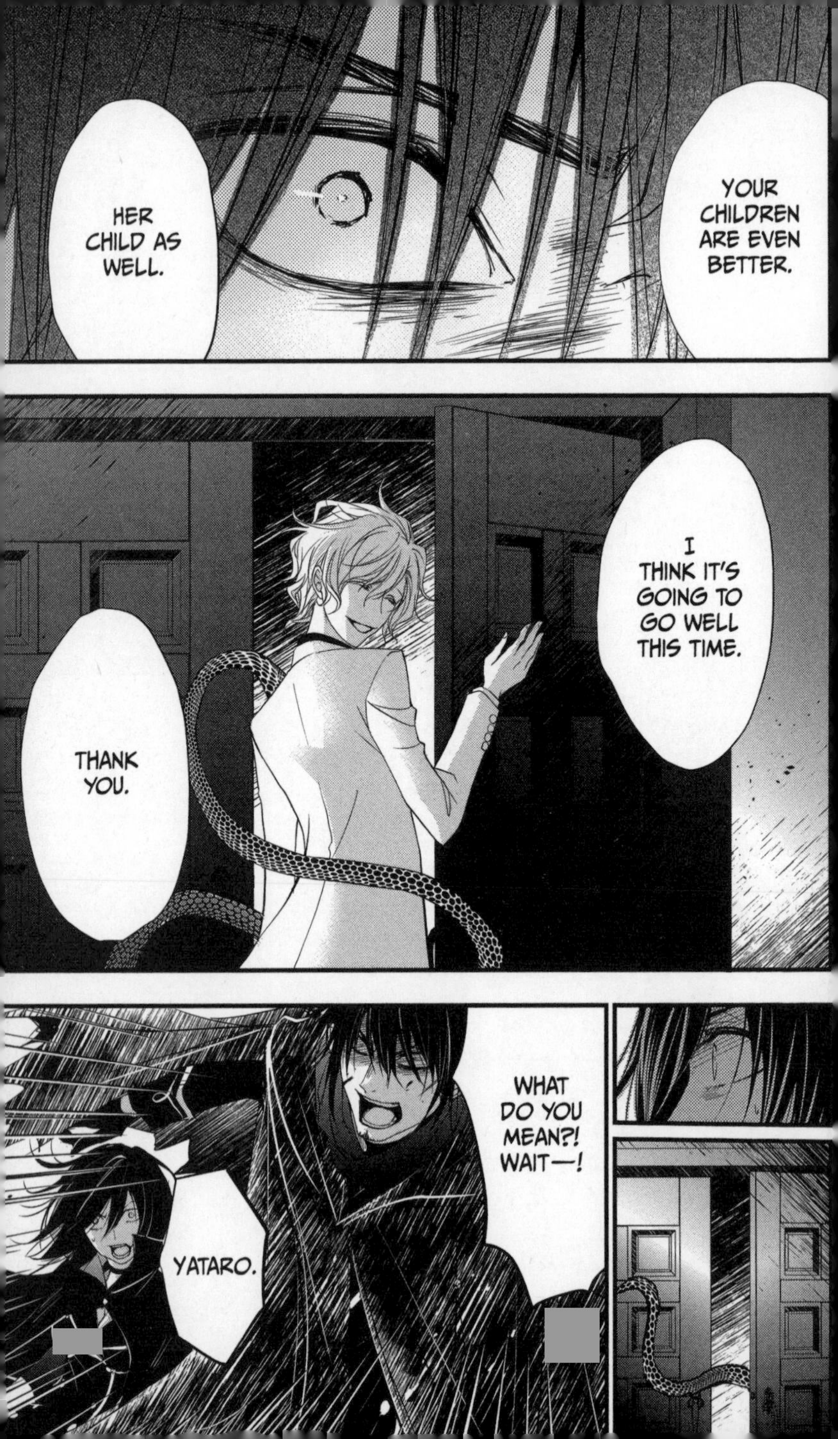
YOUR CHILDREN ARE EVEN BETTER.
HER CHILD AS WELL.
I THINK IT'S GOING TO GO WELL THIS TIME.
THANK YOU.
WHAT DO YOU MEAN?! WAIT—!
YATARO.

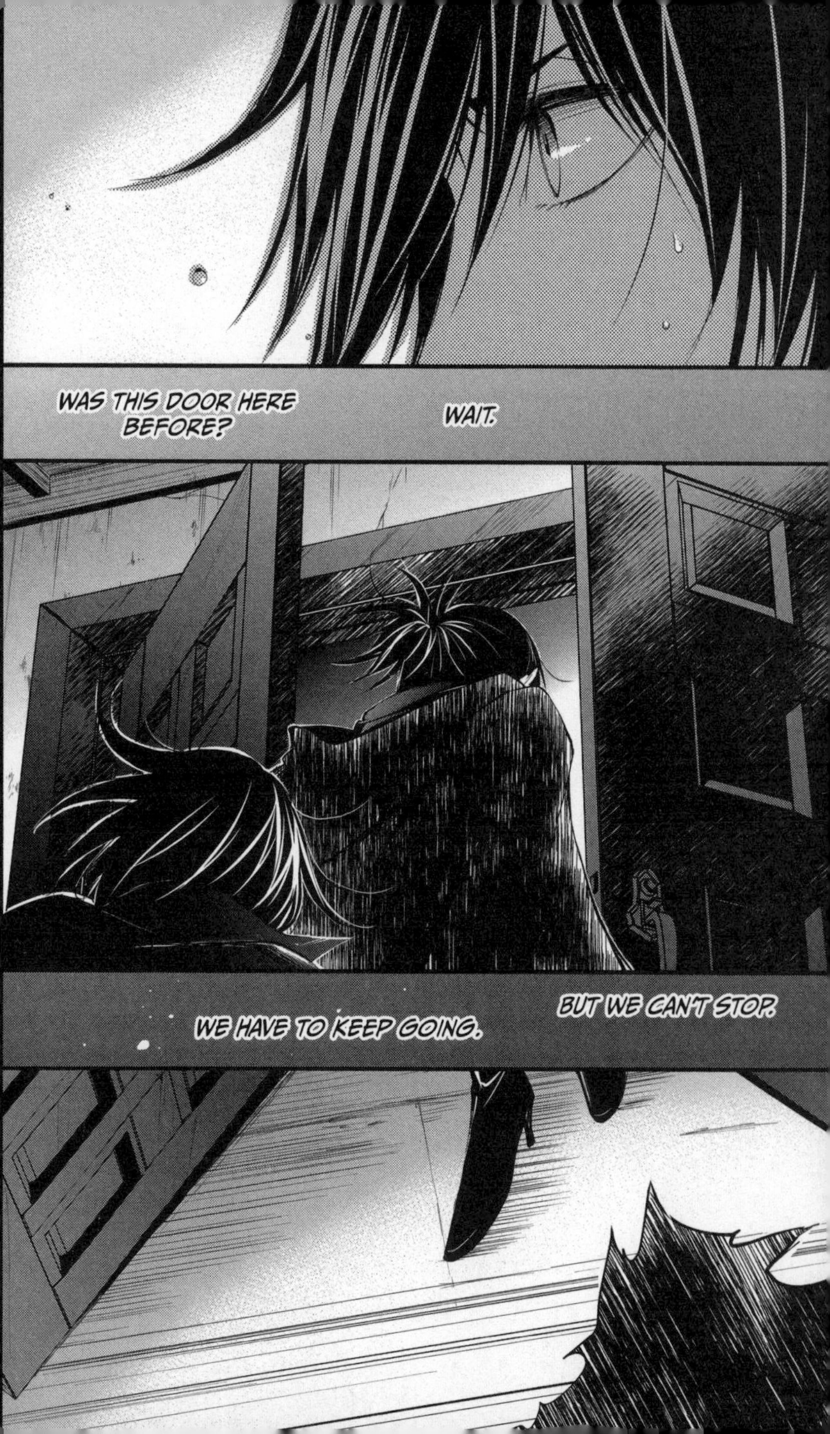
WAIT.
WAS THIS DOOR HERE BEFORE?
BUT WE CAN'T STOP.
WE HAVE TO KEEP GOING.

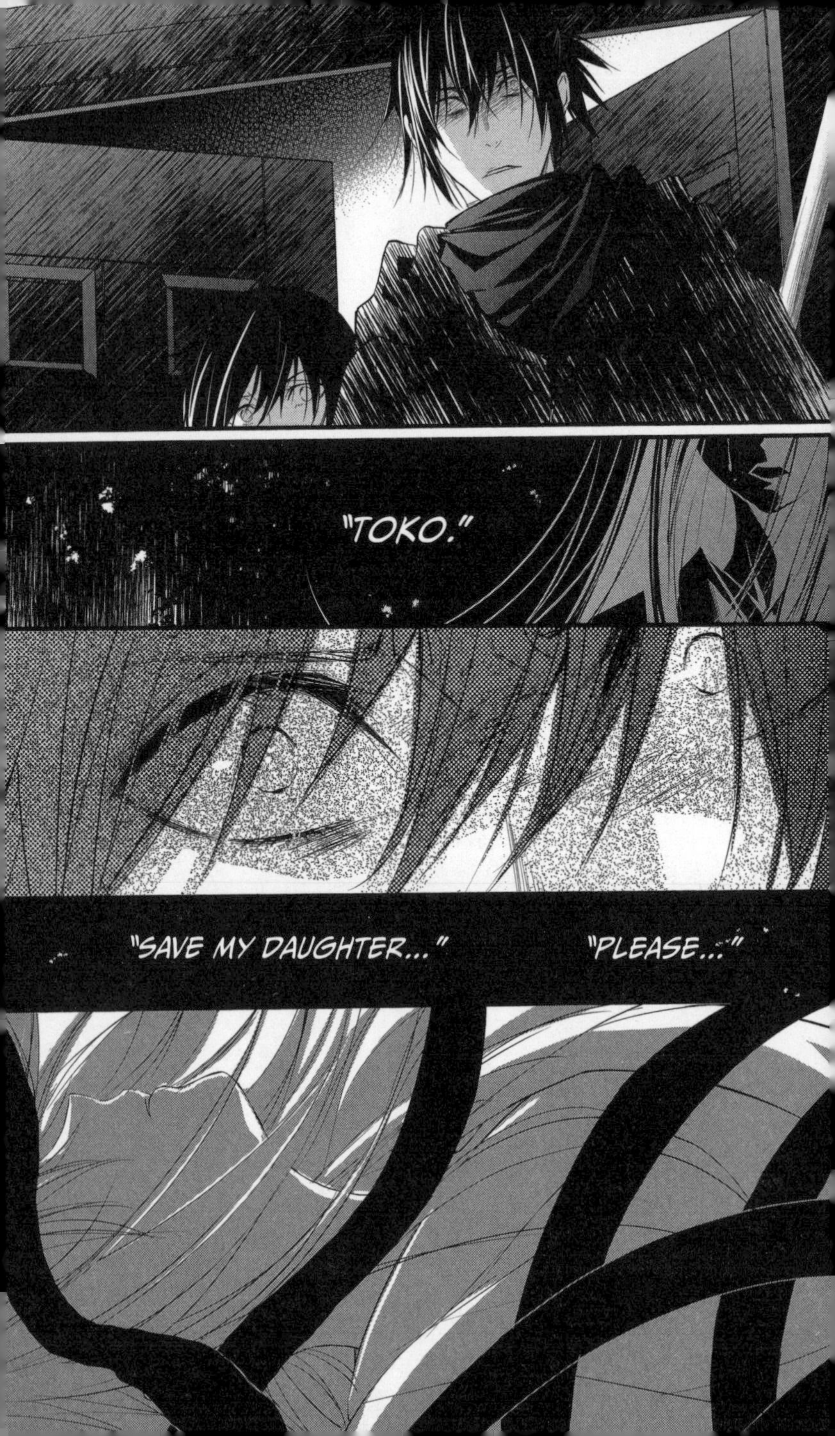
"TOKO."
"PLEASE..."
"SAVE MY DAUGHTER..."

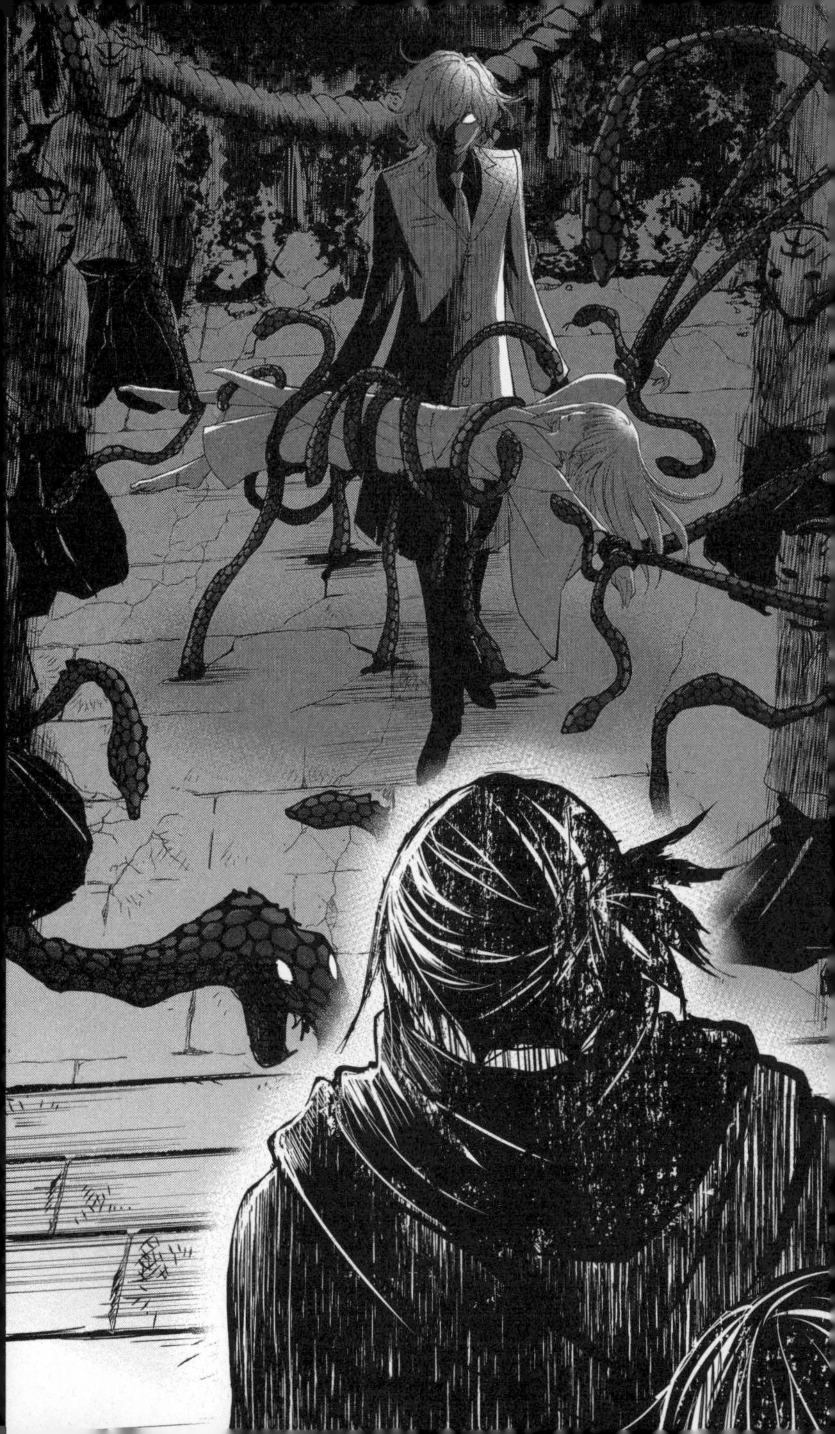

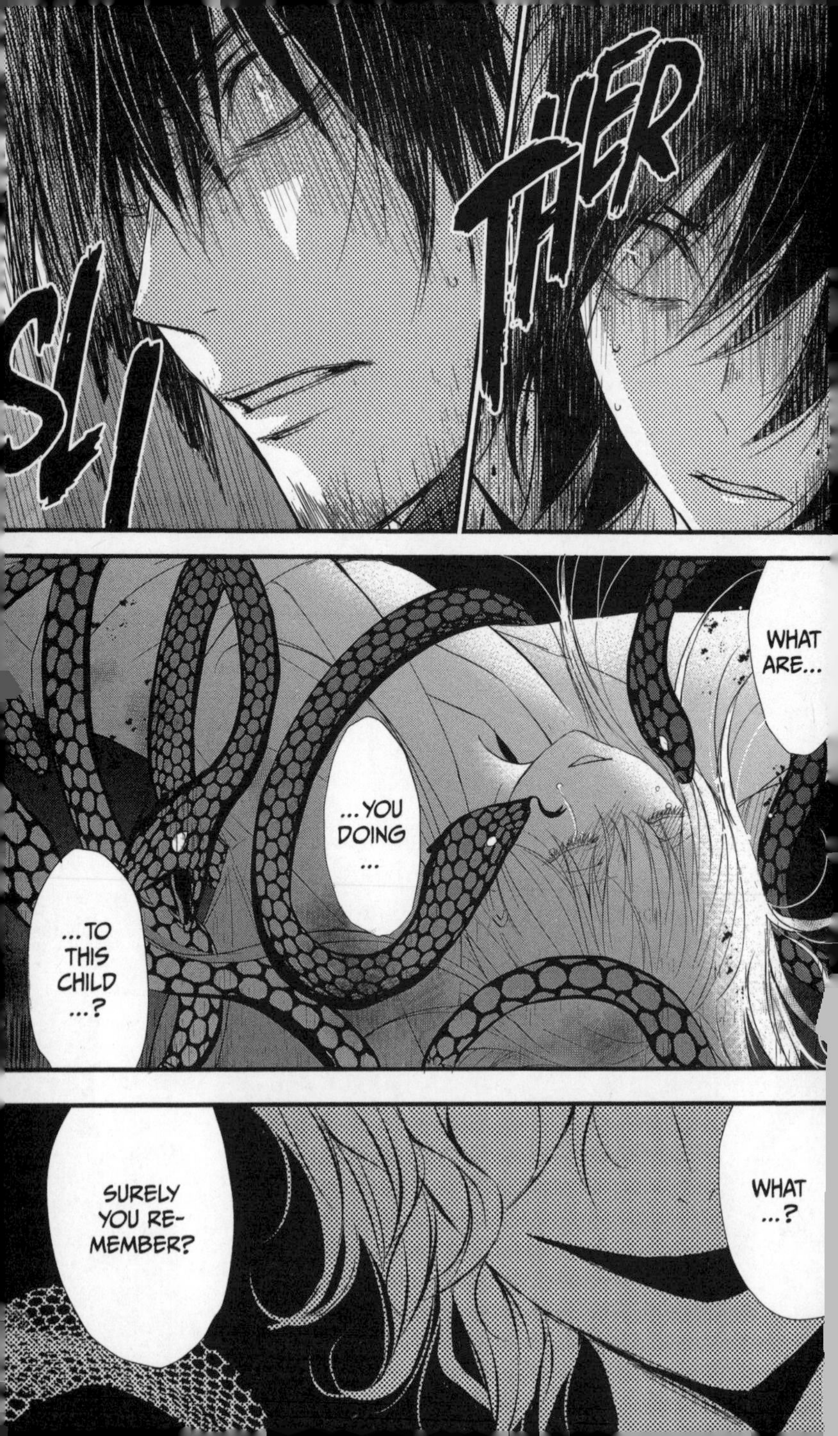
SLITHER
WHAT ARE...
...YOU DOING ...
...TO THIS CHILD ...?
WHAT ...?
SURELY YOU RE- MEMBER?

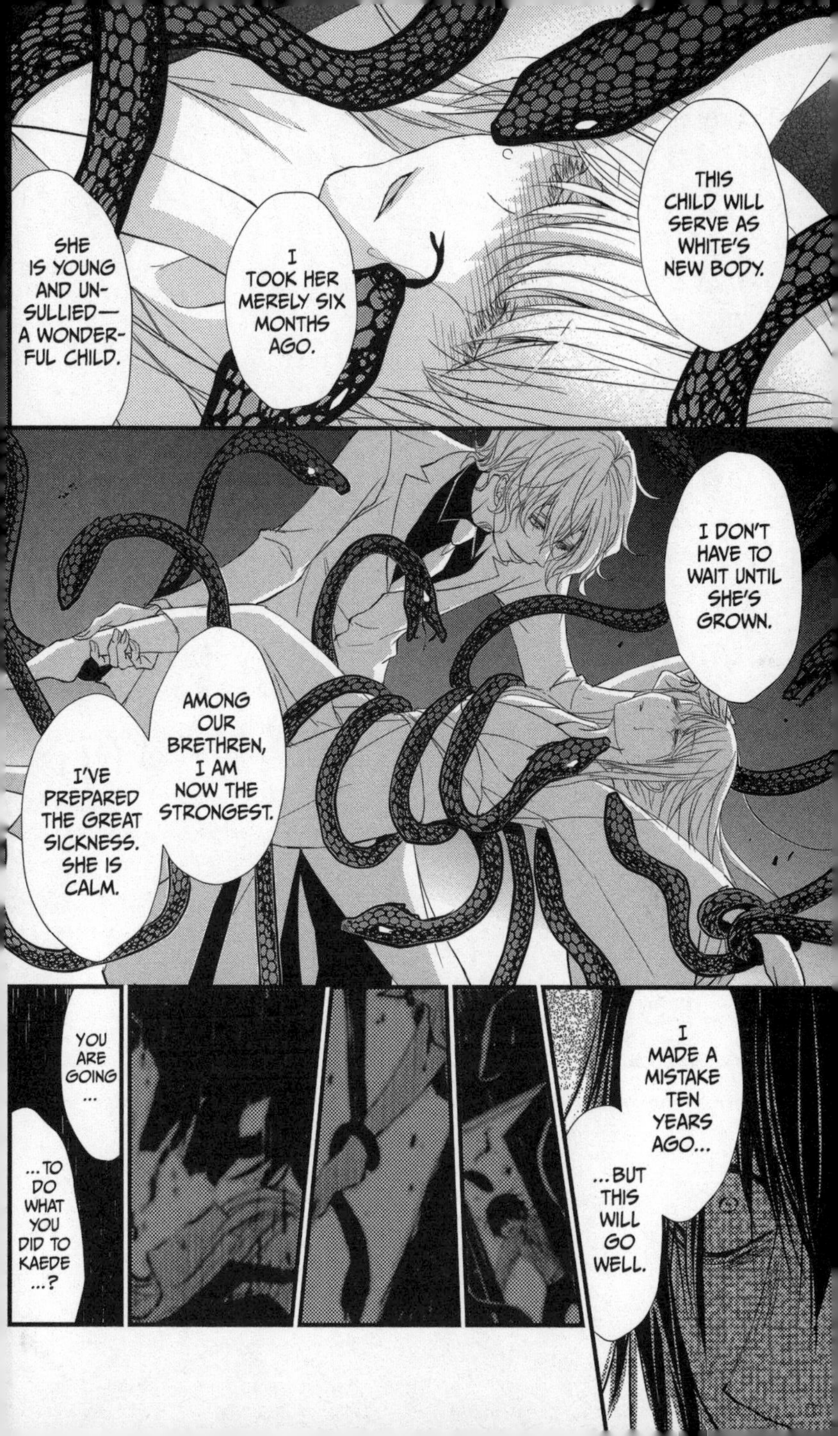
THIS CHILD WILL SERVE AS WHITE'S NEW BODY.
I TOOK HER MERELY SIX MONTHS AGO.
SHE IS YOUNG AND UN-SULLIED—A WONDERFUL CHILD.
I DON'T HAVE TO WAIT UNTIL SHE'S GROWN.
AMONG OUR BRETHREN, I AM NOW THE STRONGEST.
I'VE PREPARED THE GREAT SICKNESS. SHE IS CALM.
I MADE A MISTAKE TEN YEARS AGO...
...BUT THIS WILL GO WELL.
YOU ARE GOING...
...TO DO WHAT YOU DID TO KAEDE...?

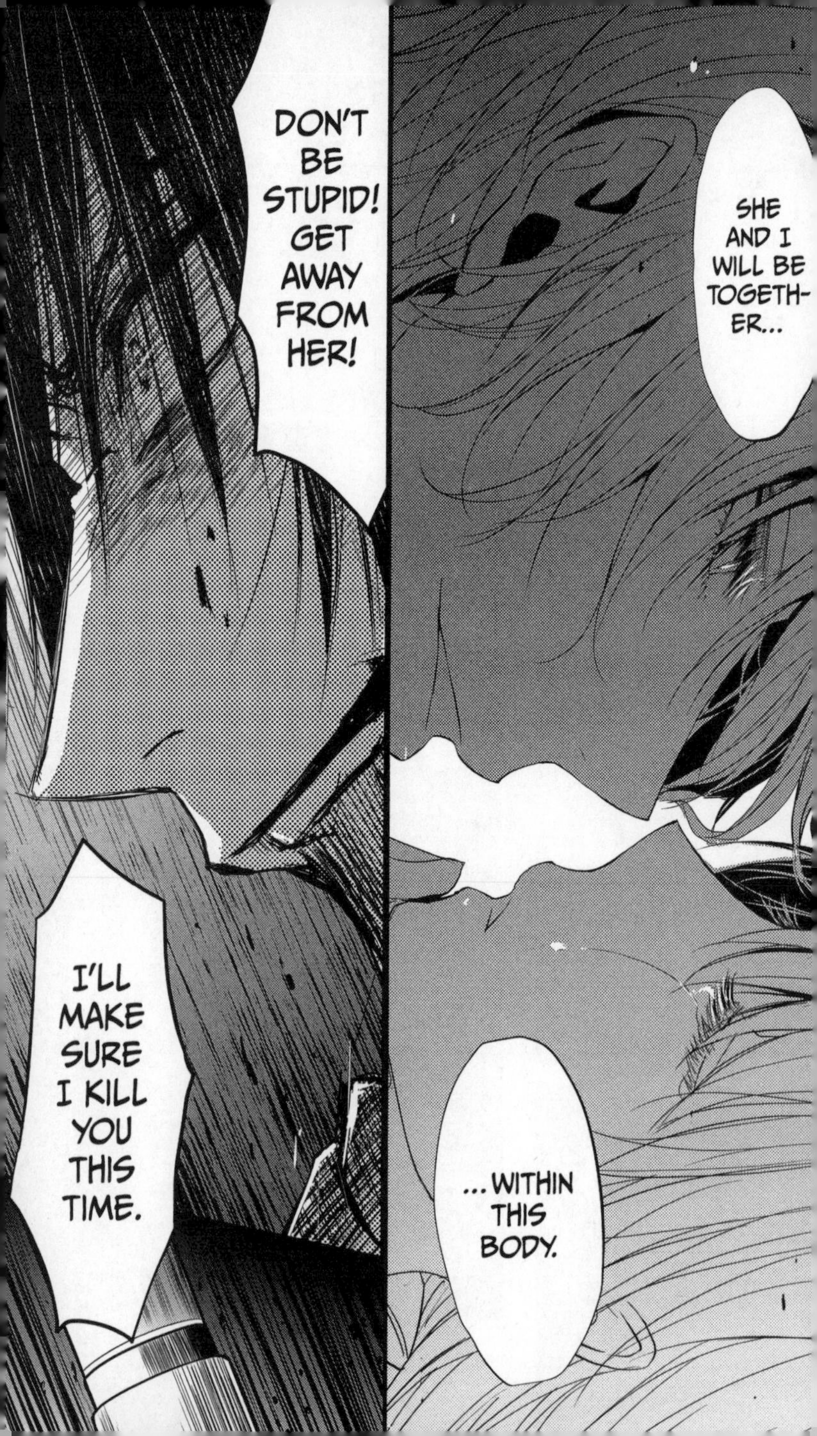
SHE AND I WILL BE TOGETHER...
...WITHIN THIS BODY.
DON'T BE STUPID! GET AWAY FROM HER!
I'LL MAKE SURE I KILL YOU THIS TIME.

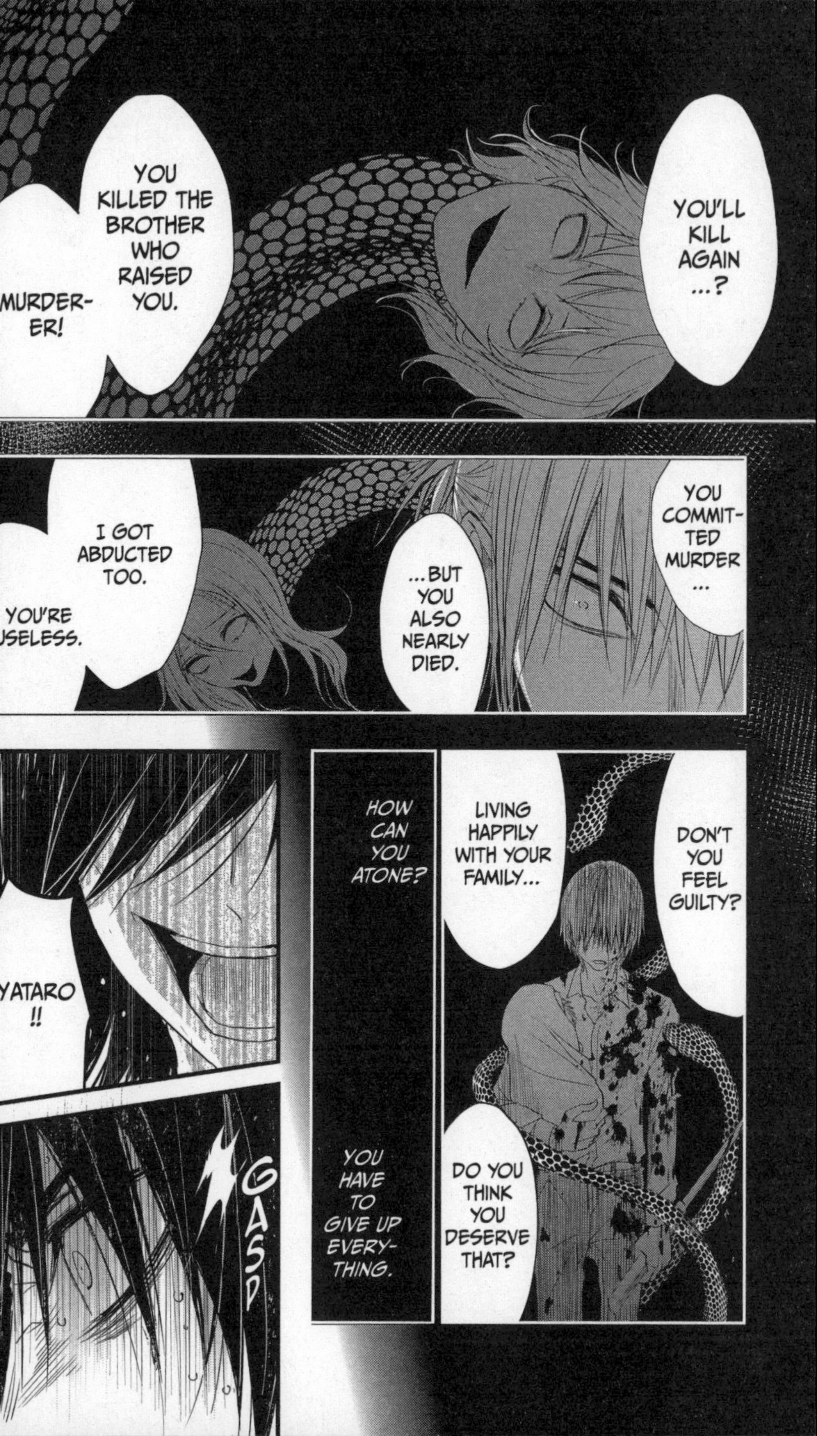
YOU'LL KILL AGAIN ...?
YOU KILLED THE BROTHER WHO RAISED YOU.
MURDER-ER!
YOU COMMIT-TED MURDER ...
...BUT YOU ALSO NEARLY DIED.
I GOT ABDUCTED TOO.
YOU'RE USELESS.
DON'T YOU FEEL GUILTY?
LIVING HAPPILY WITH YOUR FAMILY...
DO YOU THINK YOU DESERVE THAT?
HOW CAN YOU ATONE?
YOU HAVE TO GIVE UP EVERY-THING.
YATARO !!
GASP

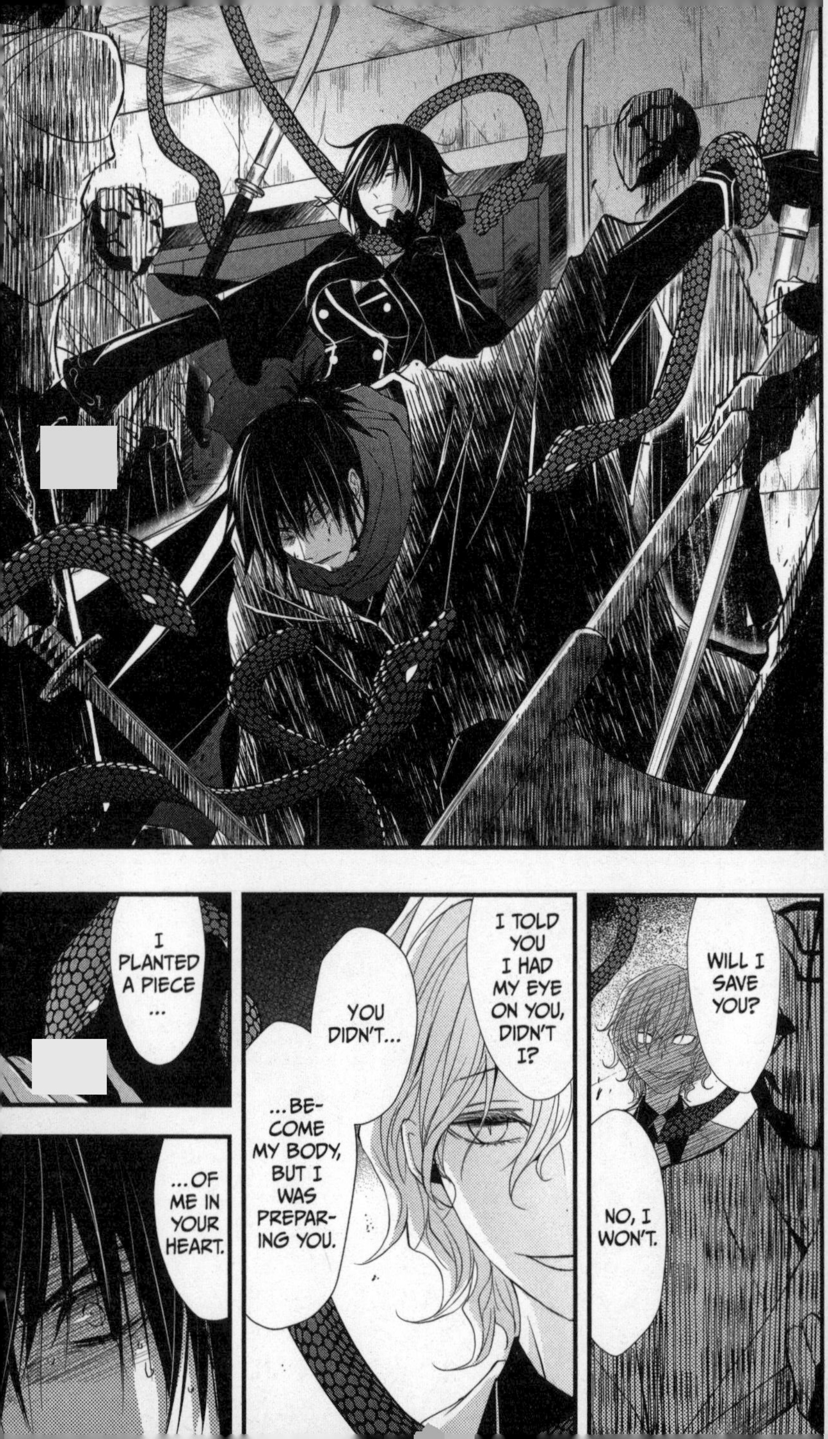
WILL I SAVE YOU?
NO, I WON'T.
I TOLD YOU I HAD MY EYE ON YOU, DIDN'T I?
YOU DIDN'T...
...BECOME MY BODY, BUT I WAS PREPARING YOU.
I PLANTED A PIECE...
...OF ME IN YOUR HEART.

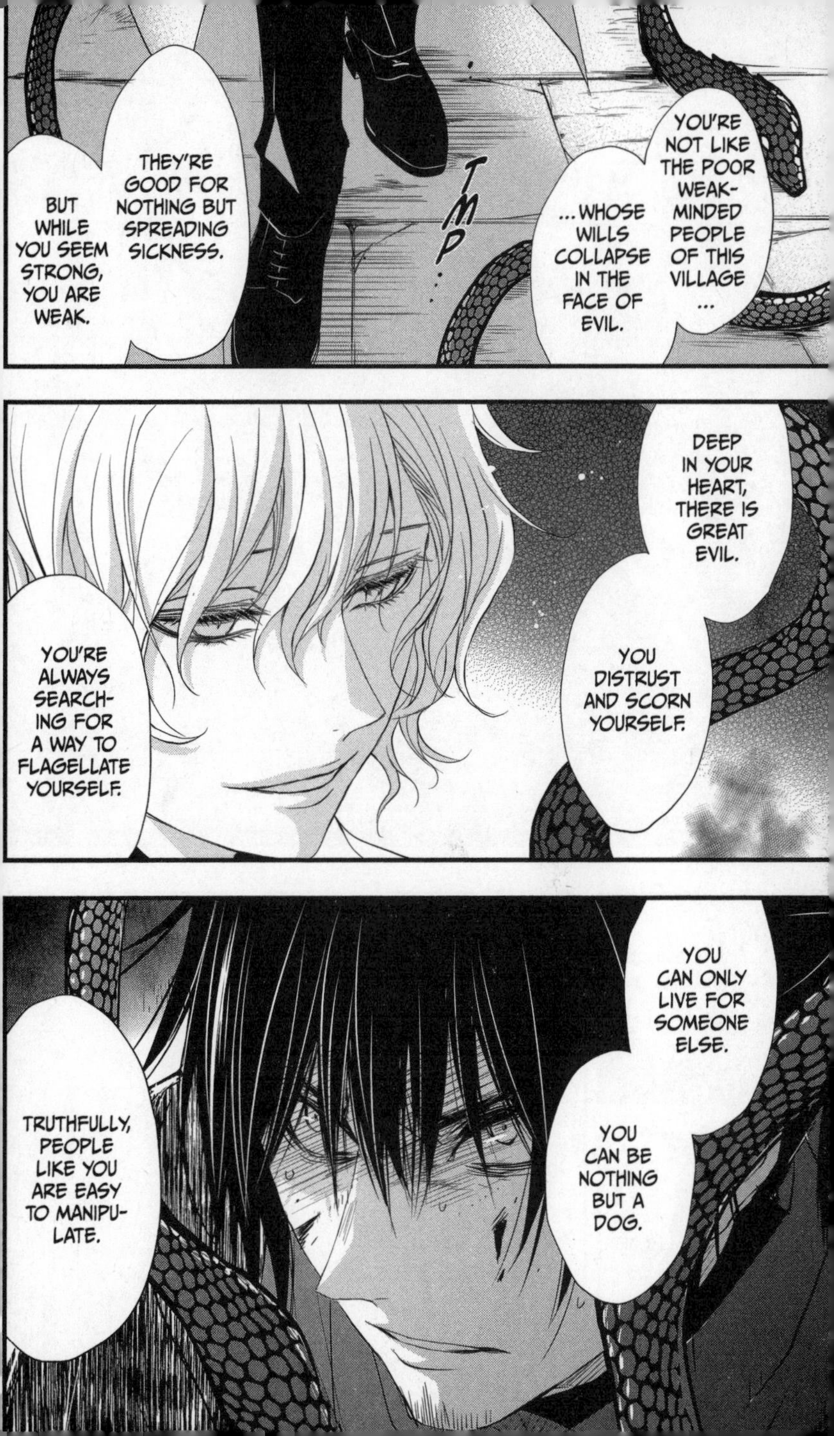
YOU'RE NOT LIKE THE POOR WEAK-MINDED PEOPLE OF THIS VILLAGE ...
...WHOSE WILLS COLLAPSE IN THE FACE OF EVIL.
TMP...
THEY'RE GOOD FOR NOTHING BUT SPREADING SICKNESS.
BUT WHILE YOU SEEM STRONG, YOU ARE WEAK.
DEEP IN YOUR HEART, THERE IS GREAT EVIL.
YOU DISTRUST AND SCORN YOURSELF.
YOU'RE ALWAYS SEARCH-ING FOR A WAY TO FLAGELLATE YOURSELF.
YOU CAN ONLY LIVE FOR SOMEONE ELSE.
YOU CAN BE NOTHING BUT A DOG.
TRUTHFULLY, PEOPLE LIKE YOU ARE EASY TO MANIPU-LATE.

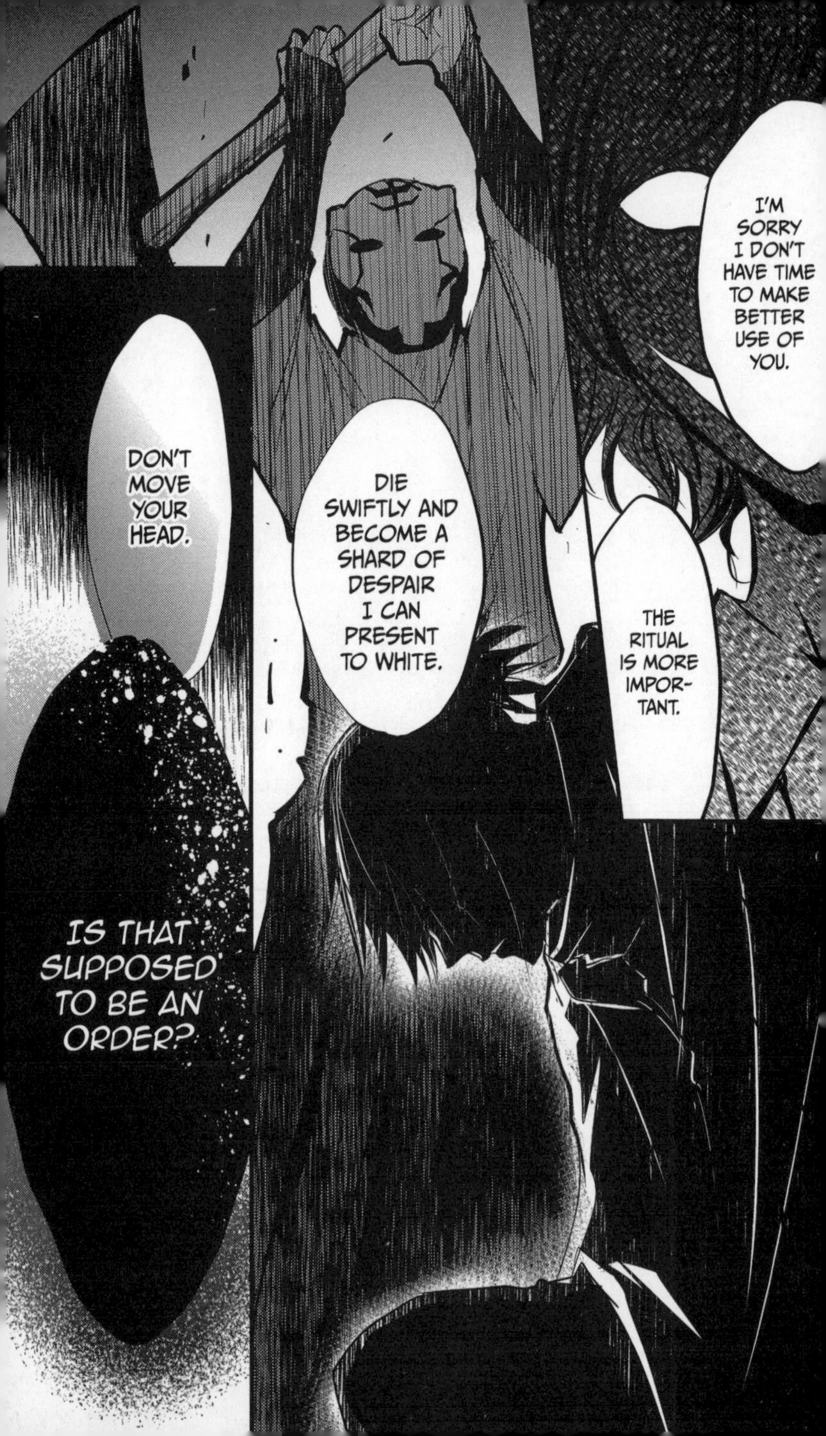
I'M SORRY I DON'T HAVE TIME TO MAKE BETTER USE OF YOU.
THE RITUAL IS MORE IMPOR-TANT.
DIE SWIFTLY AND BECOME A SHARD OF DESPAIR I CAN PRESENT TO WHITE.
DON'T MOVE YOUR HEAD.
IS THAT SUPPOSED TO BE AN ORDER?

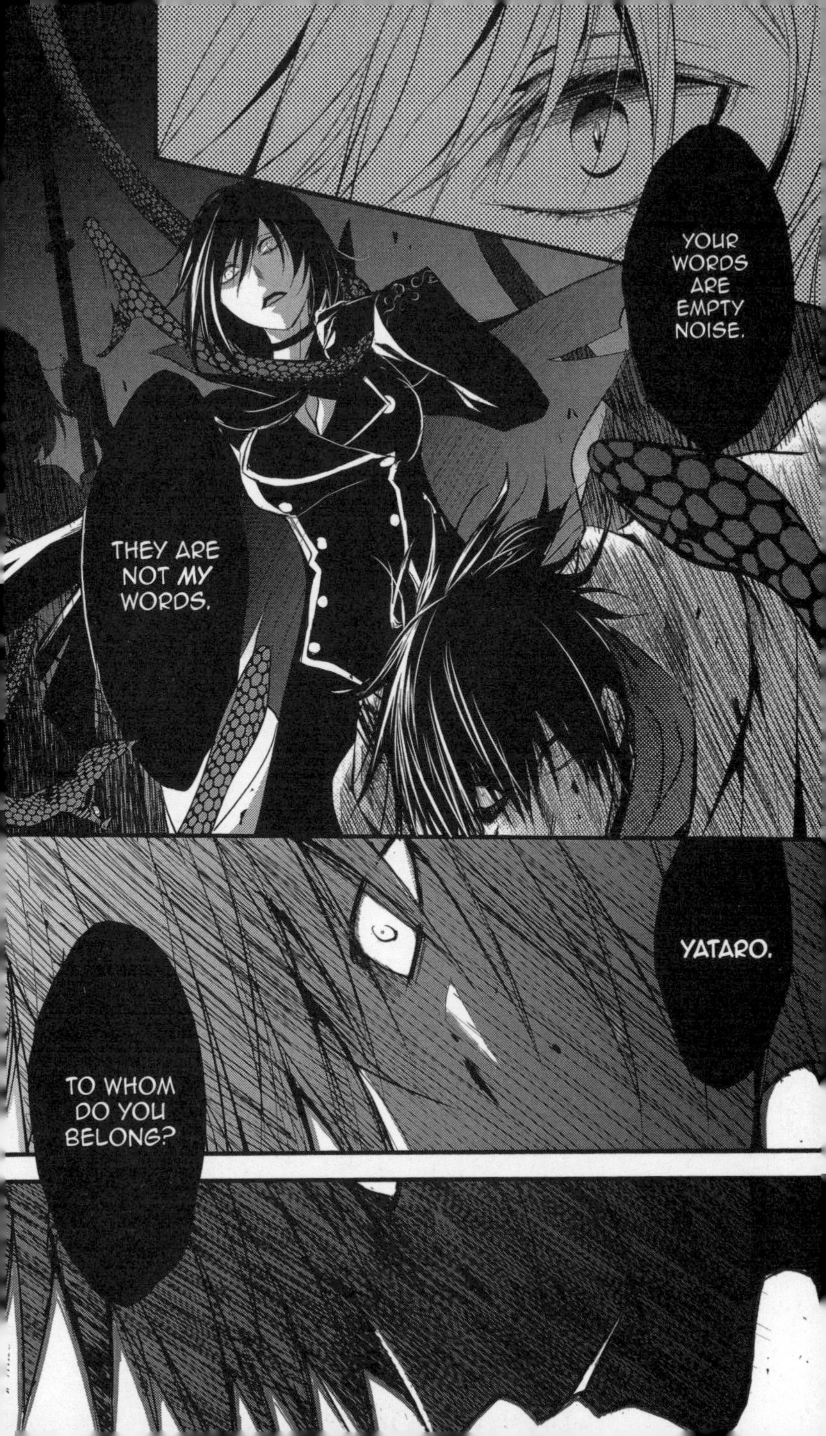
YOUR WORDS ARE EMPTY NOISE.
THEY ARE NOT MY WORDS.
YATARO.
TO WHOM DO YOU BELONG?

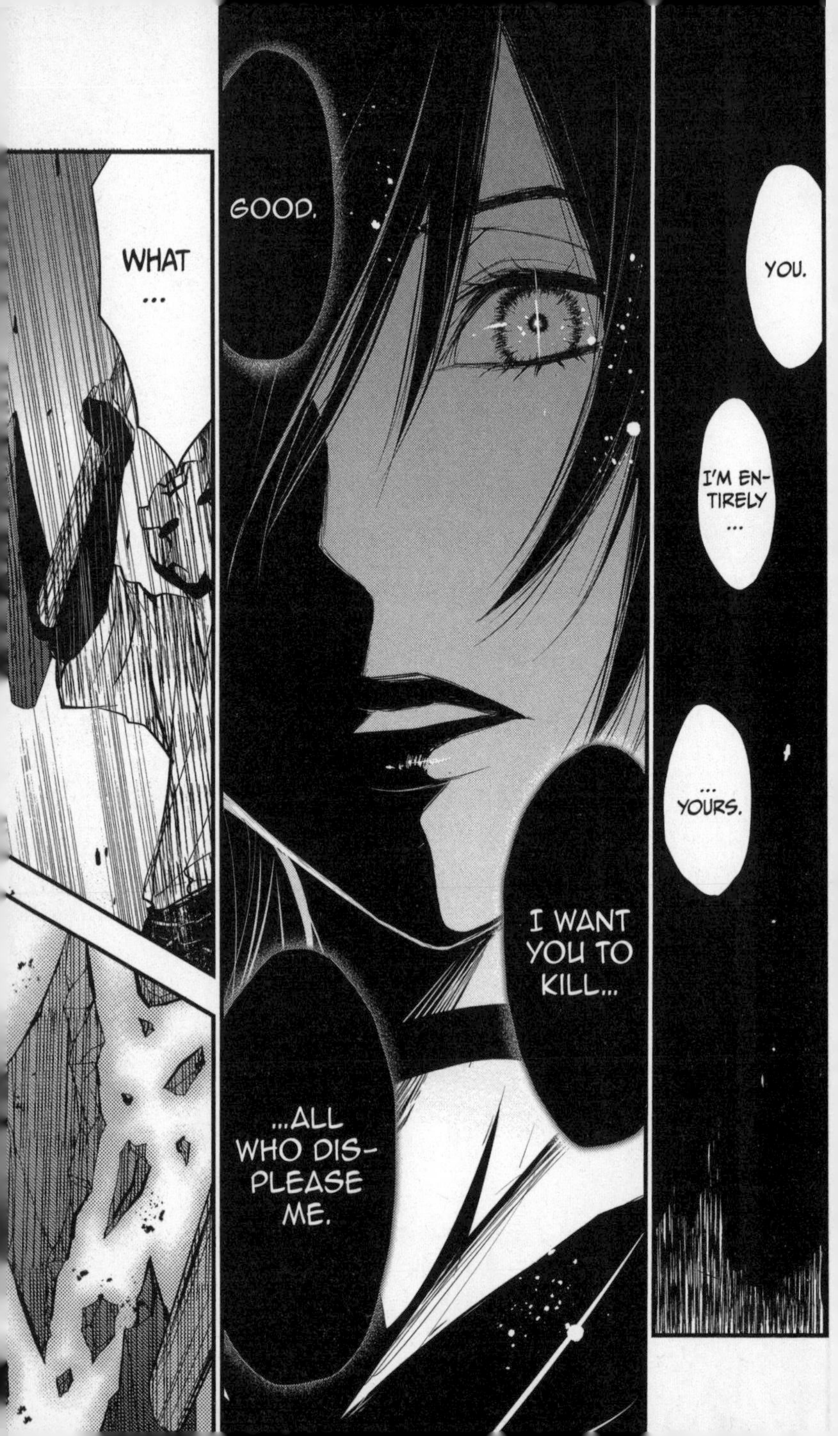
YOU.
I'M EN-TIRELY ...
... YOURS.
GOOD.
I WANT YOU TO KILL...
...ALL WHO DIS-PLEASE ME.
WHAT ...

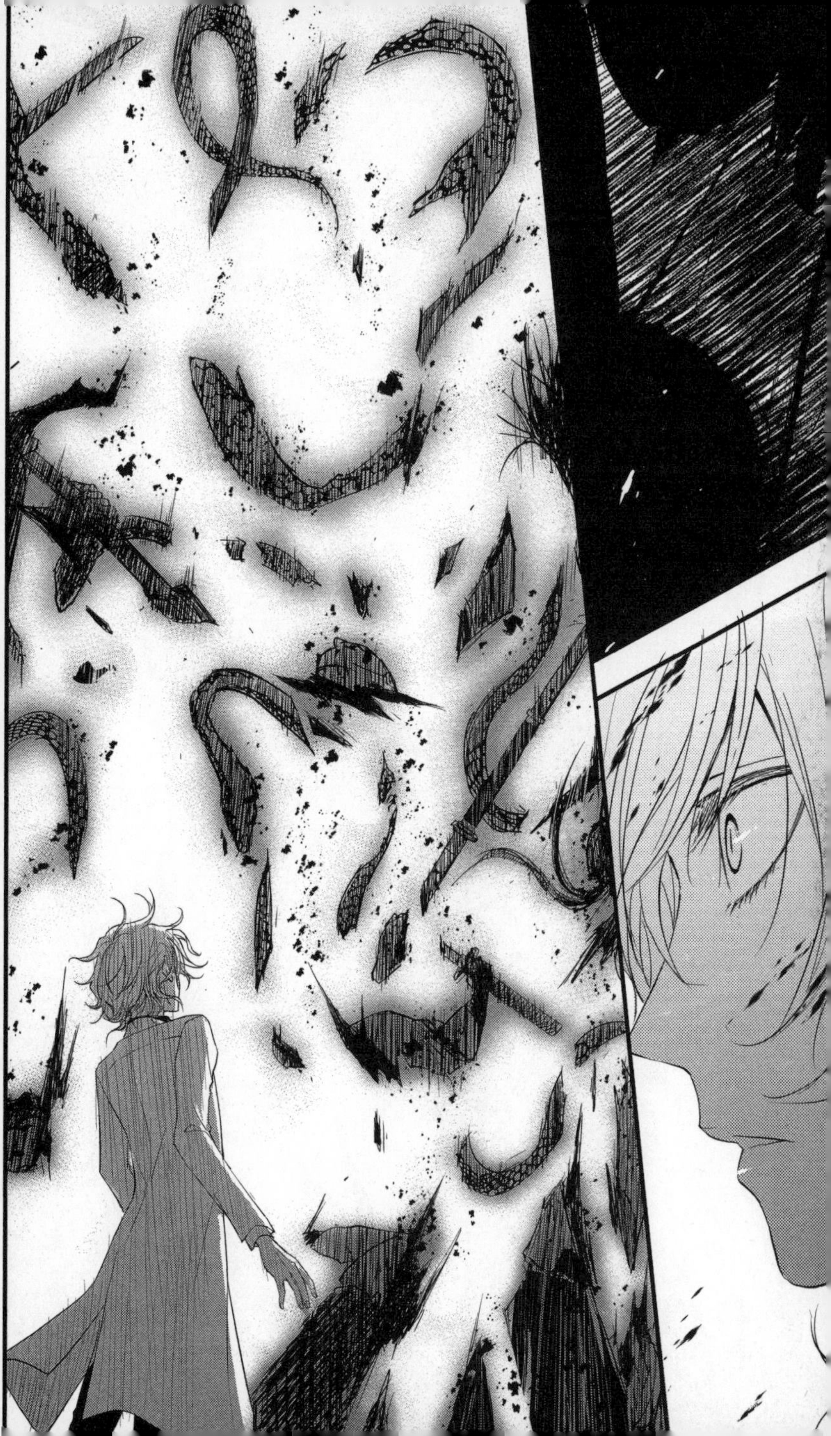

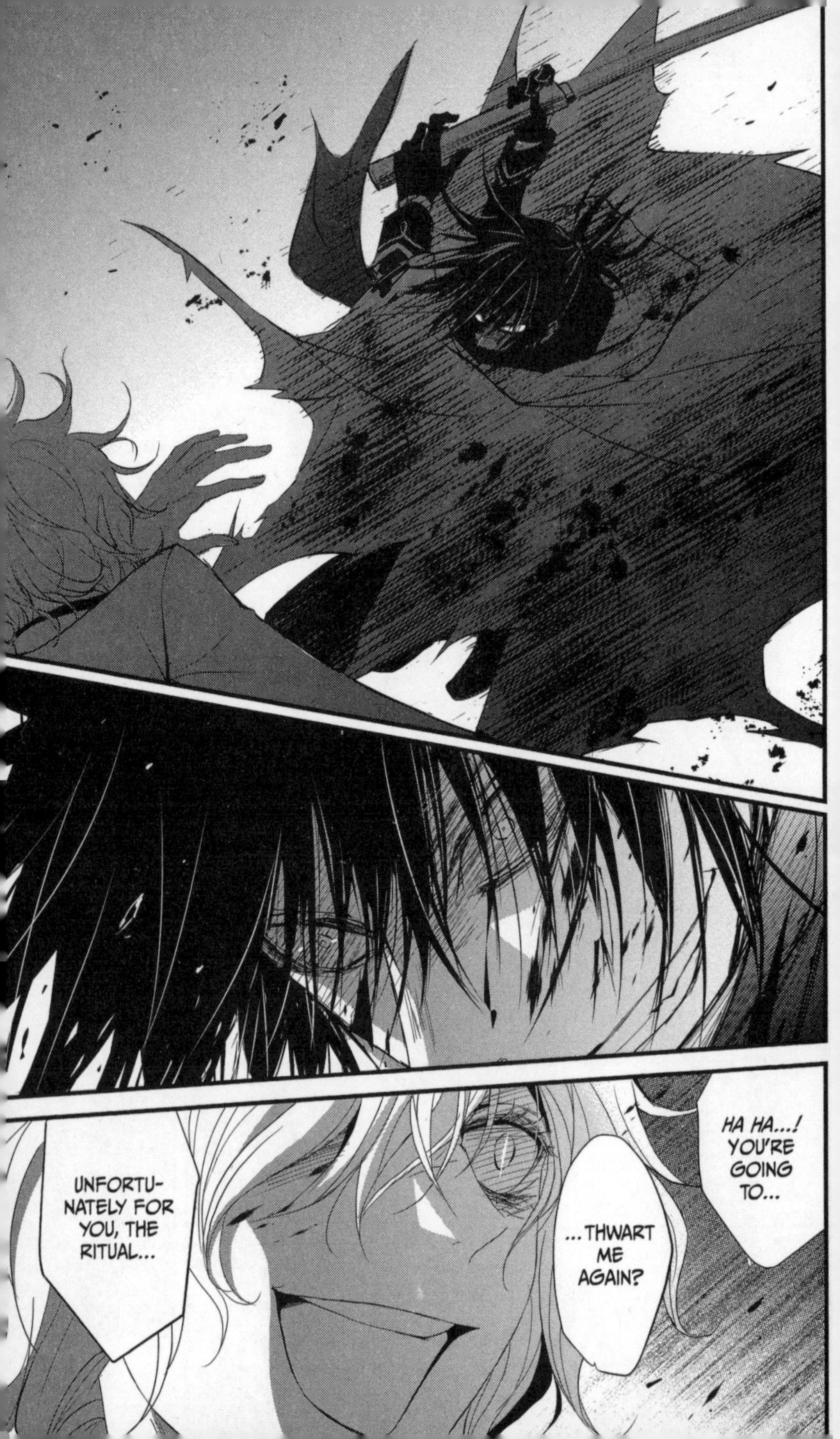
HA HA...! YOU'RE GOING TO...
...THWART ME AGAIN?
UNFORTU-NATELY FOR YOU, THE RITUAL...

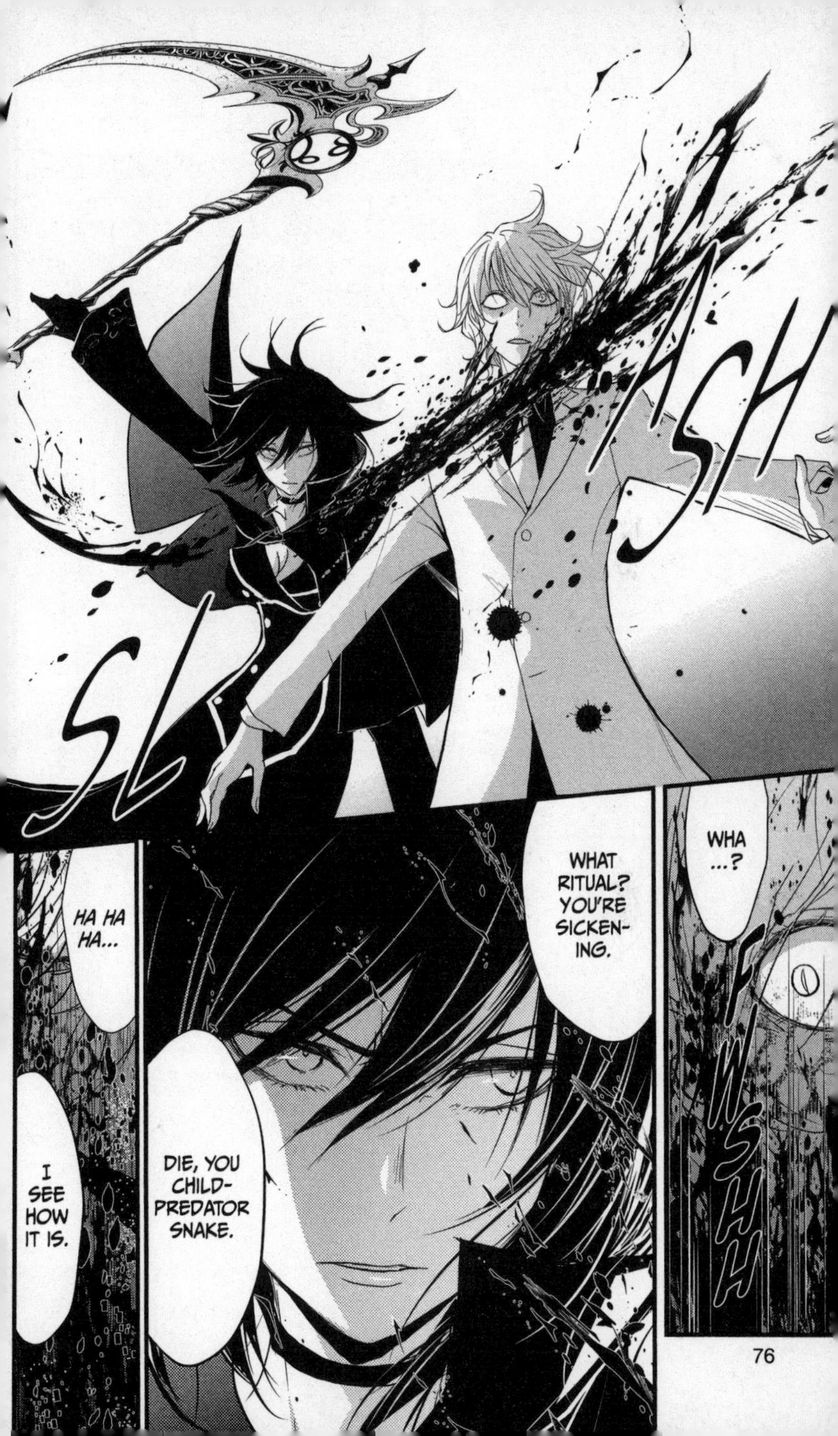
SLASH
WHA...?
WHAT RITUAL? YOU'RE SICKEN-ING.
DIE, YOU CHILD-PREDATOR SNAKE.
HA HA HA...
I SEE HOW IT IS.

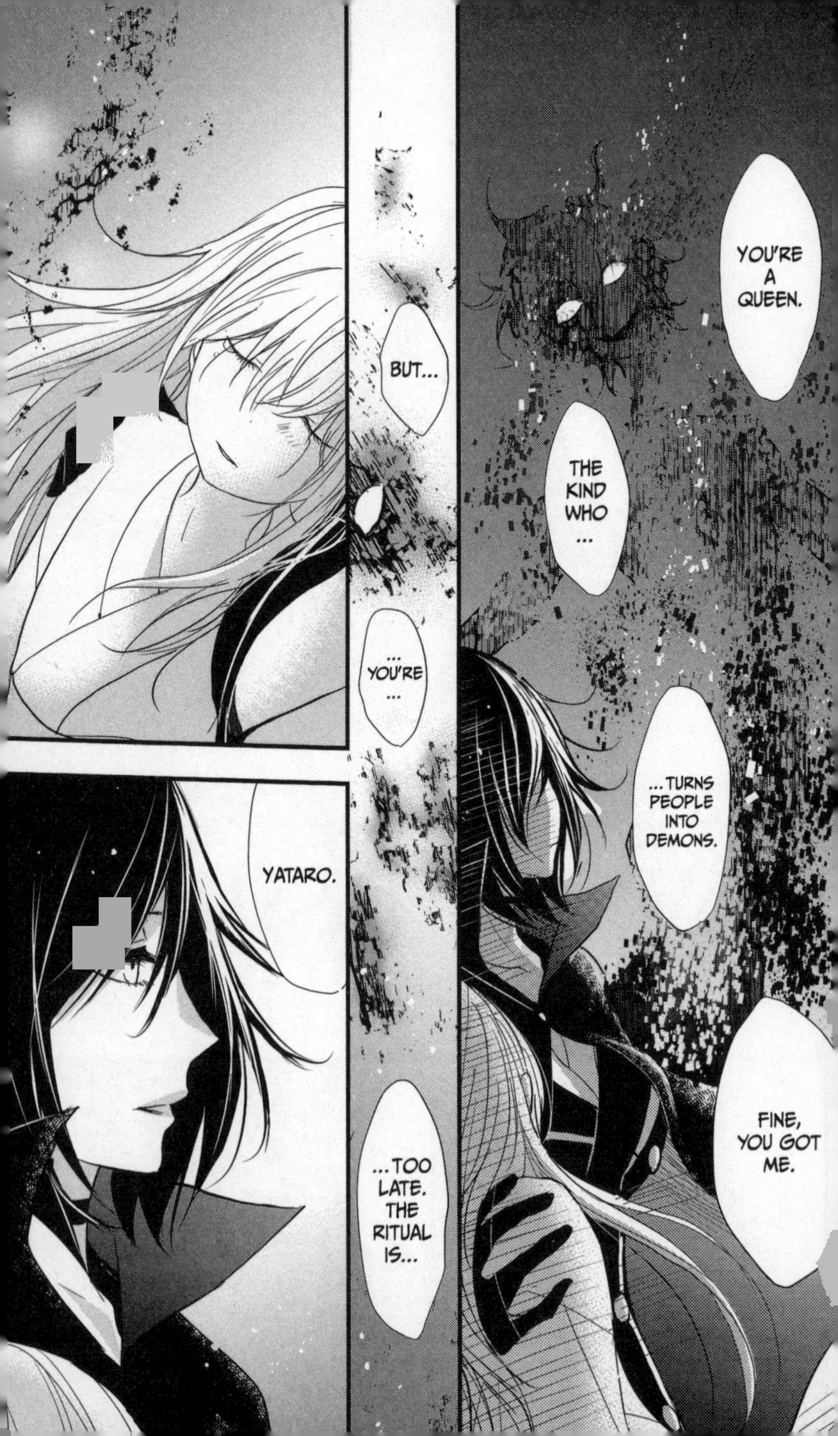
YOU'RE A QUEEN.
THE KIND WHO ...
...TURNS PEOPLE INTO DEMONS.
FINE, YOU GOT ME.
BUT...
... YOU'RE ...
...TOO LATE. THE RITUAL IS...
YATARO.

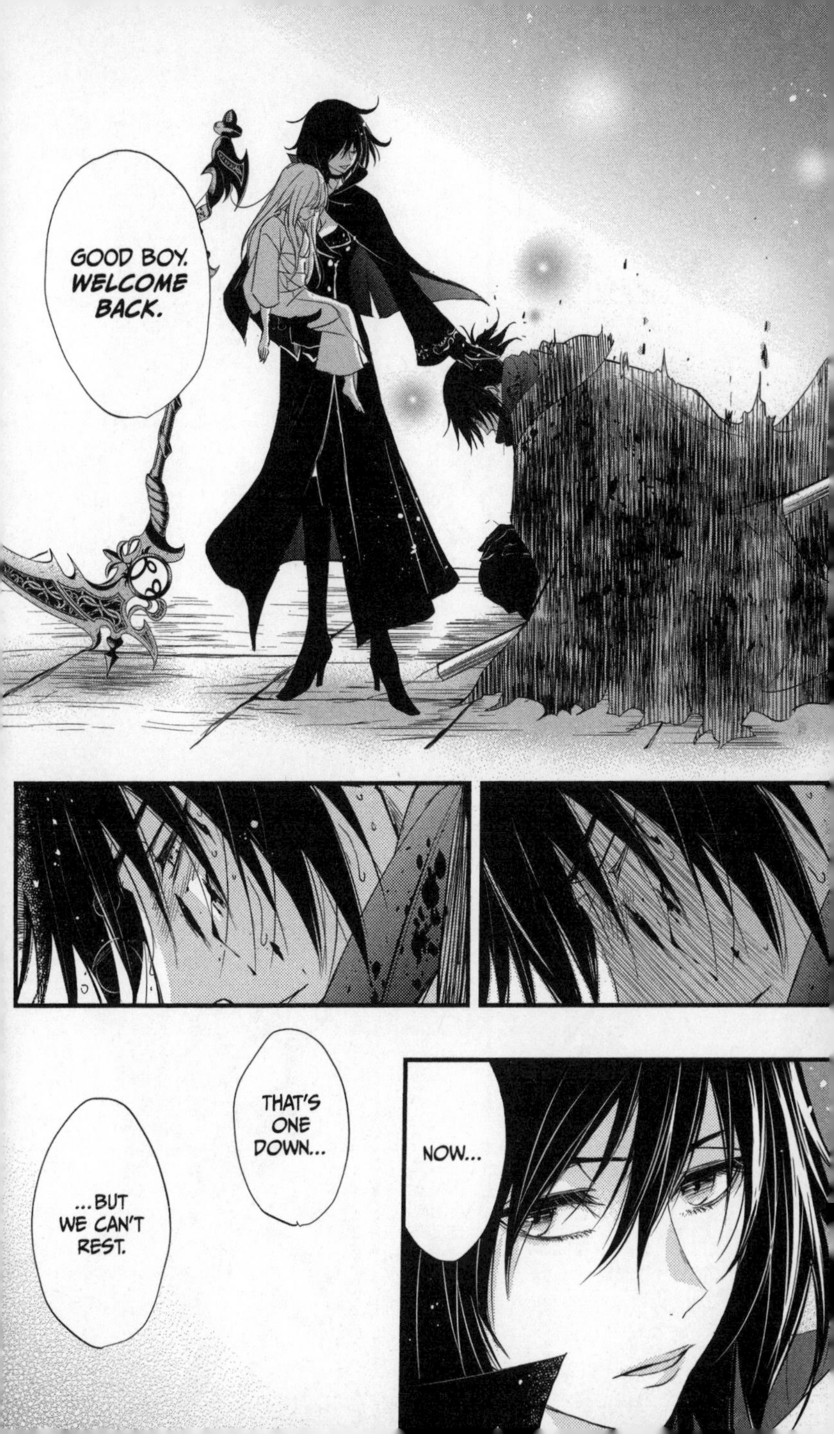
GOOD BOY. WELCOME BACK.
NOW...
THAT'S ONE DOWN...
...BUT WE CAN'T REST.

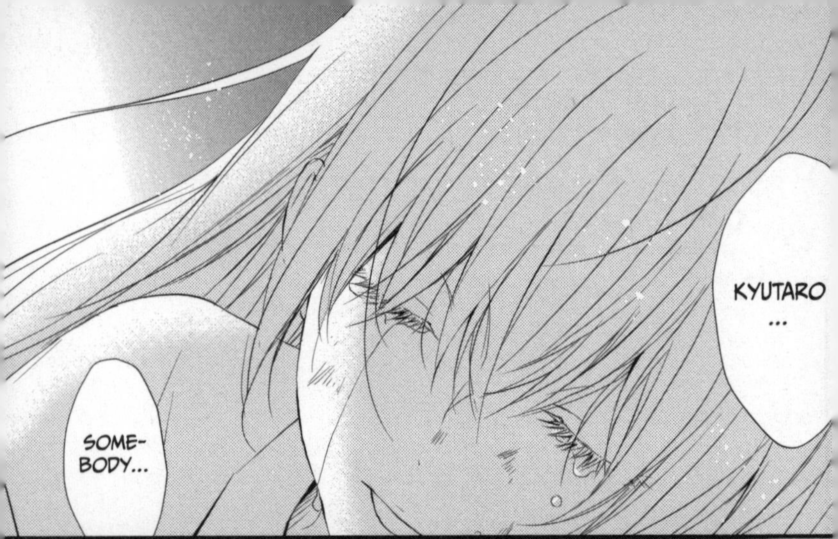
KYUTARO ...
SOME-BODY...
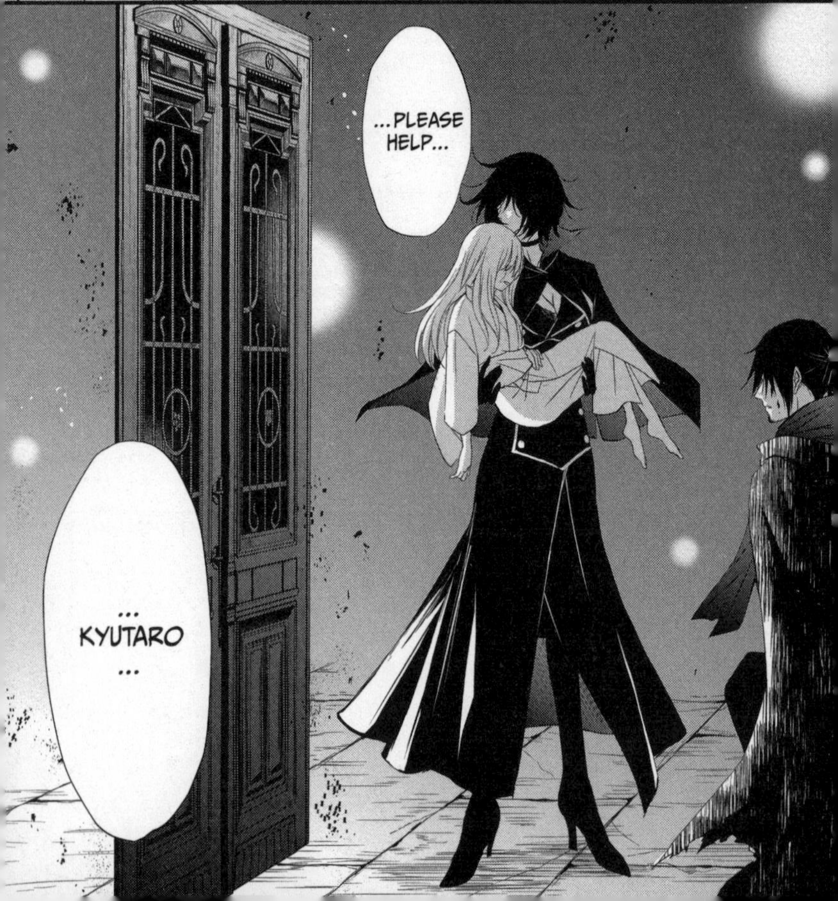
...PLEASE HELP...
... KYUTARO ...

MONTHLY BETSUCOMI SALE DATE NOTICE ON TWITTER

CHAPTER 38

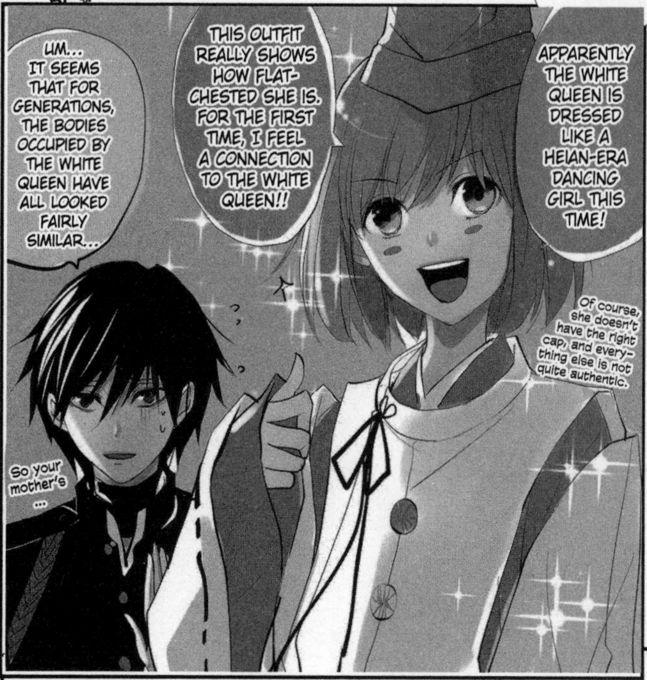
APPARENTLY THE WHITE QUEEN IS DRESSED LIKE A HEIAN-ERA DANCING GIRL THIS TIME!
THIS OUTFIT REALLY SHOWS HOW FLAT-CHESTED SHE IS. FOR THE FIRST TIME, I FEEL A CONNECTION TO THE WHITE QUEEN!!
UM... IT SEEMS THAT FOR GENERATIONS, THE BODIES OCCUPIED BY THE WHITE QUEEN HAVE ALL LOOKED FAIRLY SIMILAR...
Of course, she doesn't have the right cap, and everything else is not quite authentic.
So your mother's ...

LET'S SEE... WHAT'S UP IN *QUEEN'S QUALITY* THIS MONTH?

(1) YES. I THINK THEY SHOULD HAVE KILLED HIM. (DANGEROUS)
(2) THE WHITE QUEEN'S FASHION SENSE IS ALL OVER THE PLACE, ISN'T IT?
(3) GENBU LEADER, KUROSAKI SAID THAT IF YOU DON'T KEEP YOUR BOOBS WARM, THEY'LL SAG.

CHAPTER 38 BRINGS YOU THE CRUEL FATE OF A YOUNG BOY AND GIRL, AS WELL AS THE CRUEL COMPARISONS OF BOOBS.

(1) THE GUY I SAID THEY SHOULD'VE KILLED IS THIS SUSPICIOUS-LOOKING BONY GUY. →

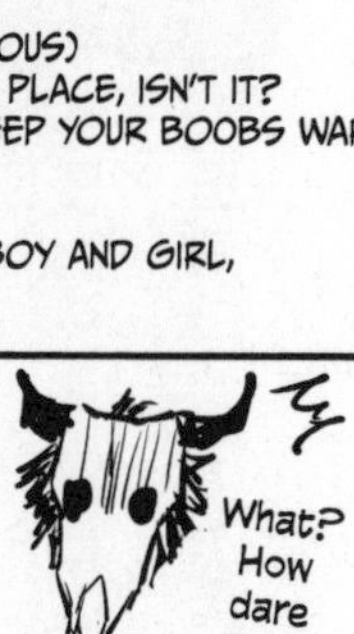
What? How dare you!

THERE WERE OTHERS WHO MIGHT HAVE BEEN KILLED IN THIS CHAPTER. I'M SORRY IF WHAT I SAID UNNERVED YOU. DRAWING BONES IS SUCH A PAIN.

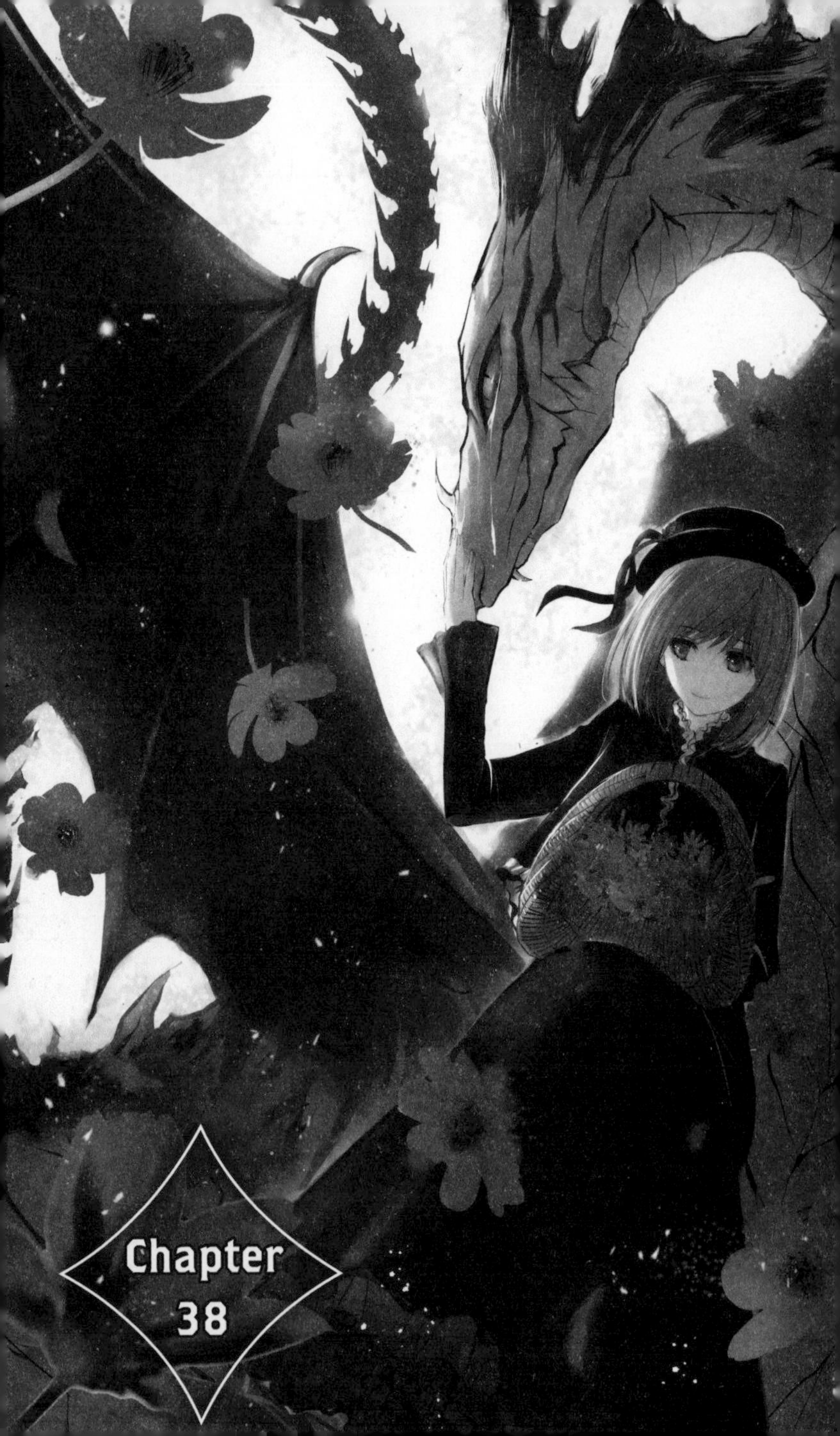
Chapter
38

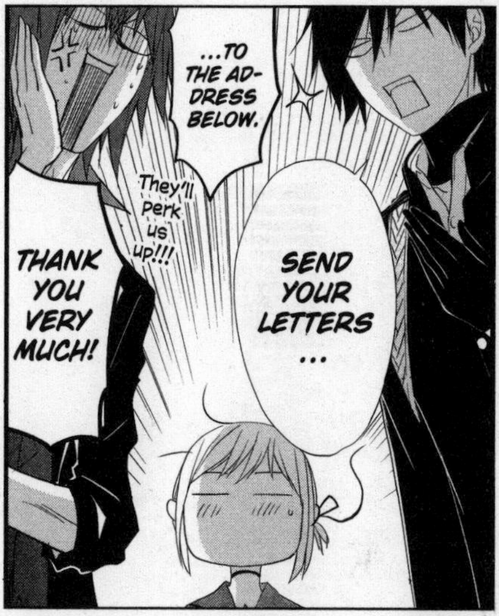
SEND YOUR LETTERS ...
...TO THE AD-DRESS BELOW.
They'll perk us up!!!
THANK YOU VERY MUCH!

KYOUSUKE MOTOMI
C/O QUEEN'S QUALITY EDITOR
VIZ MEDIA
P.O. BOX 77010
SAN FRANCISCO, CA 94107

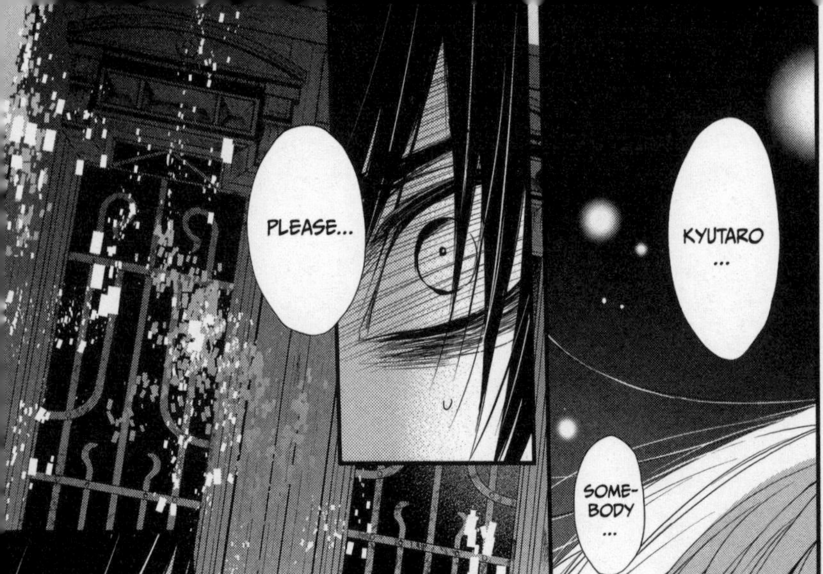
KYUTARO...
SOME-BODY...
PLEASE...
...HELP...

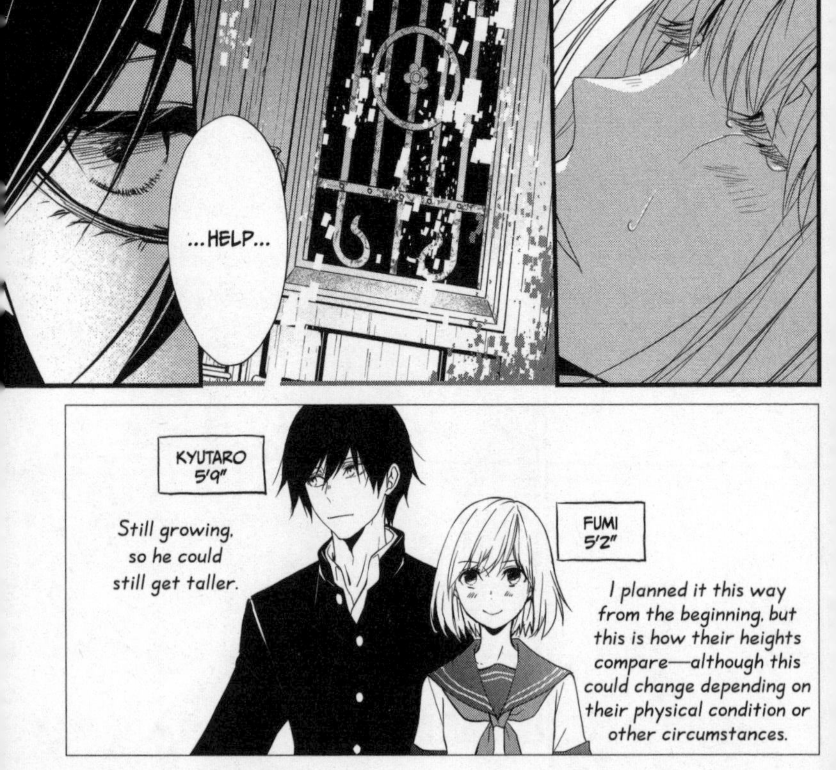
KYUTARO 5'9"
Still growing, so he could still get taller.
FUMI 5'2"
I planned it this way from the beginning, but this is how their heights compare—although this could change depending on their physical condition or other circumstances.

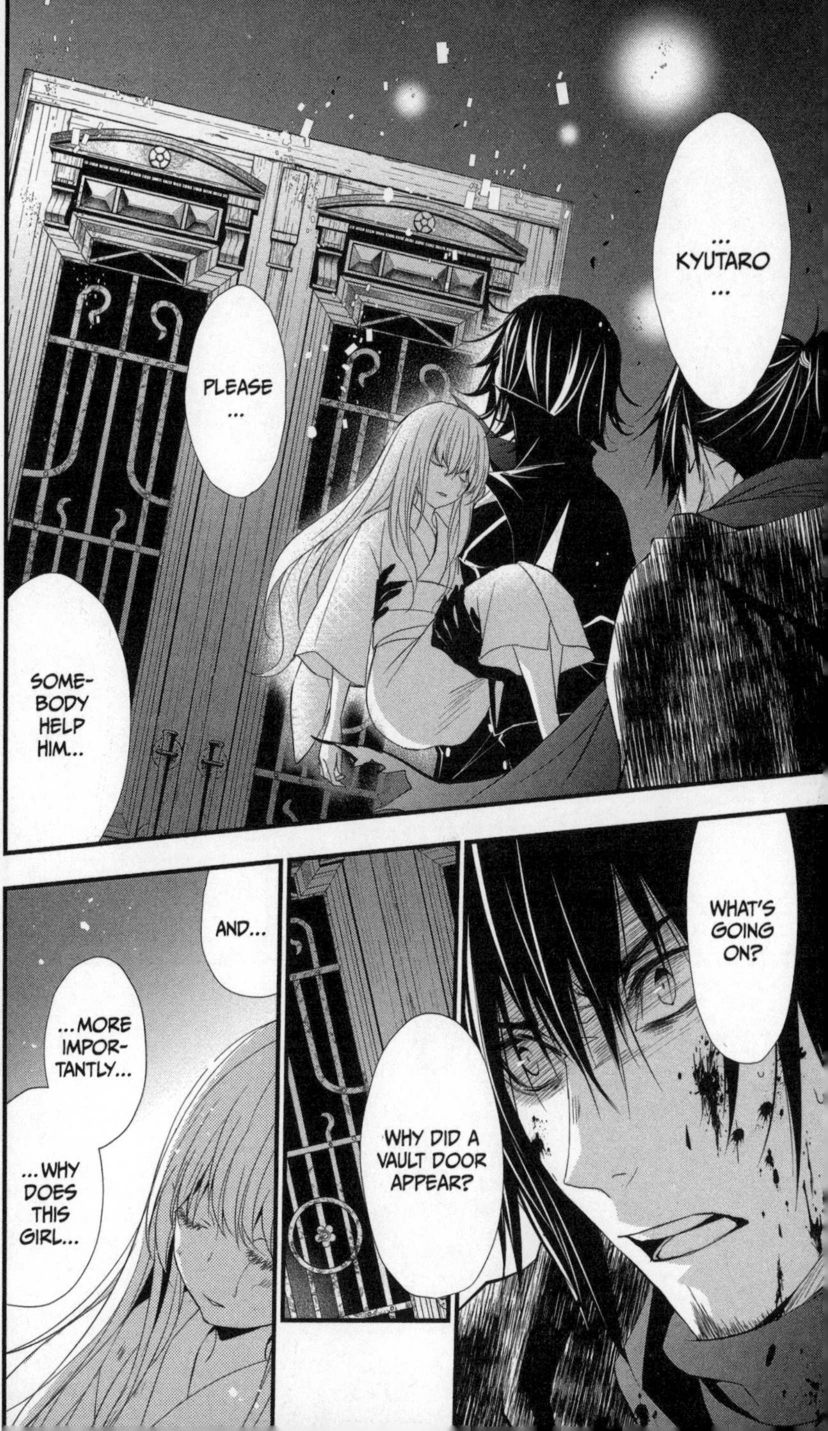

...KYUTARO...
PLEASE...
SOMEBODY HELP HIM...
WHAT'S GOING ON?
WHY DID A VAULT DOOR APPEAR?
AND...
...MORE IMPORTANTLY...
...WHY DOES THIS GIRL...

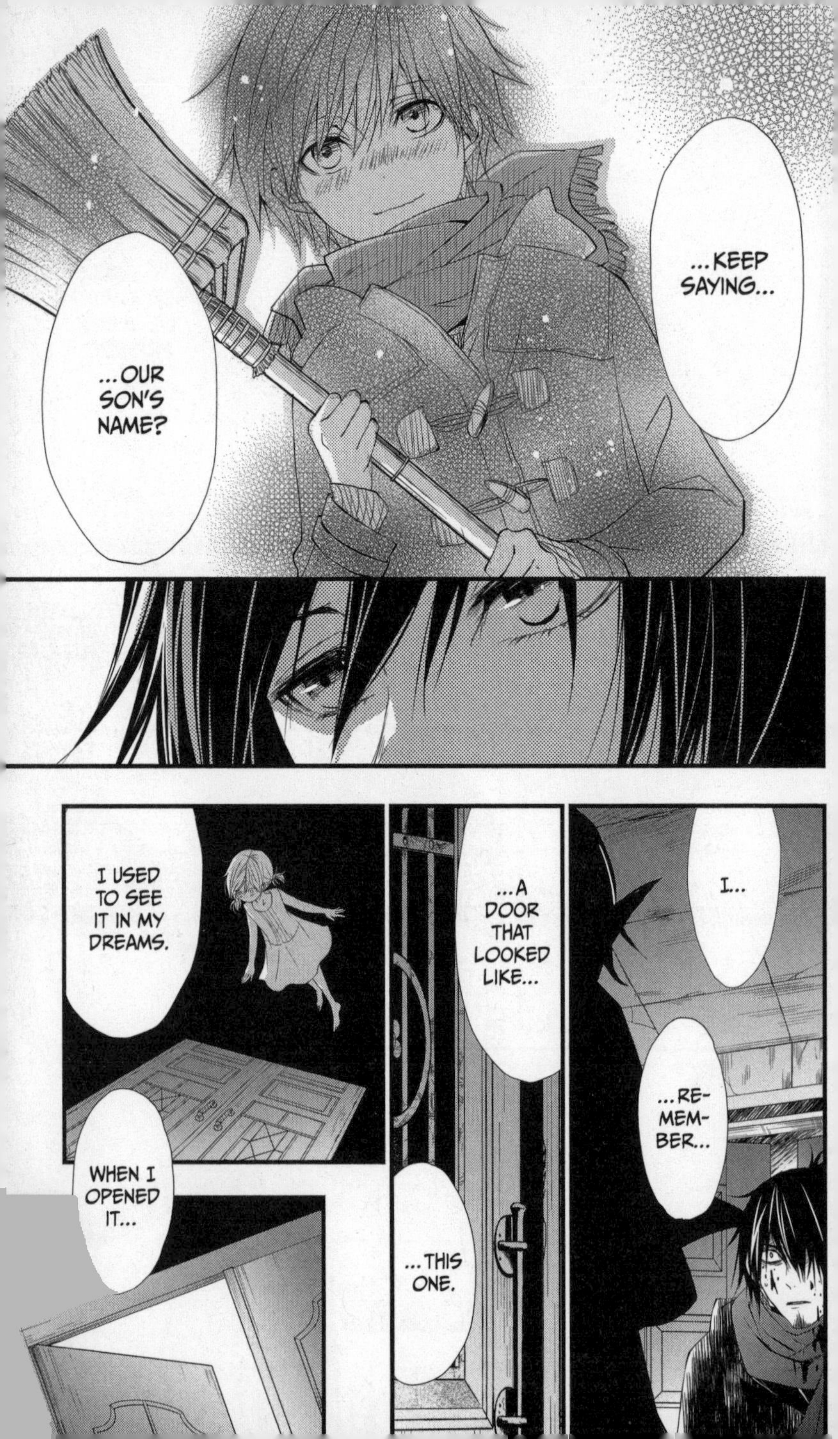
...KEEP SAYING...
...OUR SON'S NAME?
I...
...RE-MEM-BER...
...A DOOR THAT LOOKED LIKE...
...THIS ONE.
I USED TO SEE IT IN MY DREAMS.
WHEN I OPENED IT...

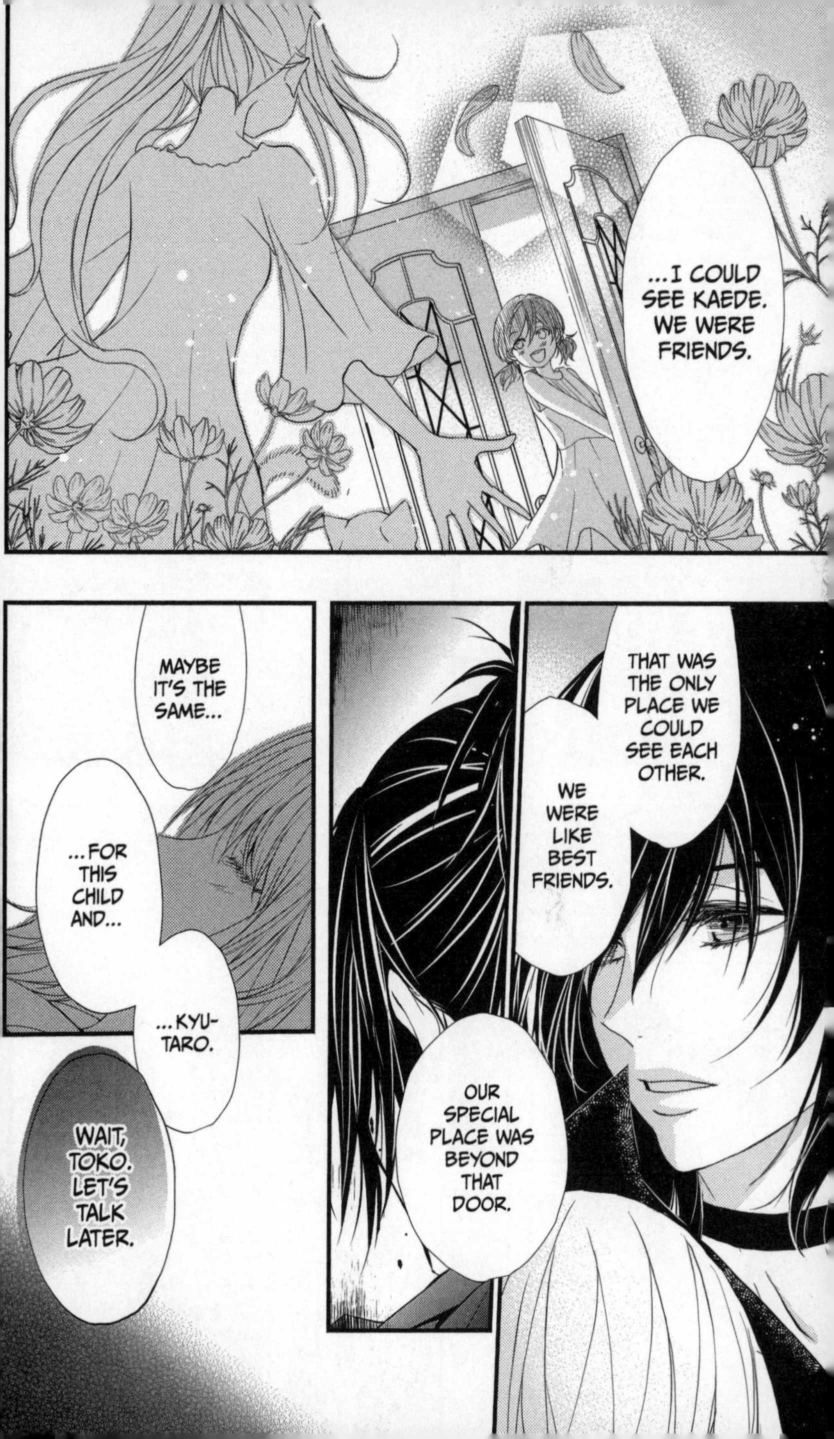
...I COULD SEE KAEDE. WE WERE FRIENDS.
THAT WAS THE ONLY PLACE WE COULD SEE EACH OTHER.
WE WERE LIKE BEST FRIENDS.
OUR SPECIAL PLACE WAS BEYOND THAT DOOR.
MAYBE IT'S THE SAME...
...FOR THIS CHILD AND...
...KYU-TARO.
WAIT, TOKO. LET'S TALK LATER.

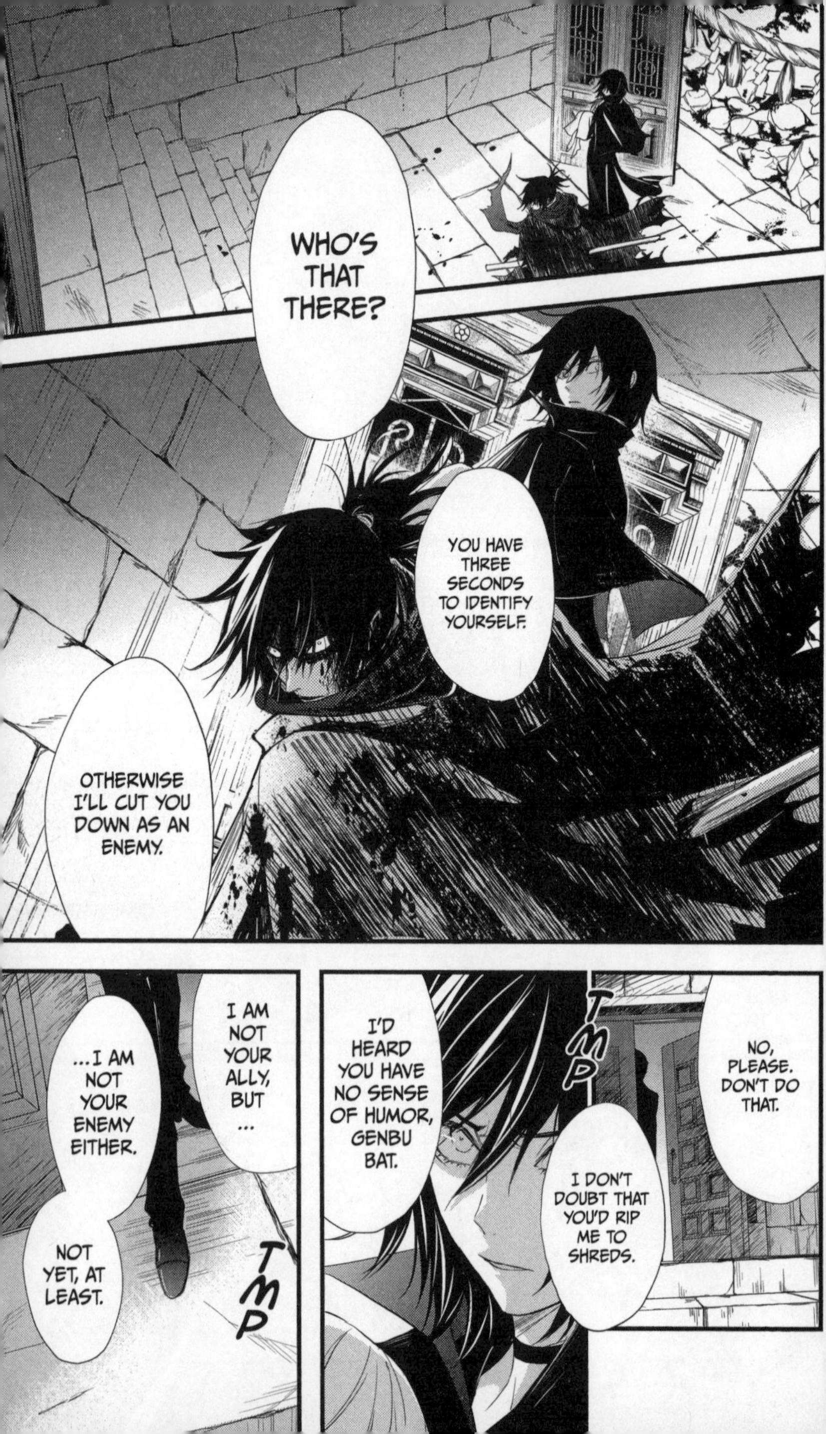
WHO'S THAT THERE?
YOU HAVE THREE SECONDS TO IDENTIFY YOURSELF.
OTHERWISE I'LL CUT YOU DOWN AS AN ENEMY.
TMP
NO, PLEASE. DON'T DO THAT.
I DON'T DOUBT THAT YOU'D RIP ME TO SHREDS.
I'D HEARD YOU HAVE NO SENSE OF HUMOR, GENBU BAT.
I AM NOT YOUR ALLY, BUT ...
...I AM NOT YOUR ENEMY EITHER.
NOT YET, AT LEAST.
TMP

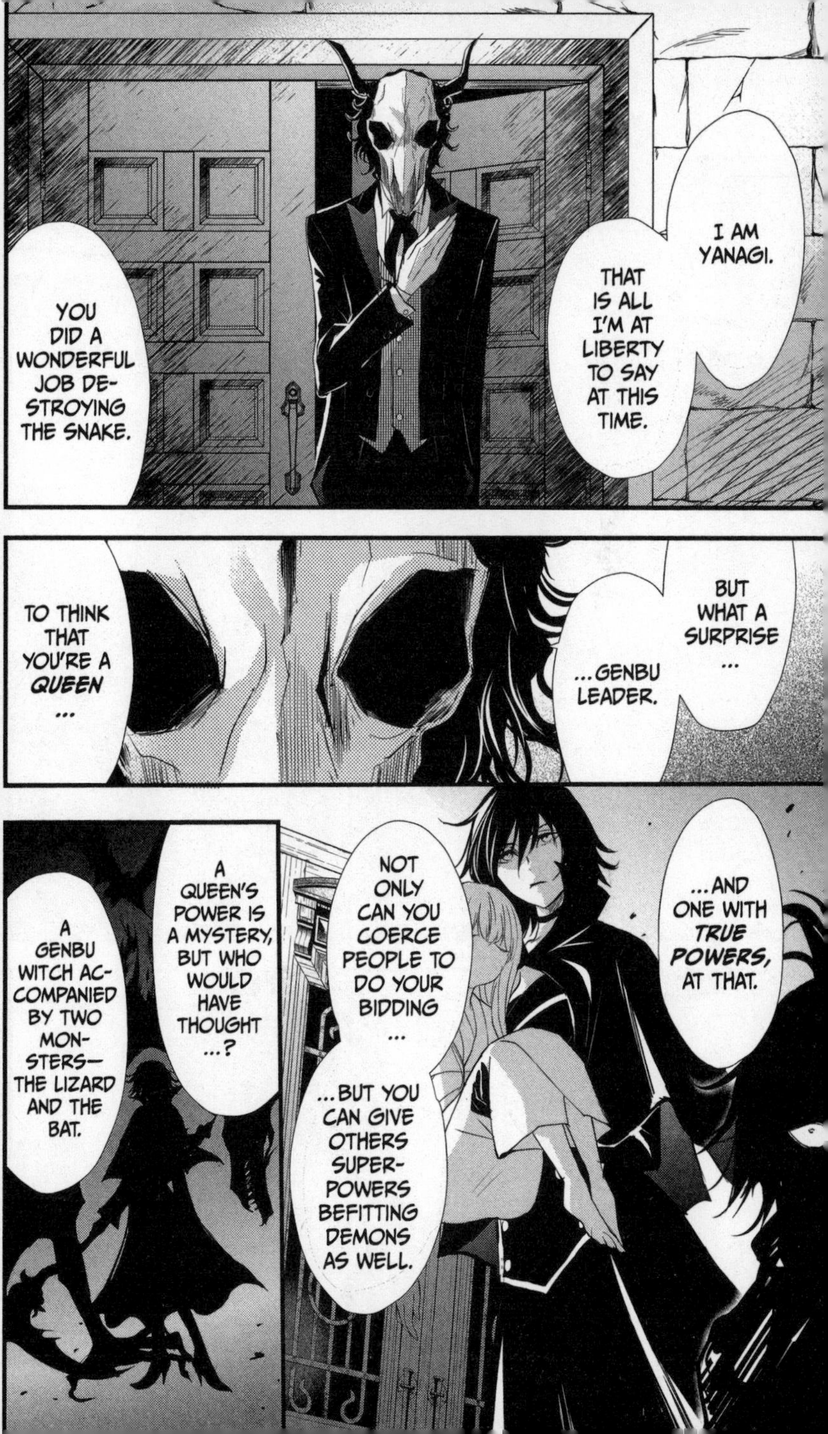
I AM YANAGI.
THAT IS ALL I'M AT LIBERTY TO SAY AT THIS TIME.
YOU DID A WONDERFUL JOB DE-STROYING THE SNAKE.
BUT WHAT A SURPRISE ...
...GENBU LEADER.
TO THINK THAT YOU'RE A *QUEEN* ...
...AND ONE WITH *TRUE POWERS*, AT THAT.
NOT ONLY CAN YOU COERCE PEOPLE TO DO YOUR BIDDING ...
...BUT YOU CAN GIVE OTHERS SUPER-POWERS BEFITTING DEMONS AS WELL.
A QUEEN'S POWER IS A MYSTERY, BUT WHO WOULD HAVE THOUGHT ...?
A GENBU WITCH AC-COMPANIED BY TWO MON-STERS— THE LIZARD AND THE BAT.

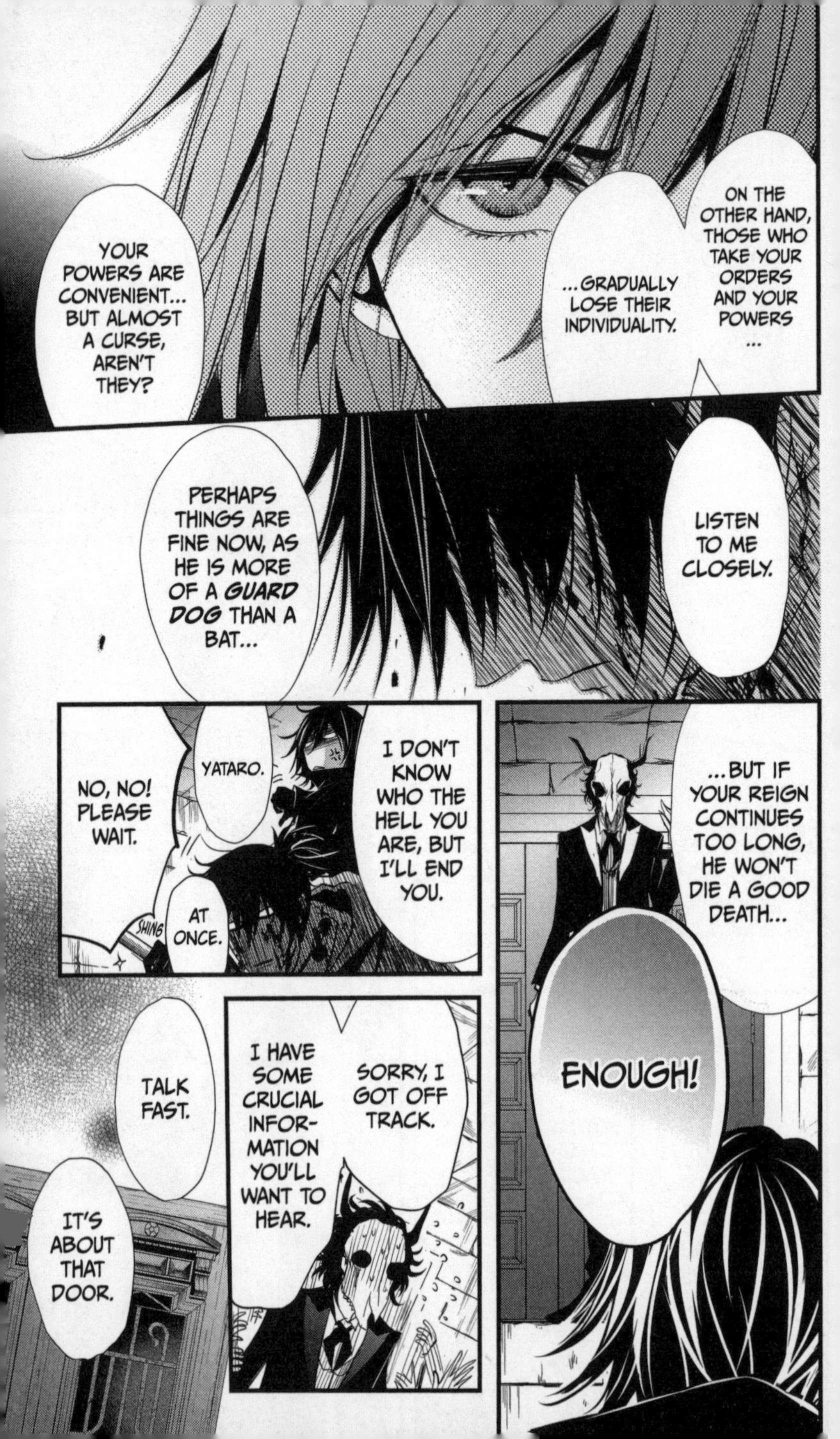
ON THE OTHER HAND, THOSE WHO TAKE YOUR ORDERS AND YOUR POWERS ...
...GRADUALLY LOSE THEIR INDIVIDUALITY.
YOUR POWERS ARE CONVENIENT... BUT ALMOST A CURSE, AREN'T THEY?
LISTEN TO ME CLOSELY.
PERHAPS THINGS ARE FINE NOW, AS HE IS MORE OF A *GUARD DOG* THAN A BAT...
...BUT IF YOUR REIGN CONTINUES TOO LONG, HE WON'T DIE A GOOD DEATH...
ENOUGH!
I DON'T KNOW WHO THE HELL YOU ARE, BUT I'LL END YOU.
YATARO.
AT ONCE.
SHING
NO, NO! PLEASE WAIT.
SORRY, I GOT OFF TRACK.
I HAVE SOME CRUCIAL INFOR-MATION YOU'LL WANT TO HEAR.
TALK FAST.
IT'S ABOUT THAT DOOR.

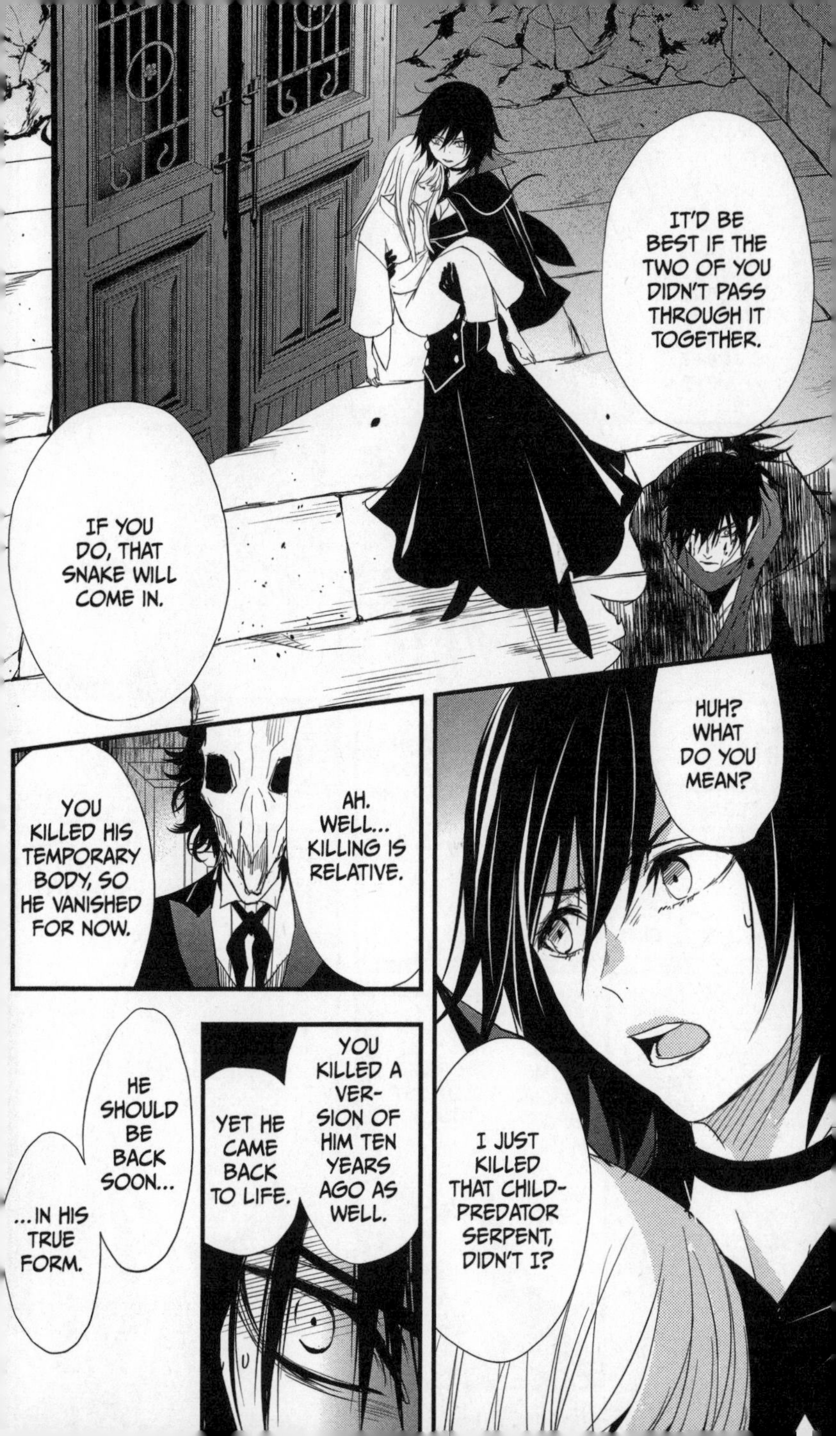
IT'D BE BEST IF THE TWO OF YOU DIDN'T PASS THROUGH IT TOGETHER.
IF YOU DO, THAT SNAKE WILL COME IN.
HUH? WHAT DO YOU MEAN?
I JUST KILLED THAT CHILD-PREDATOR SERPENT, DIDN'T I?
AH. WELL... KILLING IS RELATIVE.
YOU KILLED HIS TEMPORARY BODY, SO HE VANISHED FOR NOW.
YOU KILLED A VER-SION OF HIM TEN YEARS AGO AS WELL.
YET HE CAME BACK TO LIFE.
HE SHOULD BE BACK SOON...
...IN HIS TRUE FORM.

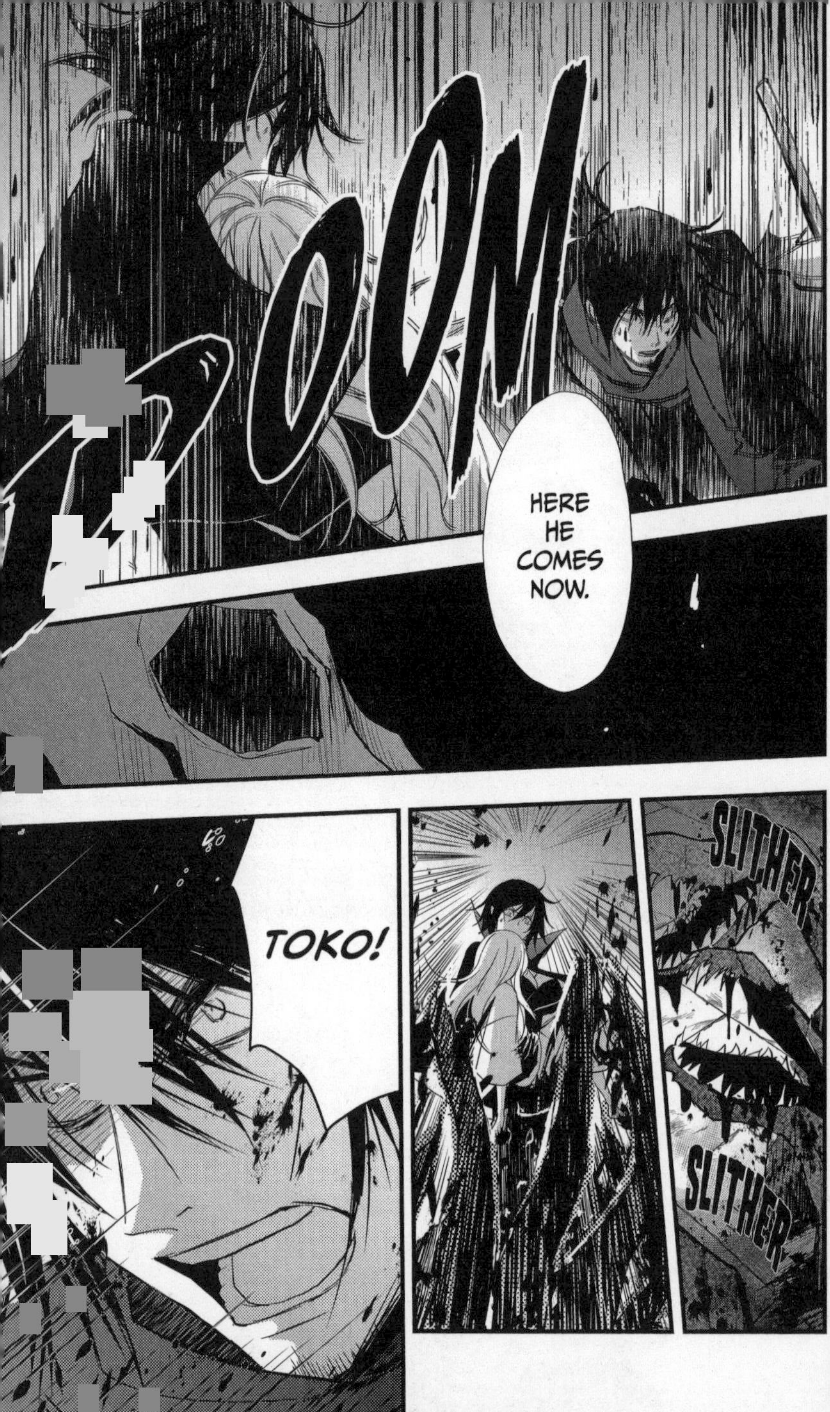
HERE HE COMES NOW.
SLITHER
SLITHER
TOKO!

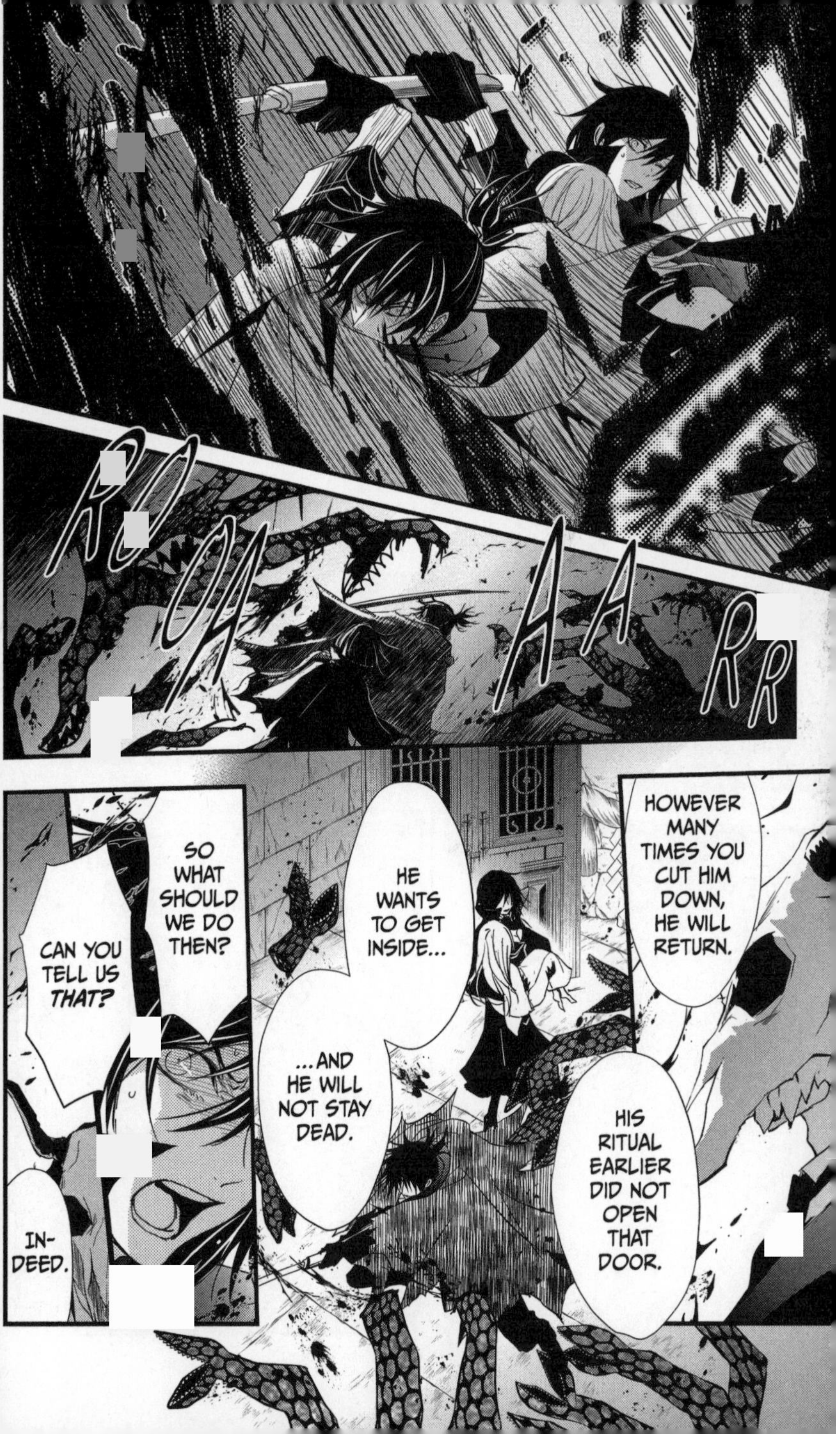
ROOAAARR
HOWEVER MANY TIMES YOU CUT HIM DOWN, HE WILL RETURN.
HIS RITUAL EARLIER DID NOT OPEN THAT DOOR.
HE WANTS TO GET INSIDE...
...AND HE WILL NOT STAY DEAD.
SO WHAT SHOULD WE DO THEN?
CAN YOU TELL US *THAT?*
IN-DEED.

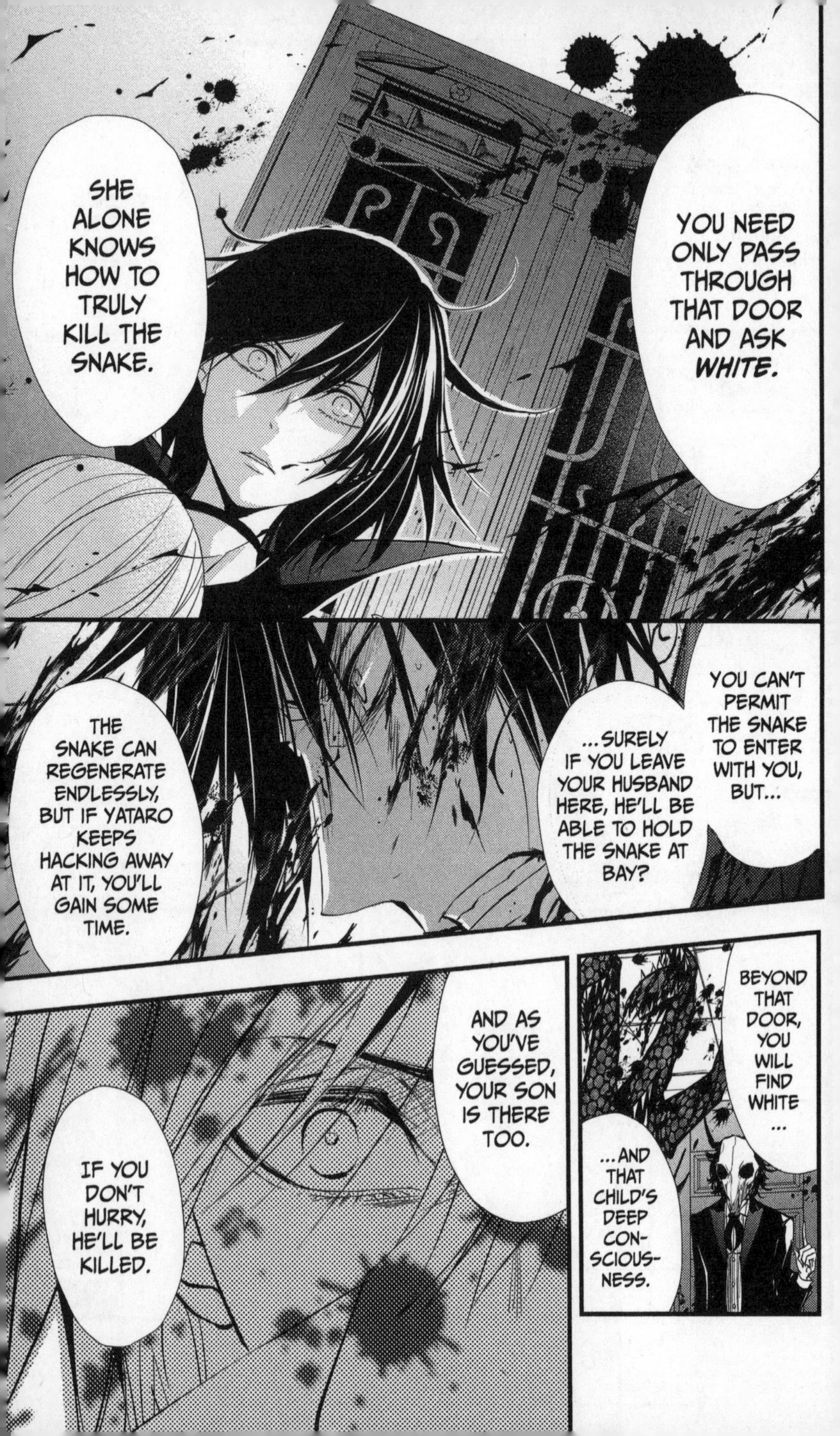
YOU NEED ONLY PASS THROUGH THAT DOOR AND ASK *WHITE.*
SHE ALONE KNOWS HOW TO TRULY KILL THE SNAKE.
YOU CAN'T PERMIT THE SNAKE TO ENTER WITH YOU, BUT...
...SURELY IF YOU LEAVE YOUR HUSBAND HERE, HE'LL BE ABLE TO HOLD THE SNAKE AT BAY?
THE SNAKE CAN REGENERATE ENDLESSLY, BUT IF YATARO KEEPS HACKING AWAY AT IT, YOU'LL GAIN SOME TIME.
BEYOND THAT DOOR, YOU WILL FIND WHITE...
...AND THAT CHILD'S DEEP CON-SCIOUS-NESS.
AND AS YOU'VE GUESSED, YOUR SON IS THERE TOO.
IF YOU DON'T HURRY, HE'LL BE KILLED.

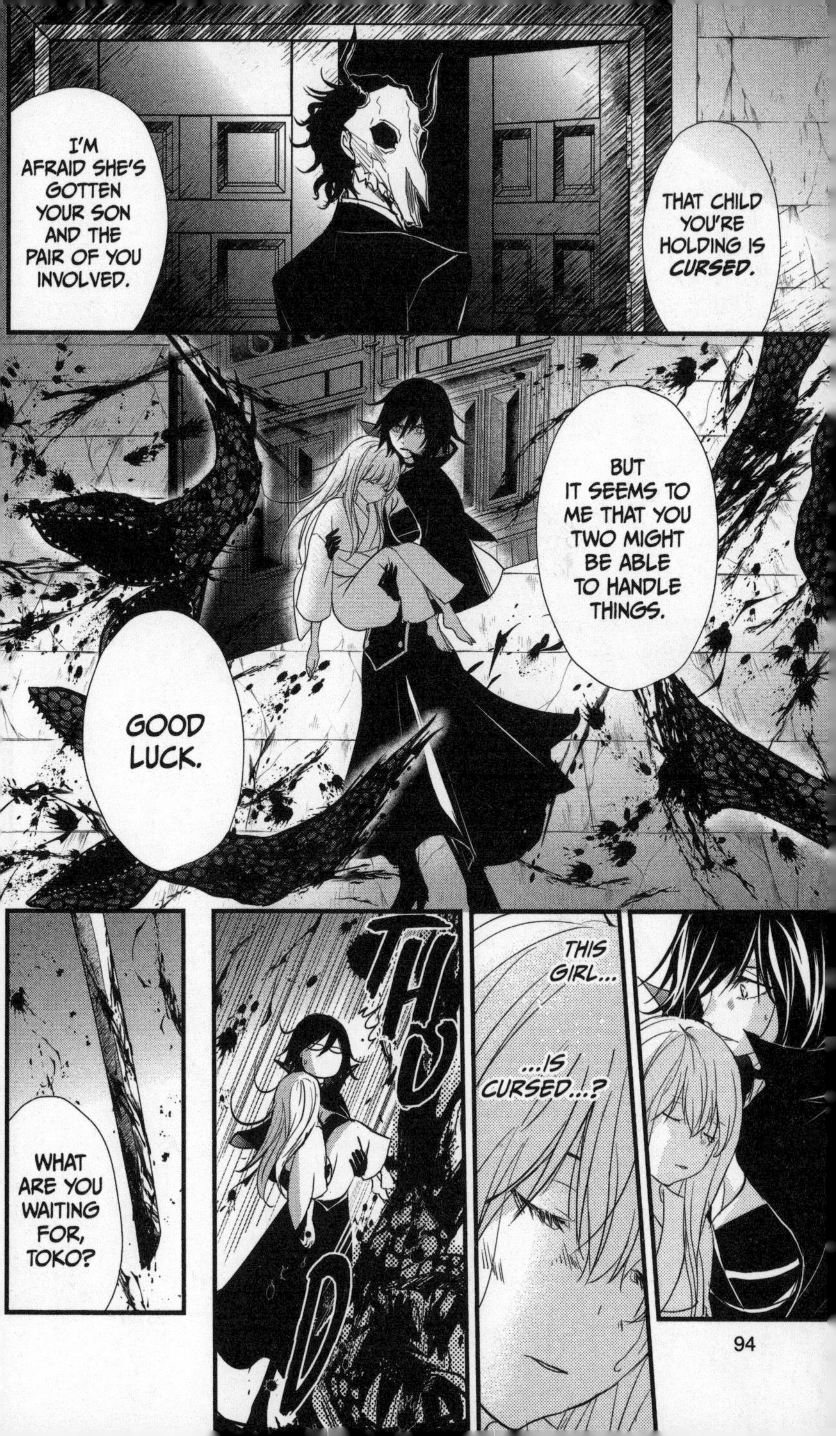
THAT CHILD YOU'RE HOLDING IS CURSED.
I'M AFRAID SHE'S GOTTEN YOUR SON AND THE PAIR OF YOU INVOLVED.
BUT IT SEEMS TO ME THAT YOU TWO MIGHT BE ABLE TO HANDLE THINGS.
GOOD LUCK.
THIS GIRL...
...IS CURSED...?
THUD
WHAT ARE YOU WAITING FOR, TOKO?

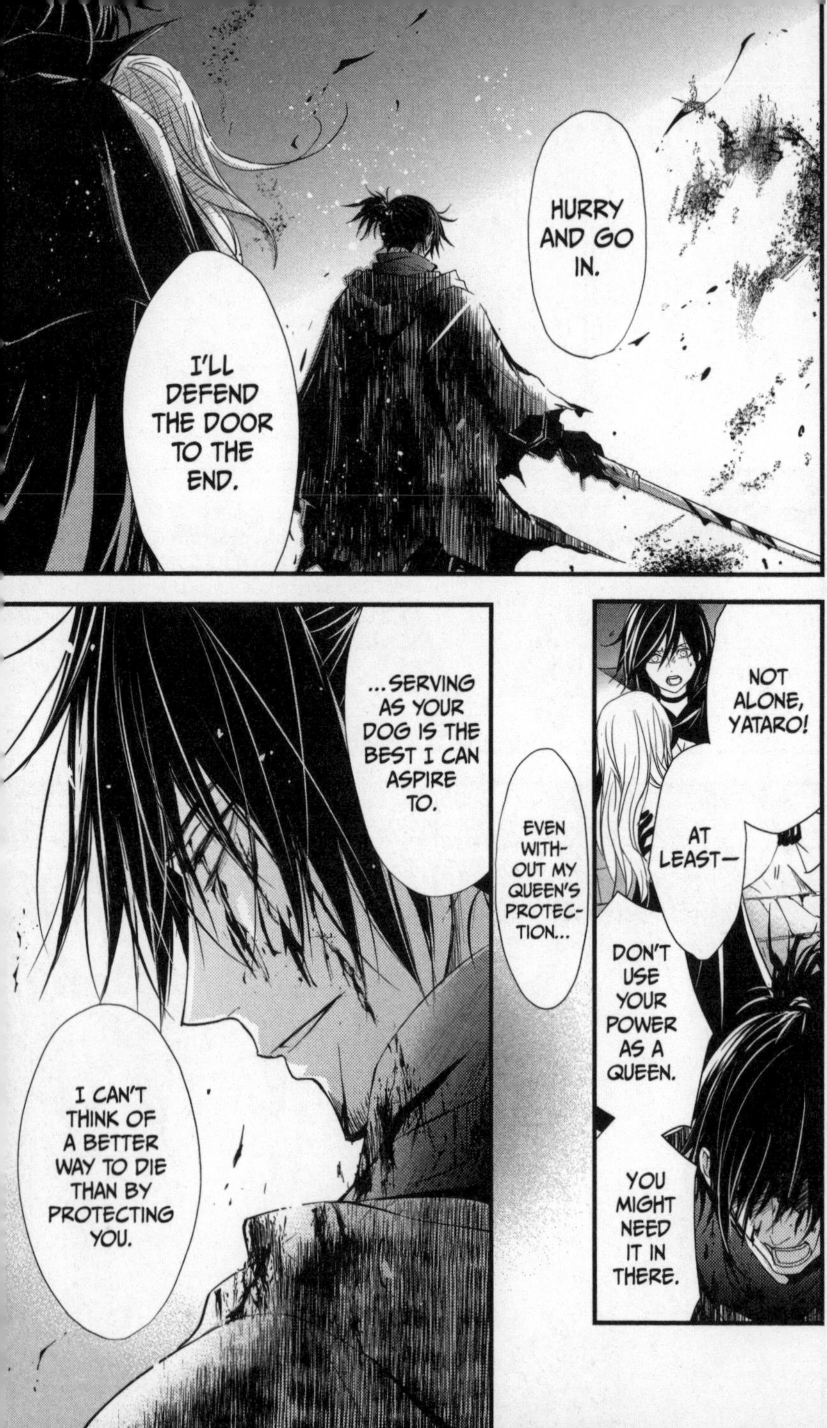
HURRY AND GO IN.
I'LL DEFEND THE DOOR TO THE END.
NOT ALONE, YATARO!
AT LEAST—
DON'T USE YOUR POWER AS A QUEEN.
YOU MIGHT NEED IT IN THERE.
EVEN WITH-OUT MY QUEEN'S PROTEC-TION...
...SERVING AS YOUR DOG IS THE BEST I CAN ASPIRE TO.
I CAN'T THINK OF A BETTER WAY TO DIE THAN BY PROTECTING YOU.

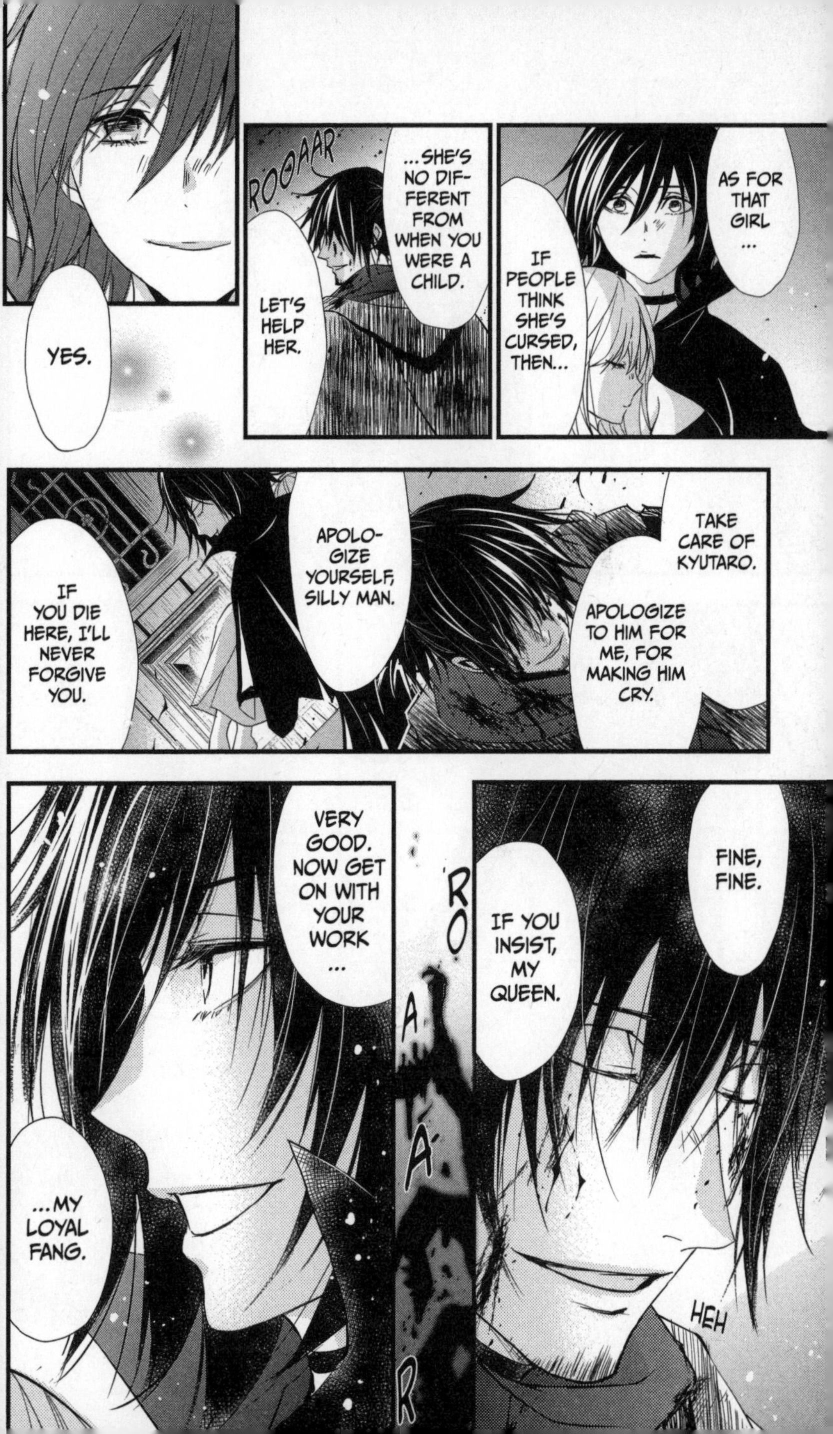
AS FOR THAT GIRL ...
IF PEOPLE THINK SHE'S CURSED, THEN...
...SHE'S NO DIF-FERENT FROM WHEN YOU WERE A CHILD.
ROOAAR
LET'S HELP HER.
YES.
TAKE CARE OF KYUTARO.
APOLOGIZE TO HIM FOR ME, FOR MAKING HIM CRY.
APOLO-GIZE YOURSELF, SILLY MAN.
IF YOU DIE HERE, I'LL NEVER FORGIVE YOU.
FINE, FINE.
IF YOU INSIST, MY QUEEN.
HEH
ROAAAR
VERY GOOD. NOW GET ON WITH YOUR WORK ...
...MY LOYAL FANG.

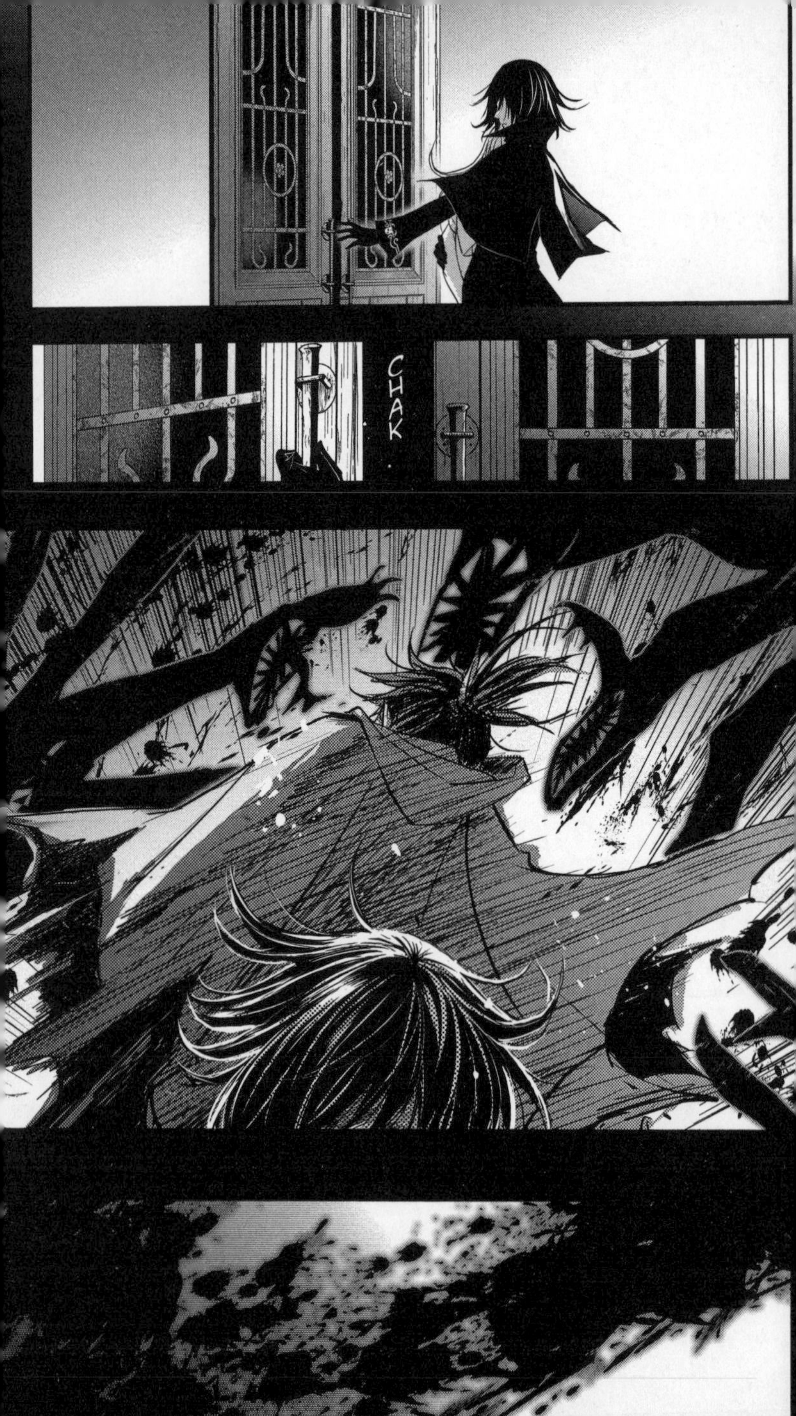
CHAK

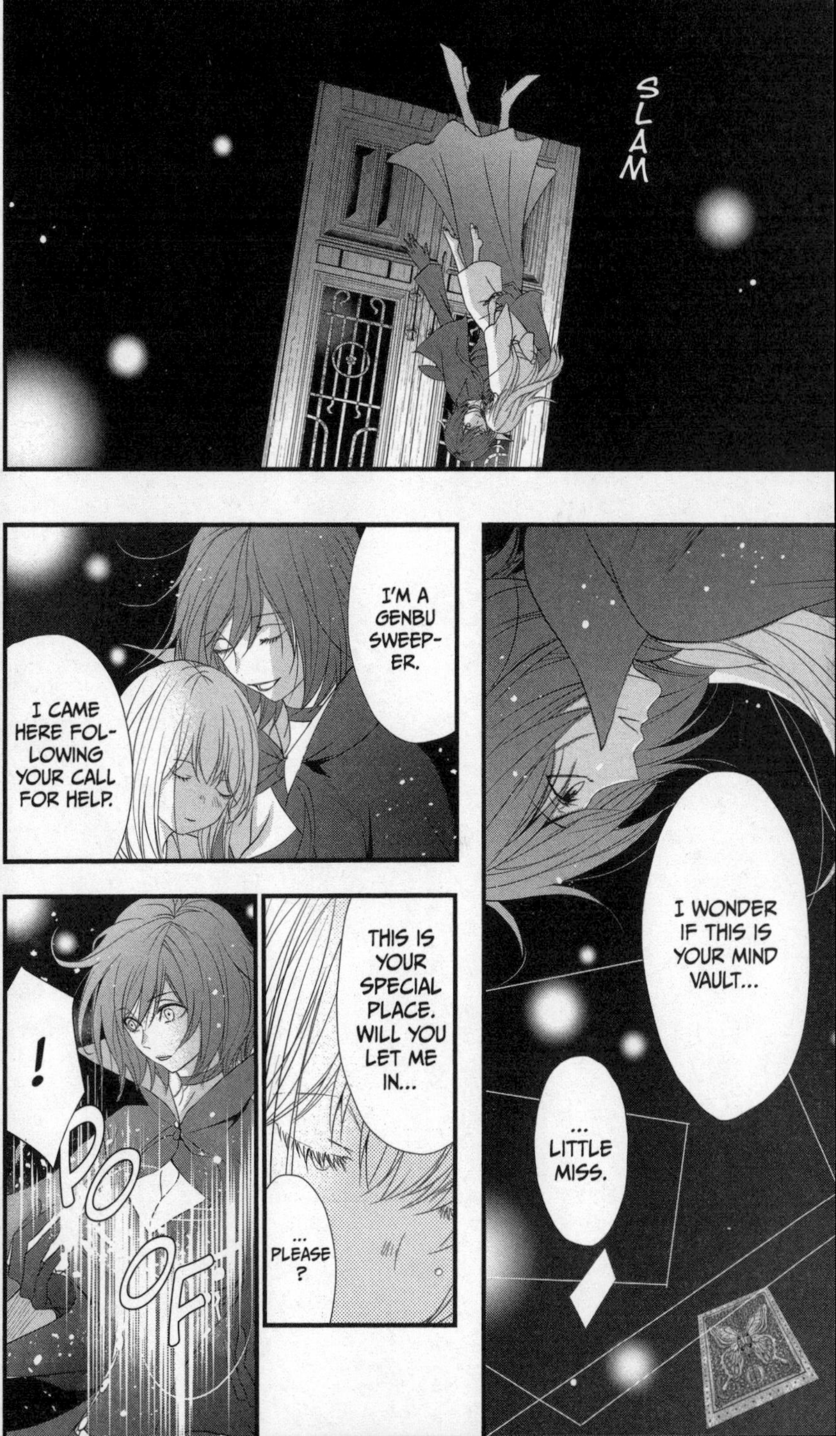
SLAM
I WONDER IF THIS IS YOUR MIND VAULT...
... LITTLE MISS.
I'M A GENBU SWEEP-ER.
I CAME HERE FOL-LOWING YOUR CALL FOR HELP.
THIS IS YOUR SPECIAL PLACE. WILL YOU LET ME IN...
... PLEASE?
!
POOF

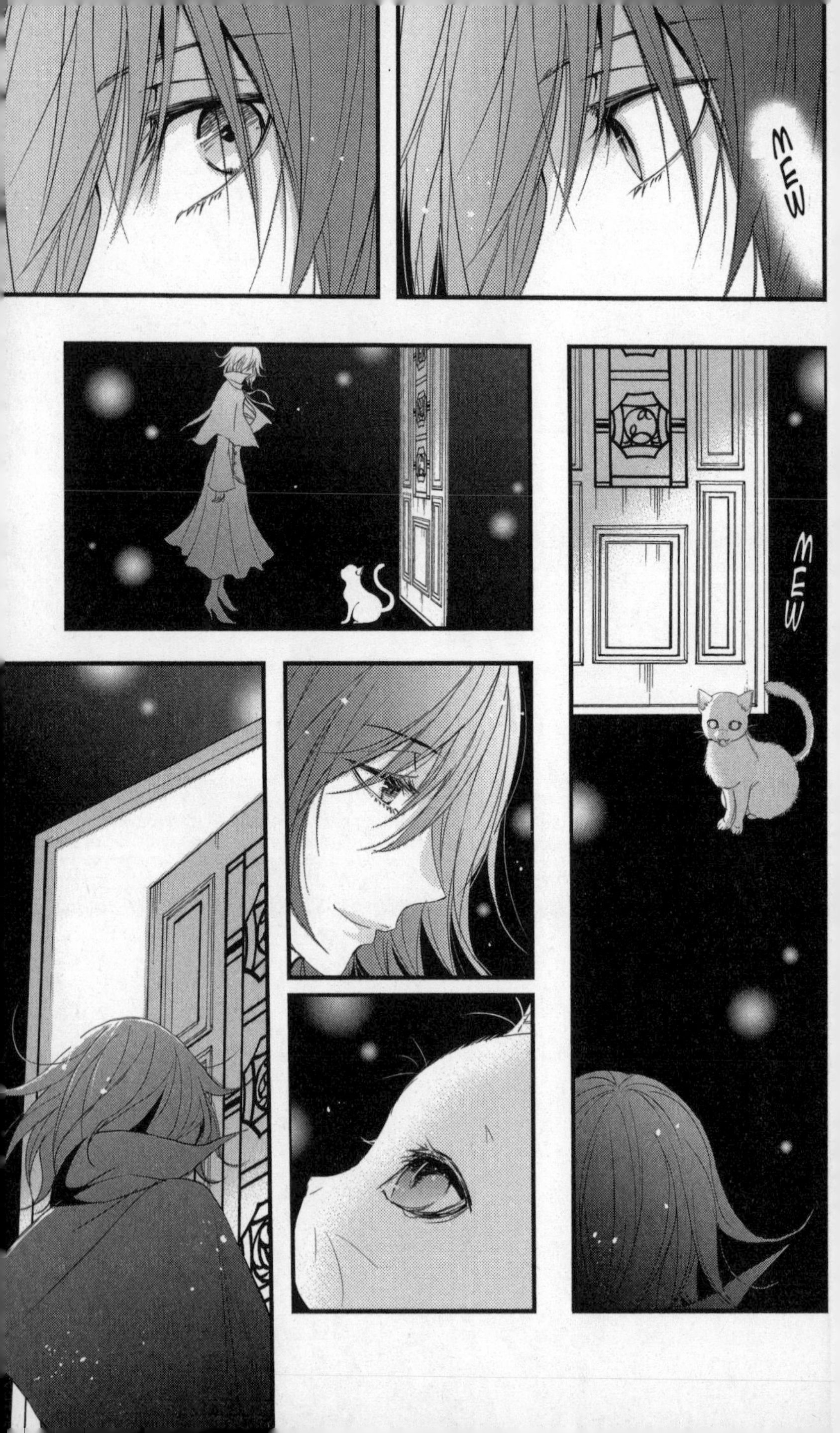
MEW
MEW

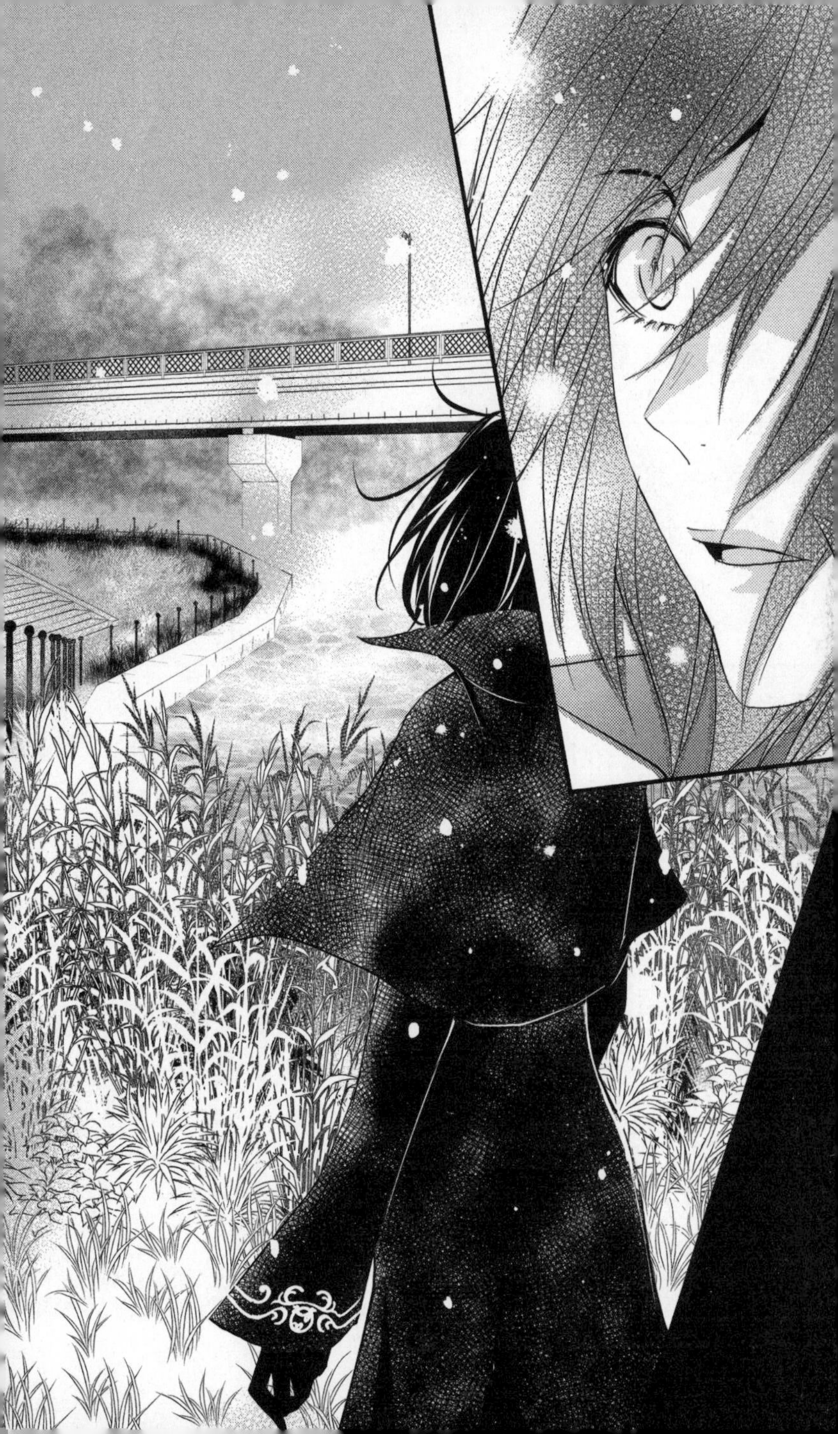

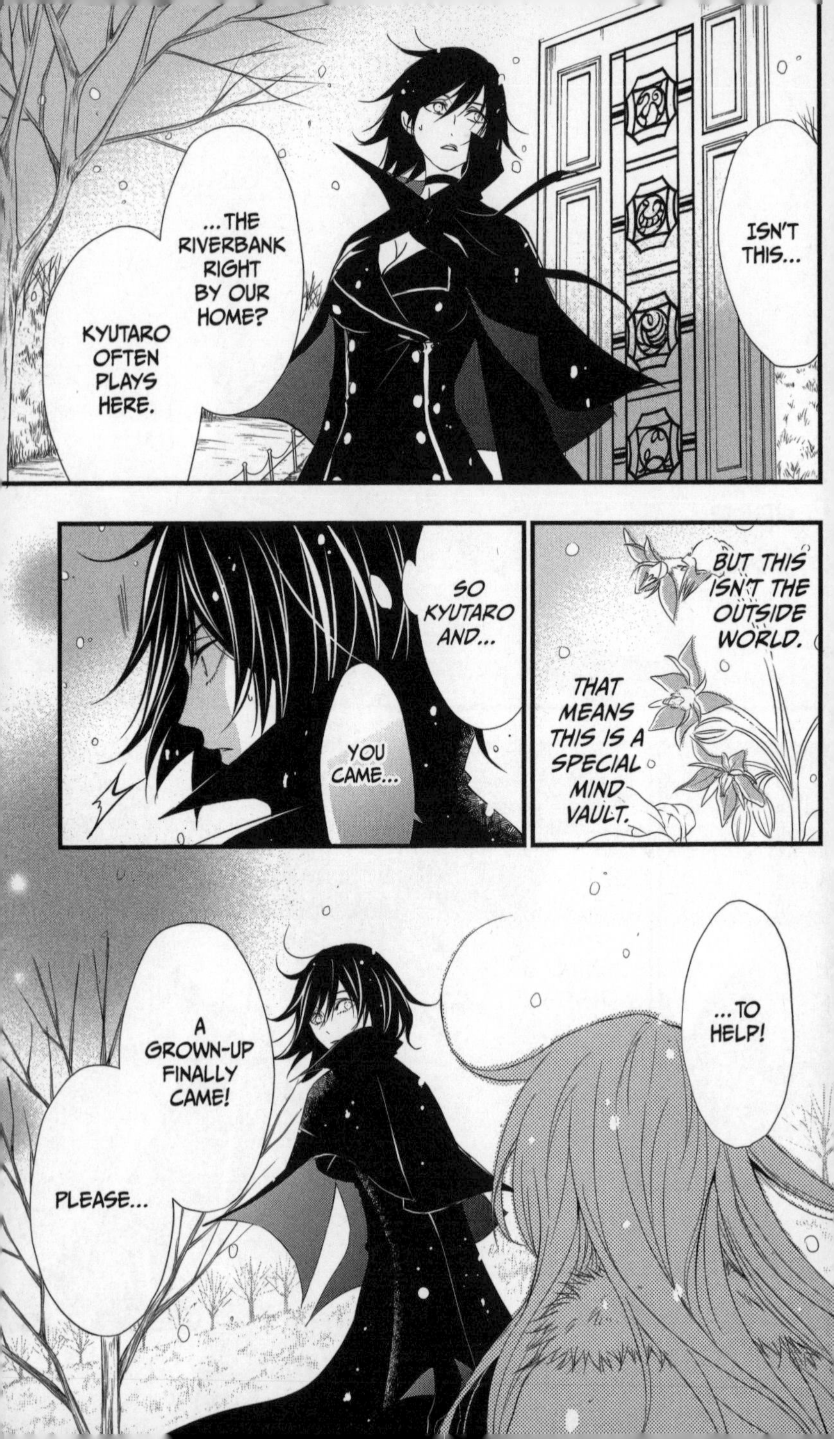
ISN'T THIS...
...THE RIVERBANK RIGHT BY OUR HOME?
KYUTARO OFTEN PLAYS HERE.
BUT THIS ISN'T THE OUTSIDE WORLD.
THAT MEANS THIS IS A SPECIAL MIND VAULT.
SO KYUTARO AND...
YOU CAME...
A GROWN-UP FINALLY CAME!
PLEASE...
...TO HELP!

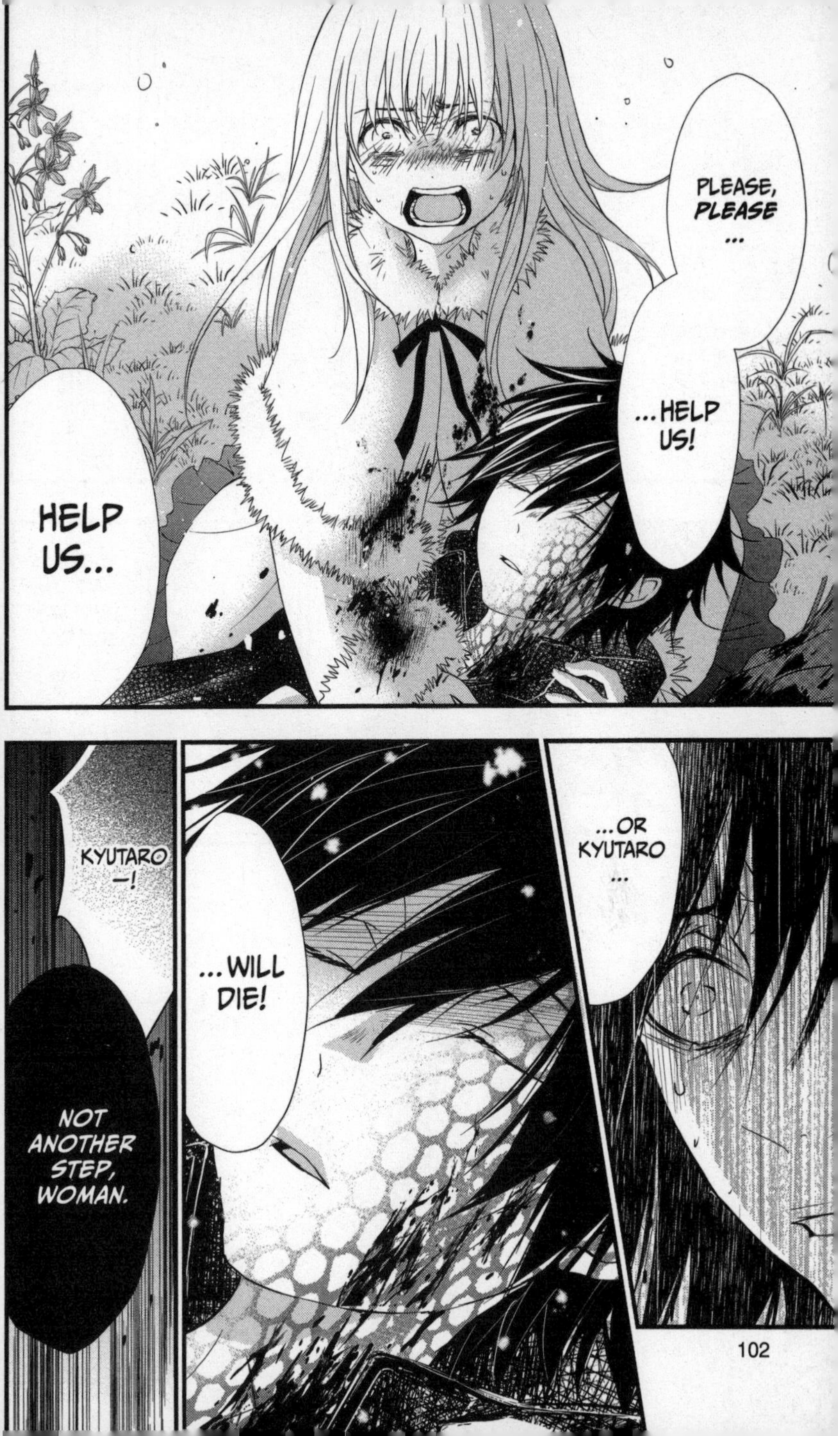
PLEASE, PLEASE ...
...HELP US!
HELP US...
...OR KYUTARO ...
...WILL DIE!
KYUTARO —!
NOT ANOTHER STEP, WOMAN.

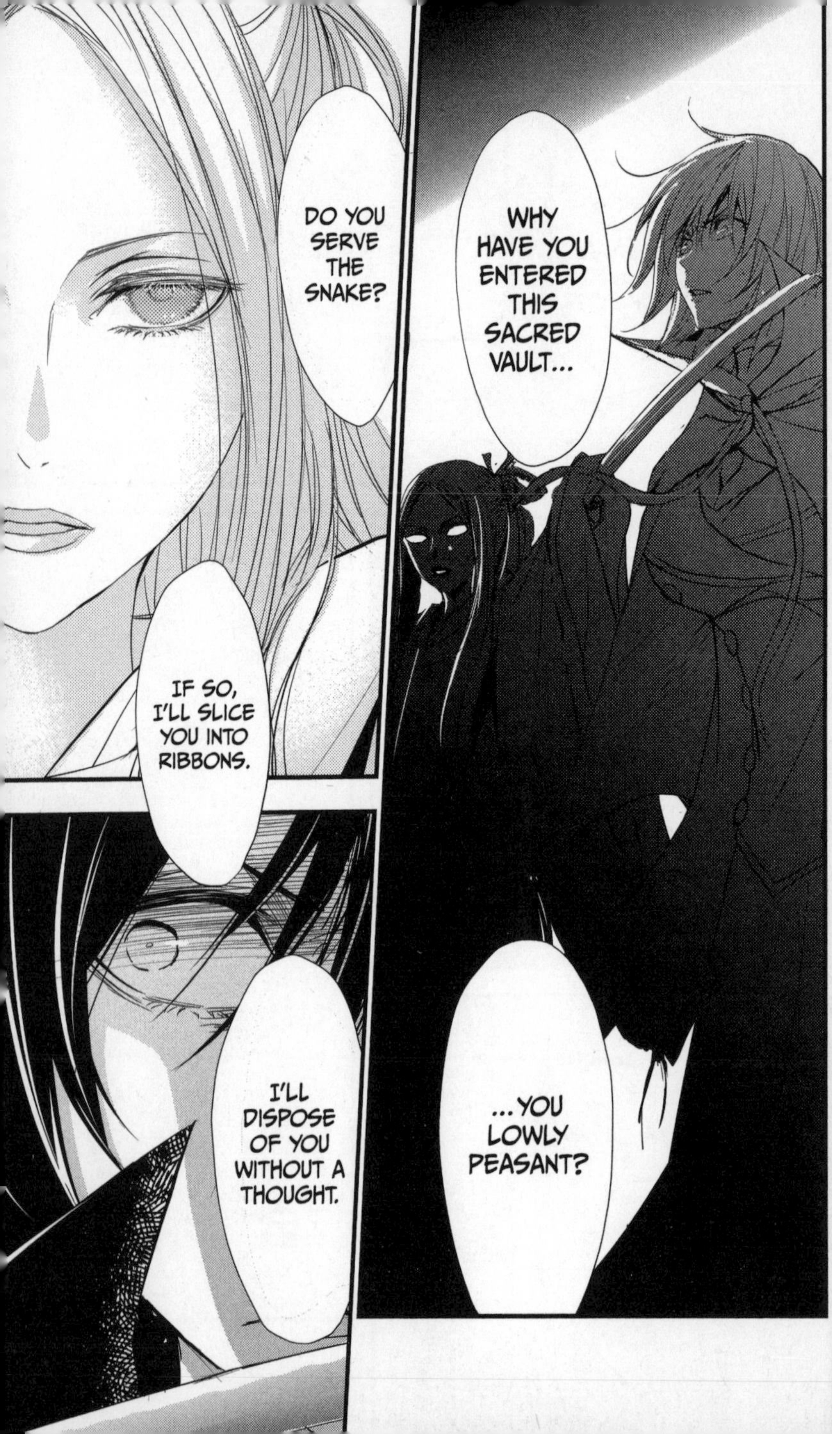
WHY HAVE YOU ENTERED THIS SACRED VAULT...
...YOU LOWLY PEASANT?
DO YOU SERVE THE SNAKE?
IF SO, I'LL SLICE YOU INTO RIBBONS.
I'LL DISPOSE OF YOU WITHOUT A THOUGHT.

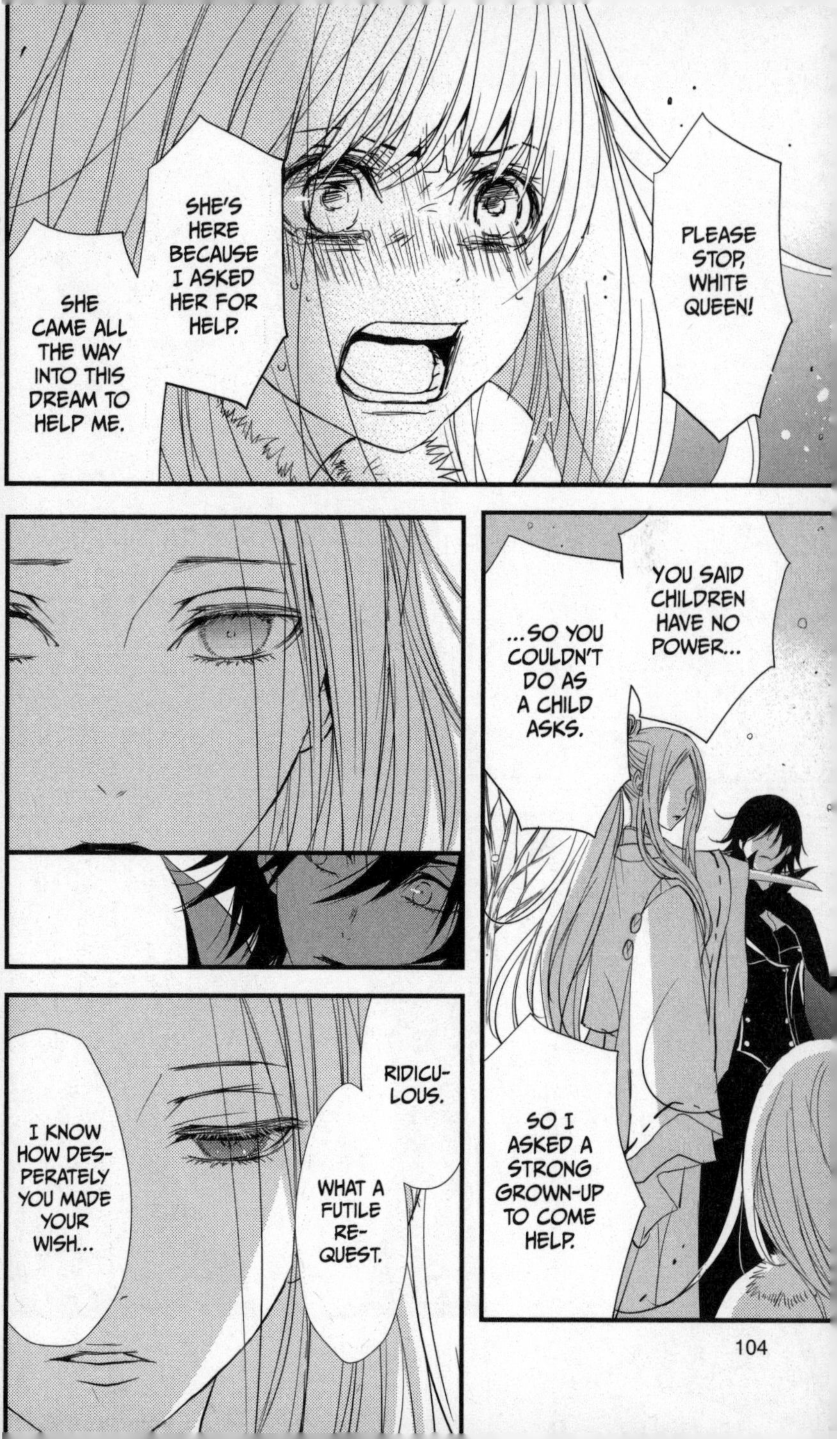
PLEASE STOP, WHITE QUEEN!
SHE'S HERE BECAUSE I ASKED HER FOR HELP.
SHE CAME ALL THE WAY INTO THIS DREAM TO HELP ME.
YOU SAID CHILDREN HAVE NO POWER...
...SO YOU COULDN'T DO AS A CHILD ASKS.
SO I ASKED A STRONG GROWN-UP TO COME HELP.
RIDICU-LOUS.
WHAT A FUTILE RE-QUEST.
I KNOW HOW DES-PERATELY YOU MADE YOUR WISH...

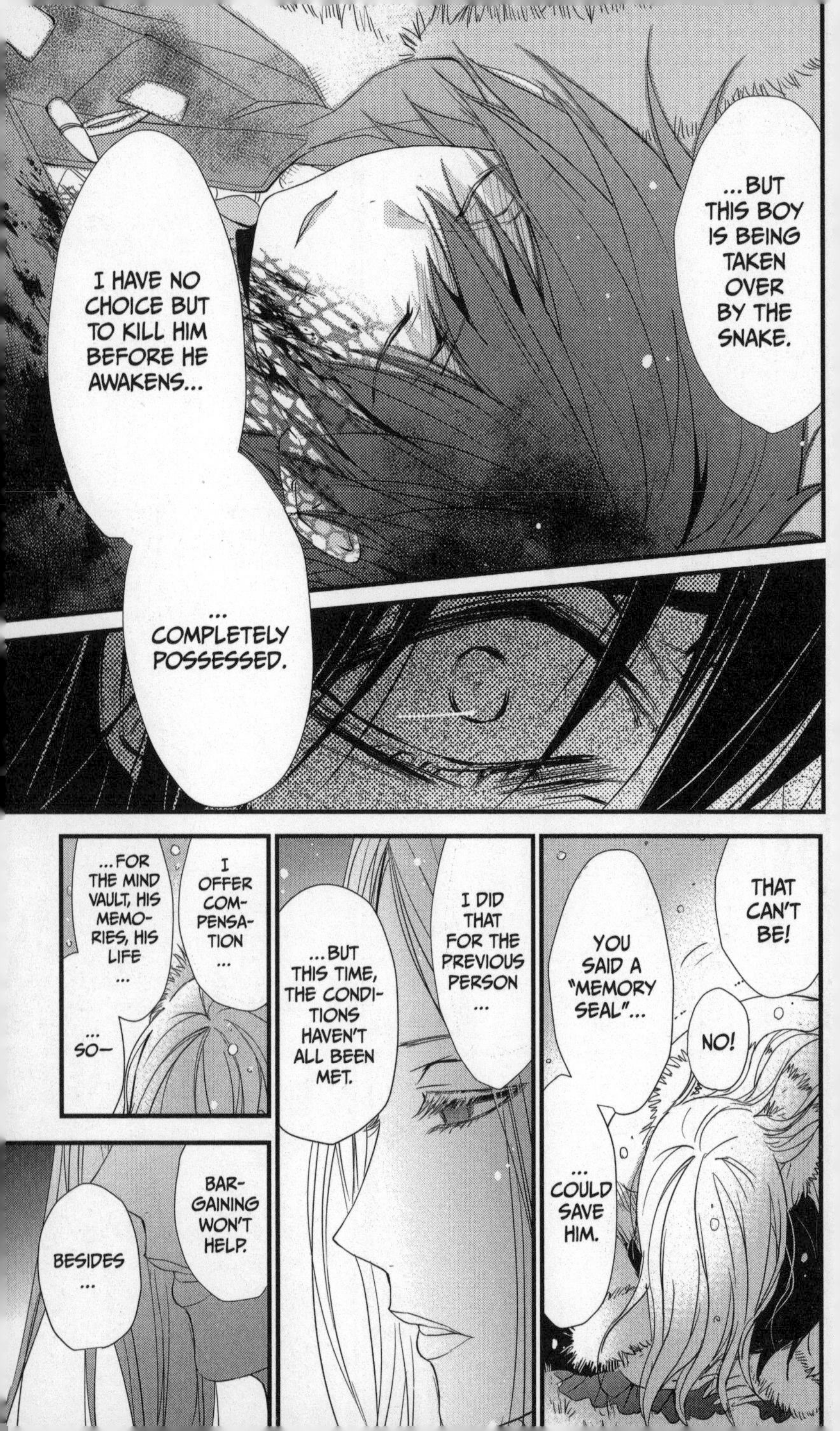
...BUT THIS BOY IS BEING TAKEN OVER BY THE SNAKE.
I HAVE NO CHOICE BUT TO KILL HIM BEFORE HE AWAKENS...
... COMPLETELY POSSESSED.
THAT CAN'T BE!
NO!
YOU SAID A "MEMORY SEAL"...
... COULD SAVE HIM.
I DID THAT FOR THE PREVIOUS PERSON ...
...BUT THIS TIME, THE CONDI-TIONS HAVEN'T ALL BEEN MET.
I OFFER COM-PENSA-TION ...
...FOR THE MIND VAULT, HIS MEMO-RIES, HIS LIFE ...
... SO—
BAR-GAINING WON'T HELP.
BESIDES ...

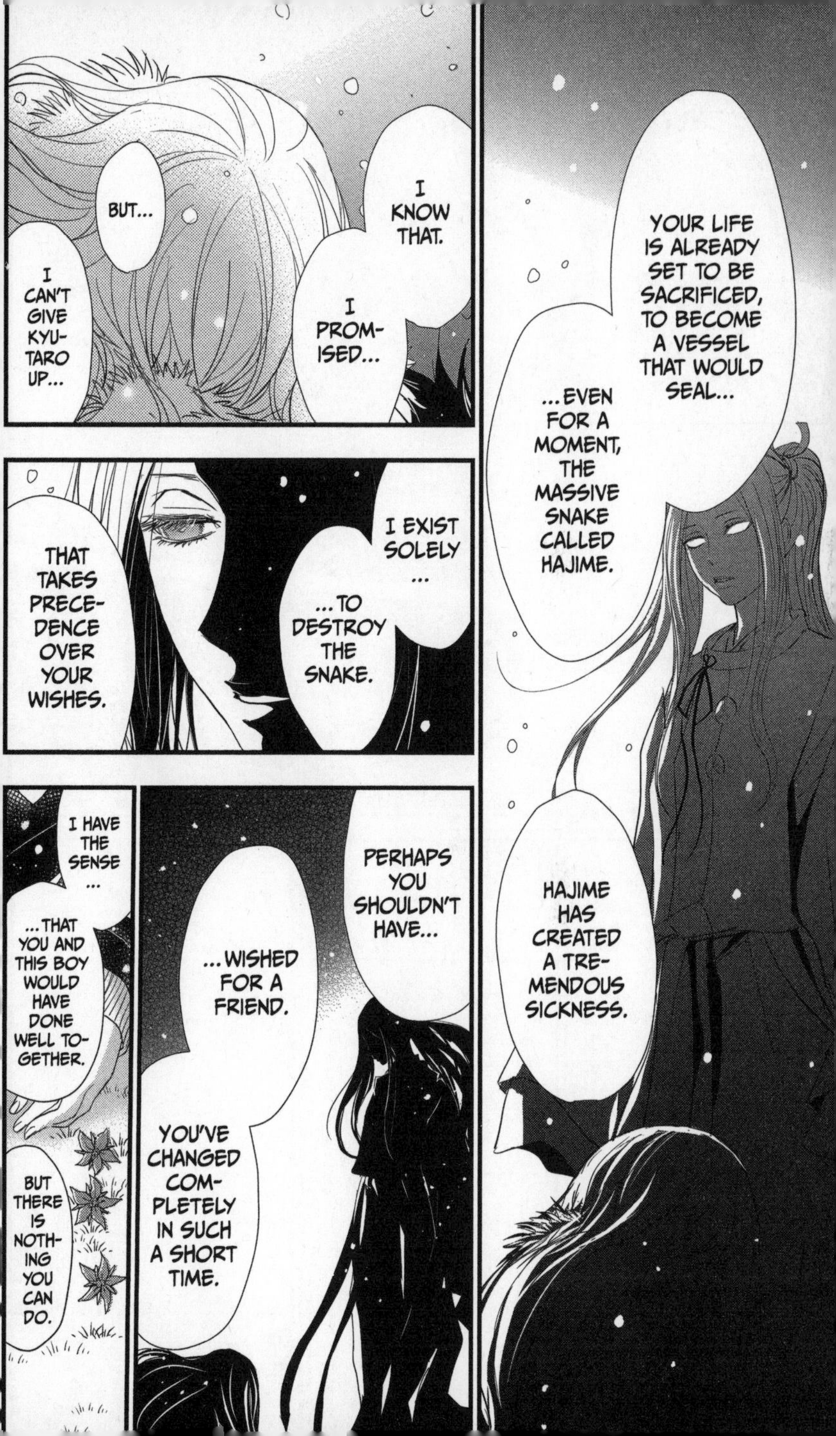
YOUR LIFE IS ALREADY SET TO BE SACRIFICED, TO BECOME A VESSEL THAT WOULD SEAL...
...EVEN FOR A MOMENT, THE MASSIVE SNAKE CALLED HAJIME.
HAJIME HAS CREATED A TREMENDOUS SICKNESS.
I KNOW THAT.
I PROMISED...
BUT...
I CAN'T GIVE KYUTARO UP...
I EXIST SOLELY...
...TO DESTROY THE SNAKE.
THAT TAKES PRECEDENCE OVER YOUR WISHES.
PERHAPS YOU SHOULDN'T HAVE...
...WISHED FOR A FRIEND.
YOU'VE CHANGED COMPLETELY IN SUCH A SHORT TIME.
I HAVE THE SENSE...
...THAT YOU AND THIS BOY WOULD HAVE DONE WELL TOGETHER.
BUT THERE IS NOTHING YOU CAN DO.

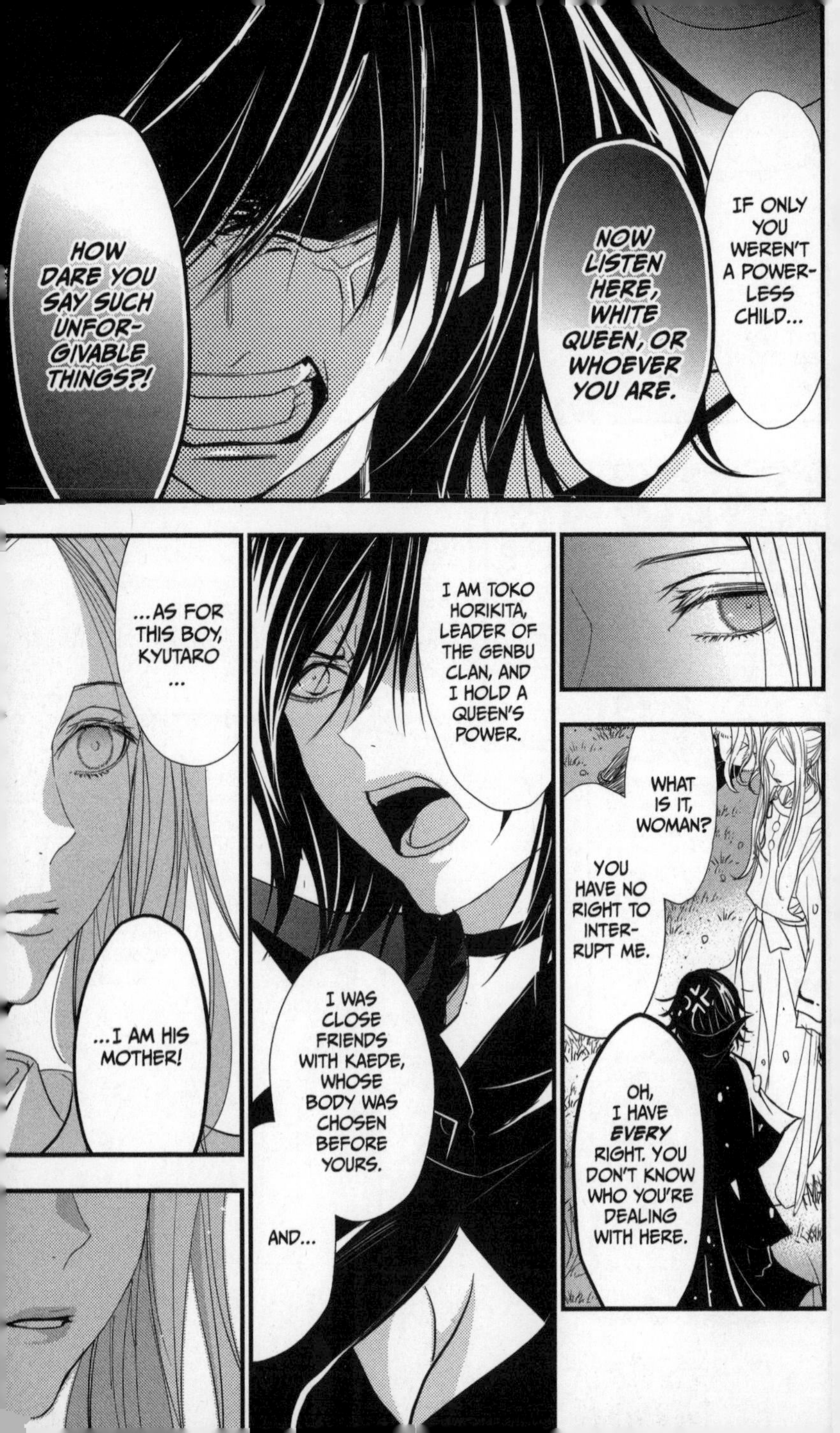
IF ONLY YOU WEREN'T A POWERLESS CHILD...
NOW LISTEN HERE, WHITE QUEEN, OR WHOEVER YOU ARE.
HOW DARE YOU SAY SUCH UNFORGIVABLE THINGS?!
WHAT IS IT, WOMAN?
YOU HAVE NO RIGHT TO INTERRUPT ME.
OH, I HAVE *EVERY* RIGHT. YOU DON'T KNOW WHO YOU'RE DEALING WITH HERE.
I AM TOKO HORIKITA, LEADER OF THE GENBU CLAN, AND I HOLD A QUEEN'S POWER.
I WAS CLOSE FRIENDS WITH KAEDE, WHOSE BODY WAS CHOSEN BEFORE YOURS.
AND...
...AS FOR THIS BOY, KYUTARO ...
...I AM HIS MOTHER!

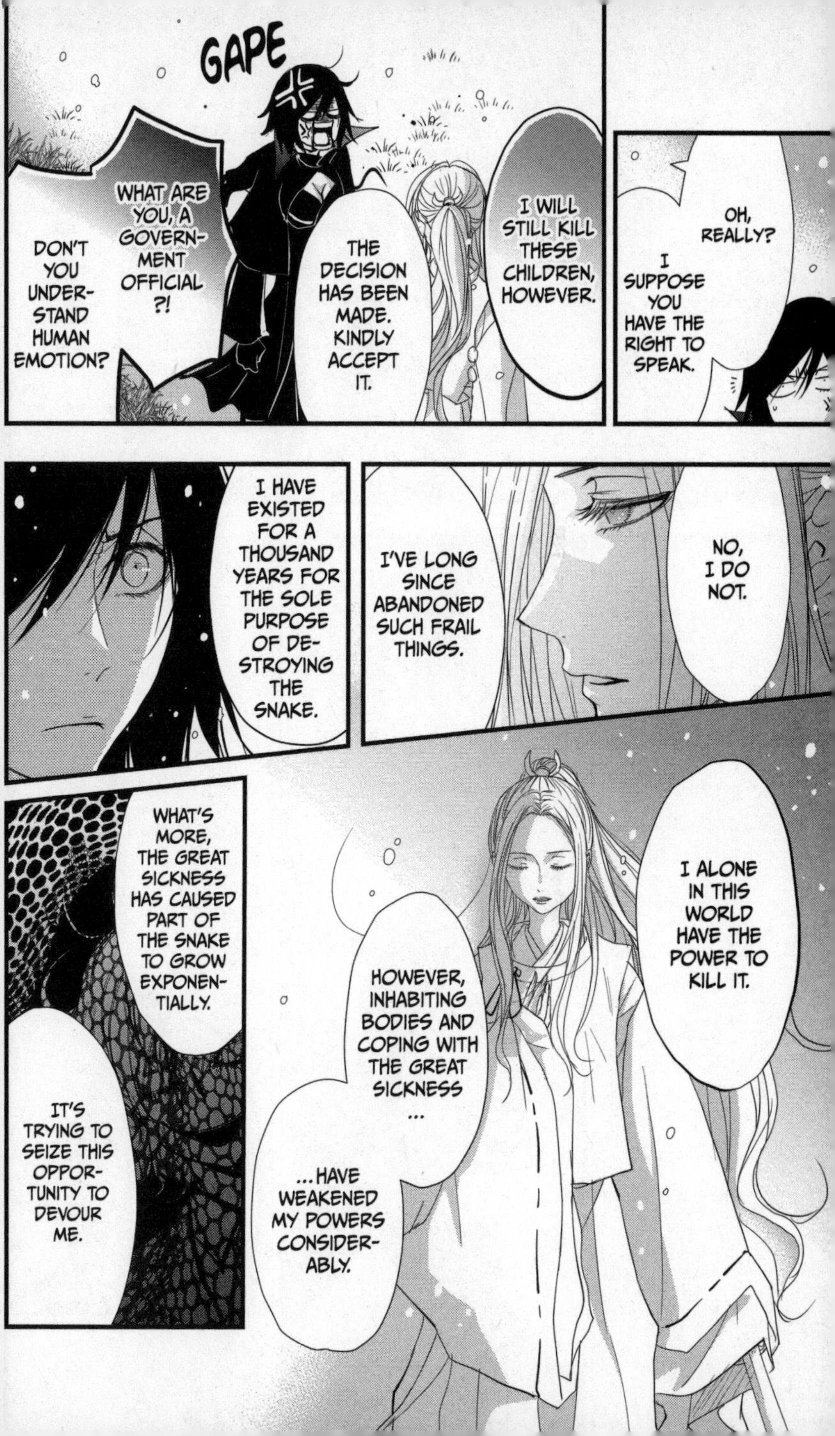
OH, REALLY?
I SUPPOSE YOU HAVE THE RIGHT TO SPEAK.
I WILL STILL KILL THESE CHILDREN, HOWEVER.
THE DECISION HAS BEEN MADE. KINDLY ACCEPT IT.
GAPE
WHAT ARE YOU, A GOVERNMENT OFFICIAL?!
DON'T YOU UNDERSTAND HUMAN EMOTION?
NO, I DO NOT.
I'VE LONG SINCE ABANDONED SUCH FRAIL THINGS.
I HAVE EXISTED FOR A THOUSAND YEARS FOR THE SOLE PURPOSE OF DESTROYING THE SNAKE.
I ALONE IN THIS WORLD HAVE THE POWER TO KILL IT.
HOWEVER, INHABITING BODIES AND COPING WITH THE GREAT SICKNESS...
...HAVE WEAKENED MY POWERS CONSIDERABLY.
WHAT'S MORE, THE GREAT SICKNESS HAS CAUSED PART OF THE SNAKE TO GROW EXPONENTIALLY.
IT'S TRYING TO SEIZE THIS OPPORTUNITY TO DEVOUR ME.

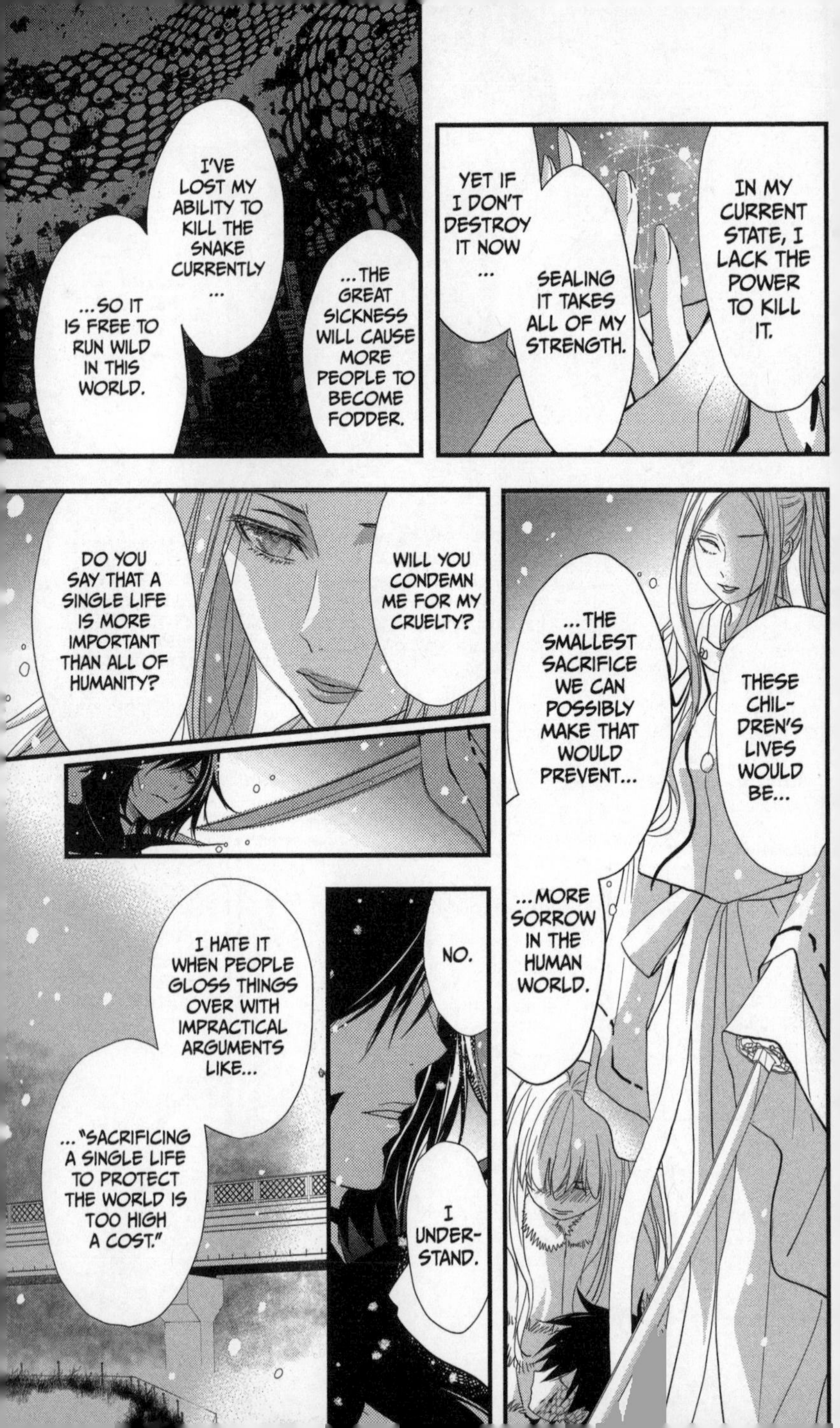
IN MY CURRENT STATE, I LACK THE POWER TO KILL IT.
SEALING IT TAKES ALL OF MY STRENGTH.
YET IF I DON'T DESTROY IT NOW ...
...THE GREAT SICKNESS WILL CAUSE MORE PEOPLE TO BECOME FODDER.
I'VE LOST MY ABILITY TO KILL THE SNAKE CURRENTLY ...
...SO IT IS FREE TO RUN WILD IN THIS WORLD.
THESE CHIL-DREN'S LIVES WOULD BE...
...THE SMALLEST SACRIFICE WE CAN POSSIBLY MAKE THAT WOULD PREVENT...
...MORE SORROW IN THE HUMAN WORLD.
WILL YOU CONDEMN ME FOR MY CRUELTY?
DO YOU SAY THAT A SINGLE LIFE IS MORE IMPORTANT THAN ALL OF HUMANITY?
NO.
I HATE IT WHEN PEOPLE GLOSS THINGS OVER WITH IMPRACTICAL ARGUMENTS LIKE...
..."SACRIFICING A SINGLE LIFE TO PROTECT THE WORLD IS TOO HIGH A COST."
I UNDER-STAND.

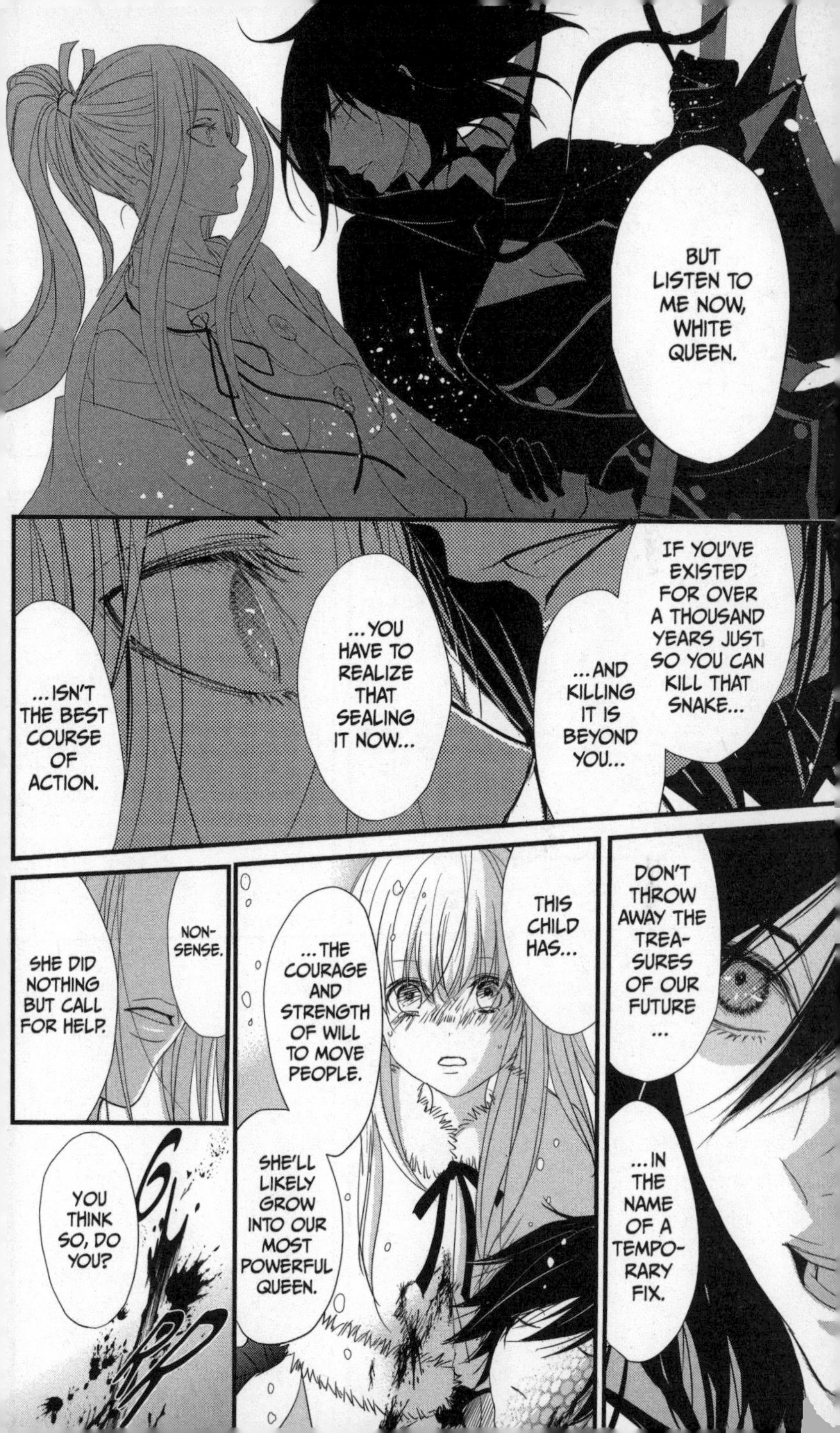
BUT LISTEN TO ME NOW, WHITE QUEEN.
IF YOU'VE EXISTED FOR OVER A THOUSAND YEARS JUST SO YOU CAN KILL THAT SNAKE...
...AND KILLING IT IS BEYOND YOU...
...YOU HAVE TO REALIZE THAT SEALING IT NOW...
...ISN'T THE BEST COURSE OF ACTION.
DON'T THROW AWAY THE TREASURES OF OUR FUTURE...
...IN THE NAME OF A TEMPORARY FIX.
THIS CHILD HAS...
...THE COURAGE AND STRENGTH OF WILL TO MOVE PEOPLE.
SHE'LL LIKELY GROW INTO OUR MOST POWERFUL QUEEN.
NON-SENSE.
SHE DID NOTHING BUT CALL FOR HELP.
YOU THINK SO, DO YOU?

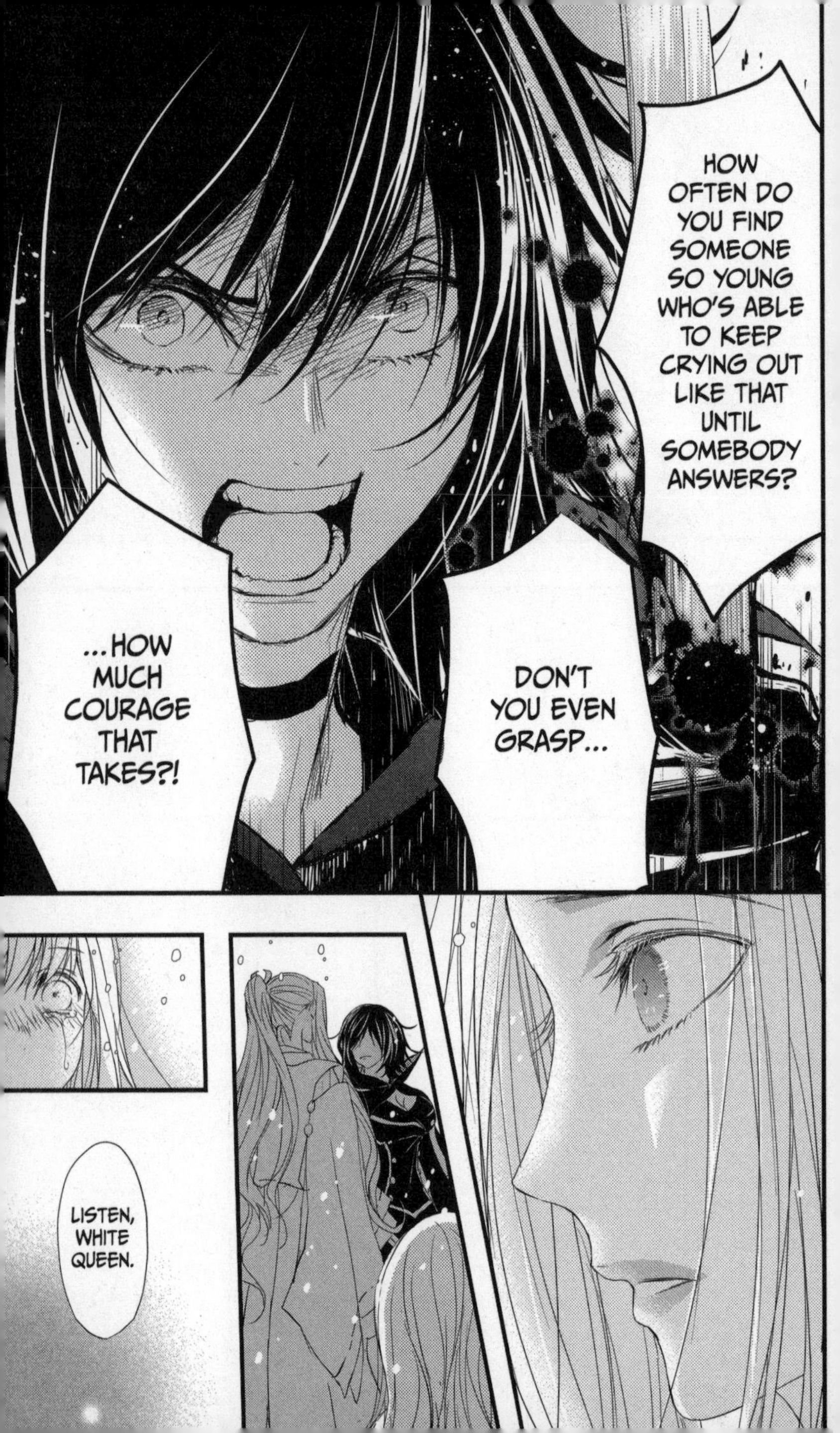
HOW OFTEN DO YOU FIND SOMEONE SO YOUNG WHO'S ABLE TO KEEP CRYING OUT LIKE THAT UNTIL SOMEBODY ANSWERS?
DON'T YOU EVEN GRASP...
...HOW MUCH COURAGE THAT TAKES?!
LISTEN, WHITE QUEEN.

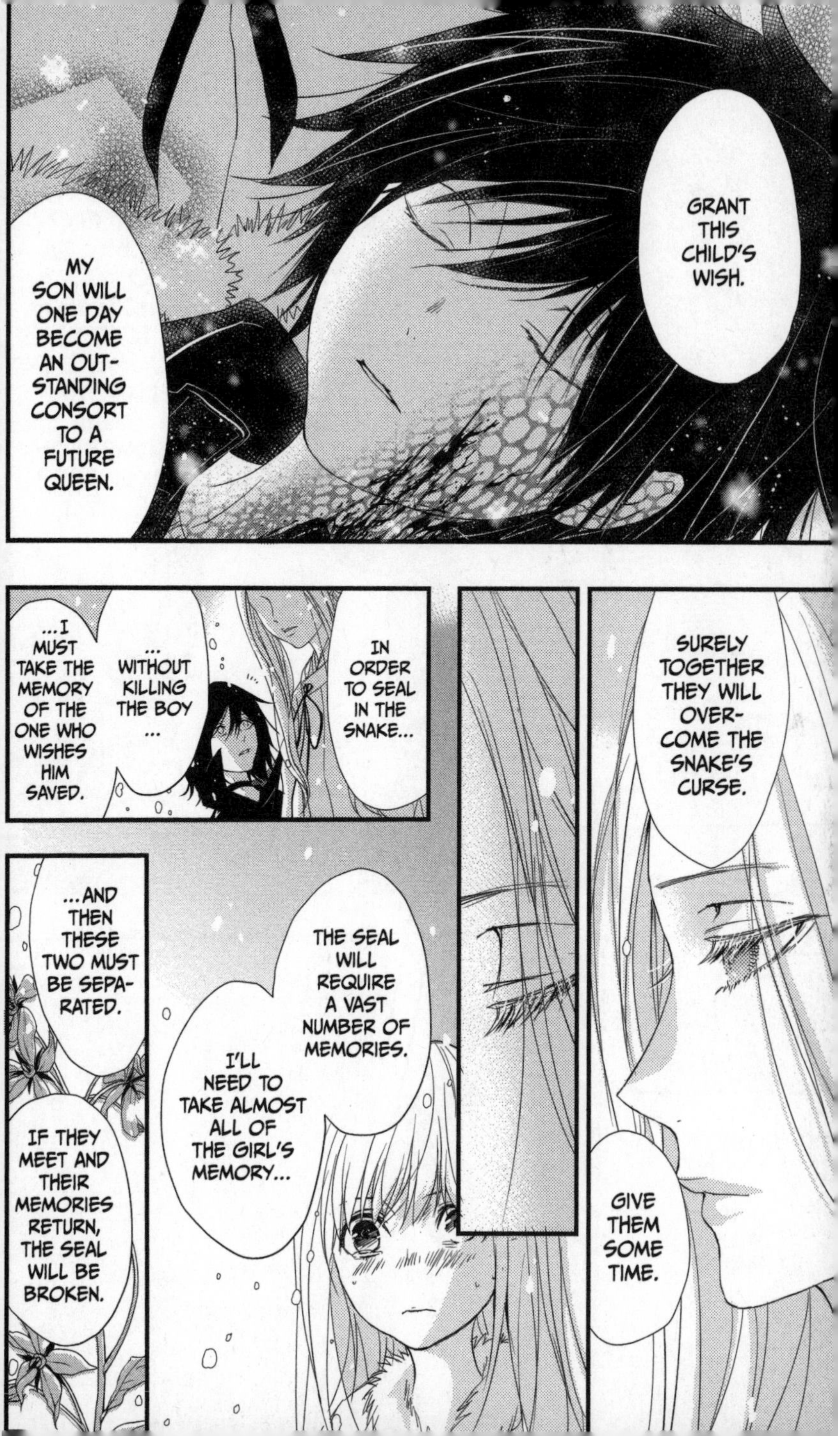
GRANT THIS CHILD'S WISH.
MY SON WILL ONE DAY BECOME AN OUTSTANDING CONSORT TO A FUTURE QUEEN.
SURELY TOGETHER THEY WILL OVERCOME THE SNAKE'S CURSE.
GIVE THEM SOME TIME.
IN ORDER TO SEAL IN THE SNAKE...
...WITHOUT KILLING THE BOY...
...I MUST TAKE THE MEMORY OF THE ONE WHO WISHES HIM SAVED.
THE SEAL WILL REQUIRE A VAST NUMBER OF MEMORIES.
I'LL NEED TO TAKE ALMOST ALL OF THE GIRL'S MEMORY...
...AND THEN THESE TWO MUST BE SEPARATED.
IF THEY MEET AND THEIR MEMORIES RETURN, THE SEAL WILL BE BROKEN.

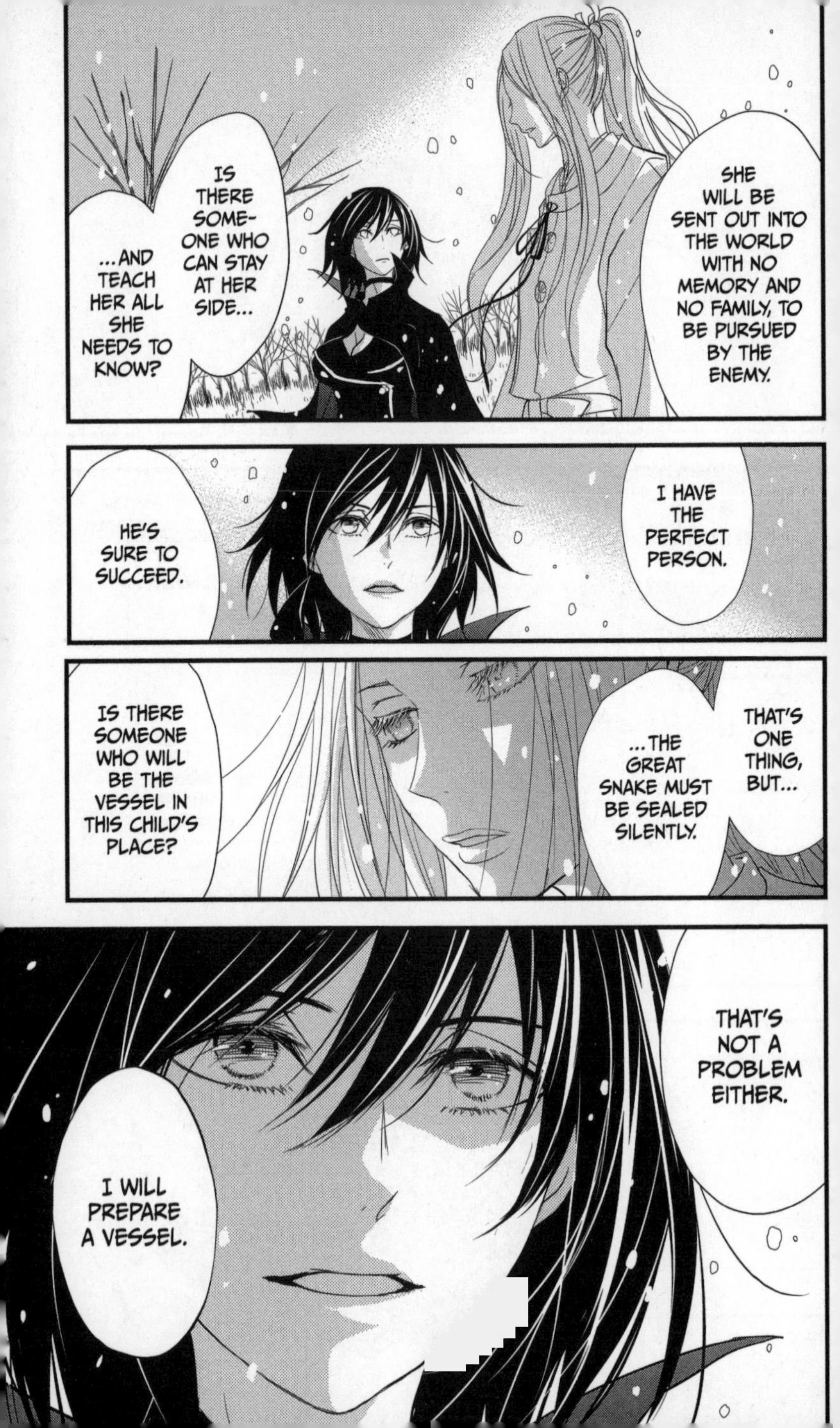
SHE WILL BE SENT OUT INTO THE WORLD WITH NO MEMORY AND NO FAMILY, TO BE PURSUED BY THE ENEMY.
IS THERE SOME-ONE WHO CAN STAY AT HER SIDE...
...AND TEACH HER ALL SHE NEEDS TO KNOW?
I HAVE THE PERFECT PERSON.
HE'S SURE TO SUCCEED.
THAT'S ONE THING, BUT...
...THE GREAT SNAKE MUST BE SEALED SILENTLY.
IS THERE SOMEONE WHO WILL BE THE VESSEL IN THIS CHILD'S PLACE?
THAT'S NOT A PROBLEM EITHER.
I WILL PREPARE A VESSEL.

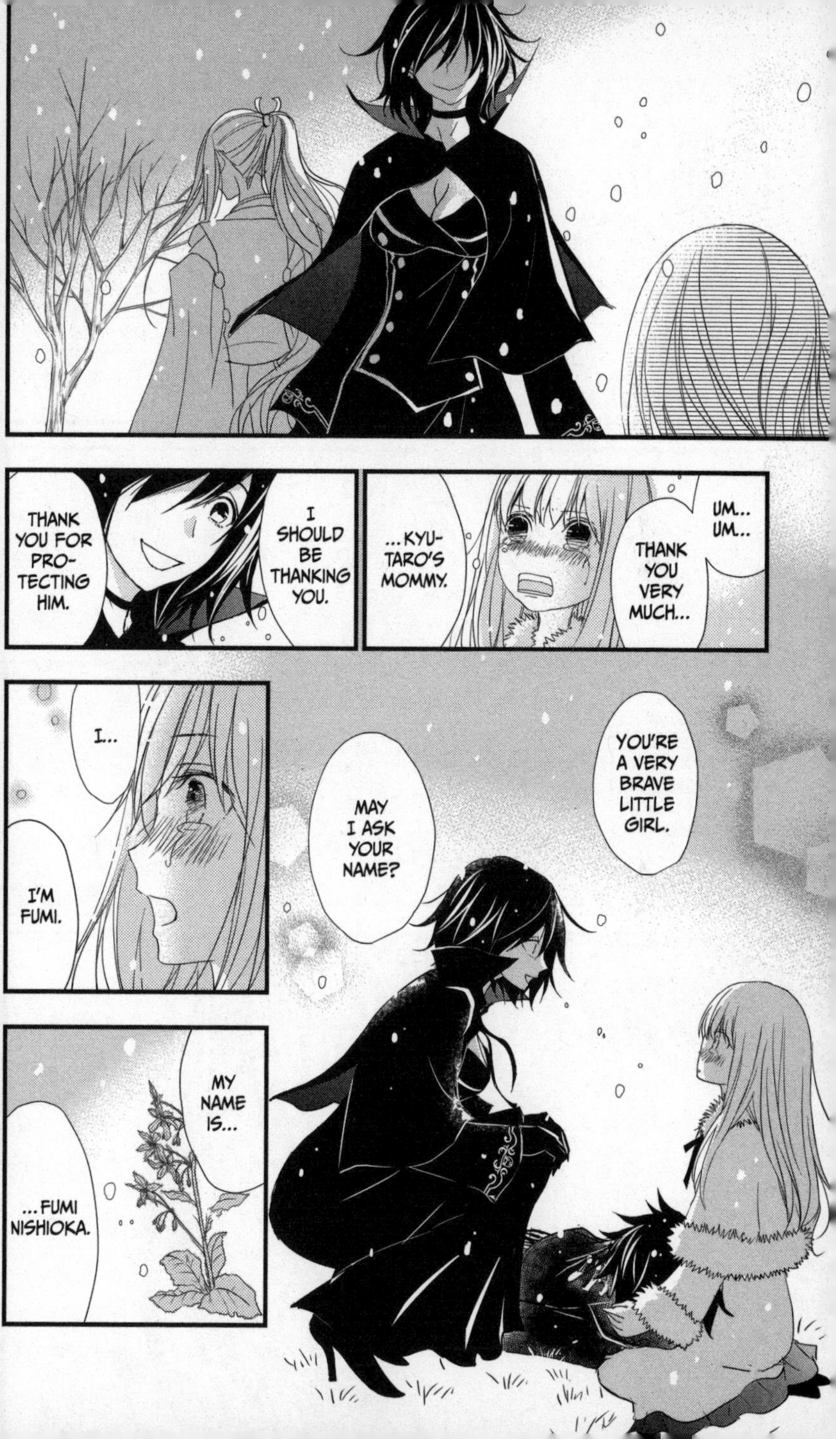
UM... UM...
THANK YOU VERY MUCH...
...KYU-TARO'S MOMMY.
I SHOULD BE THANKING YOU.
THANK YOU FOR PRO-TECTING HIM.
YOU'RE A VERY BRAVE LITTLE GIRL.
MAY I ASK YOUR NAME?
I...
I'M FUMI.
MY NAME IS...
...FUMI NISHIOKA.

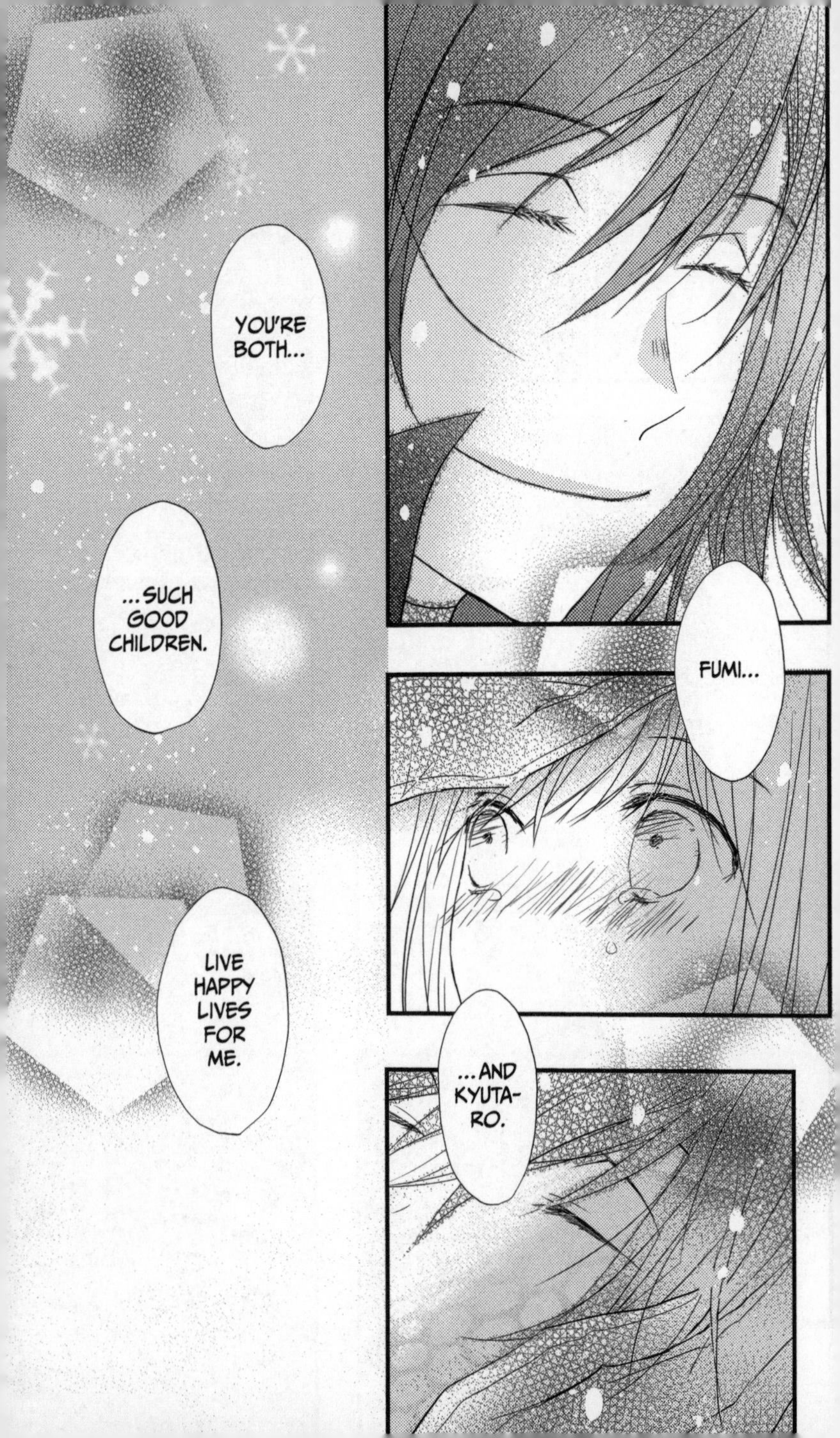
FUMI...
...AND KYUTA-RO.
YOU'RE BOTH...
...SUCH GOOD CHILDREN.
LIVE HAPPY LIVES FOR ME.

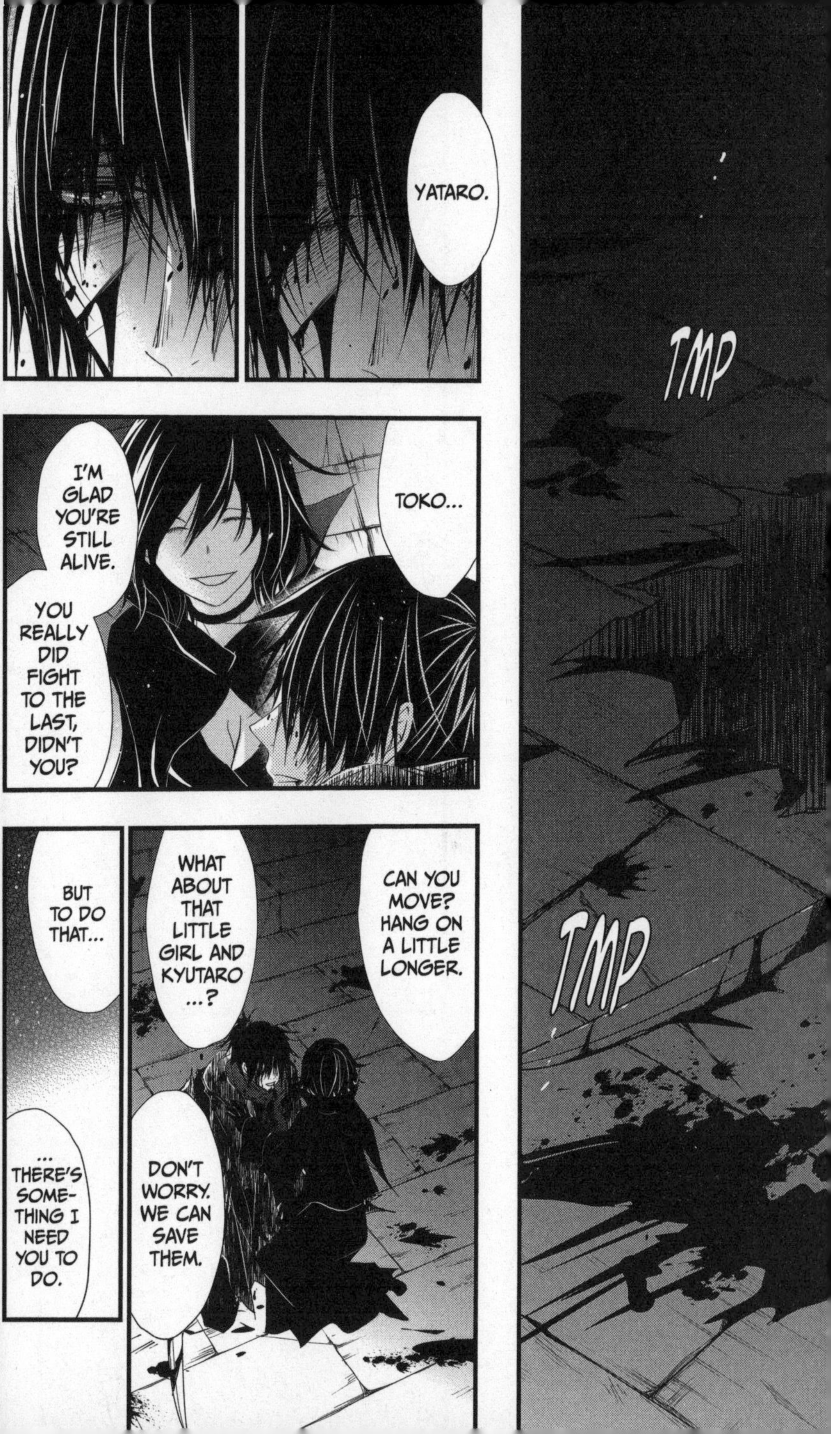
TMP
TMP
YATARO.
TOKO...
I'M GLAD YOU'RE STILL ALIVE.
YOU REALLY DID FIGHT TO THE LAST, DIDN'T YOU?
CAN YOU MOVE? HANG ON A LITTLE LONGER.
WHAT ABOUT THAT LITTLE GIRL AND KYUTARO ...?
DON'T WORRY. WE CAN SAVE THEM.
BUT TO DO THAT...
... THERE'S SOME-THING I NEED YOU TO DO.

I'M SO SORRY, YATARO.
I HAVE TO ASK YOU...
...TO KILL ME...
...WITH YOUR OWN HANDS.

MONTHLY BETSUCOMI SALE DATE NOTICE ON TWITTER

CHAPTER 39

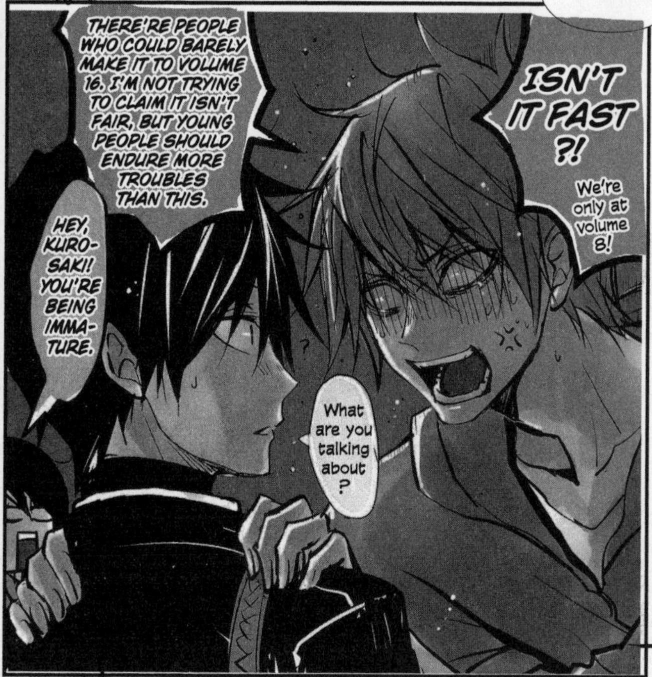
ISN'T IT FAST?!
We're only at volume 8!
THERE'RE PEOPLE WHO COULD BARELY MAKE IT TO VOLUME 16. I'M NOT TRYING TO CLAIM IT ISN'T FAIR, BUT YOUNG PEOPLE SHOULD ENDURE MORE TROUBLES THAN THIS.
What are you talking about?
HEY, KURO-SAKI! YOU'RE BEING IMMA-TURE.

LET'S SEE... WHAT'S UP IN *QUEEN'S QUALITY* THIS MONTH?

(1) I WISH HE'D MAKE IT CLEAR WHETHER HE'S A BAT OR A DOG.
(2) NO MATTER HOW SERIOUS THE SITUATION, THE SCRUB BRUSH WILL ELICIT A GIGGLE.
(3) THAT NONCOMPOOP IS NEVER FAZED BY KUROSAKI.

CHAPTER 39 IS THE LAST OF THE FLASHBACK ARC!

ONCE AGAIN, KUROSAKI OF *DENGEKI DAISY* GETS INVOLVED...

DENGEKI DAISY WAS 16 VOLUMES LONG. EVEN IF I ADD THE THREE VOLUMES OF *QQ SWEEPER* TO THIS SERIES, KYUTARO'S STORY IS COMING ALONG SLIGHTLY FASTER. WELL, ACTUALLY, BOTH ARE SLOW. (SORRY.)

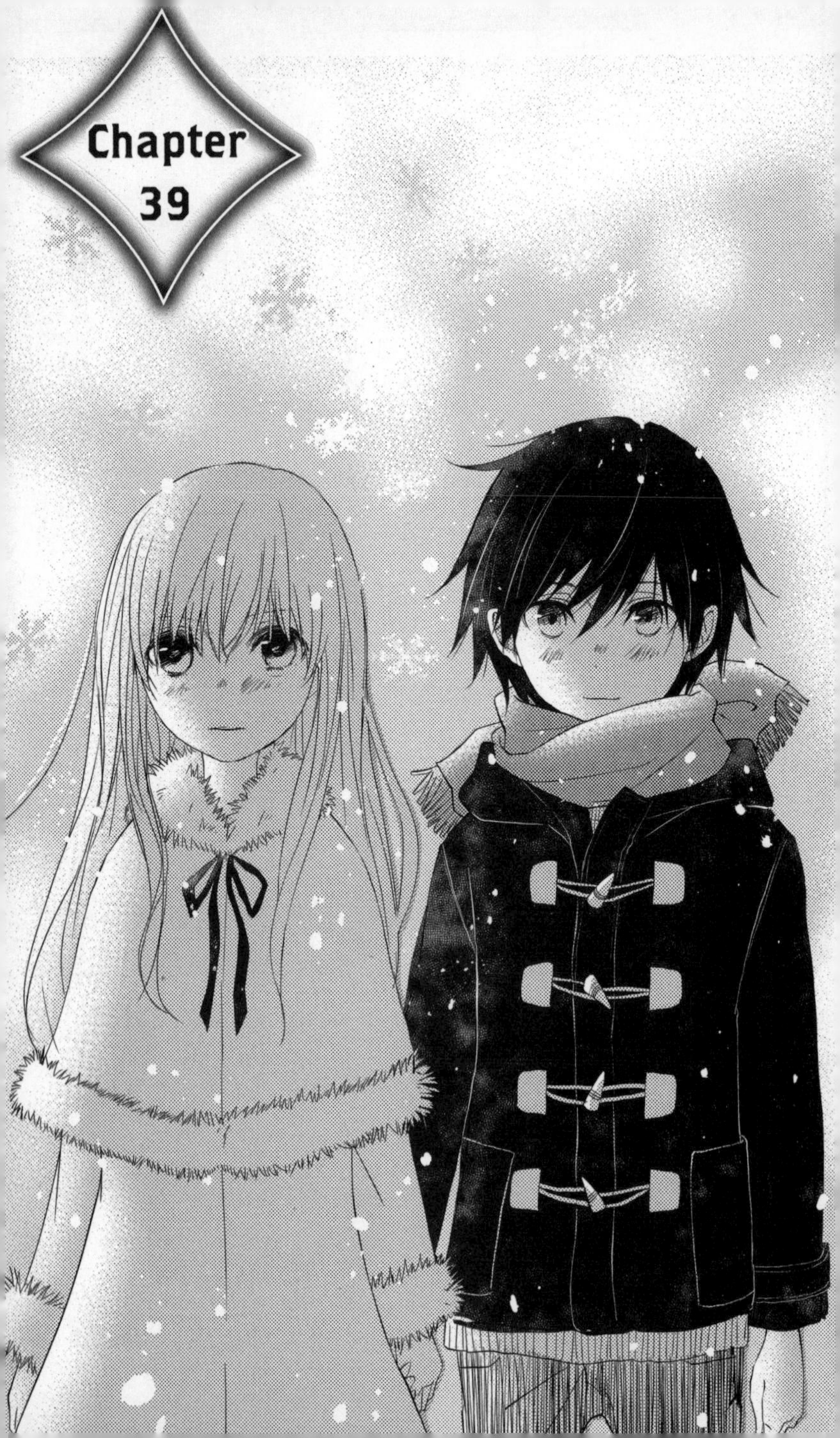
Chapter
39

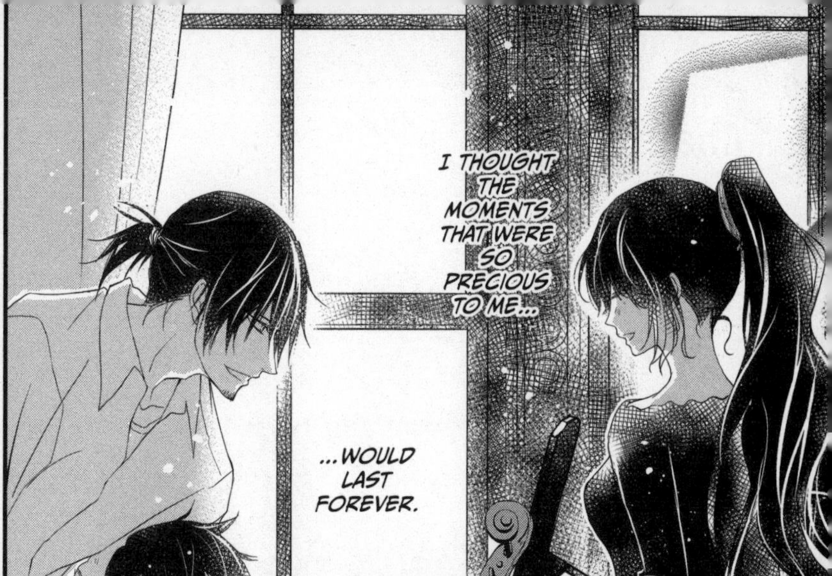
I THOUGHT THE MOMENTS THAT WERE SO PRECIOUS TO ME...
...WOULD LAST FOREVER.

Since this story is about cleaning, let me talk a little bit about that! I like Wave dusters. They're disposable, so they aren't "green," but they are very convenient. I have a wool duster too, but I don't like to get it dirty, so I just use it around my bed. I have dusters tucked away like secret ninja weapons—in my workplace, near my TV, my bookcase, the bathroom, the kitchen—and use them when I feel like it.

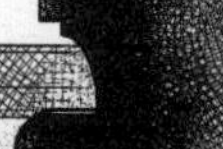
FLUFFY

In the morning, when I'm reheating my second cup of coffee for 30 seconds, I dust the area around my microwave.

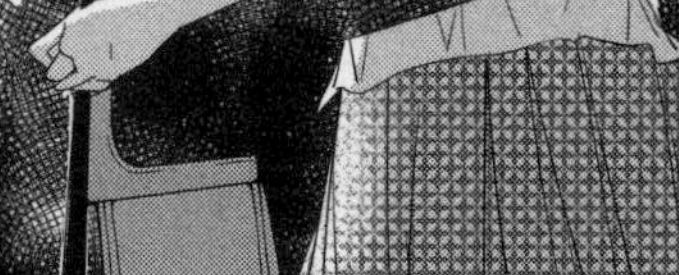
VRRR

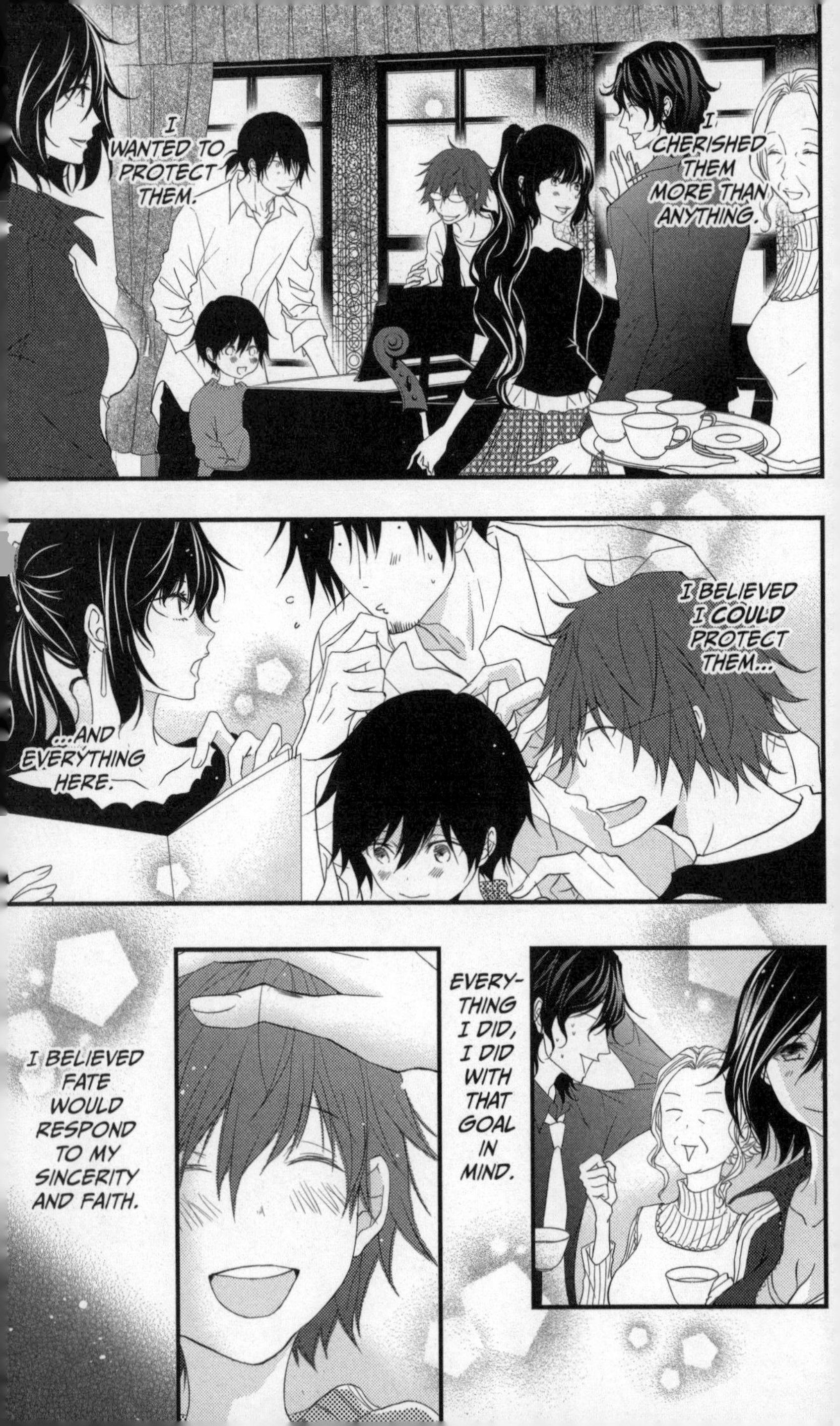
I CHERISHED THEM MORE THAN ANYTHING.
I WANTED TO PROTECT THEM.
I BELIEVED I COULD PROTECT THEM...
...AND EVERYTHING HERE.
EVERY-THING I DID, I DID WITH THAT GOAL IN MIND.
I BELIEVED FATE WOULD RESPOND TO MY SINCERITY AND FAITH.

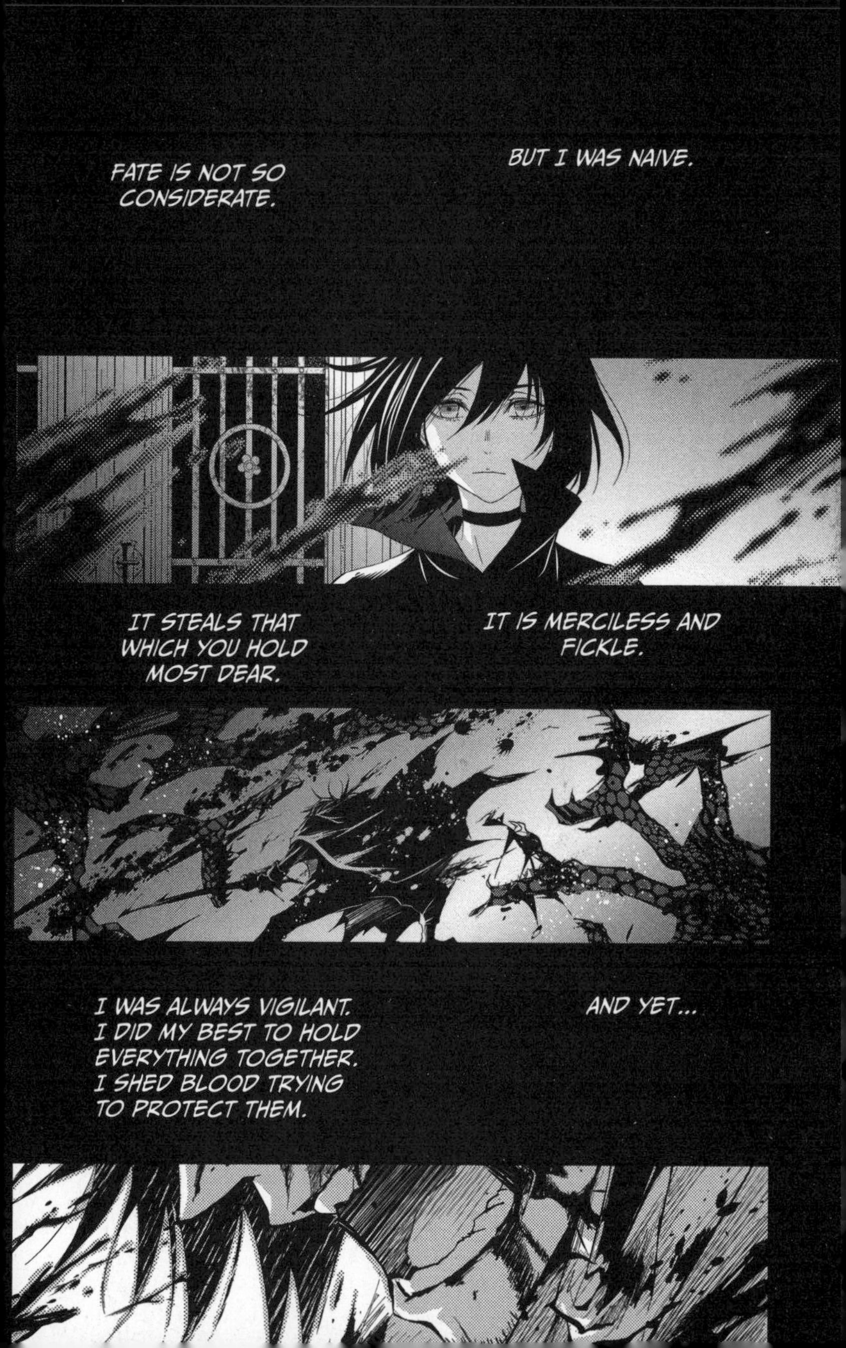
BUT I WAS NAIVE.
FATE IS NOT SO CONSIDERATE.
IT IS MERCILESS AND FICKLE.
IT STEALS THAT WHICH YOU HOLD MOST DEAR.
AND YET...
I WAS ALWAYS VIGILANT. I DID MY BEST TO HOLD EVERYTHING TOGETHER. I SHED BLOOD TRYING TO PROTECT THEM.

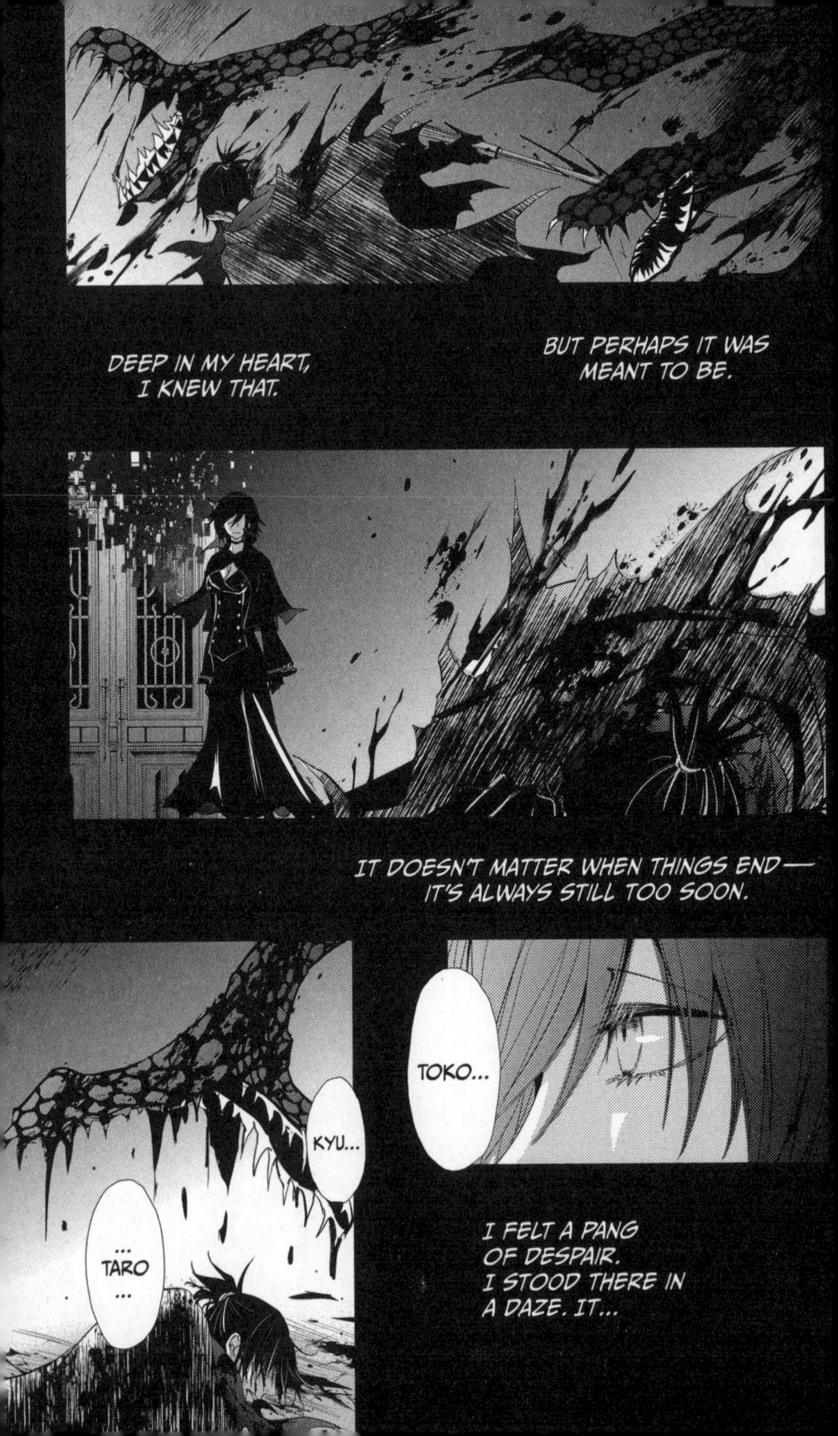
BUT PERHAPS IT WAS MEANT TO BE.
DEEP IN MY HEART, I KNEW THAT.
IT DOESN'T MATTER WHEN THINGS END— IT'S ALWAYS STILL TOO SOON.
TOKO...
I FELT A PANG OF DESPAIR. I STOOD THERE IN A DAZE. IT...
KYU...
...TARO...

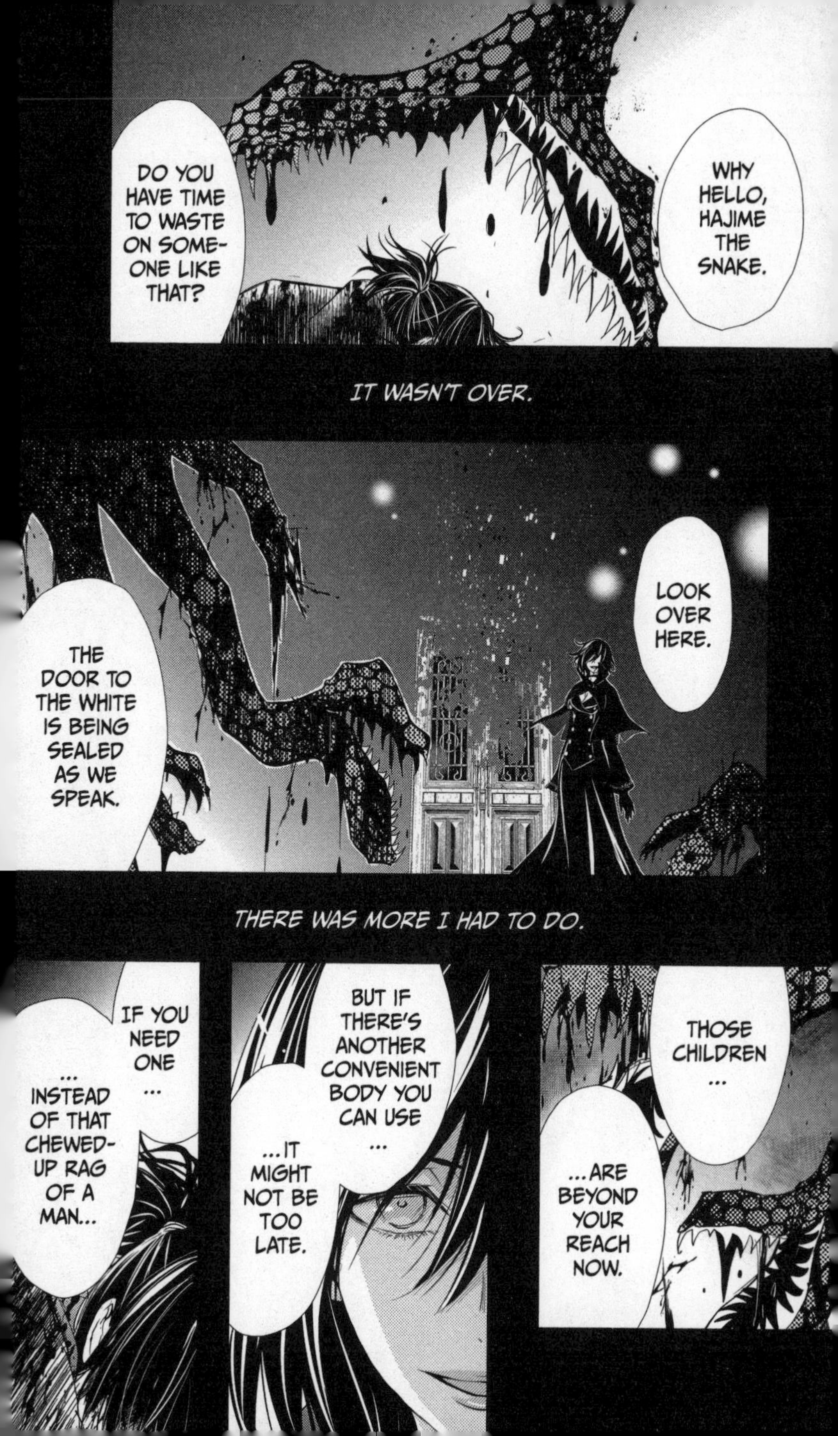
WHY HELLO, HAJIME THE SNAKE.
DO YOU HAVE TIME TO WASTE ON SOME-ONE LIKE THAT?
IT WASN'T OVER.
LOOK OVER HERE.
THE DOOR TO THE WHITE IS BEING SEALED AS WE SPEAK.
THERE WAS MORE I HAD TO DO.
THOSE CHILDREN ...
...ARE BEYOND YOUR REACH NOW.
BUT IF THERE'S ANOTHER CONVENIENT BODY YOU CAN USE ...
...IT MIGHT NOT BE TOO LATE.
IF YOU NEED ONE ...
... INSTEAD OF THAT CHEWED-UP RAG OF A MAN...

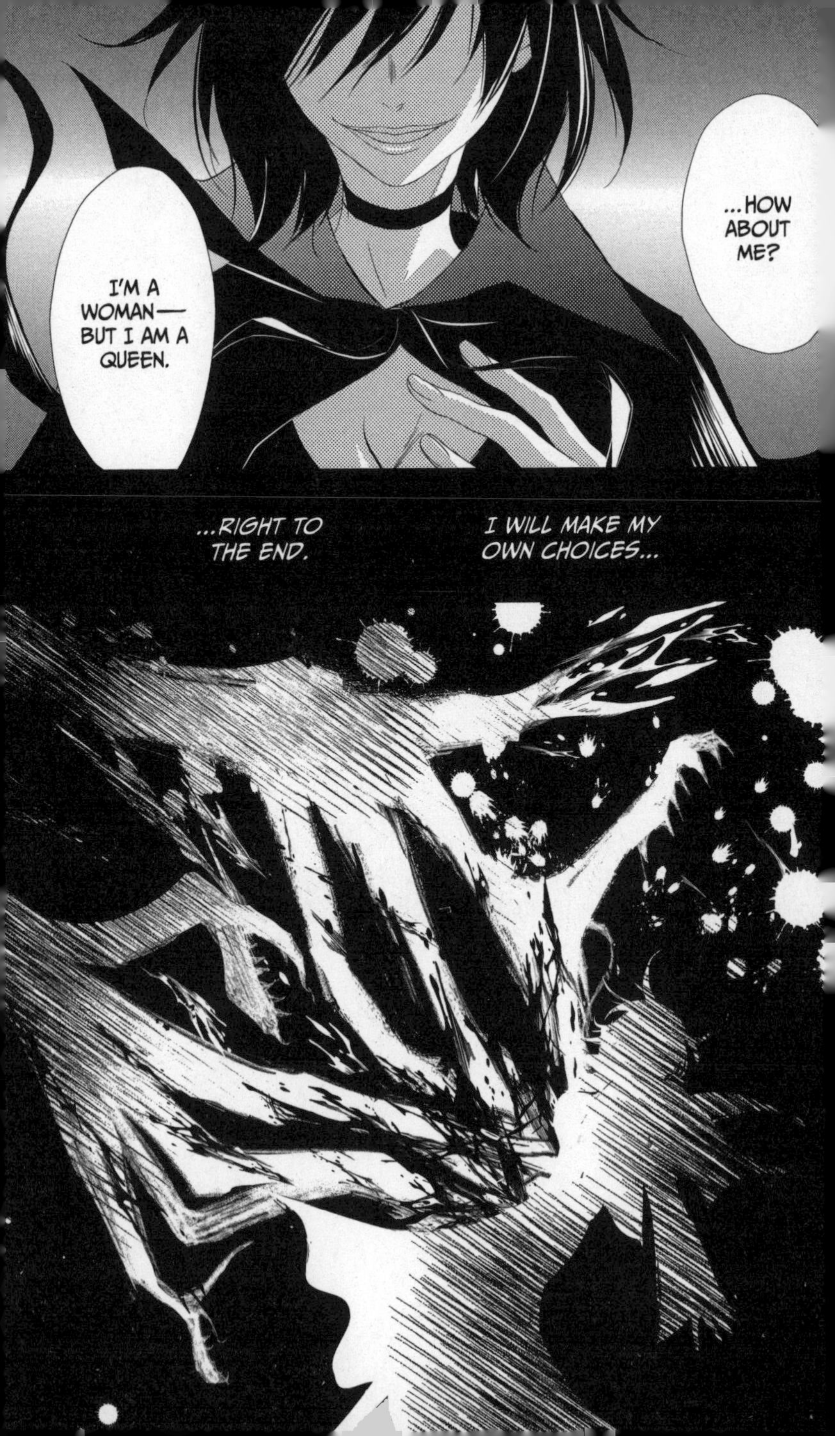
...HOW ABOUT ME?
I'M A WOMAN— BUT I AM A QUEEN.
I WILL MAKE MY OWN CHOICES...
...RIGHT TO THE END.

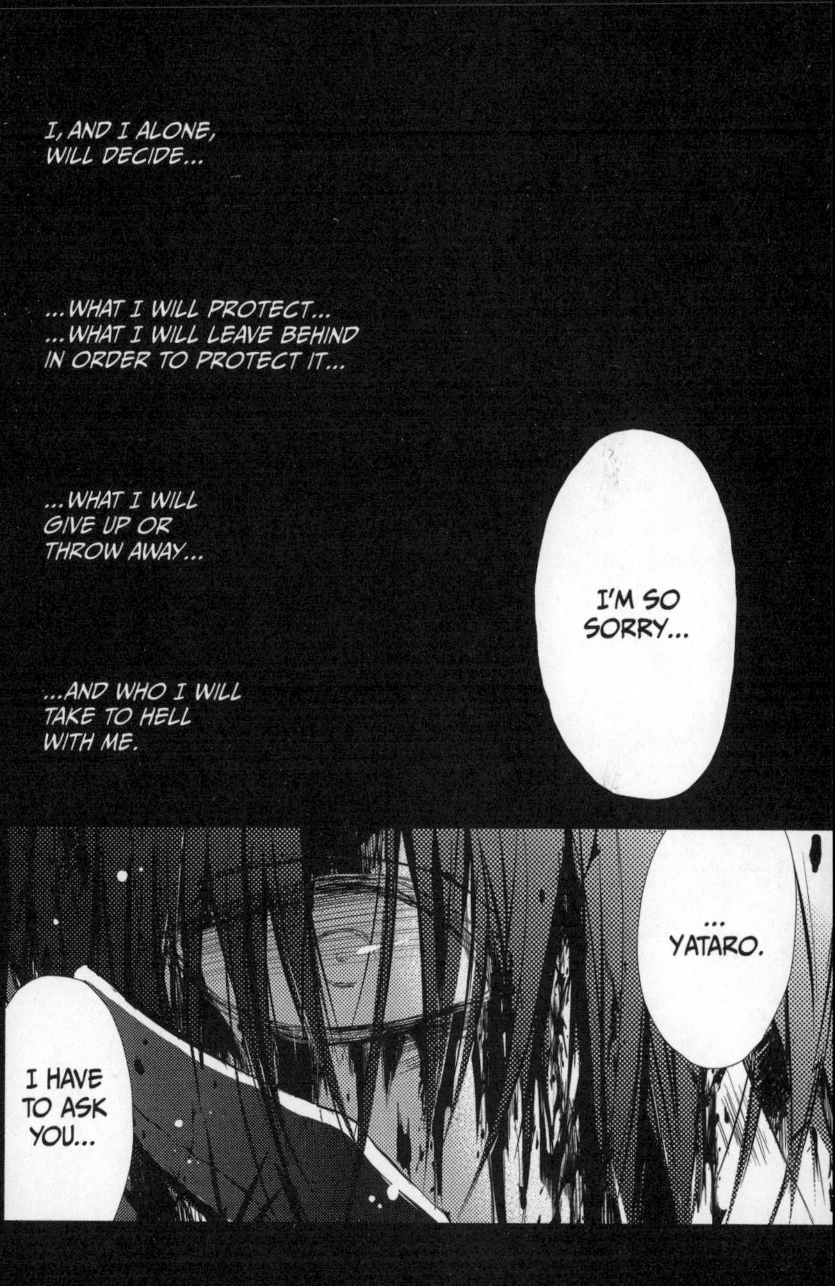
I, AND I ALONE, WILL DECIDE...
...WHAT I WILL PROTECT... ...WHAT I WILL LEAVE BEHIND IN ORDER TO PROTECT IT...
...WHAT I WILL GIVE UP OR THROW AWAY...
...AND WHO I WILL TAKE TO HELL WITH ME.
I'M SO SORRY...
... YATARO.
I HAVE TO ASK YOU...

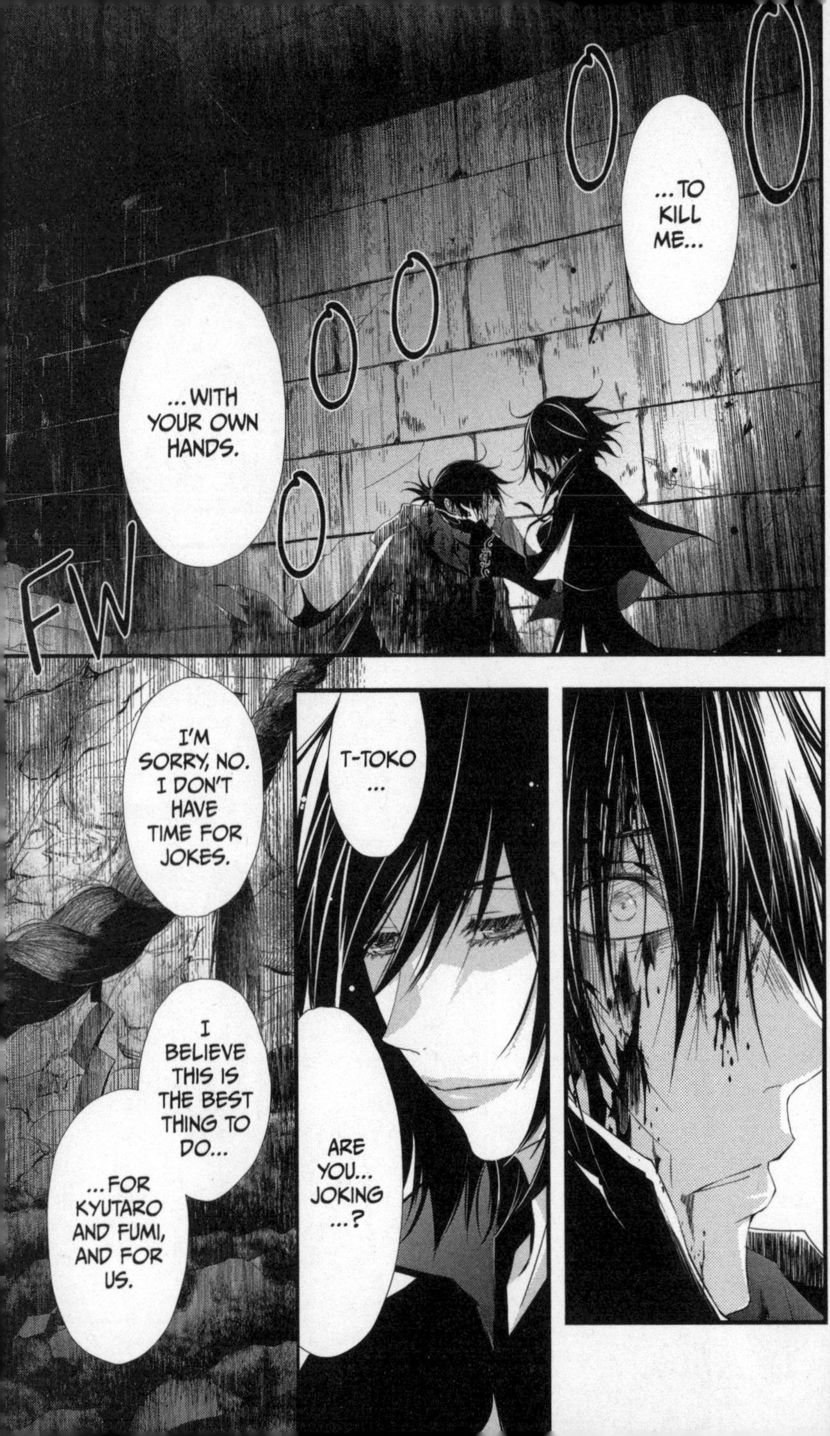
...TO KILL ME...
...WITH YOUR OWN HANDS.
FWOOOOO
T-TOKO ...
ARE YOU... JOKING ...?
I'M SORRY, NO. I DON'T HAVE TIME FOR JOKES.
I BELIEVE THIS IS THE BEST THING TO DO...
...FOR KYUTARO AND FUMI, AND FOR US.

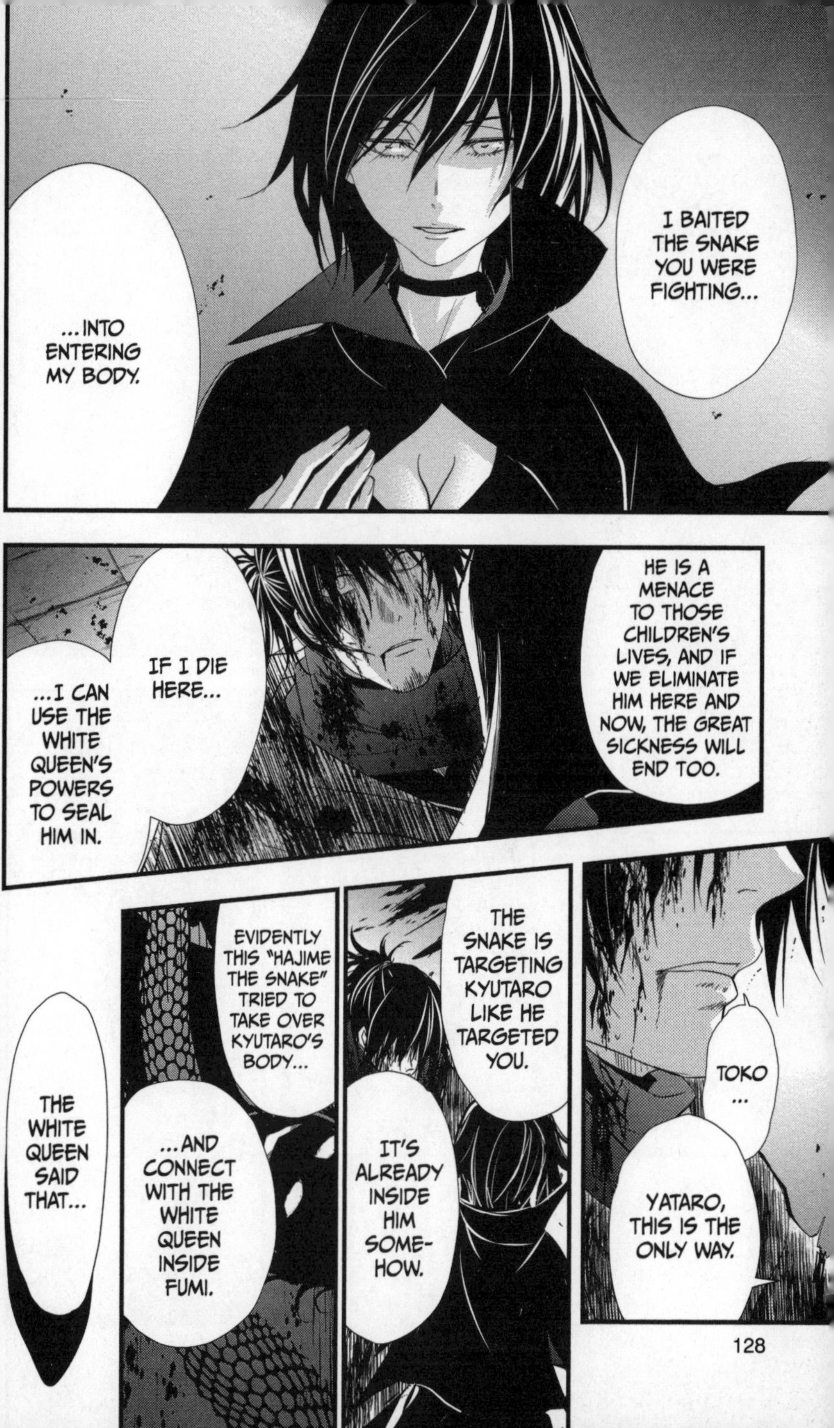
I BAITED THE SNAKE YOU WERE FIGHTING...
...INTO ENTERING MY BODY.
HE IS A MENACE TO THOSE CHILDREN'S LIVES, AND IF WE ELIMINATE HIM HERE AND NOW, THE GREAT SICKNESS WILL END TOO.
IF I DIE HERE...
...I CAN USE THE WHITE QUEEN'S POWERS TO SEAL HIM IN.
TOKO...
YATARO, THIS IS THE ONLY WAY.
THE SNAKE IS TARGETING KYUTARO LIKE HE TARGETED YOU.
IT'S ALREADY INSIDE HIM SOME-HOW.
EVIDENTLY THIS "HAJIME THE SNAKE" TRIED TO TAKE OVER KYUTARO'S BODY...
...AND CONNECT WITH THE WHITE QUEEN INSIDE FUMI.
THE WHITE QUEEN SAID THAT...

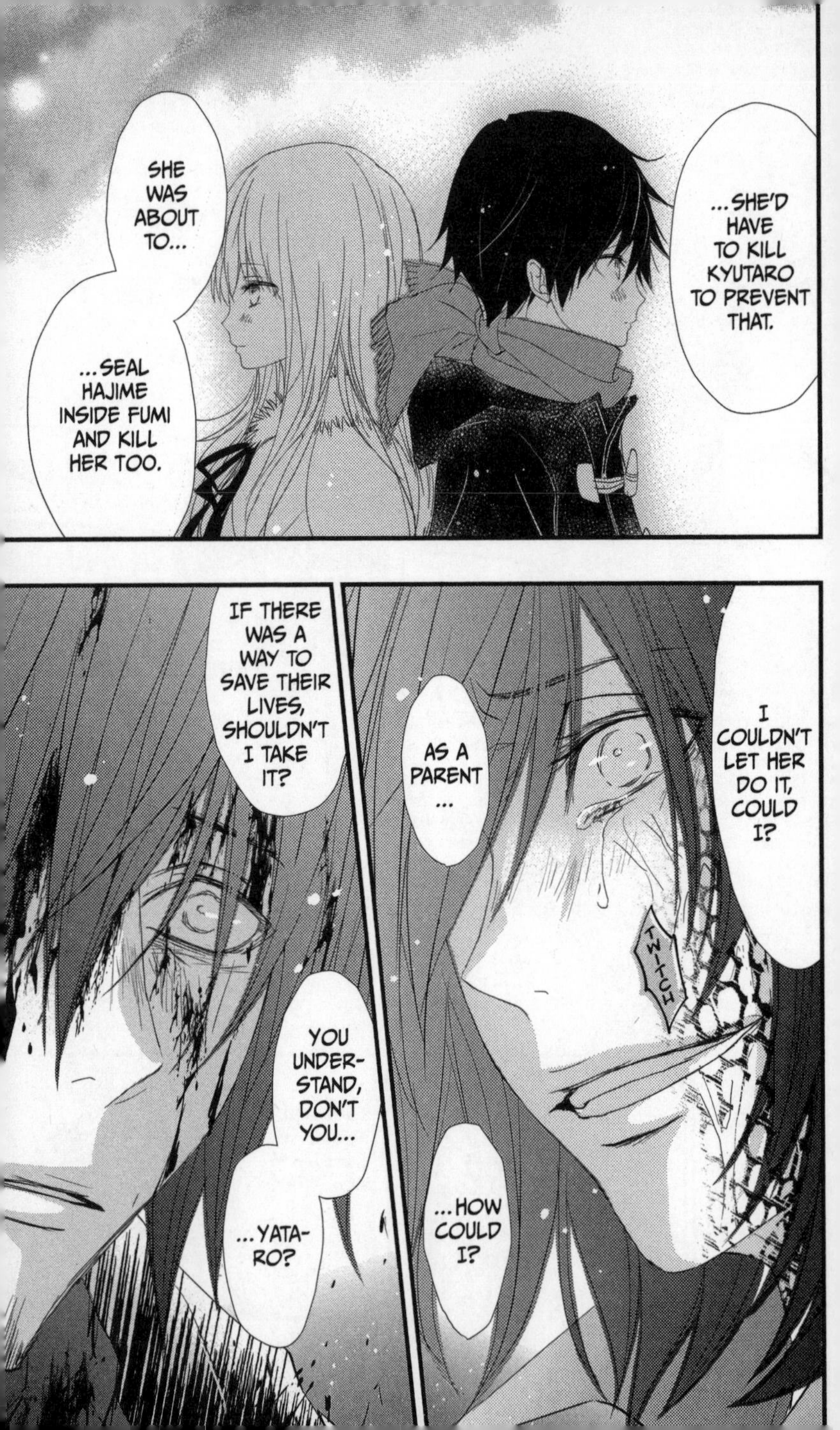
...SHE'D HAVE TO KILL KYUTARO TO PREVENT THAT.
SHE WAS ABOUT TO...
...SEAL HAJIME INSIDE FUMI AND KILL HER TOO.
I COULDN'T LET HER DO IT, COULD I?
AS A PARENT...
TWITCH
...HOW COULD I?
IF THERE WAS A WAY TO SAVE THEIR LIVES, SHOULDN'T I TAKE IT?
YOU UNDER-STAND, DON'T YOU...
...YATA-RO?

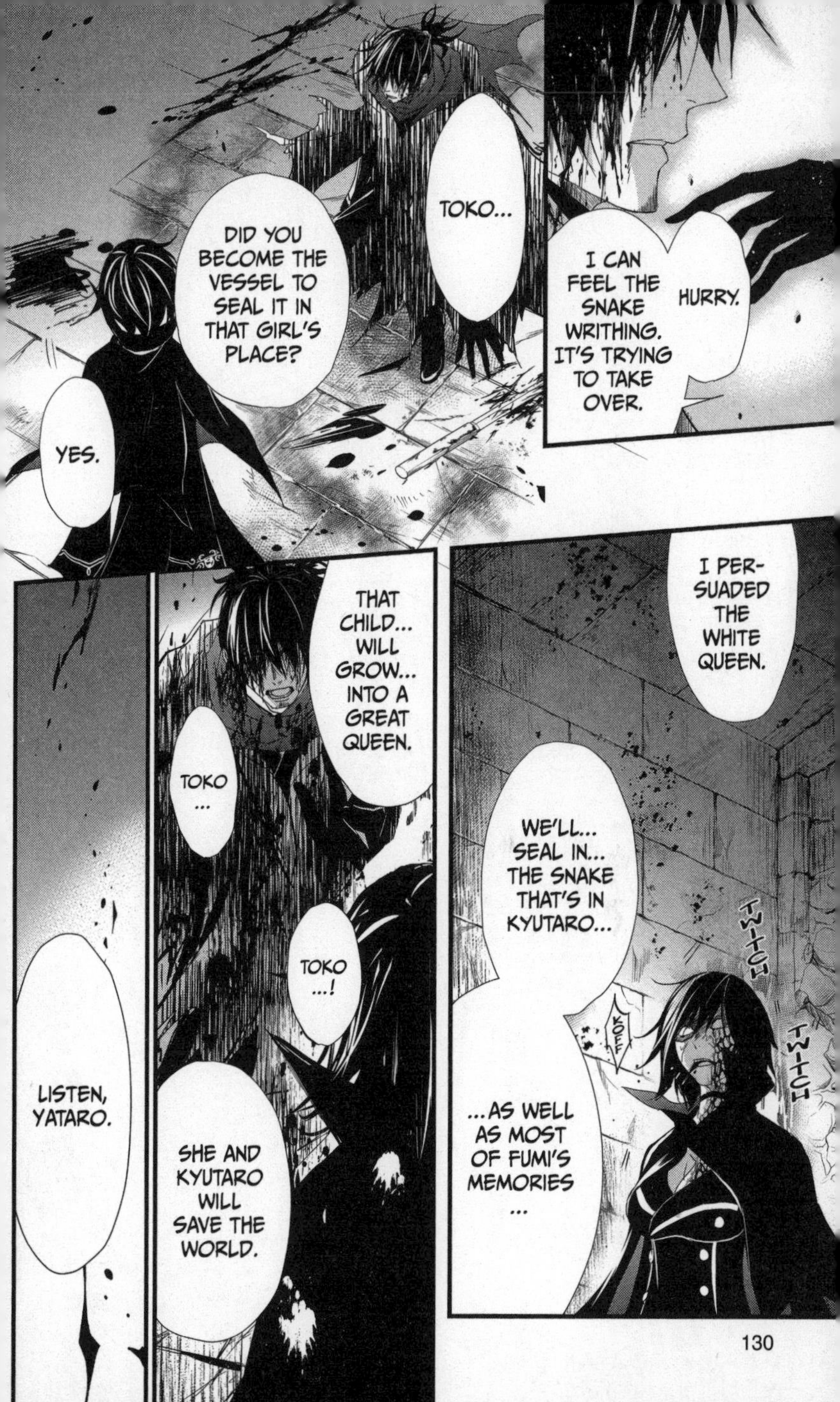
I CAN FEEL THE SNAKE WRITHING. IT'S TRYING TO TAKE OVER.
HURRY.
TOKO...
DID YOU BECOME THE VESSEL TO SEAL IT IN THAT GIRL'S PLACE?
YES.
I PER-SUADED THE WHITE QUEEN.
WE'LL... SEAL IN... THE SNAKE THAT'S IN KYUTARO...
TWITCH
TWITCH
KOFF
...AS WELL AS MOST OF FUMI'S MEMORIES ...
THAT CHILD... WILL GROW... INTO A GREAT QUEEN.
TOKO ...
TOKO ...!
SHE AND KYUTARO WILL SAVE THE WORLD.
LISTEN, YATARO.

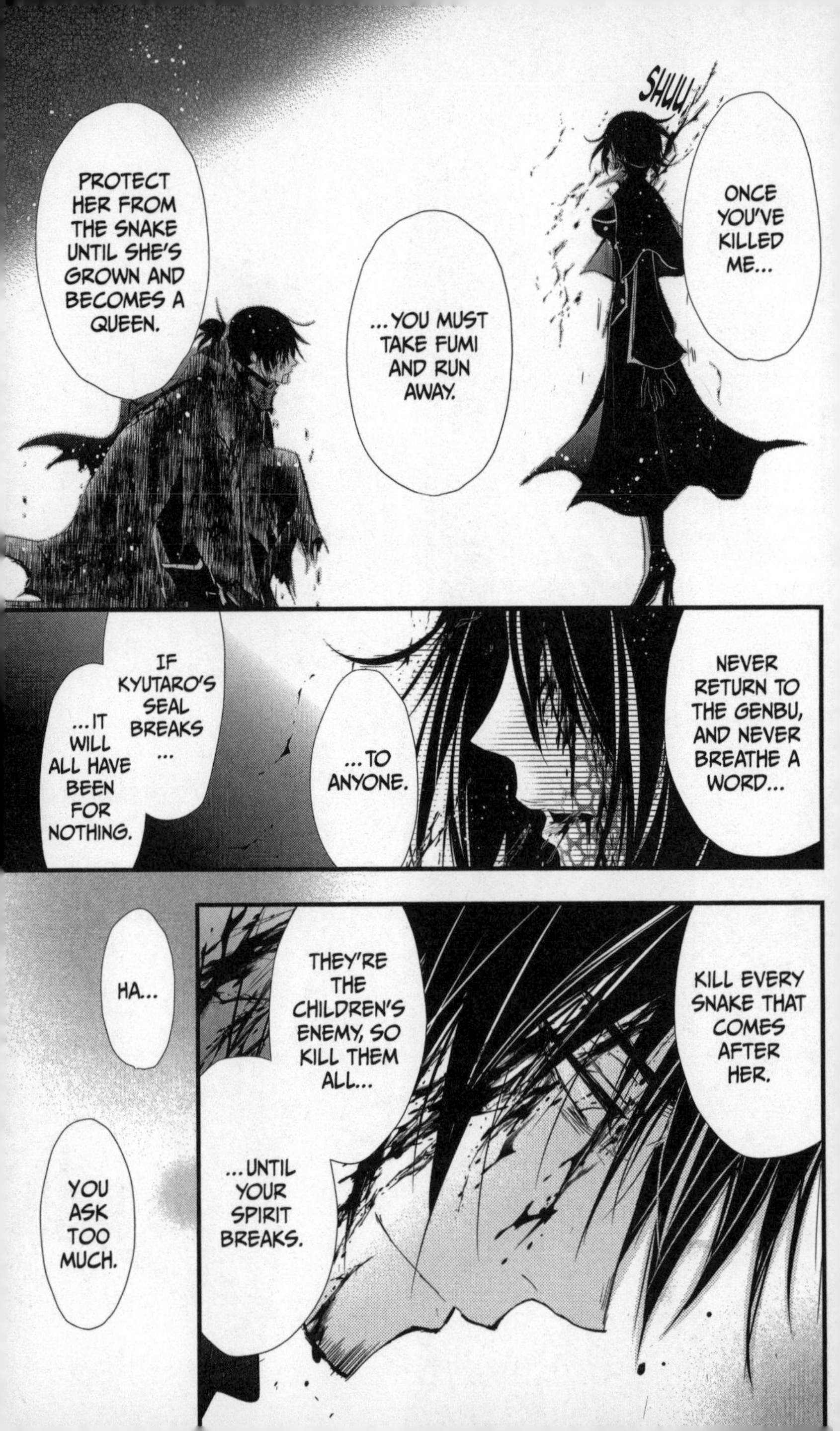
SHUU
ONCE YOU'VE KILLED ME...
...YOU MUST TAKE FUMI AND RUN AWAY.
PROTECT HER FROM THE SNAKE UNTIL SHE'S GROWN AND BECOMES A QUEEN.
NEVER RETURN TO THE GENBU, AND NEVER BREATHE A WORD...
...TO ANYONE.
IF KYUTARO'S SEAL BREAKS...
...IT WILL ALL HAVE BEEN FOR NOTHING.
KILL EVERY SNAKE THAT COMES AFTER HER.
THEY'RE THE CHILDREN'S ENEMY, SO KILL THEM ALL...
...UNTIL YOUR SPIRIT BREAKS.
HA...
YOU ASK TOO MUCH.

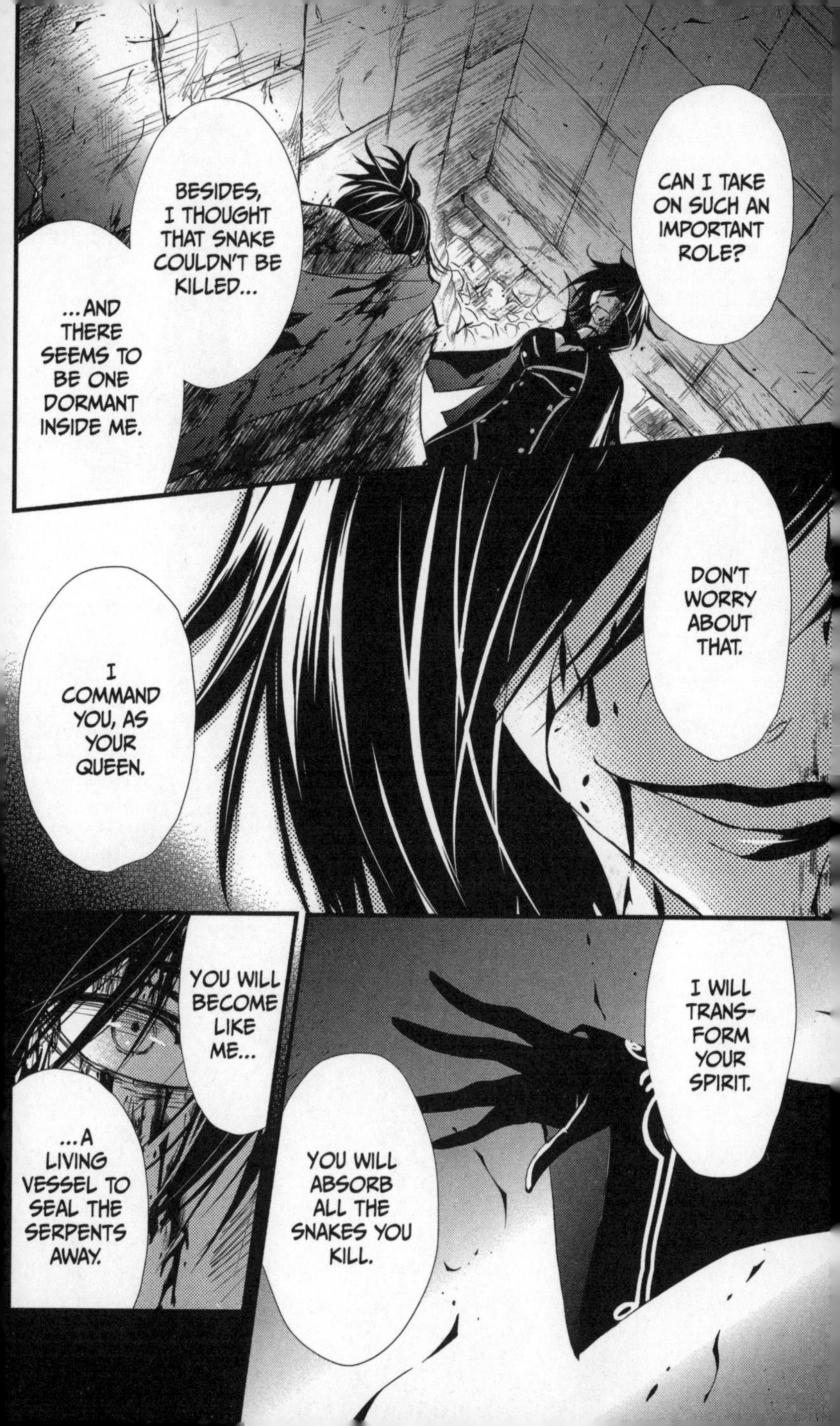
CAN I TAKE ON SUCH AN IMPORTANT ROLE?
BESIDES, I THOUGHT THAT SNAKE COULDN'T BE KILLED...
...AND THERE SEEMS TO BE ONE DORMANT INSIDE ME.
DON'T WORRY ABOUT THAT.
I COMMAND YOU, AS YOUR QUEEN.
I WILL TRANS-FORM YOUR SPIRIT.
YOU WILL ABSORB ALL THE SNAKES YOU KILL.
YOU WILL BECOME LIKE ME...
...A LIVING VESSEL TO SEAL THE SERPENTS AWAY.

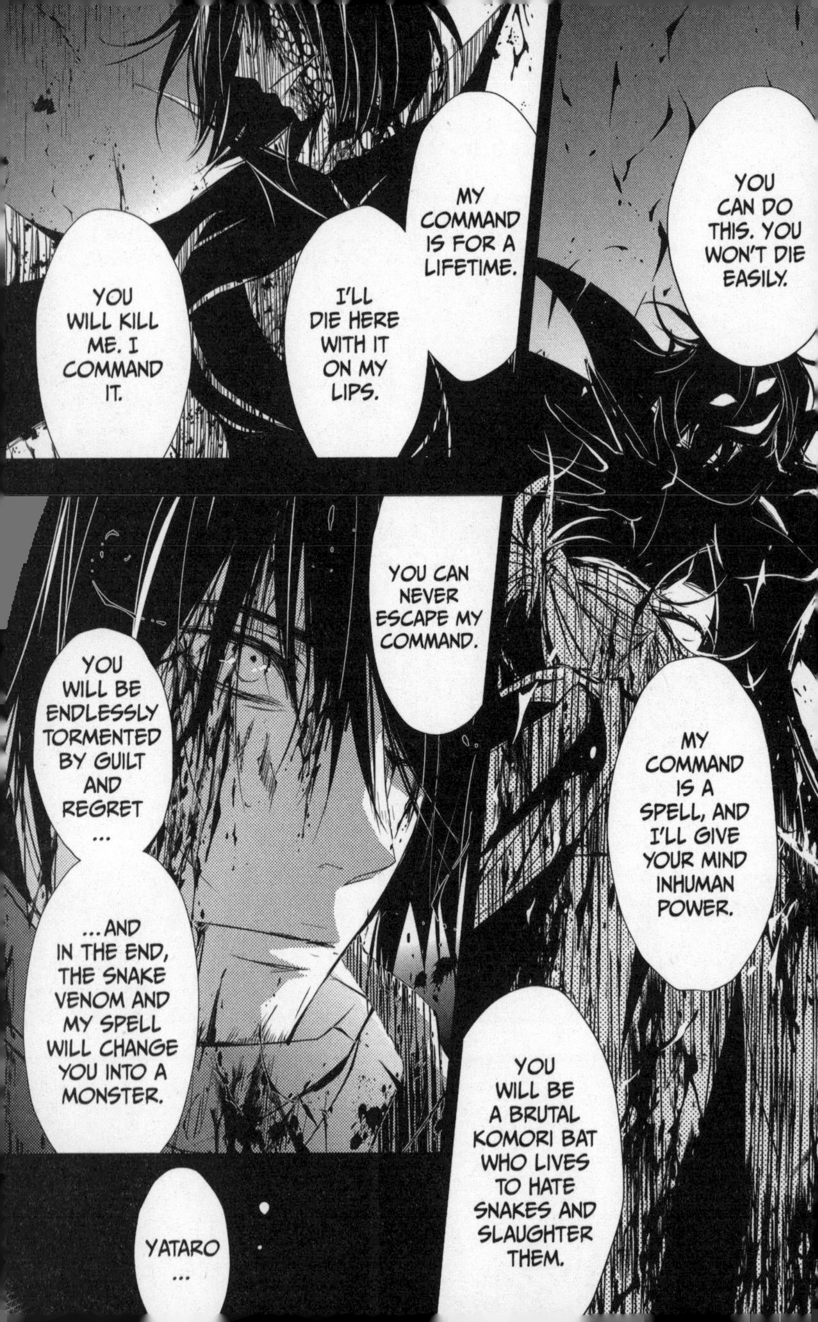
YOU CAN DO THIS. YOU WON'T DIE EASILY.
MY COMMAND IS FOR A LIFETIME.
I'LL DIE HERE WITH IT ON MY LIPS.
YOU WILL KILL ME. I COMMAND IT.
YOU CAN NEVER ESCAPE MY COMMAND.
MY COMMAND IS A SPELL, AND I'LL GIVE YOUR MIND INHUMAN POWER.
YOU WILL BE ENDLESSLY TORMENTED BY GUILT AND REGRET...
...AND IN THE END, THE SNAKE VENOM AND MY SPELL WILL CHANGE YOU INTO A MONSTER.
YOU WILL BE A BRUTAL KOMORI BAT WHO LIVES TO HATE SNAKES AND SLAUGHTER THEM.
YATARO...

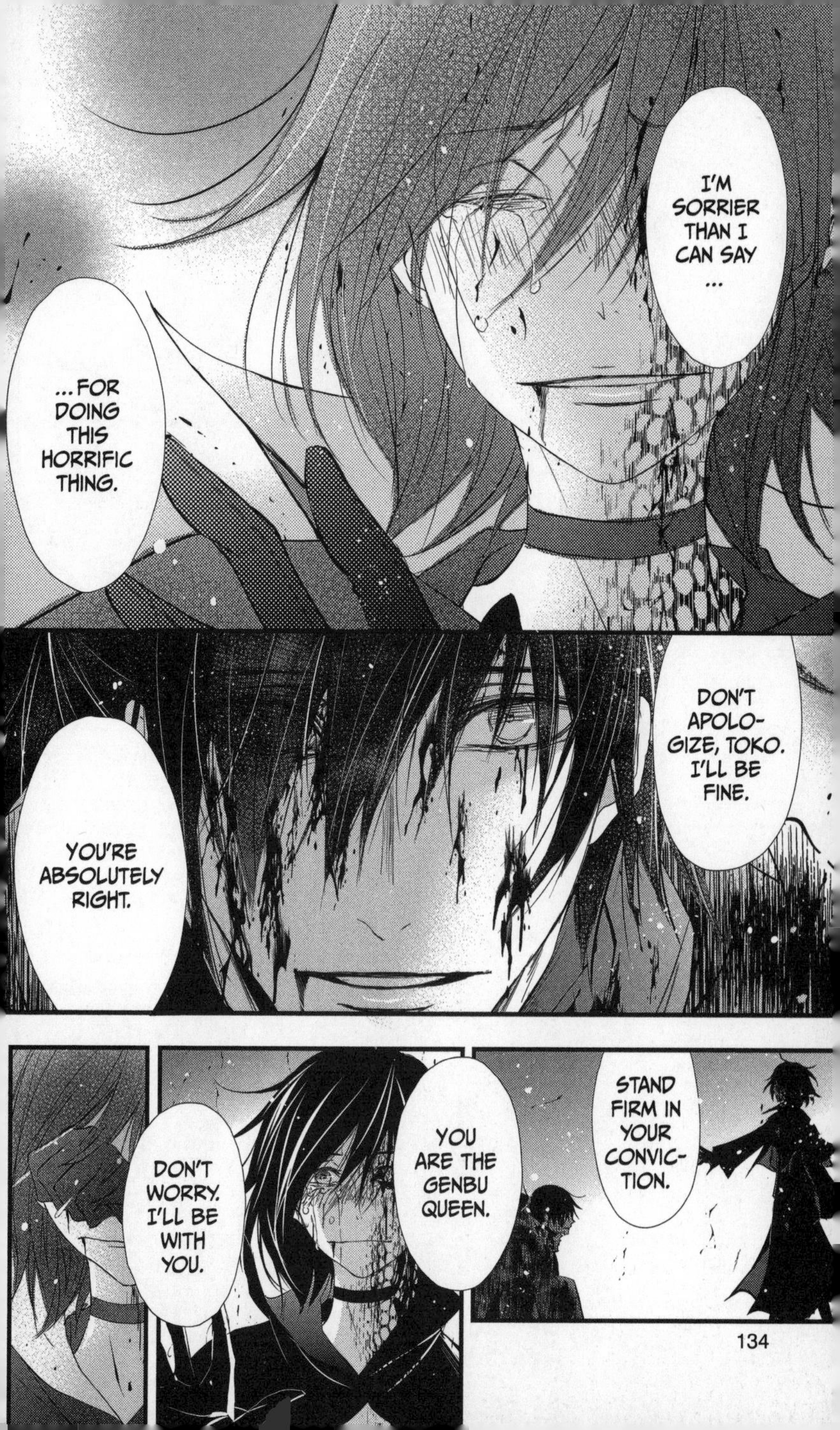
I'M SORRIER THAN I CAN SAY ...
...FOR DOING THIS HORRIFIC THING.
DON'T APOLOGIZE, TOKO. I'LL BE FINE.
YOU'RE ABSOLUTELY RIGHT.
STAND FIRM IN YOUR CONVICTION.
YOU ARE THE GENBU QUEEN.
DON'T WORRY. I'LL BE WITH YOU.

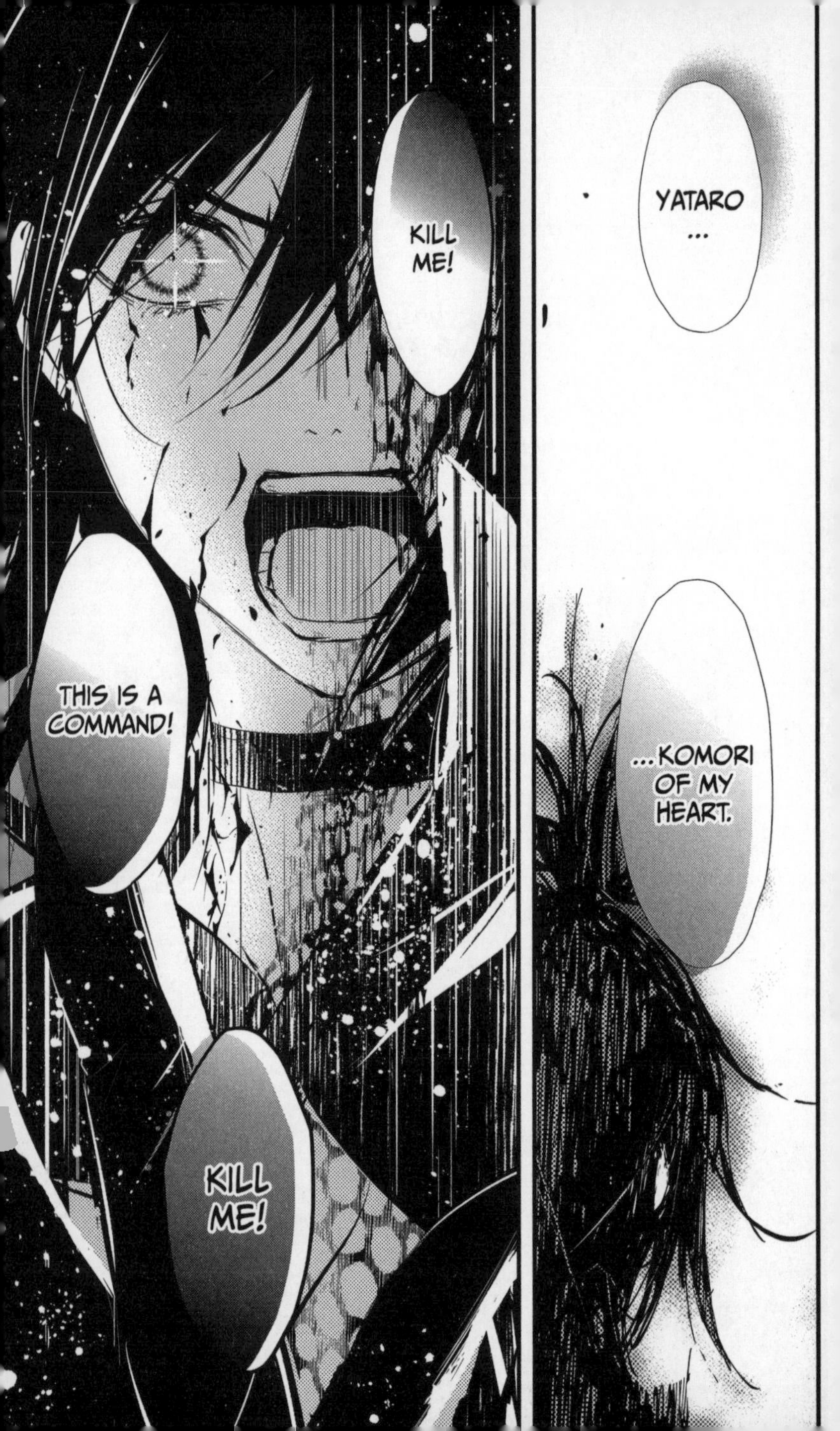
YATARO ...
...KOMORI OF MY HEART.
KILL ME!
THIS IS A COMMAND!
KILL ME!

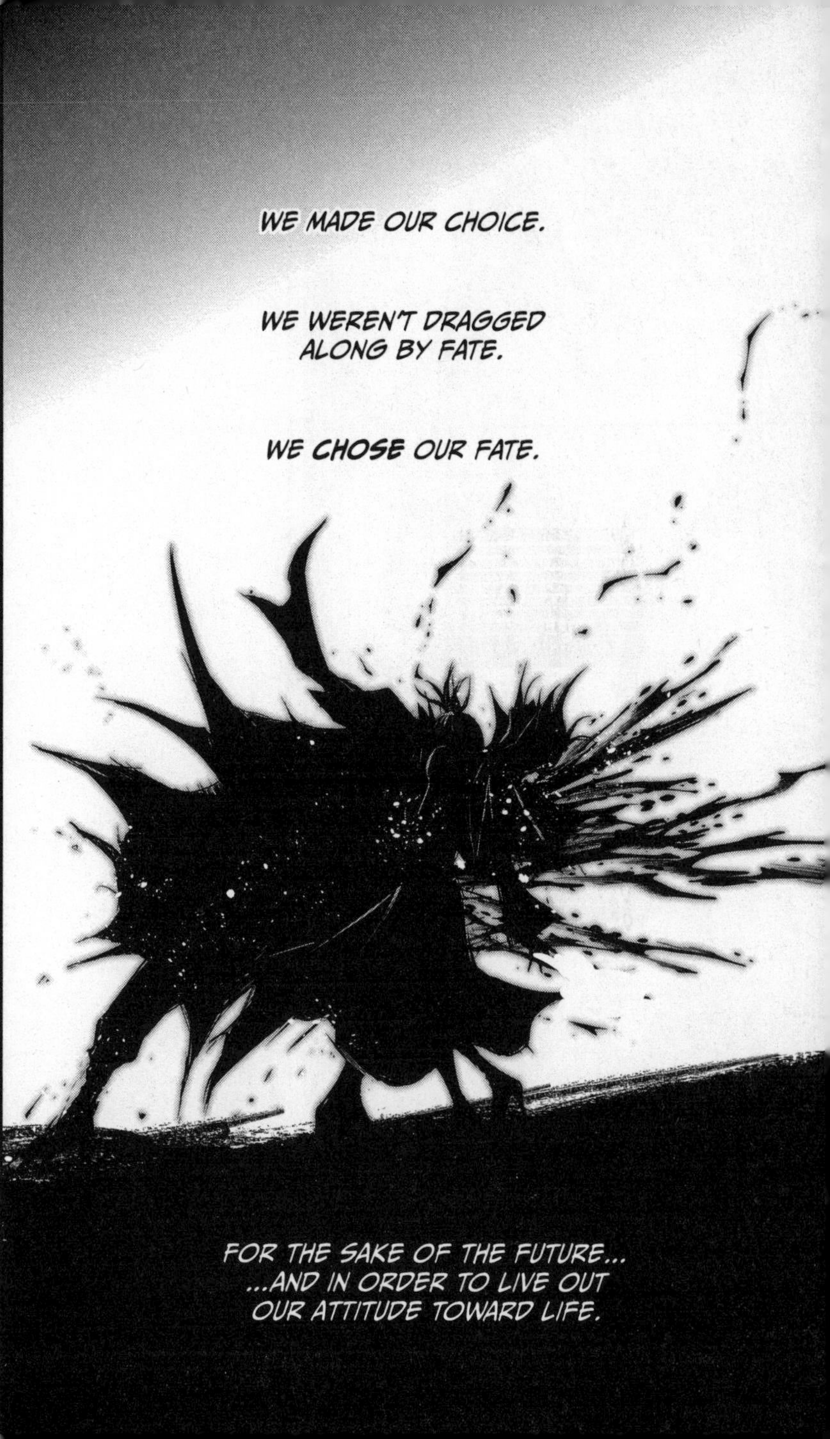
WE MADE OUR CHOICE.
WE WEREN'T DRAGGED ALONG BY FATE.
WE **CHOSE** OUR FATE.
FOR THE SAKE OF THE FUTURE...
...AND IN ORDER TO LIVE OUT OUR ATTITUDE TOWARD LIFE.

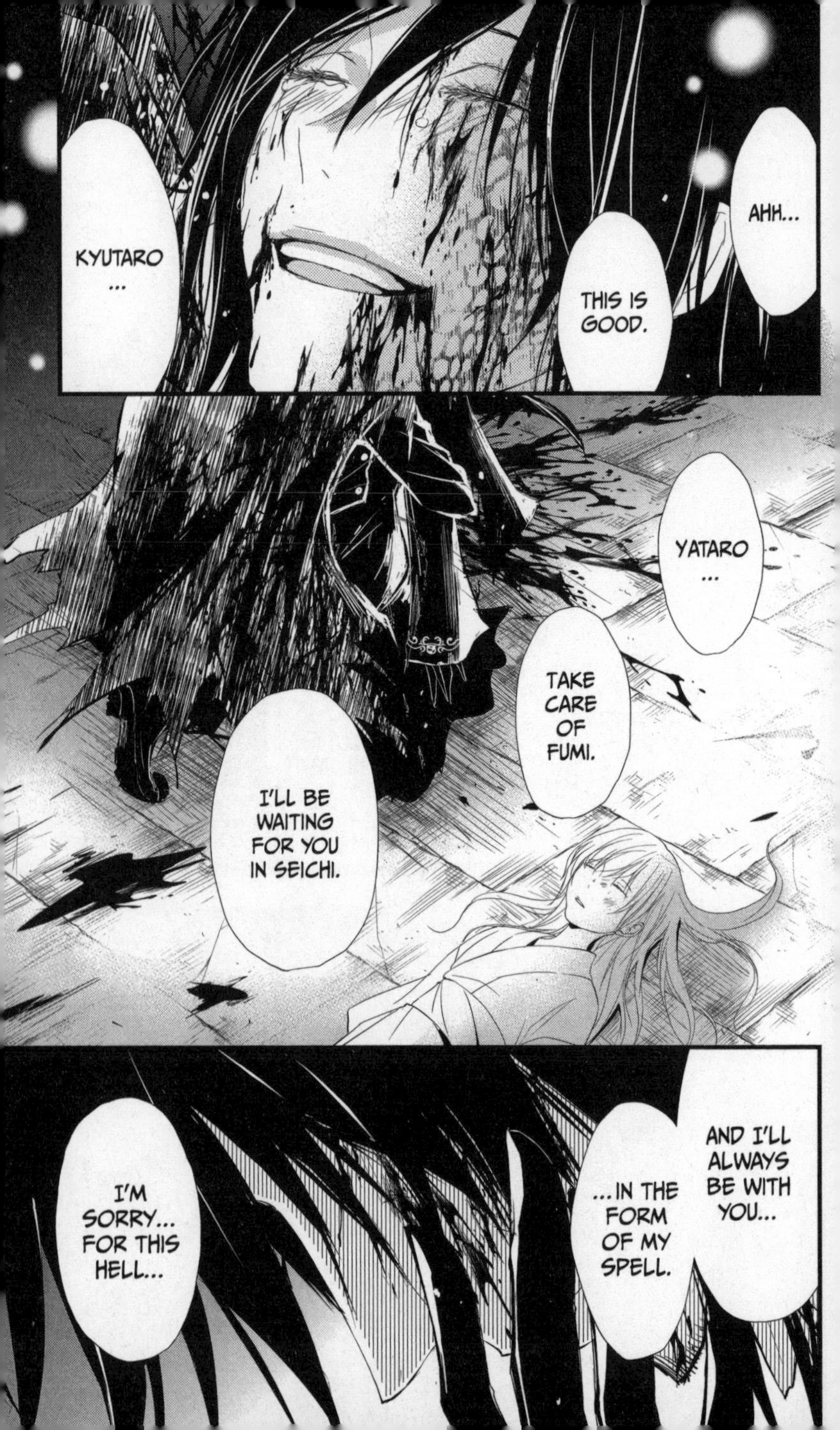
AHH...
THIS IS GOOD.
KYUTARO ...
YATARO ...
TAKE CARE OF FUMI.
I'LL BE WAITING FOR YOU IN SEICHI.
AND I'LL ALWAYS BE WITH YOU...
...IN THE FORM OF MY SPELL.
I'M SORRY... FOR THIS HELL...

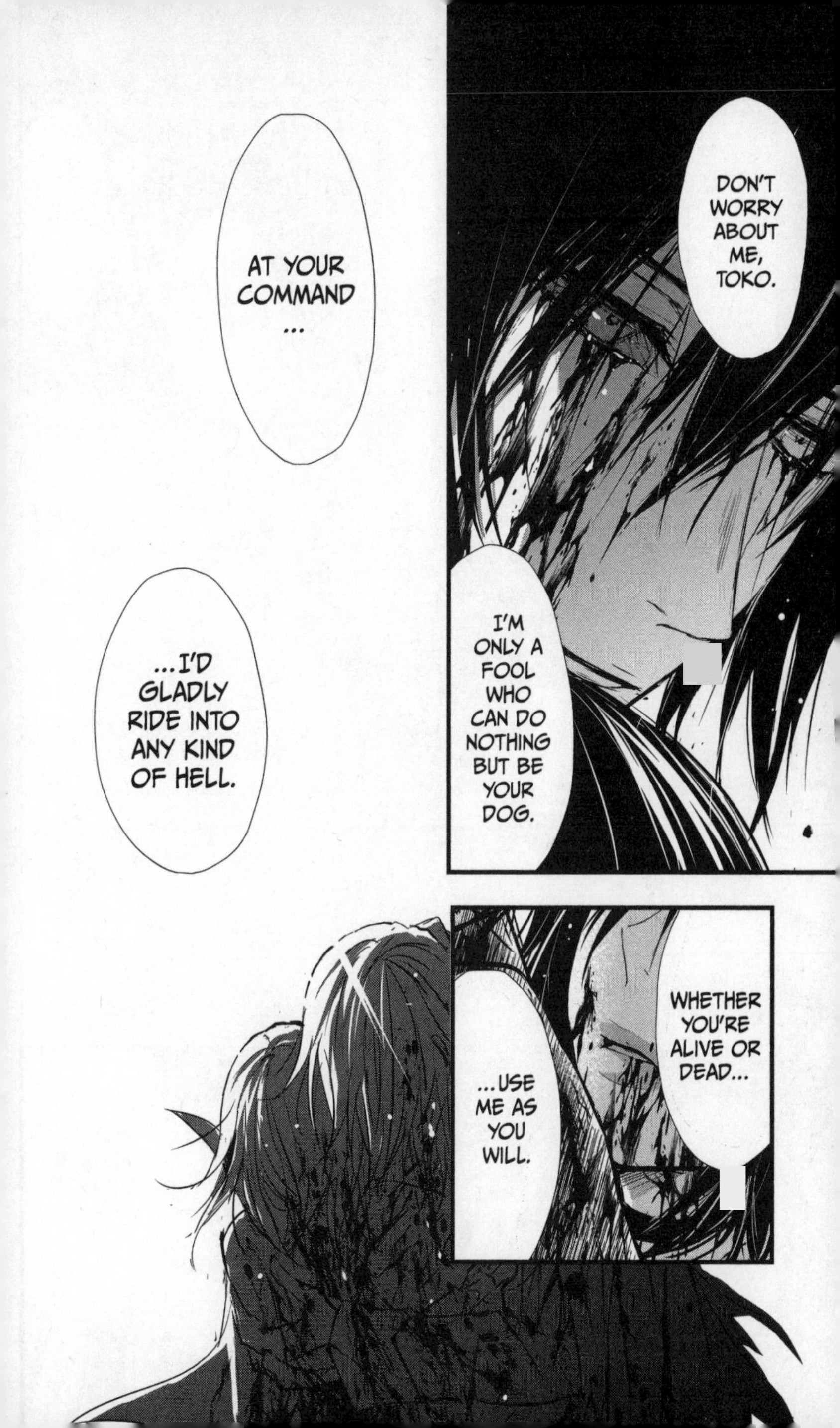
DON'T WORRY ABOUT ME, TOKO.
I'M ONLY A FOOL WHO CAN DO NOTHING BUT BE YOUR DOG.
WHETHER YOU'RE ALIVE OR DEAD...
...USE ME AS YOU WILL.
AT YOUR COMMAND ...
...I'D GLADLY RIDE INTO ANY KIND OF HELL.

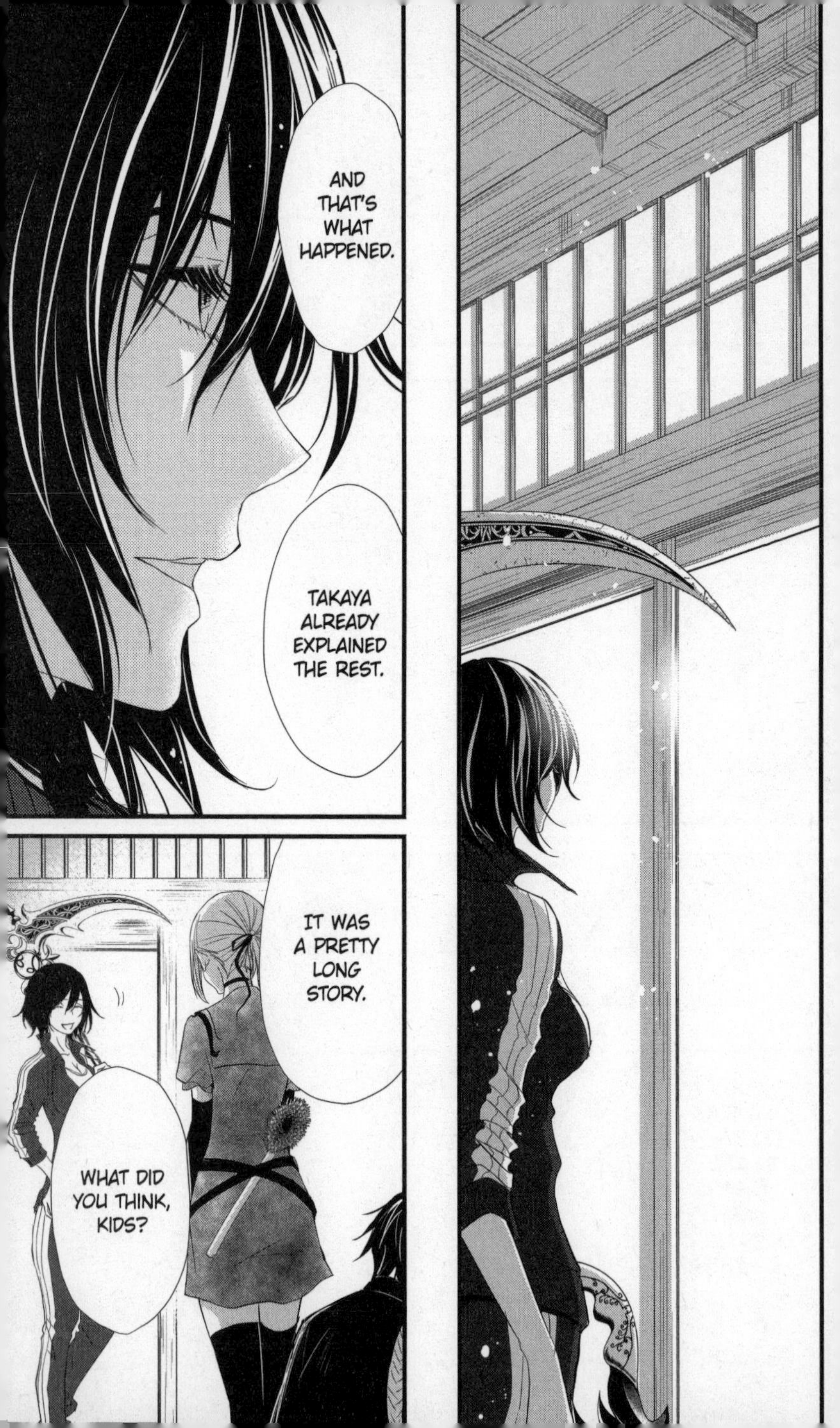
AND THAT'S WHAT HAPPENED.
TAKAYA ALREADY EXPLAINED THE REST.
IT WAS A PRETTY LONG STORY.
WHAT DID YOU THINK, KIDS?

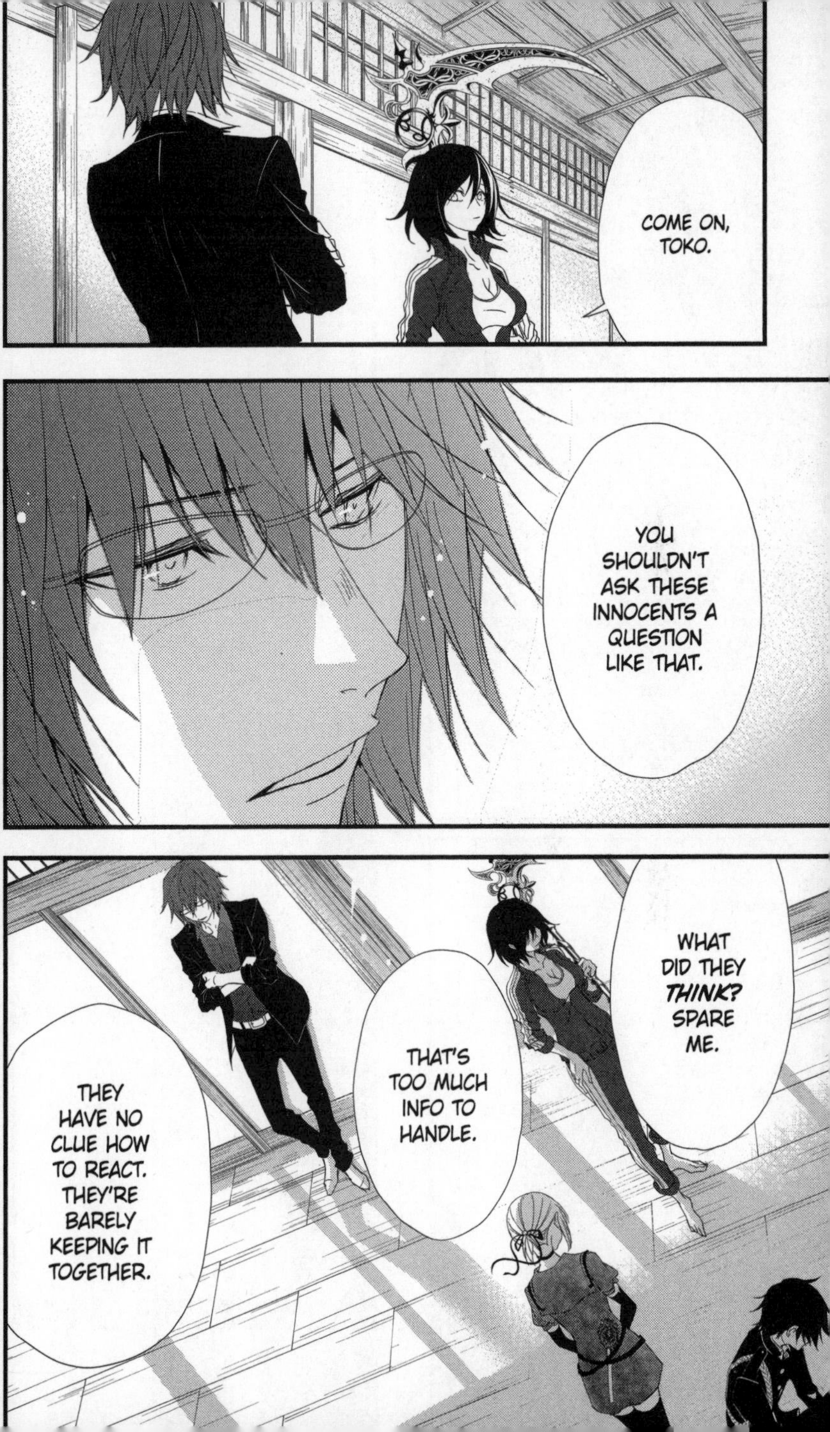
COME ON, TOKO.
YOU SHOULDN'T ASK THESE INNOCENTS A QUESTION LIKE THAT.
WHAT DID THEY *THINK*? SPARE ME.
THAT'S TOO MUCH INFO TO HANDLE.
THEY HAVE NO CLUE HOW TO REACT. THEY'RE BARELY KEEPING IT TOGETHER.

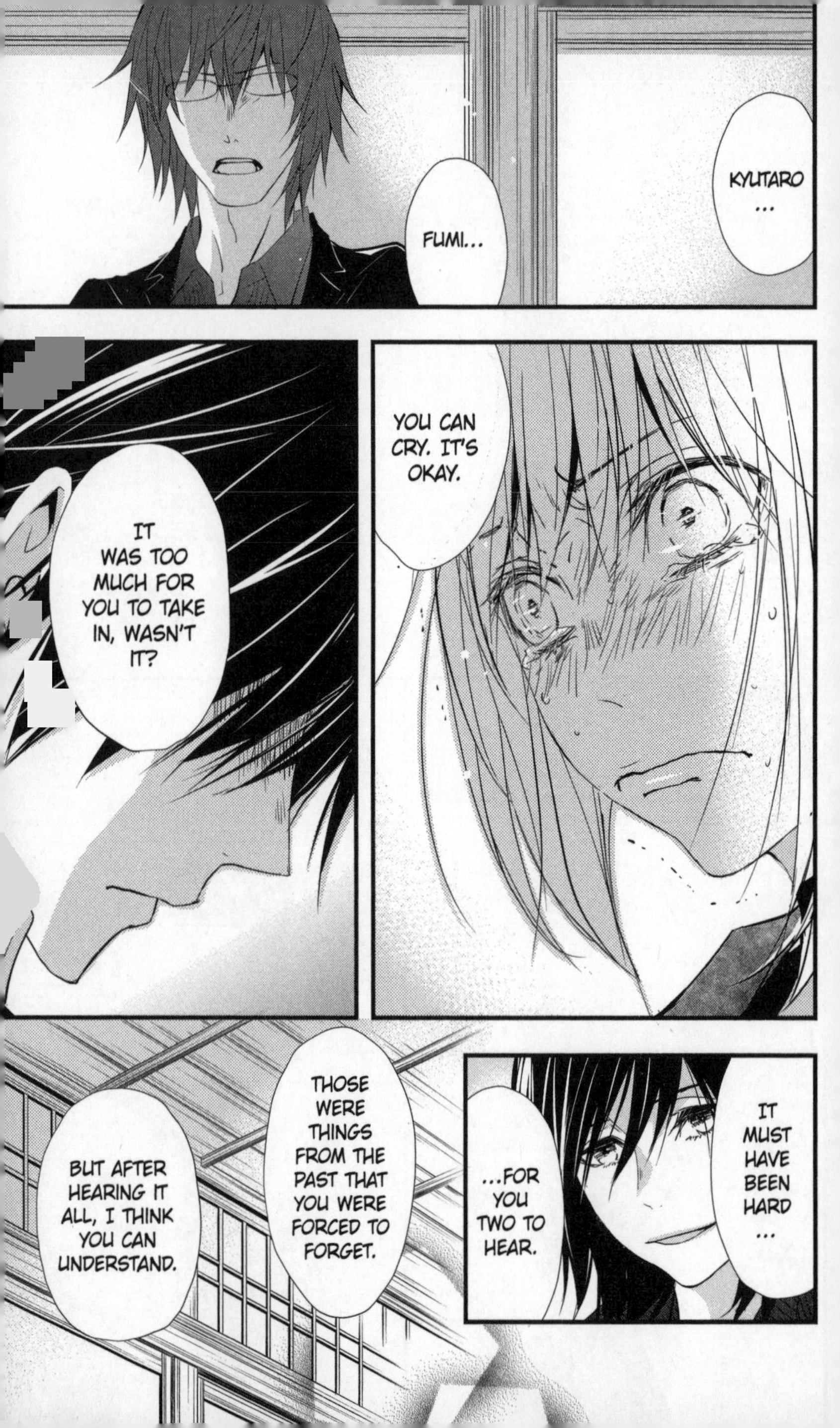
KYUTARO ...
FUMI...
YOU CAN CRY. IT'S OKAY.
IT WAS TOO MUCH FOR YOU TO TAKE IN, WASN'T IT?
IT MUST HAVE BEEN HARD ...
...FOR YOU TWO TO HEAR.
THOSE WERE THINGS FROM THE PAST THAT YOU WERE FORCED TO FORGET.
BUT AFTER HEARING IT ALL, I THINK YOU CAN UNDERSTAND.

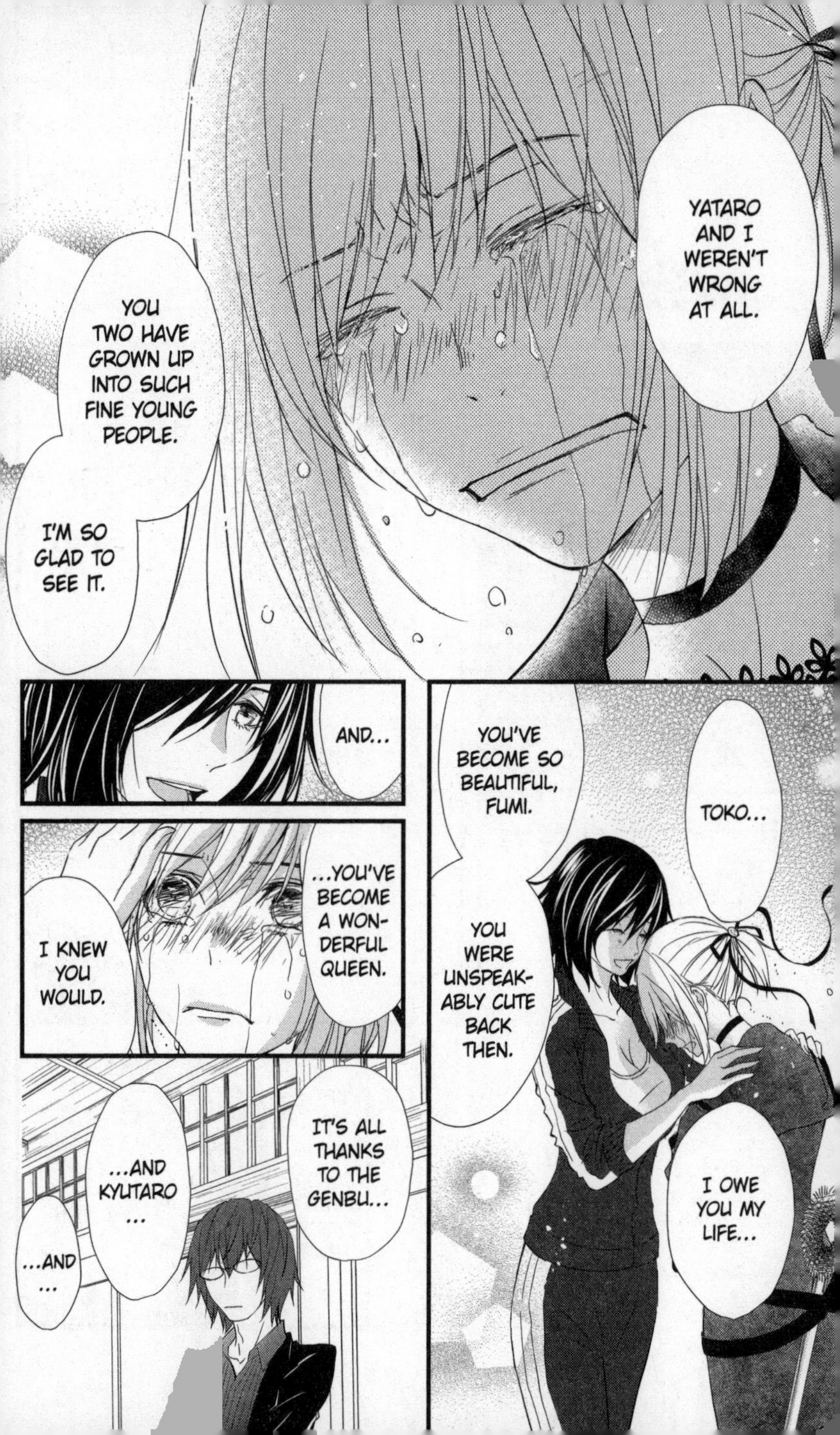
YATARO AND I WEREN'T WRONG AT ALL.
YOU TWO HAVE GROWN UP INTO SUCH FINE YOUNG PEOPLE.
I'M SO GLAD TO SEE IT.
TOKO...
YOU'VE BECOME SO BEAUTIFUL, FUMI.
YOU WERE UNSPEAK-ABLY CUTE BACK THEN.
I OWE YOU MY LIFE...
AND...
...YOU'VE BECOME A WON-DERFUL QUEEN.
I KNEW YOU WOULD.
IT'S ALL THANKS TO THE GENBU...
...AND KYUTARO ...
...AND ...

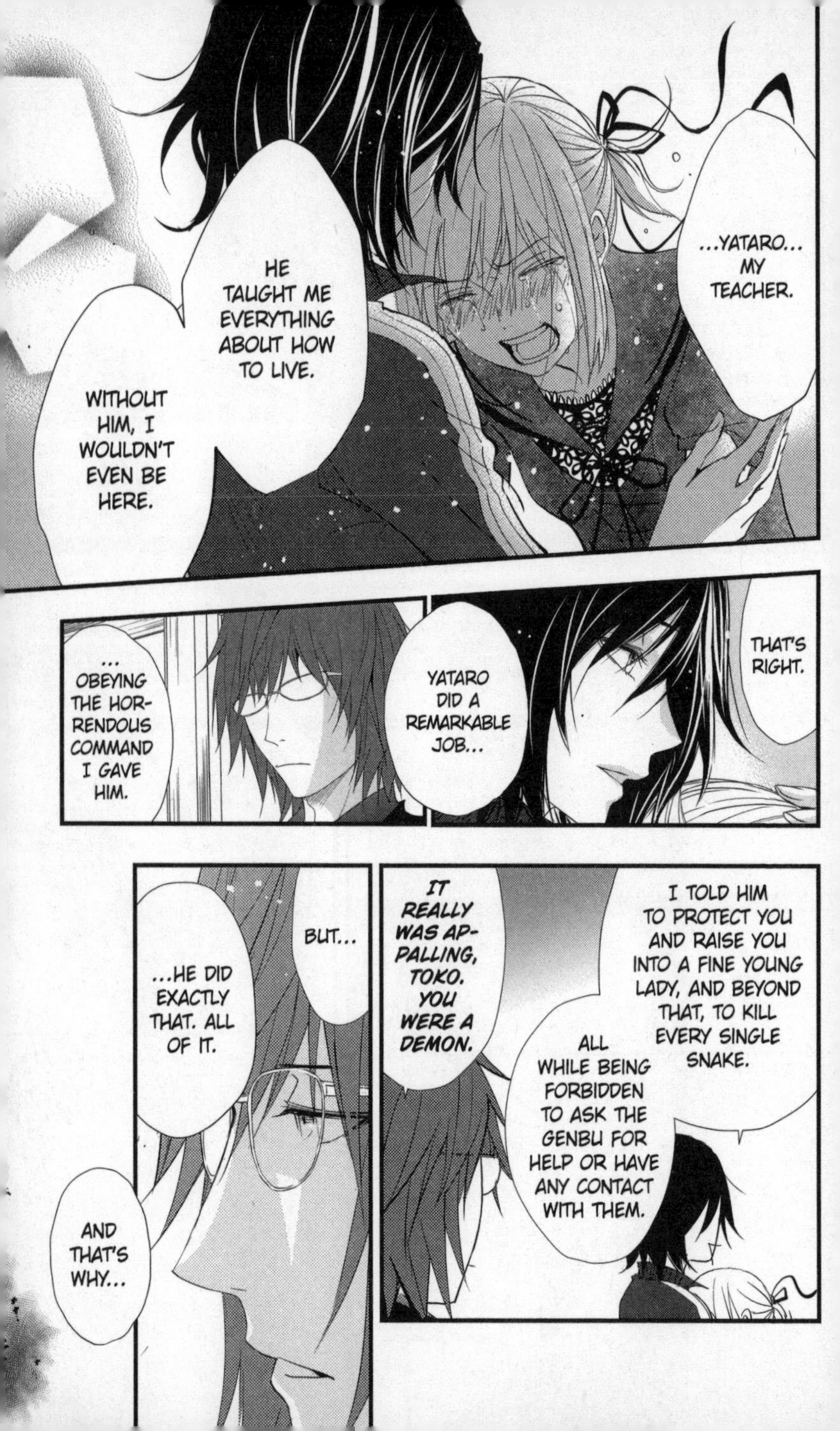
...YATARO... MY TEACHER.
HE TAUGHT ME EVERYTHING ABOUT HOW TO LIVE.
WITHOUT HIM, I WOULDN'T EVEN BE HERE.
THAT'S RIGHT.
YATARO DID A REMARKABLE JOB...
...OBEYING THE HORRENDOUS COMMAND I GAVE HIM.
I TOLD HIM TO PROTECT YOU AND RAISE YOU INTO A FINE YOUNG LADY, AND BEYOND THAT, TO KILL EVERY SINGLE SNAKE.
ALL WHILE BEING FORBIDDEN TO ASK THE GENBU FOR HELP OR HAVE ANY CONTACT WITH THEM.
IT REALLY WAS APPALLING, TOKO. YOU WERE A DEMON.
BUT...
...HE DID EXACTLY THAT. ALL OF IT.
AND THAT'S WHY...

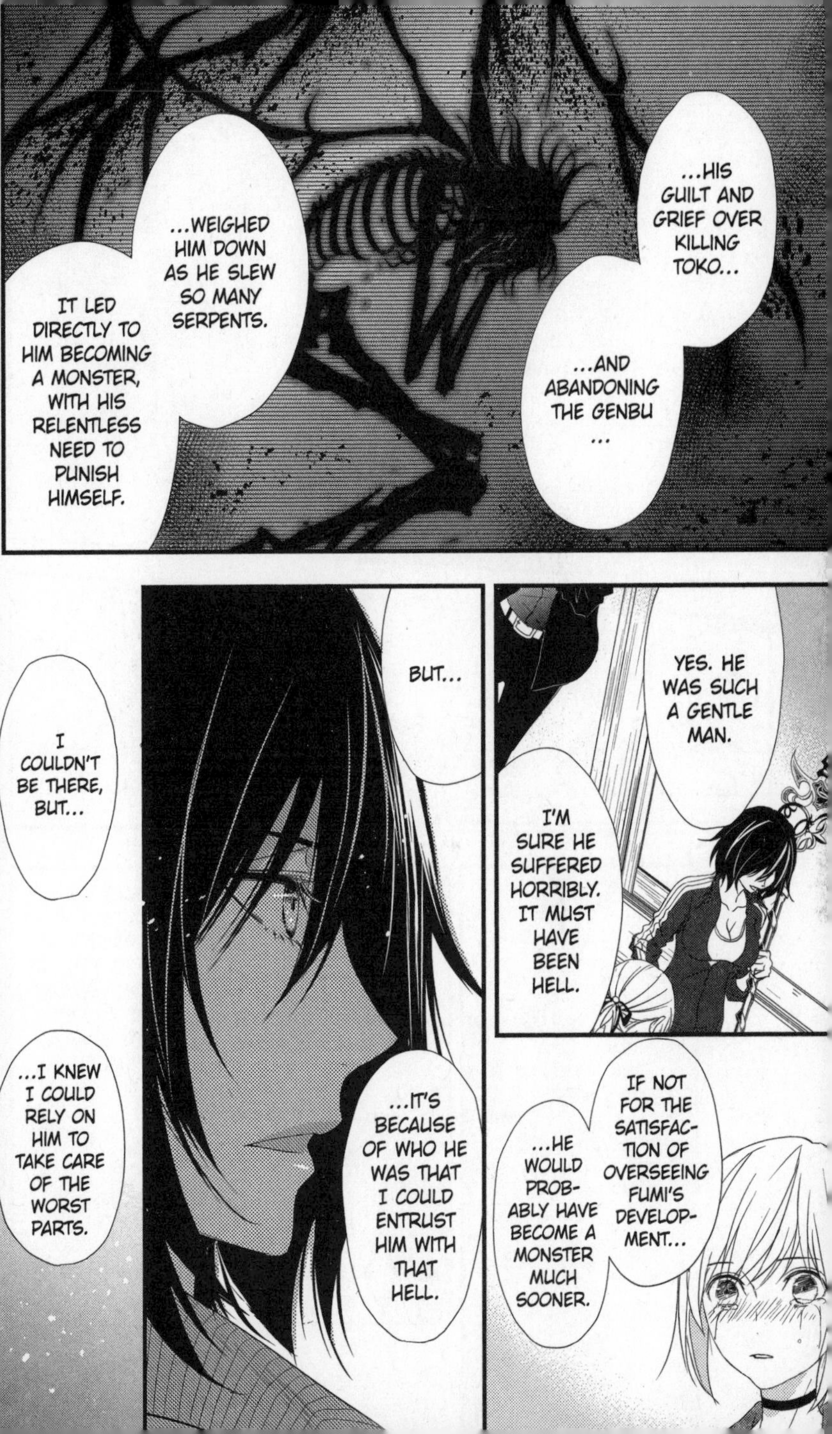
...HIS GUILT AND GRIEF OVER KILLING TOKO...
...AND ABANDONING THE GENBU...
...WEIGHED HIM DOWN AS HE SLEW SO MANY SERPENTS.
IT LED DIRECTLY TO HIM BECOMING A MONSTER, WITH HIS RELENTLESS NEED TO PUNISH HIMSELF.
YES. HE WAS SUCH A GENTLE MAN.
I'M SURE HE SUFFERED HORRIBLY. IT MUST HAVE BEEN HELL.
IF NOT FOR THE SATISFAC-TION OF OVERSEEING FUMI'S DEVELOP-MENT...
...HE WOULD PROB-ABLY HAVE BECOME A MONSTER MUCH SOONER.
BUT...
...IT'S BECAUSE OF WHO HE WAS THAT I COULD ENTRUST HIM WITH THAT HELL.
I COULDN'T BE THERE, BUT...
...I KNEW I COULD RELY ON HIM TO TAKE CARE OF THE WORST PARTS.

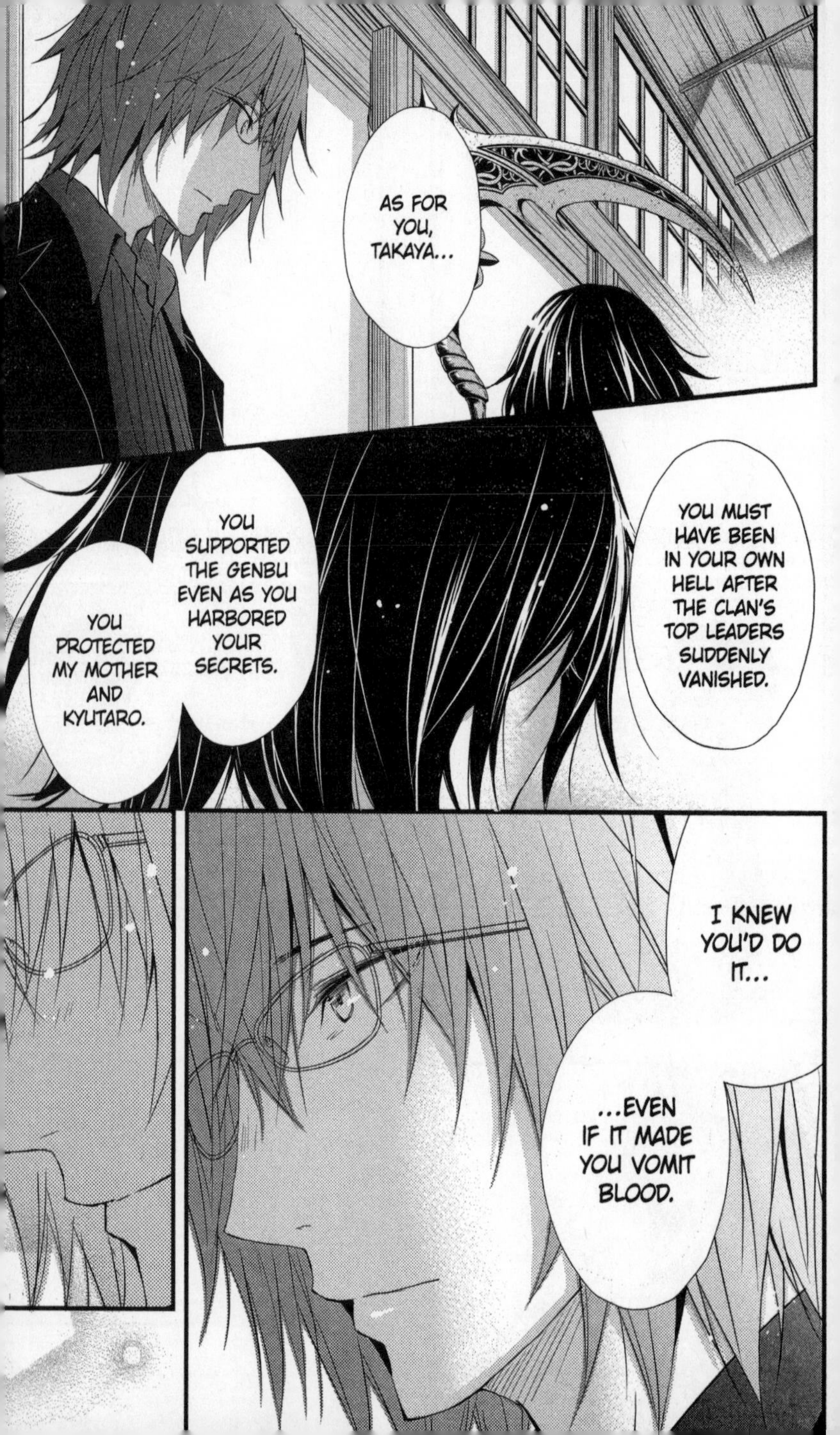
AS FOR YOU, TAKAYA...
YOU MUST HAVE BEEN IN YOUR OWN HELL AFTER THE CLAN'S TOP LEADERS SUDDENLY VANISHED.
YOU SUPPORTED THE GENBU EVEN AS YOU HARBORED YOUR SECRETS.
YOU PROTECTED MY MOTHER AND KYUTARO.
I KNEW YOU'D DO IT...
...EVEN IF IT MADE YOU VOMIT BLOOD.

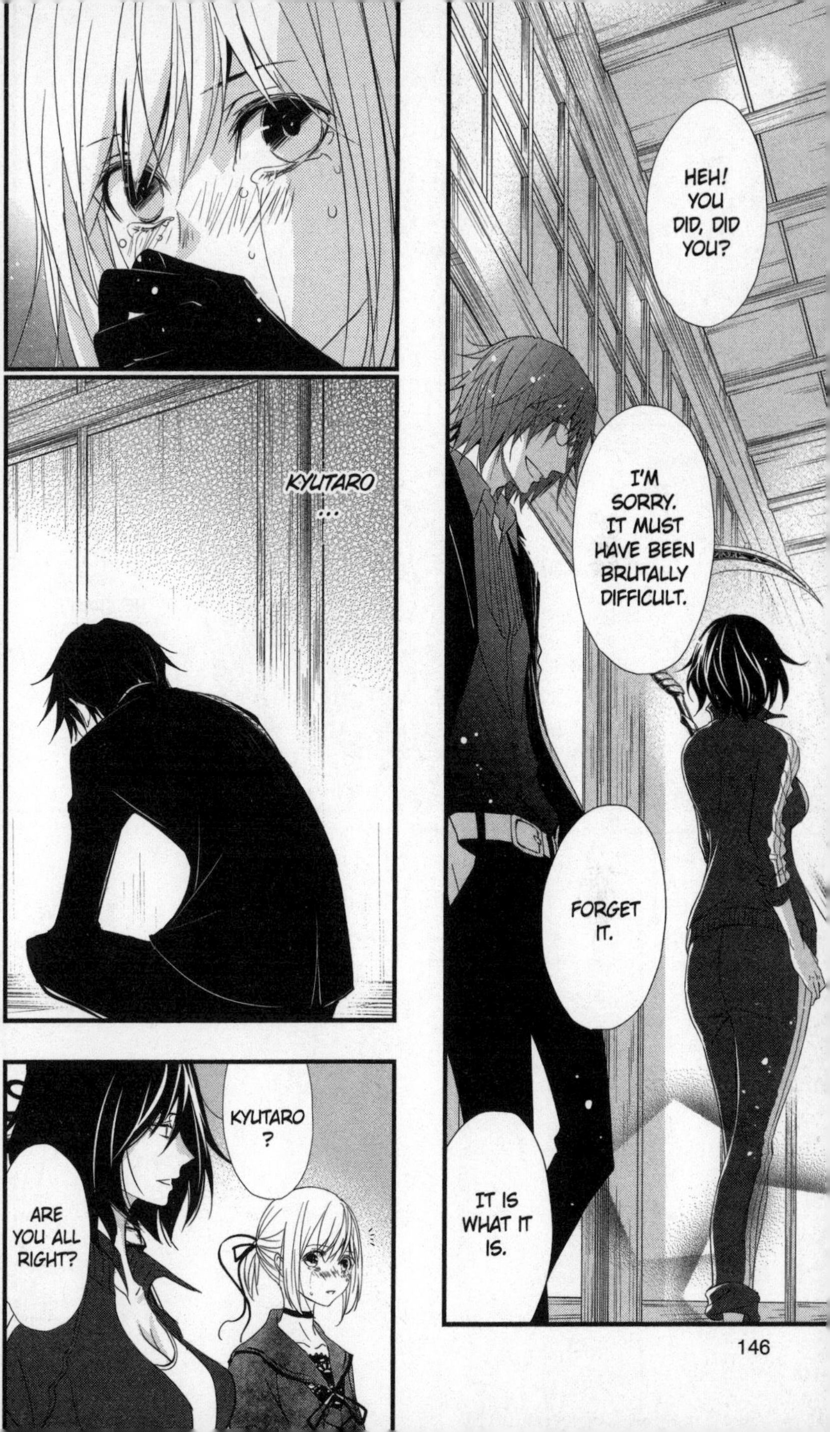
HEH! YOU DID, DID YOU?
I'M SORRY. IT MUST HAVE BEEN BRUTALLY DIFFICULT.
FORGET IT.
IT IS WHAT IT IS.
KYUTARO...
KYUTARO?
ARE YOU ALL RIGHT?

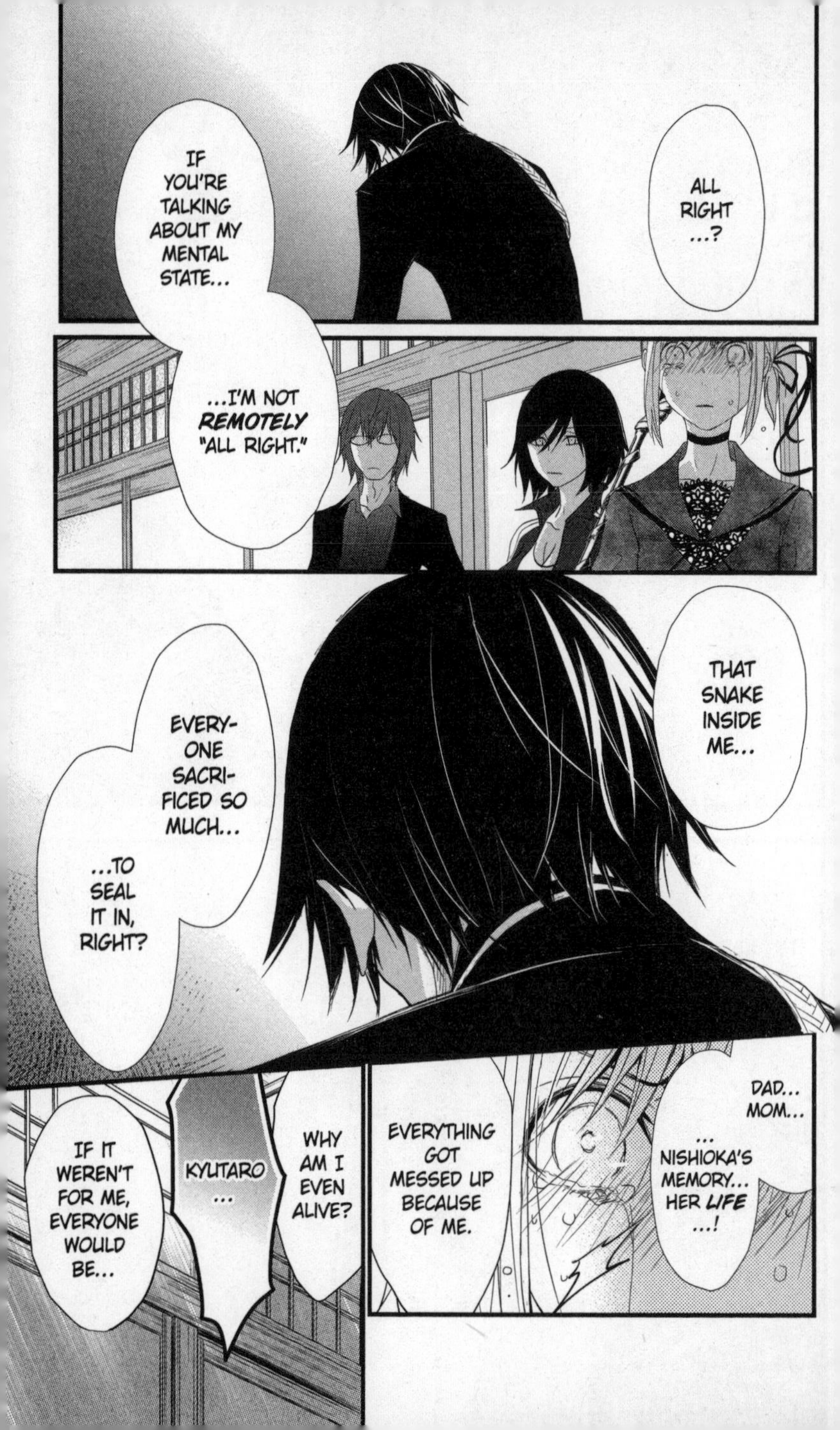
ALL RIGHT ...?
IF YOU'RE TALKING ABOUT MY MENTAL STATE...
...I'M NOT *REMOTELY* "ALL RIGHT."
THAT SNAKE INSIDE ME...
EVERY-ONE SACRI-FICED SO MUCH...
...TO SEAL IT IN, RIGHT?
DAD... MOM... ...NISHIOKA'S MEMORY... HER *LIFE* ...!
EVERYTHING GOT MESSED UP BECAUSE OF ME.
WHY AM I EVEN ALIVE?
KYUTARO ...
IF IT WEREN'T FOR ME, EVERYONE WOULD BE...

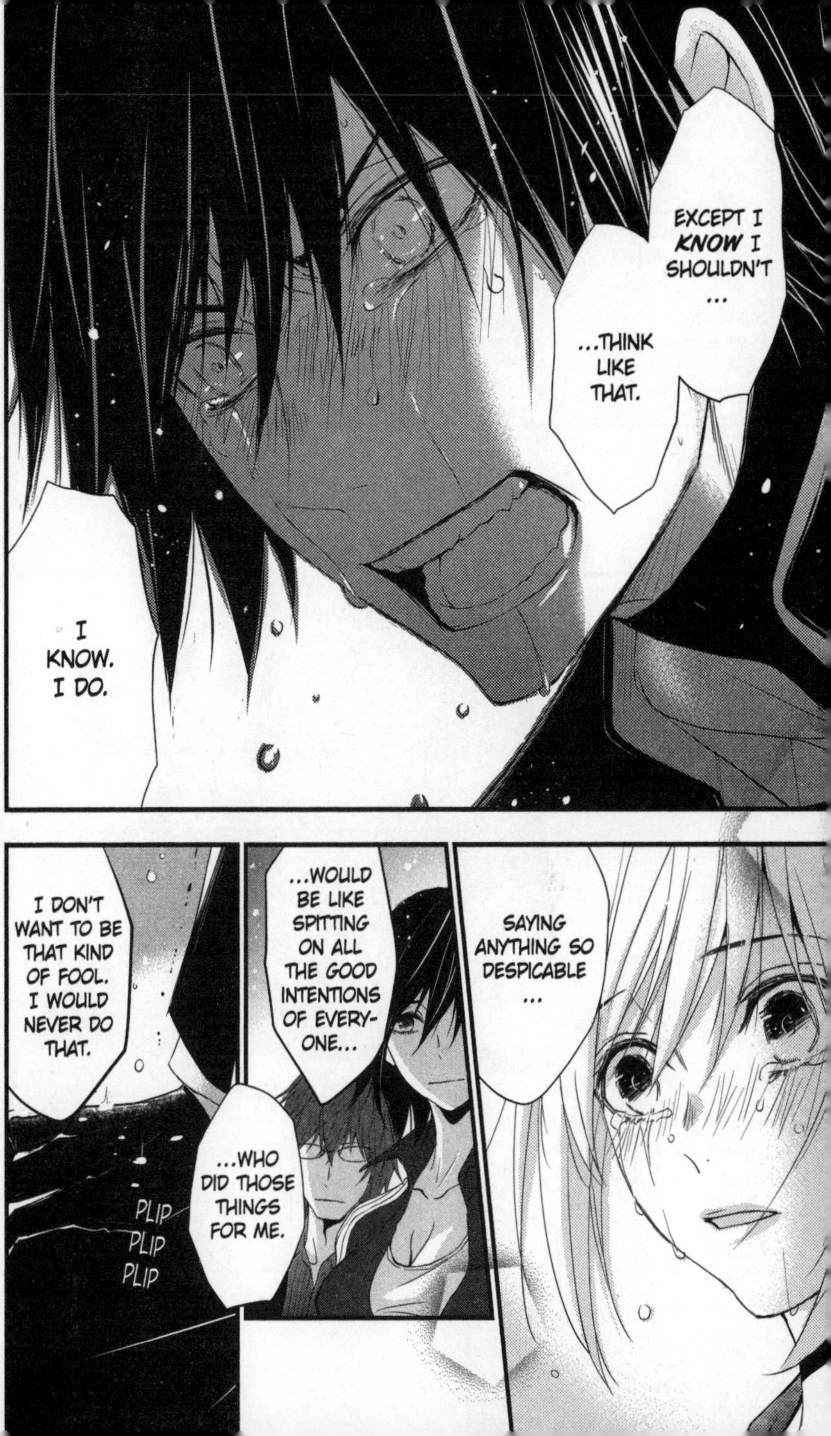
EXCEPT I KNOW I SHOULDN'T ...
...THINK LIKE THAT.
I KNOW. I DO.
SAYING ANYTHING SO DESPICABLE ...
...WOULD BE LIKE SPITTING ON ALL THE GOOD INTENTIONS OF EVERYONE...
...WHO DID THOSE THINGS FOR ME.
I DON'T WANT TO BE THAT KIND OF FOOL. I WOULD NEVER DO THAT.
PLIP PLIP PLIP

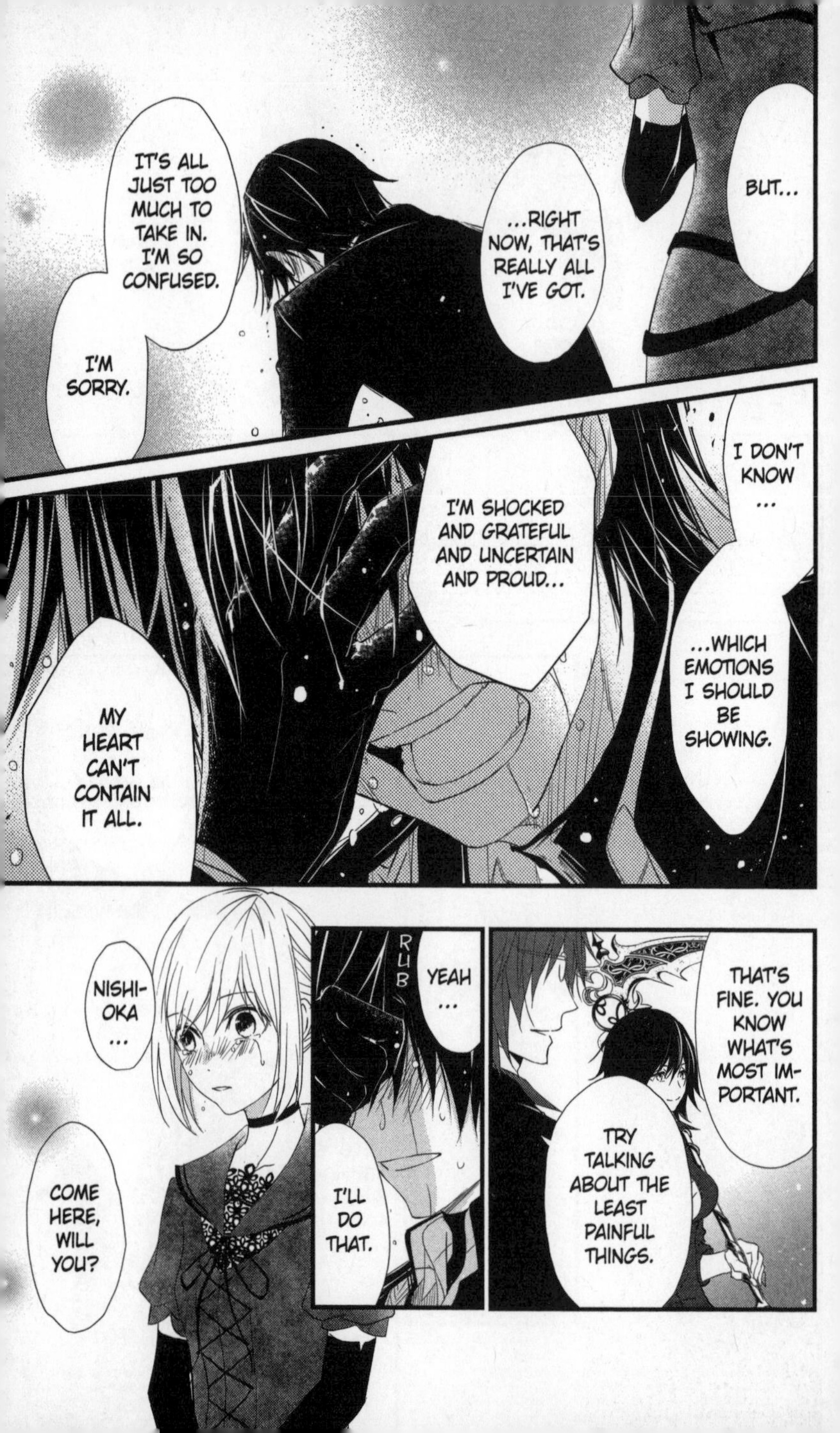
BUT...
...RIGHT NOW, THAT'S REALLY ALL I'VE GOT.
IT'S ALL JUST TOO MUCH TO TAKE IN. I'M SO CONFUSED.
I'M SORRY.
I DON'T KNOW ...
...WHICH EMOTIONS I SHOULD BE SHOWING.
I'M SHOCKED AND GRATEFUL AND UNCERTAIN AND PROUD...
MY HEART CAN'T CONTAIN IT ALL.
THAT'S FINE. YOU KNOW WHAT'S MOST IMPORTANT.
TRY TALKING ABOUT THE LEAST PAINFUL THINGS.
RUB
YEAH ...
I'LL DO THAT.
NISHIOKA ...
COME HERE, WILL YOU?

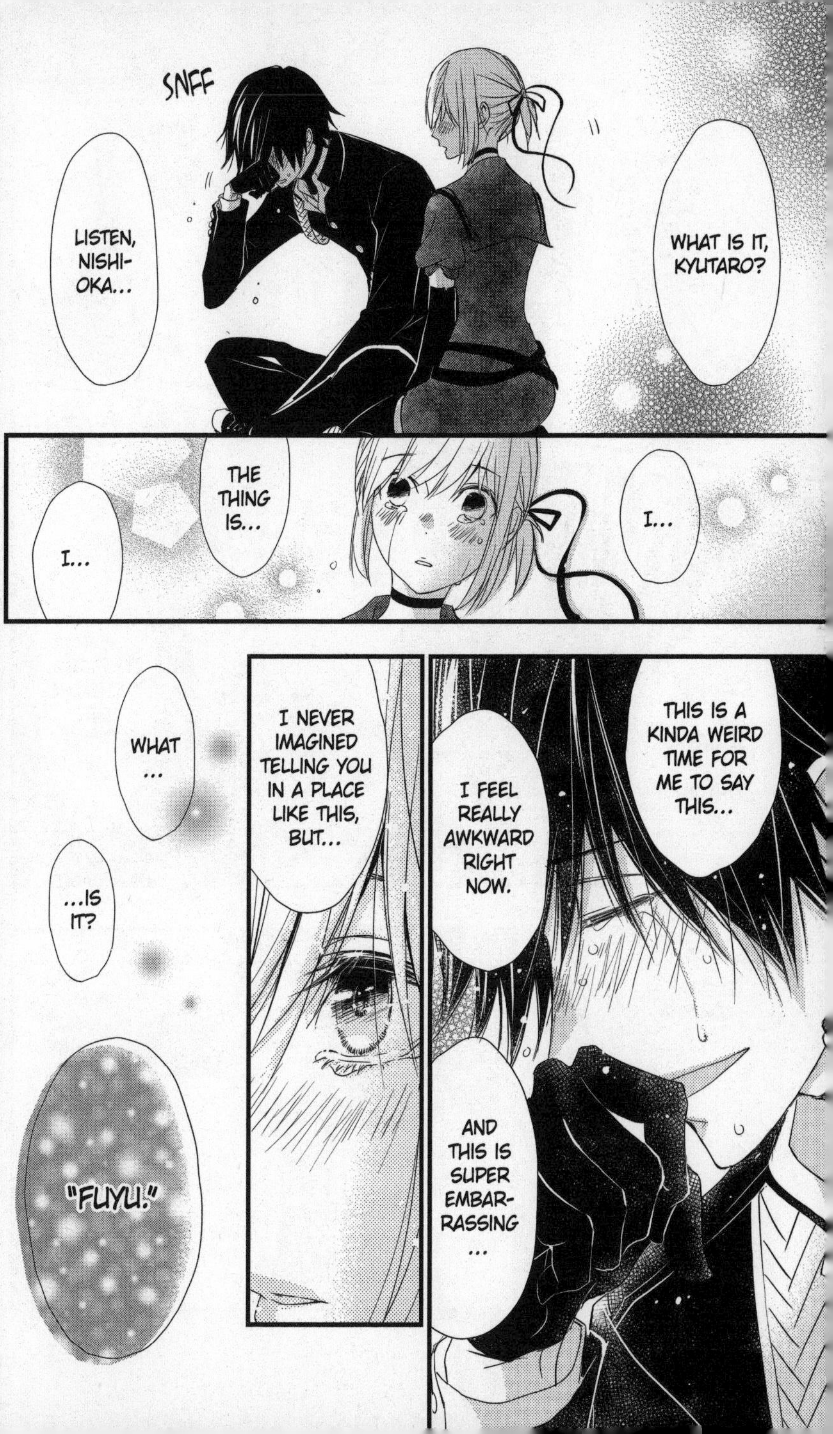
WHAT IS IT, KYUTARO?
SNFF
LISTEN, NISHI-OKA...
I...
THE THING IS...
I...
THIS IS A KINDA WEIRD TIME FOR ME TO SAY THIS...
I FEEL REALLY AWKWARD RIGHT NOW.
AND THIS IS SUPER EMBAR-RASSING...
I NEVER IMAGINED TELLING YOU IN A PLACE LIKE THIS, BUT...
WHAT...
...IS IT?
"FUYU."

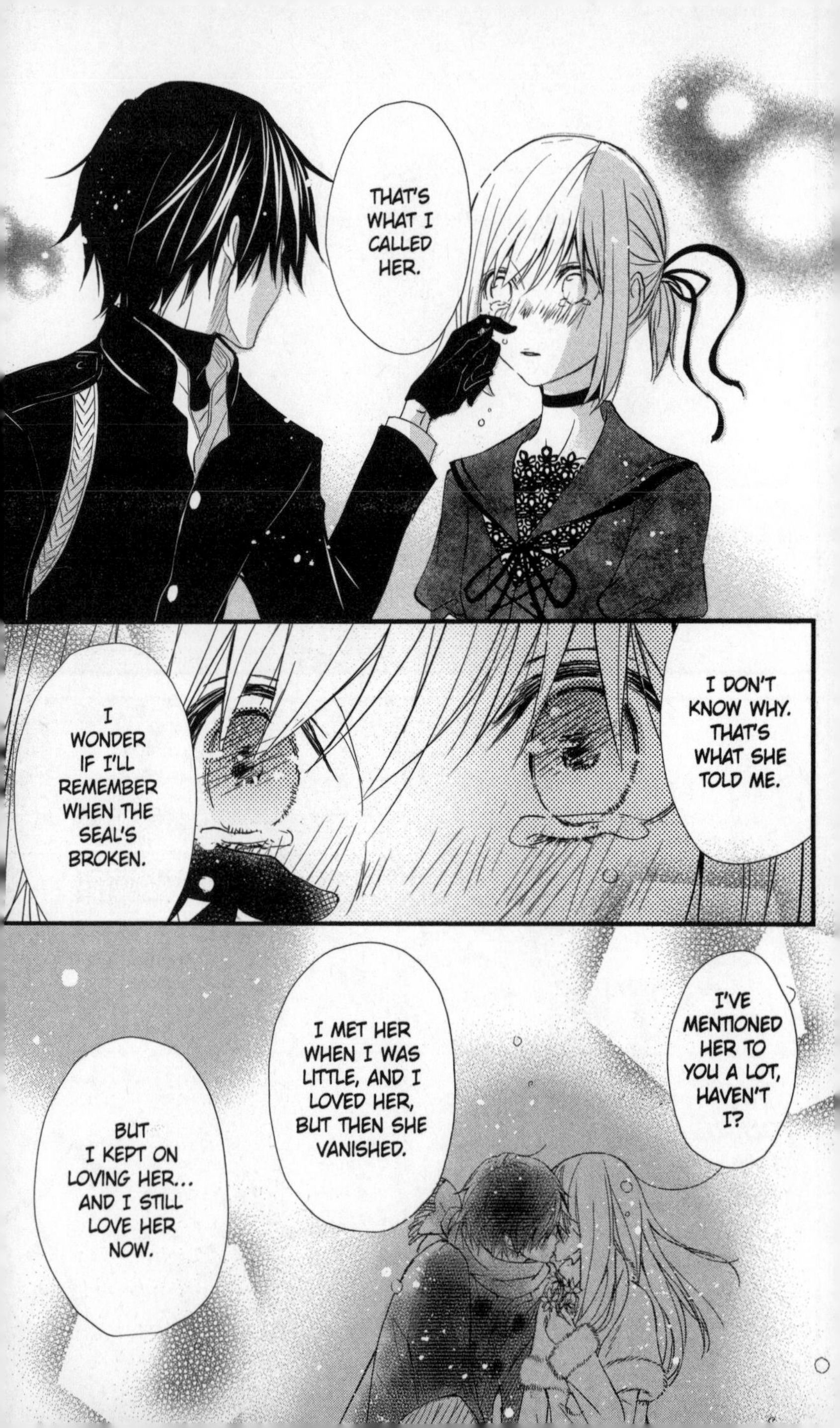
THAT'S WHAT I CALLED HER.
I DON'T KNOW WHY. THAT'S WHAT SHE TOLD ME.
I WONDER IF I'LL REMEMBER WHEN THE SEAL'S BROKEN.
I'VE MENTIONED HER TO YOU A LOT, HAVEN'T I?
I MET HER WHEN I WAS LITTLE, AND I LOVED HER, BUT THEN SHE VANISHED.
BUT I KEPT ON LOVING HER... AND I STILL LOVE HER NOW.

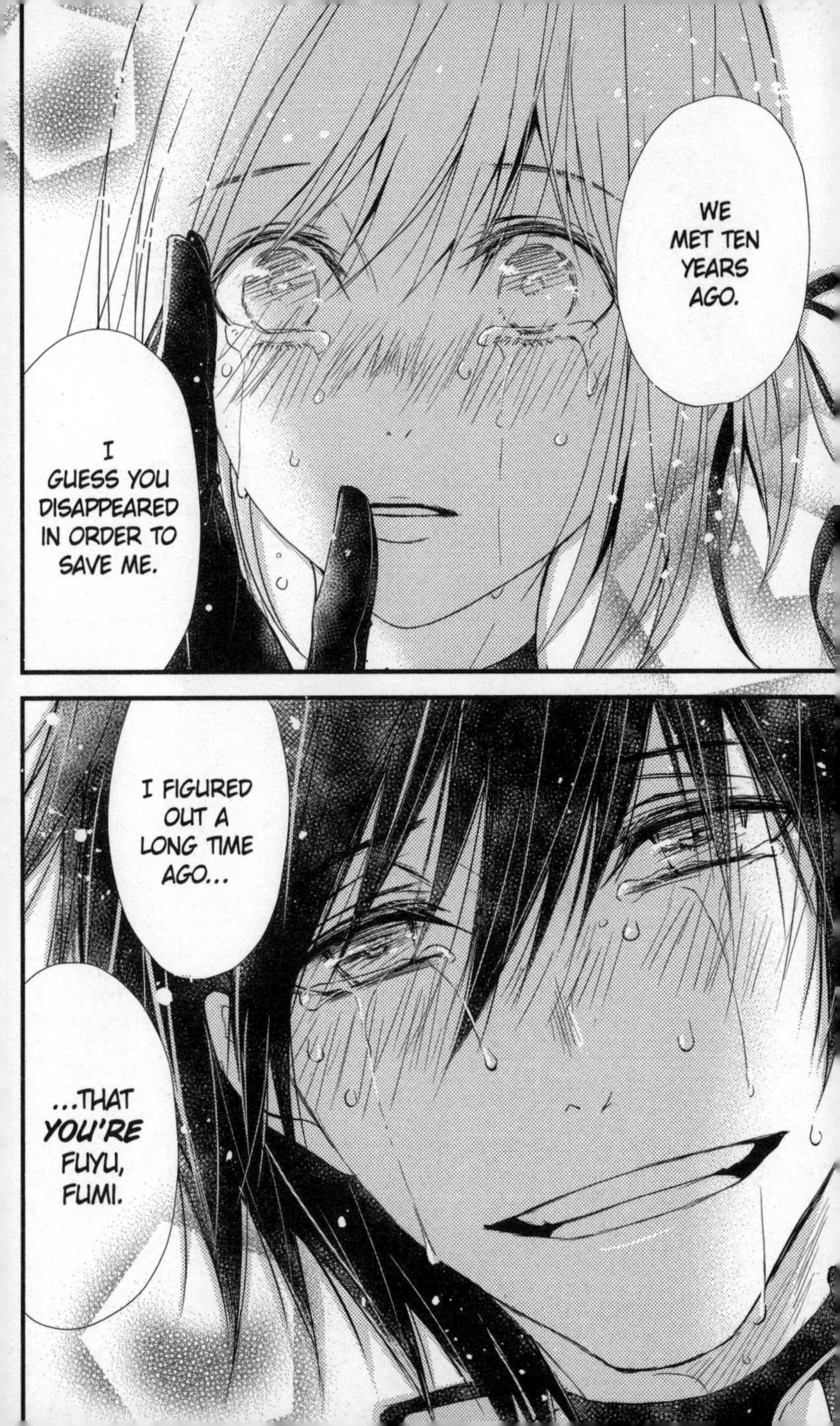
WE MET TEN YEARS AGO.
I GUESS YOU DISAPPEARED IN ORDER TO SAVE ME.
I FIGURED OUT A LONG TIME AGO...
...THAT *YOU'RE* FUYU, FUMI.

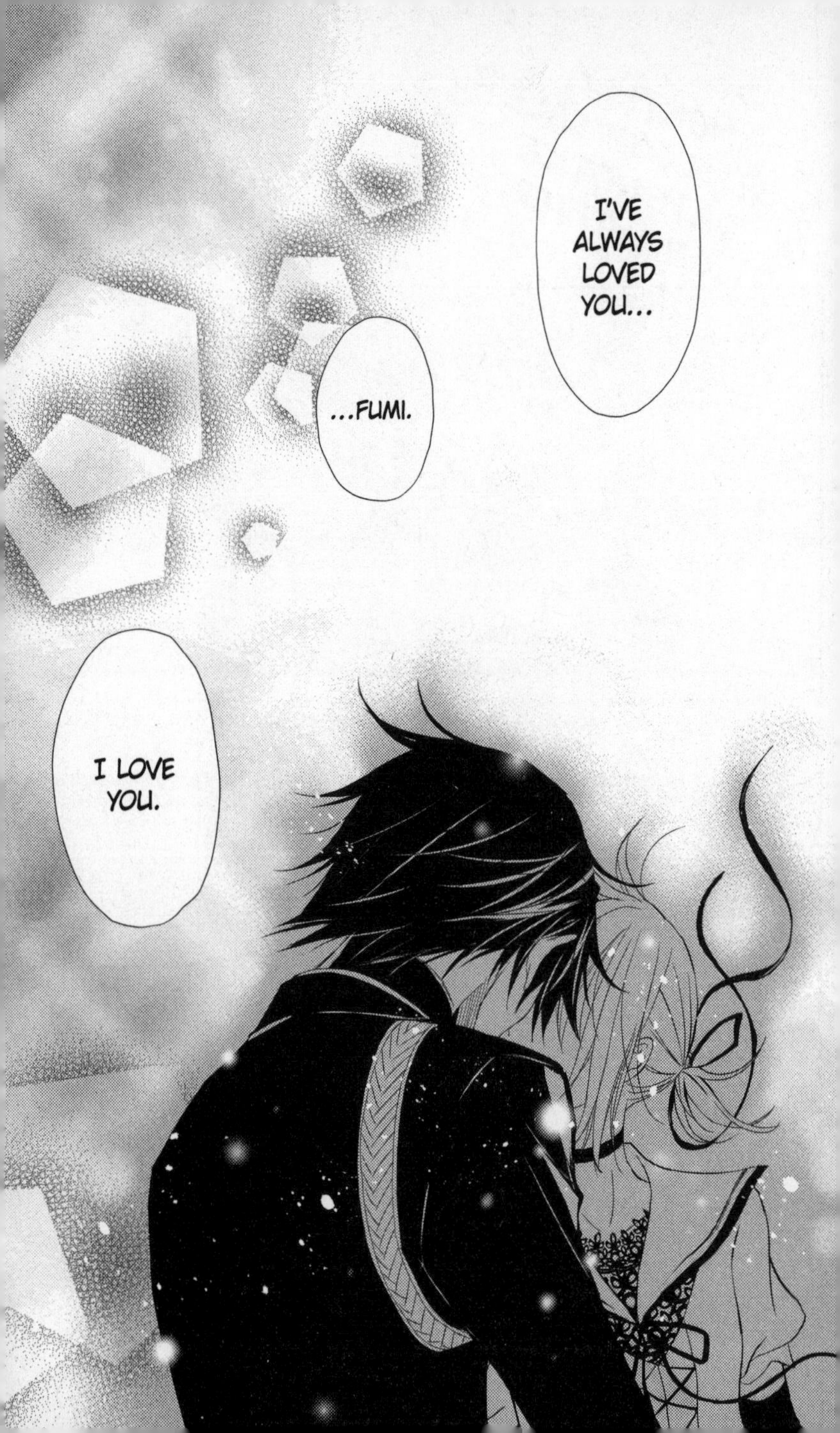
I'VE ALWAYS LOVED YOU...
...FUMI.
I LOVE YOU.

MONTHLY BETSUCOMI SALE DATE NOTICE ON TWITTER

CHAPTER 40

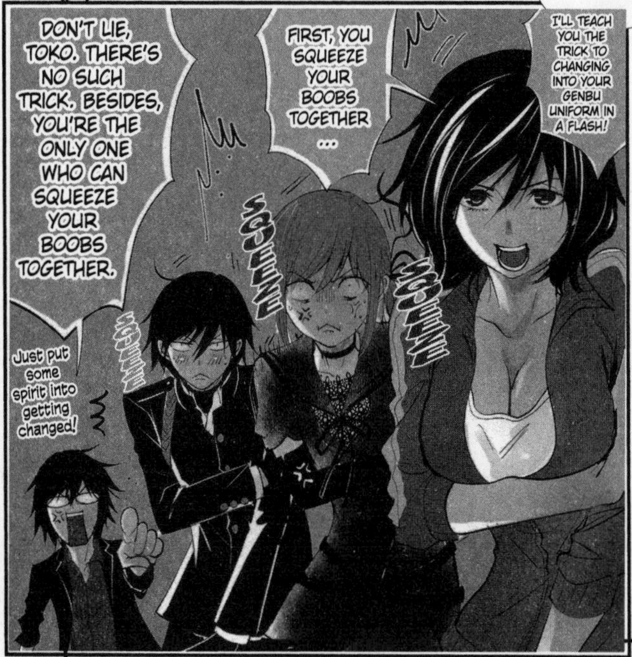
I'LL TEACH YOU THE TRICK TO CHANGING INTO YOUR GENBU UNIFORM IN A FLASH!
SQUEEZE
FIRST, YOU SQUEEZE YOUR BOOBS TOGETHER ...
SQUEEZE
DON'T LIE, TOKO. THERE'S NO SUCH TRICK. BESIDES, YOU'RE THE ONLY ONE WHO CAN SQUEEZE YOUR BOOBS TOGETHER.
Just put some spirit into getting changed!

LET'S SEE... WHAT'S UP IN *QUEEN'S QUALITY* THIS MONTH?

(1) DID ANYONE NOTICE THE REPEATING GAG FROM *QUEEN'S QUALITY* CHAPTER 3?
(2) HIS MOTHER DIDN'T SEEM VERY EMBARRASSED AT ALL.
(3) THE GENBU SWEEPERS (ORGANIZATION)—THEY CHANGED INTO THEIR FORMALS IN AN INSTANT!

IT WAS DIFFICULT DRAWING THE GENBU UNIFORMS (SO MANY BUTTONS) IN CHAPTER 40!

(1) THIS WAS THE REPEATING GAG (SEE VOLUME 1, CHAPTER 3) →

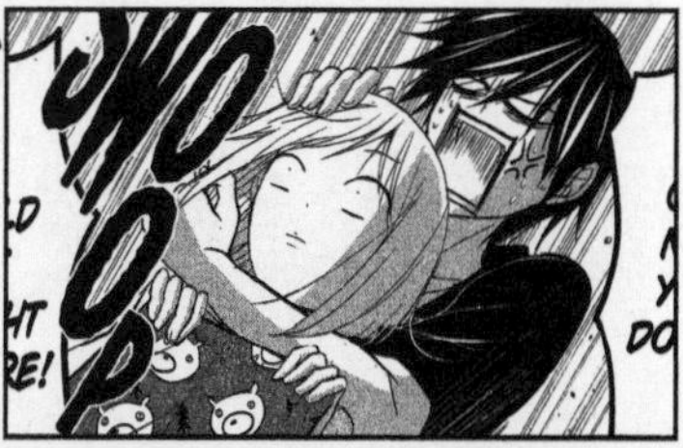
SHOOP

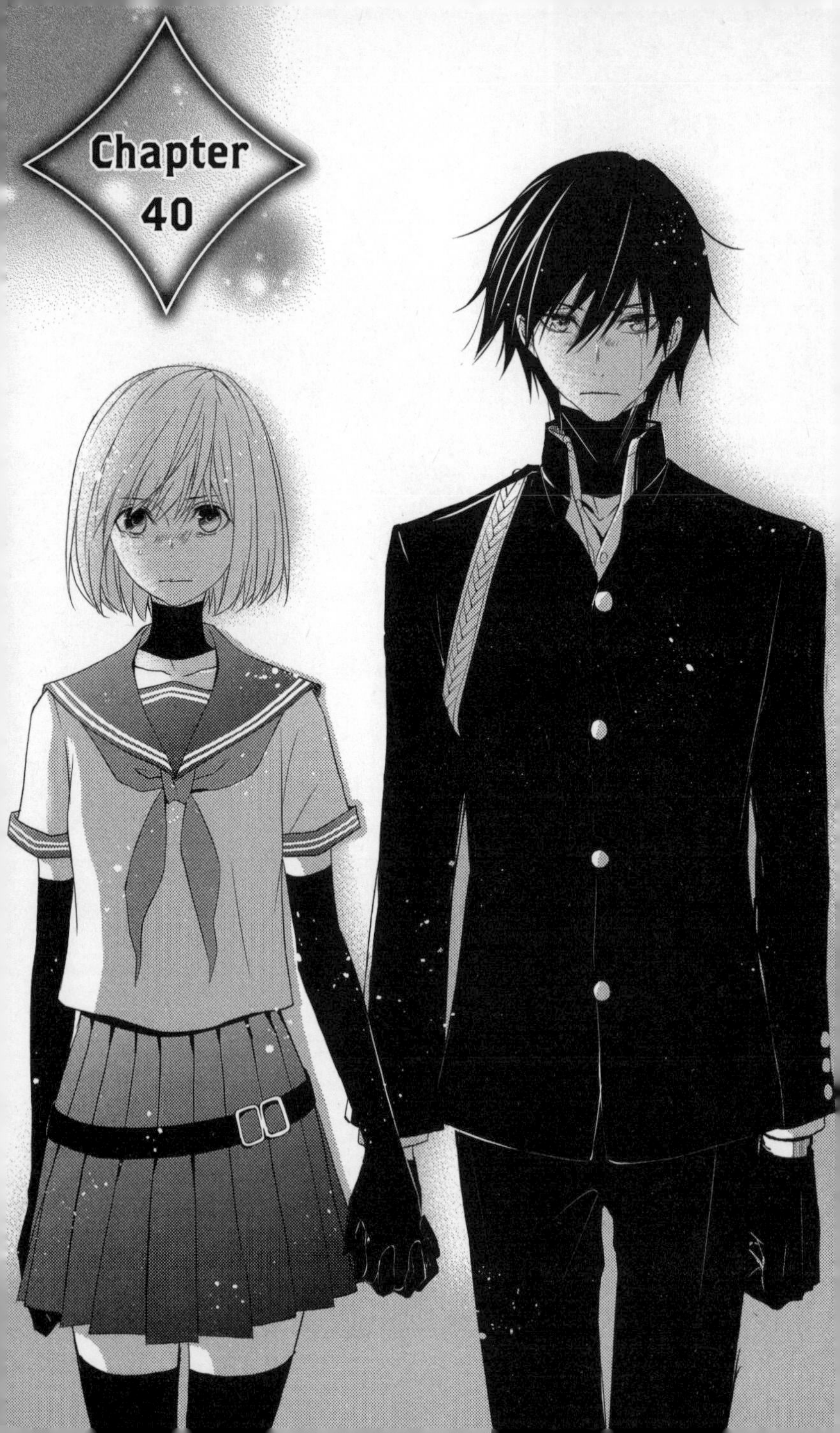
Chapter
40

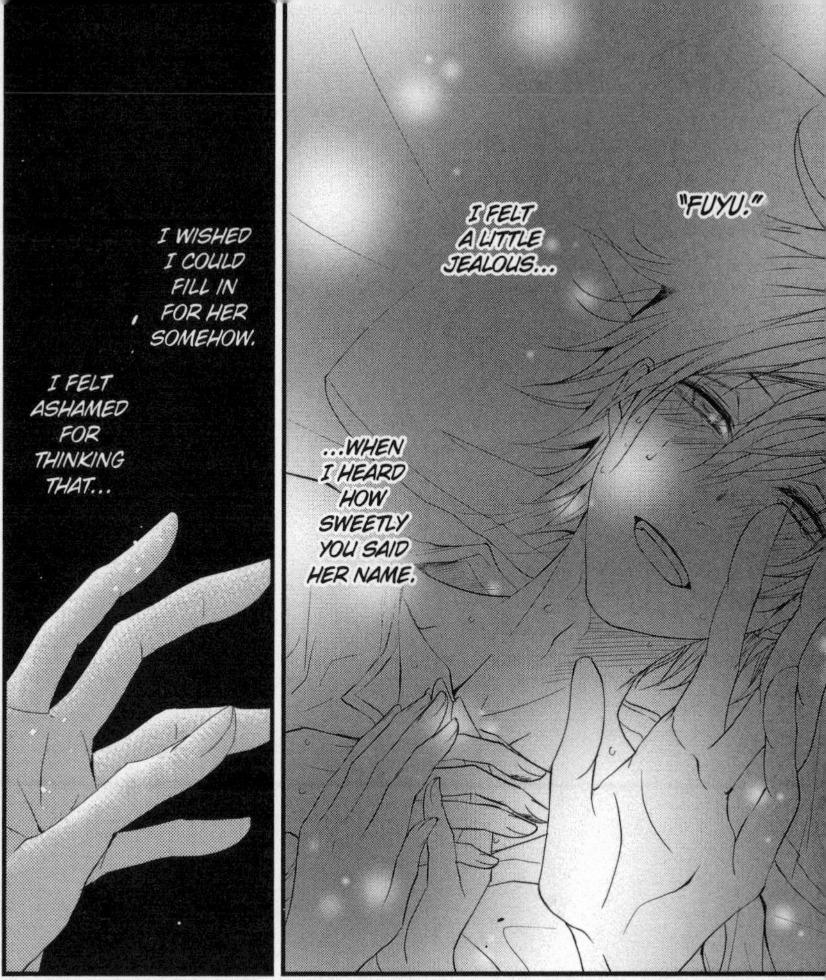
"FUYU."
I FELT A LITTLE JEALOUS...
...WHEN I HEARD HOW SWEETLY YOU SAID HER NAME.
I WISHED I COULD FILL IN FOR HER SOMEHOW.
I FELT ASHAMED FOR THINKING THAT...

In my last volume, I wrote about the problem I seemed to be having drawing breasts. As time went on, I noticed that Toko's and Ataru's breasts seem to have grown. Maybe Sarara's too. That's all. Huh? Yes. That's all.

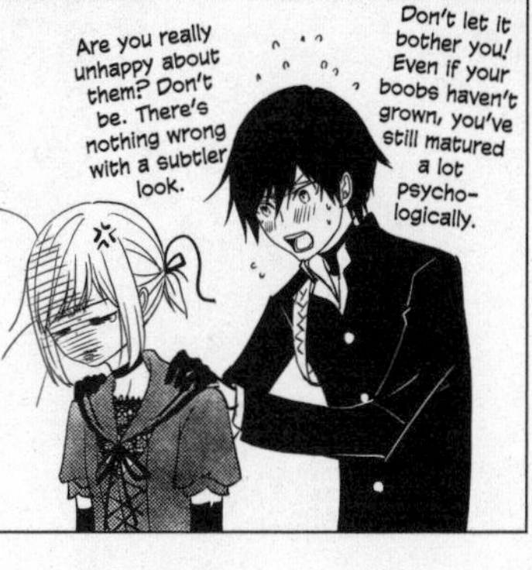
Don't let it bother you! Even if your boobs haven't grown, you've still matured a lot psycho-logically.
Are you really unhappy about them? Don't be. There's nothing wrong with a subtler look.

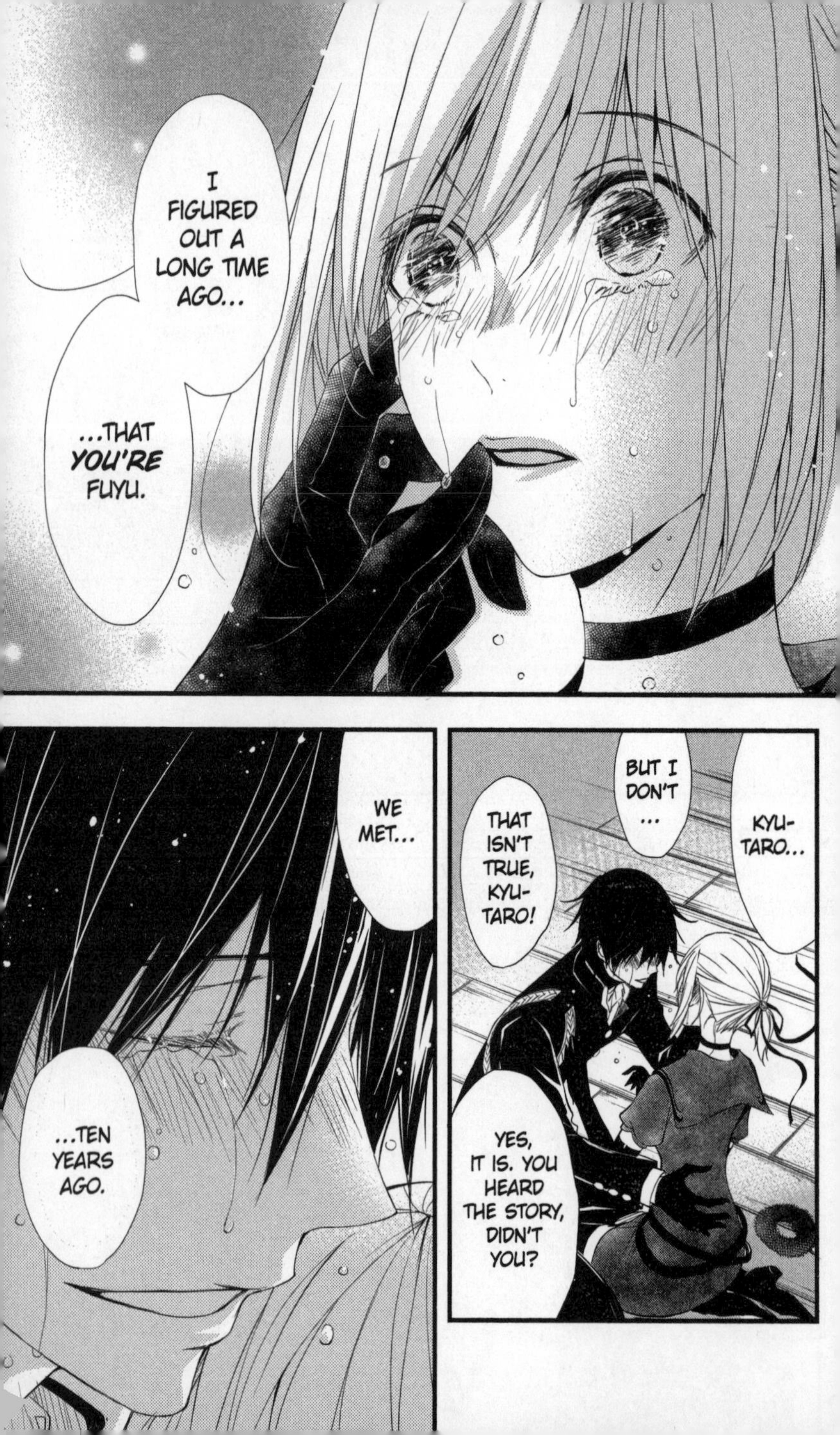
I FIGURED OUT A LONG TIME AGO...
...THAT *YOU'RE* FUYU.
KYU-TARO...
BUT I DON'T ...
THAT ISN'T TRUE, KYU-TARO!
YES, IT IS. YOU HEARD THE STORY, DIDN'T YOU?
WE MET...
...TEN YEARS AGO.

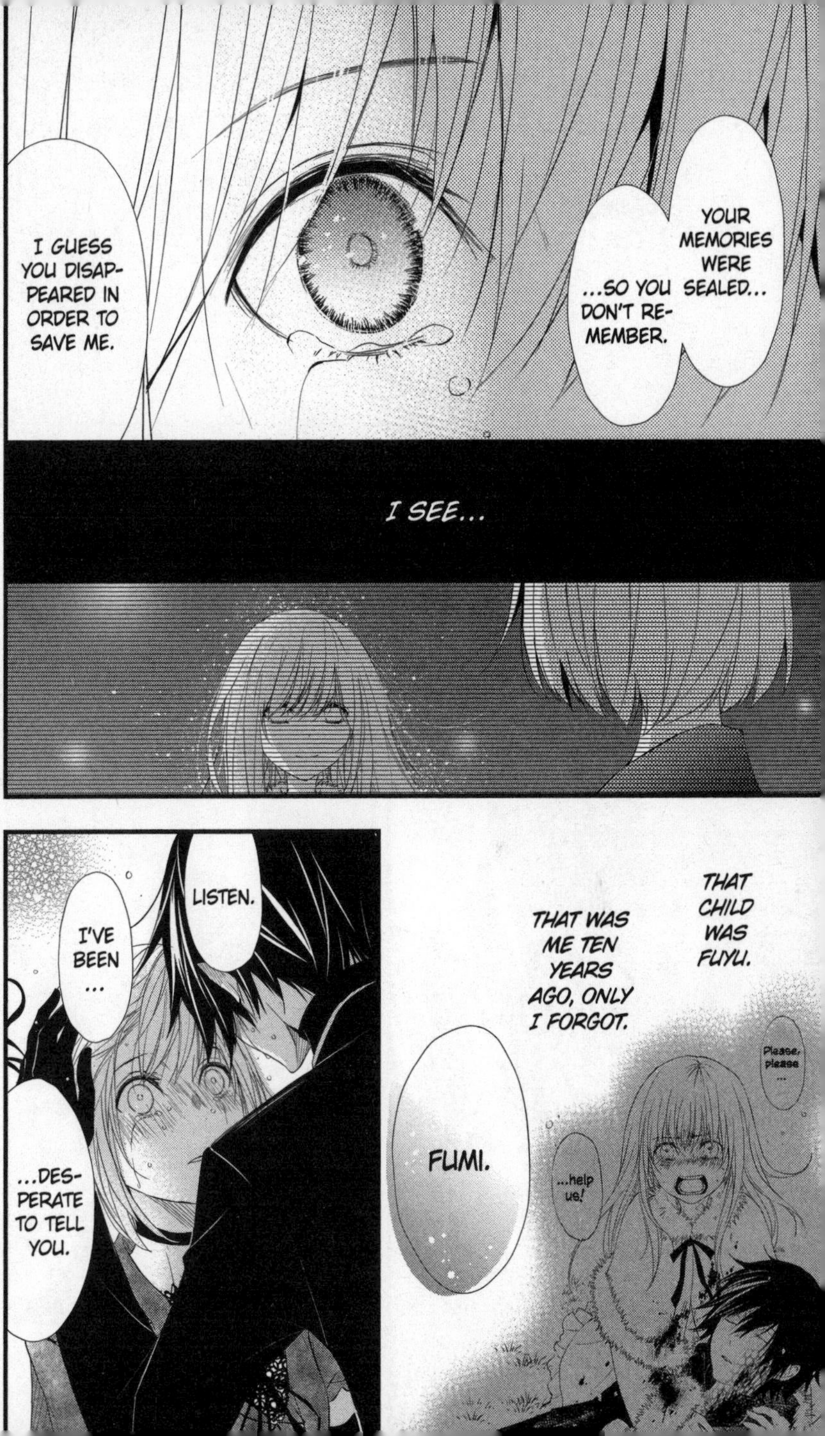
YOUR MEMORIES WERE SEALED...
...SO YOU DON'T REMEMBER.
I GUESS YOU DISAPPEARED IN ORDER TO SAVE ME.
I SEE...
THAT CHILD WAS FUYU.
THAT WAS ME TEN YEARS AGO, ONLY I FORGOT.
Please, please ...
...help us!
FUMI.
LISTEN.
I'VE BEEN ...
...DESPERATE TO TELL YOU.

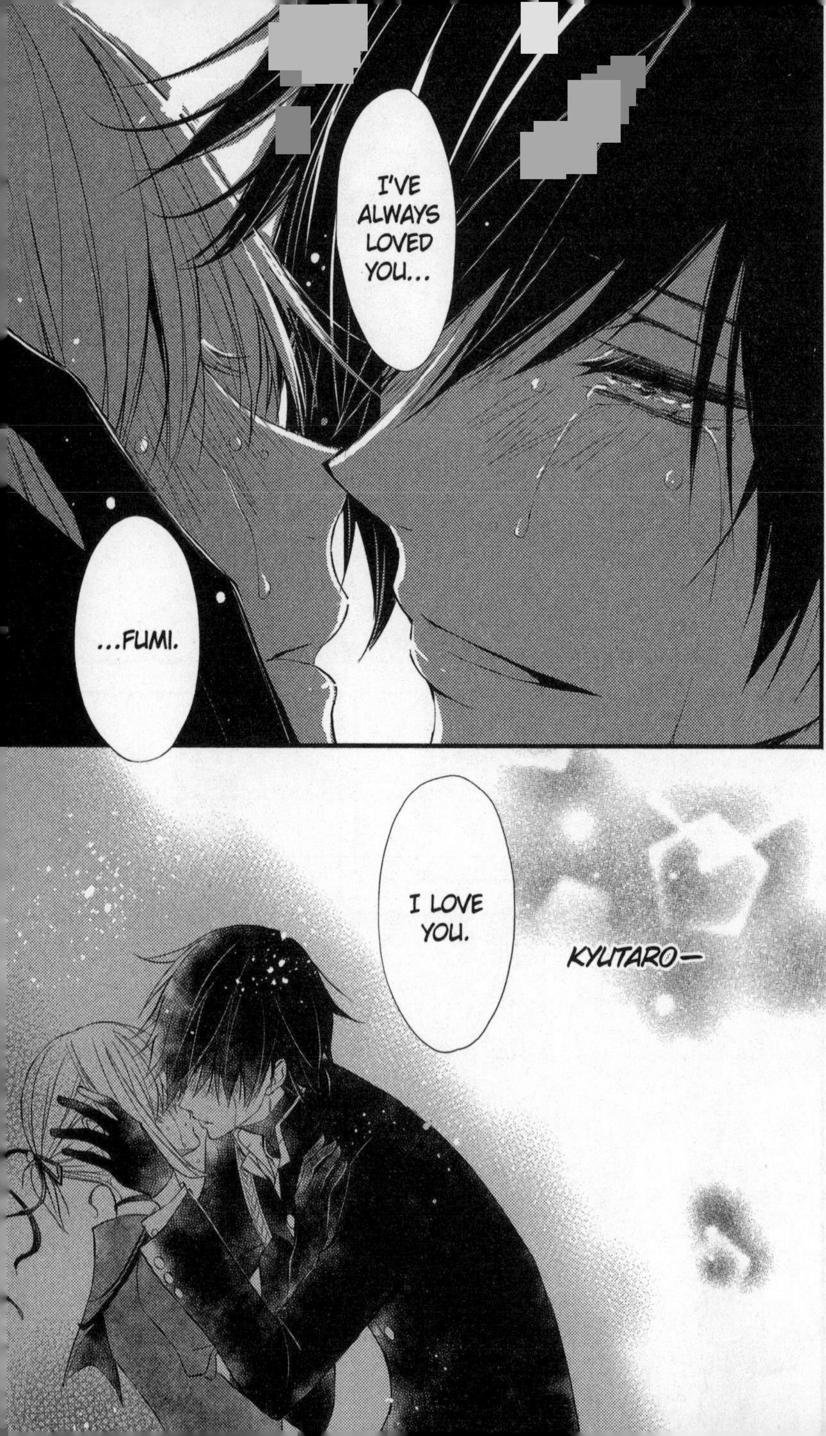
I'VE ALWAYS LOVED YOU...
...FUMI.
KYUTARO—
I LOVE YOU.

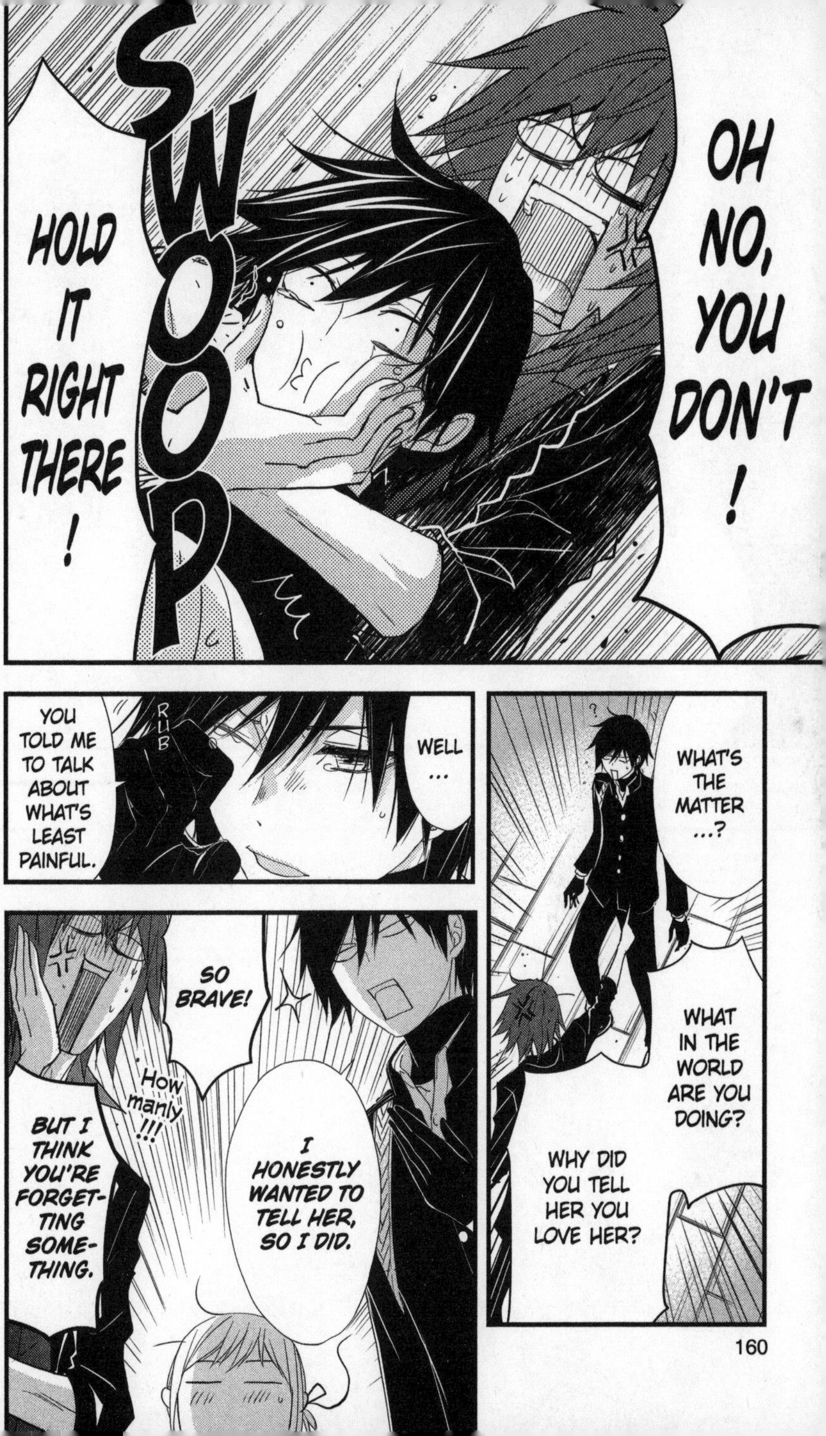
OH NO, YOU DON'T!
SWOOP
HOLD IT RIGHT THERE!
WHAT'S THE MATTER ...?
WHAT IN THE WORLD ARE YOU DOING?
WHY DID YOU TELL HER YOU LOVE HER?
WELL ...
RUB
YOU TOLD ME TO TALK ABOUT WHAT'S LEAST PAINFUL.
I HONESTLY WANTED TO TELL HER, SO I DID.
SO BRAVE!
How manly!!!
BUT I THINK YOU'RE FORGET-TING SOME-THING.

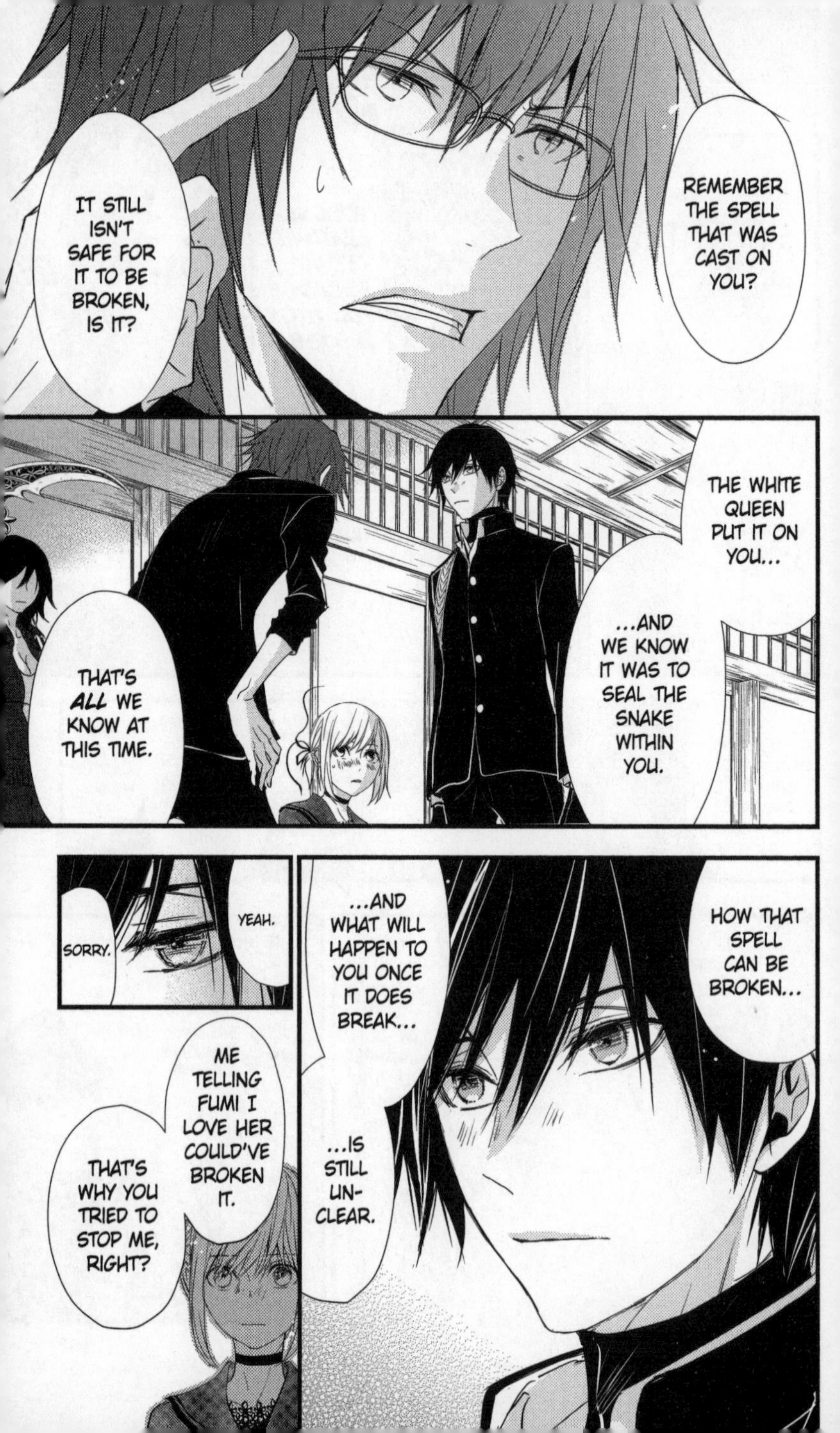
REMEMBER THE SPELL THAT WAS CAST ON YOU?
IT STILL ISN'T SAFE FOR IT TO BE BROKEN, IS IT?
THE WHITE QUEEN PUT IT ON YOU...
...AND WE KNOW IT WAS TO SEAL THE SNAKE WITHIN YOU.
THAT'S *ALL* WE KNOW AT THIS TIME.
HOW THAT SPELL CAN BE BROKEN...
...AND WHAT WILL HAPPEN TO YOU ONCE IT DOES BREAK...
...IS STILL UN-CLEAR.
YEAH.
SORRY.
ME TELLING FUMI I LOVE HER COULD'VE BROKEN IT.
THAT'S WHY YOU TRIED TO STOP ME, RIGHT?

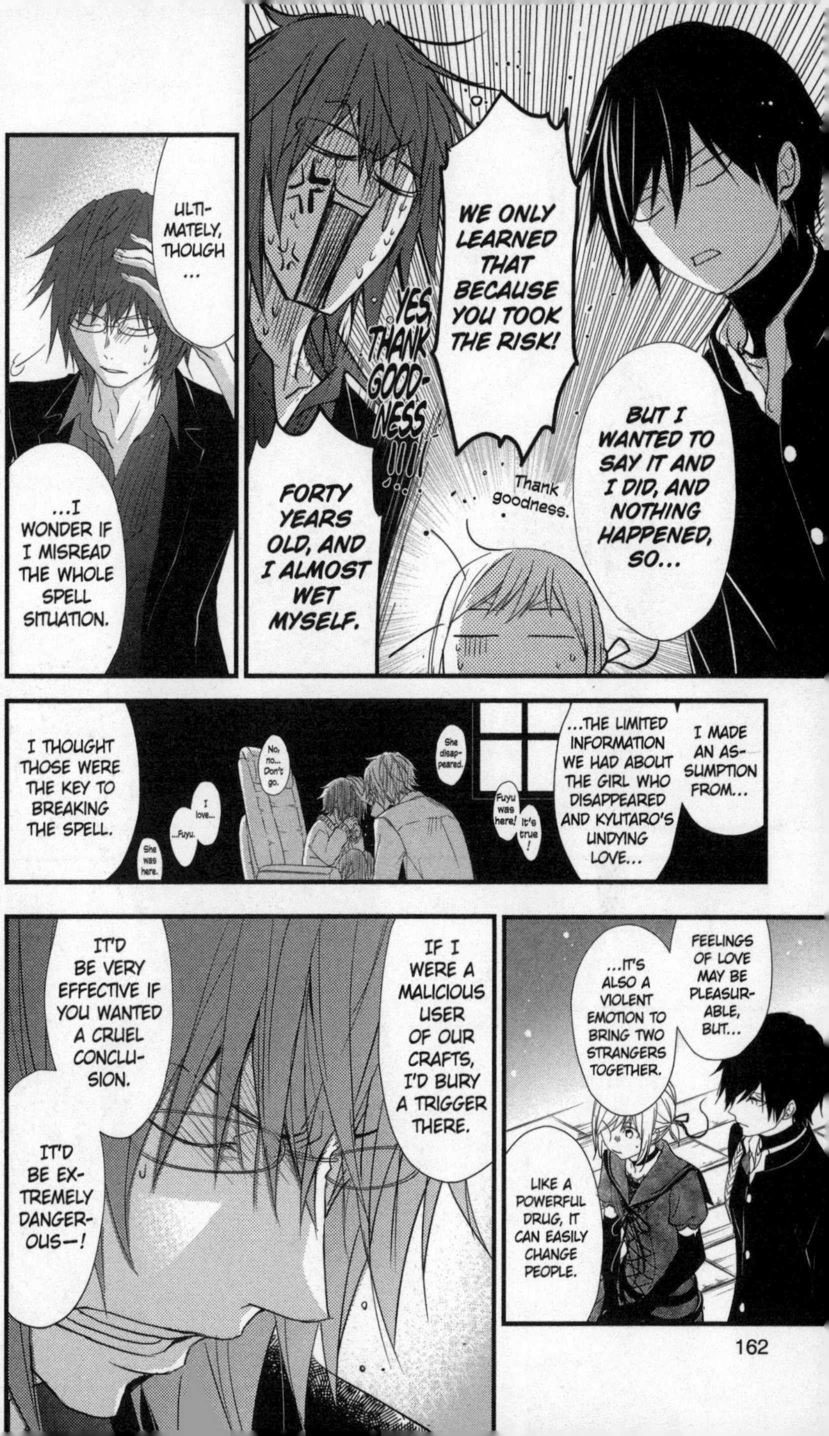
WE ONLY LEARNED THAT BECAUSE YOU TOOK THE RISK!
BUT I WANTED TO SAY IT AND I DID, AND NOTHING HAPPENED, SO...
Thank goodness.
YES, THANK GOODNESS!!!
FORTY YEARS OLD, AND I ALMOST WET MYSELF.
ULTI-MATELY, THOUGH...
...I WONDER IF I MISREAD THE WHOLE SPELL SITUATION.
I MADE AN AS-SUMPTION FROM...
...THE LIMITED INFORMATION WE HAD ABOUT THE GIRL WHO DISAPPEARED AND KYUTARO'S UNDYING LOVE...
She disap-peared.
Fuyu was here!
It's true!
No, no... Don't go.
I love...
...Fuyu.
She was here.
I THOUGHT THOSE WERE THE KEY TO BREAKING THE SPELL.
FEELINGS OF LOVE MAY BE PLEASUR-ABLE, BUT...
...IT'S ALSO A VIOLENT EMOTION TO BRING TWO STRANGERS TOGETHER.
LIKE A POWERFUL DRUG, IT CAN EASILY CHANGE PEOPLE.
IF I WERE A MALICIOUS USER OF OUR CRAFTS, I'D BURY A TRIGGER THERE.
IT'D BE VERY EFFECTIVE IF YOU WANTED A CRUEL CONCLU-SION.
IT'D BE EX-TREMELY DANGER-OUS—!

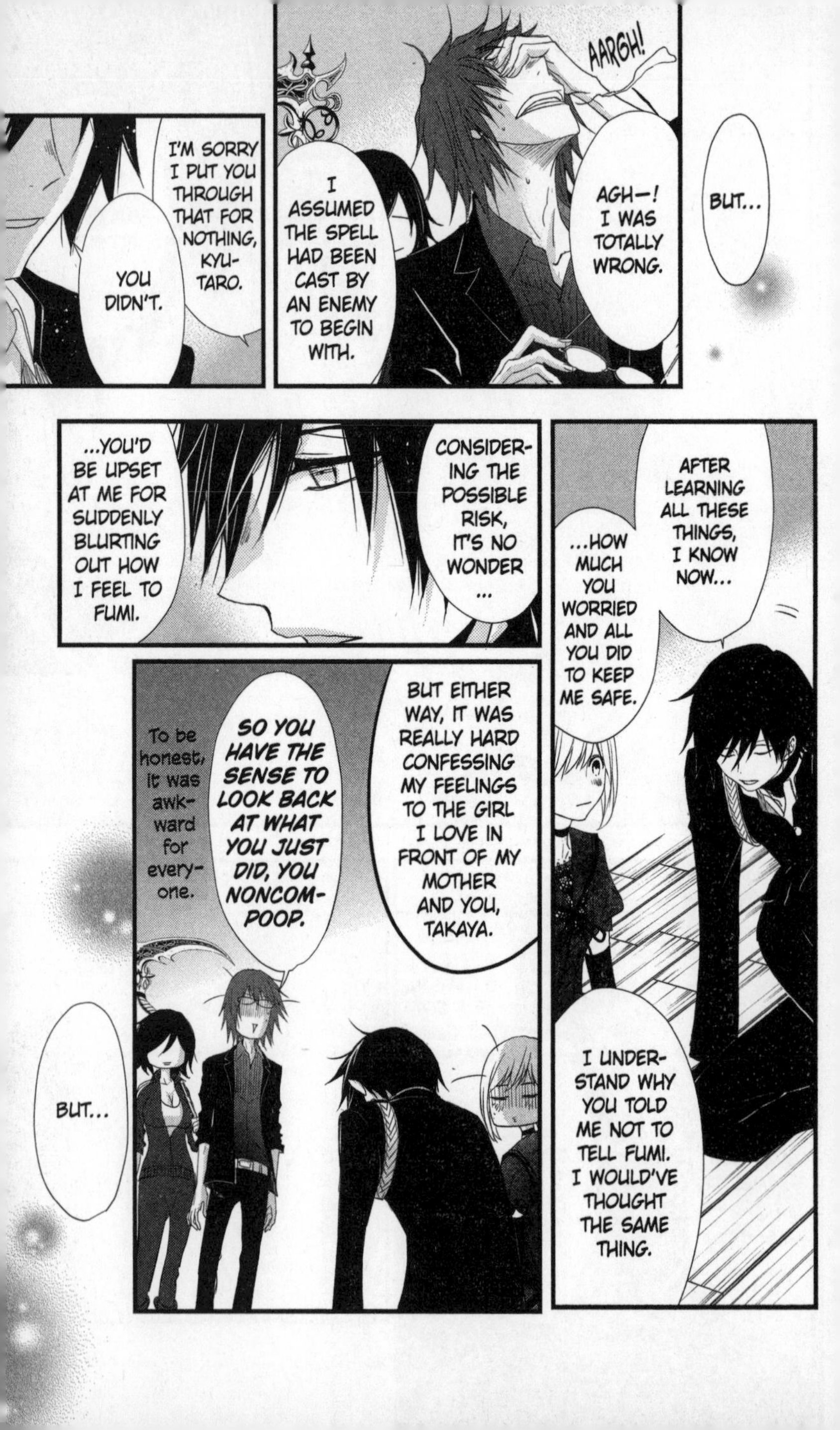
BUT...
AARGH!
AGH—! I WAS TOTALLY WRONG.
I ASSUMED THE SPELL HAD BEEN CAST BY AN ENEMY TO BEGIN WITH.
I'M SORRY I PUT YOU THROUGH THAT FOR NOTHING, KYU-TARO.
YOU DIDN'T.
AFTER LEARNING ALL THESE THINGS, I KNOW NOW...
...HOW MUCH YOU WORRIED AND ALL YOU DID TO KEEP ME SAFE.
I UNDERSTAND WHY YOU TOLD ME NOT TO TELL FUMI. I WOULD'VE THOUGHT THE SAME THING.
CONSIDERING THE POSSIBLE RISK, IT'S NO WONDER...
...YOU'D BE UPSET AT ME FOR SUDDENLY BLURTING OUT HOW I FEEL TO FUMI.
BUT EITHER WAY, IT WAS REALLY HARD CONFESSING MY FEELINGS TO THE GIRL I LOVE IN FRONT OF MY MOTHER AND YOU, TAKAYA.
SO YOU HAVE THE SENSE TO LOOK BACK AT WHAT YOU JUST DID, YOU NONCOMPOOP.
To be honest, it was awkward for everyone.
BUT...

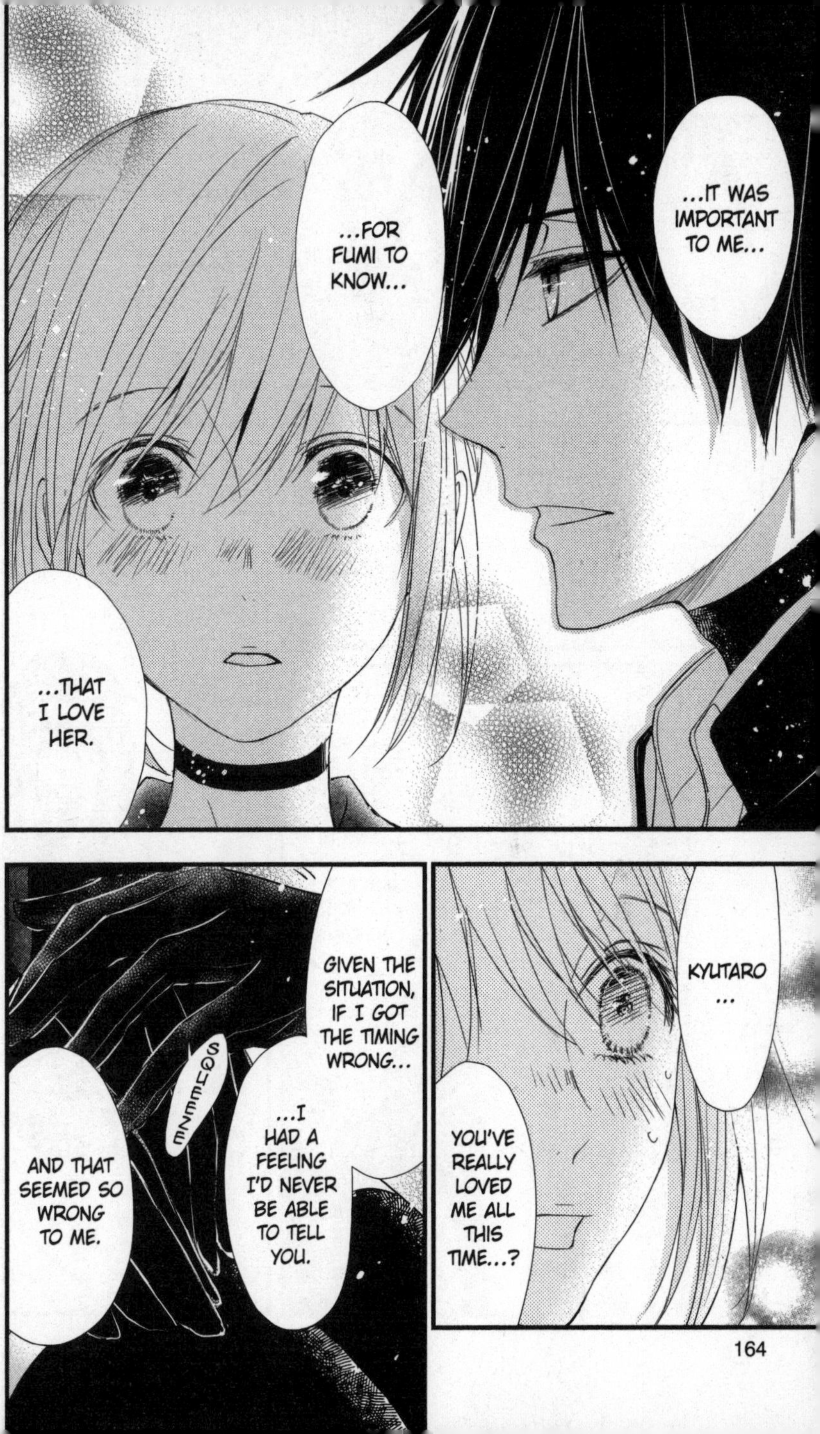
...IT WAS IMPORTANT TO ME...
...FOR FUMI TO KNOW...
...THAT I LOVE HER.
KYUTARO ...
YOU'VE REALLY LOVED ME ALL THIS TIME...?
GIVEN THE SITUATION, IF I GOT THE TIMING WRONG...
SQUEEEZE
...I HAD A FEELING I'D NEVER BE ABLE TO TELL YOU.
AND THAT SEEMED SO WRONG TO ME.

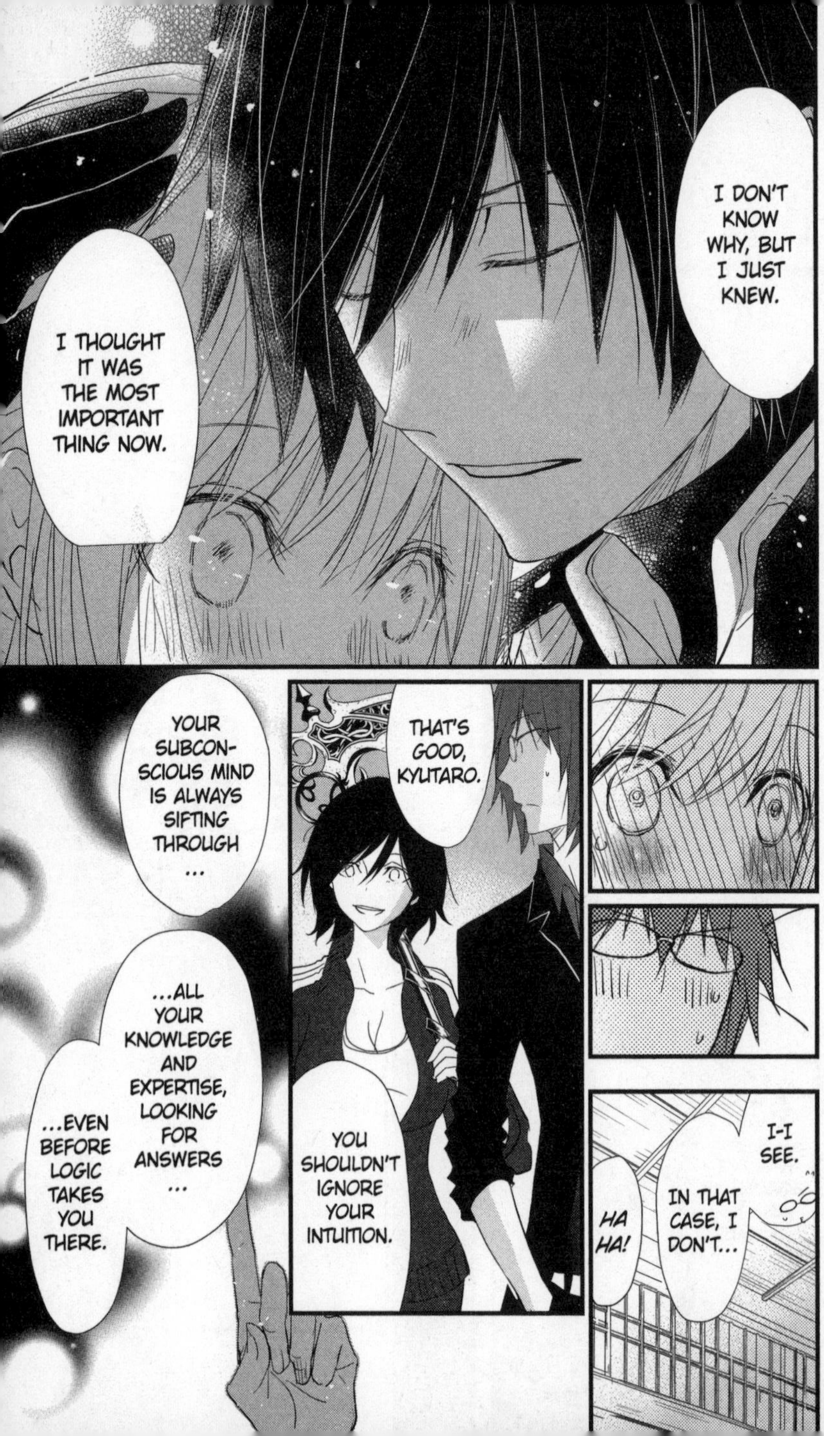
I DON'T KNOW WHY, BUT I JUST KNEW.
I THOUGHT IT WAS THE MOST IMPORTANT THING NOW.
I-I SEE.
IN THAT CASE, I DON'T...
HA HA!
THAT'S GOOD, KYUTARO.
YOU SHOULDN'T IGNORE YOUR INTUITION.
YOUR SUBCONSCIOUS MIND IS ALWAYS SIFTING THROUGH ...
...ALL YOUR KNOWLEDGE AND EXPERTISE, LOOKING FOR ANSWERS ...
...EVEN BEFORE LOGIC TAKES YOU THERE.

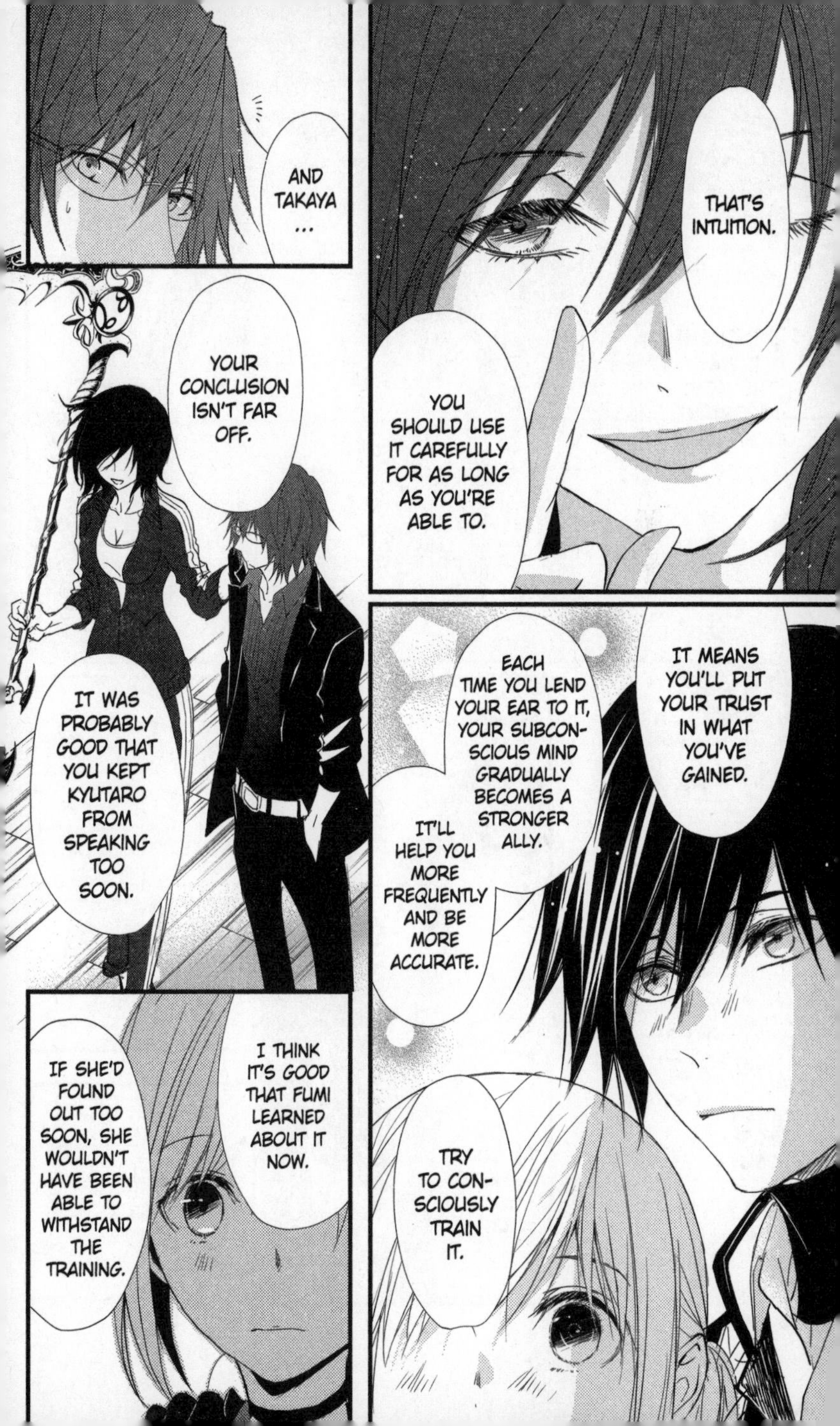
THAT'S INTUITION.
YOU SHOULD USE IT CAREFULLY FOR AS LONG AS YOU'RE ABLE TO.
AND TAKAYA ...
YOUR CONCLUSION ISN'T FAR OFF.
IT WAS PROBABLY GOOD THAT YOU KEPT KYUTARO FROM SPEAKING TOO SOON.
IT MEANS YOU'LL PUT YOUR TRUST IN WHAT YOU'VE GAINED.
EACH TIME YOU LEND YOUR EAR TO IT, YOUR SUBCON-SCIOUS MIND GRADUALLY BECOMES A STRONGER ALLY.
IT'LL HELP YOU MORE FREQUENTLY AND BE MORE ACCURATE.
TRY TO CON-SCIOUSLY TRAIN IT.
I THINK IT'S GOOD THAT FUMI LEARNED ABOUT IT NOW.
IF SHE'D FOUND OUT TOO SOON, SHE WOULDN'T HAVE BEEN ABLE TO WITHSTAND THE TRAINING.

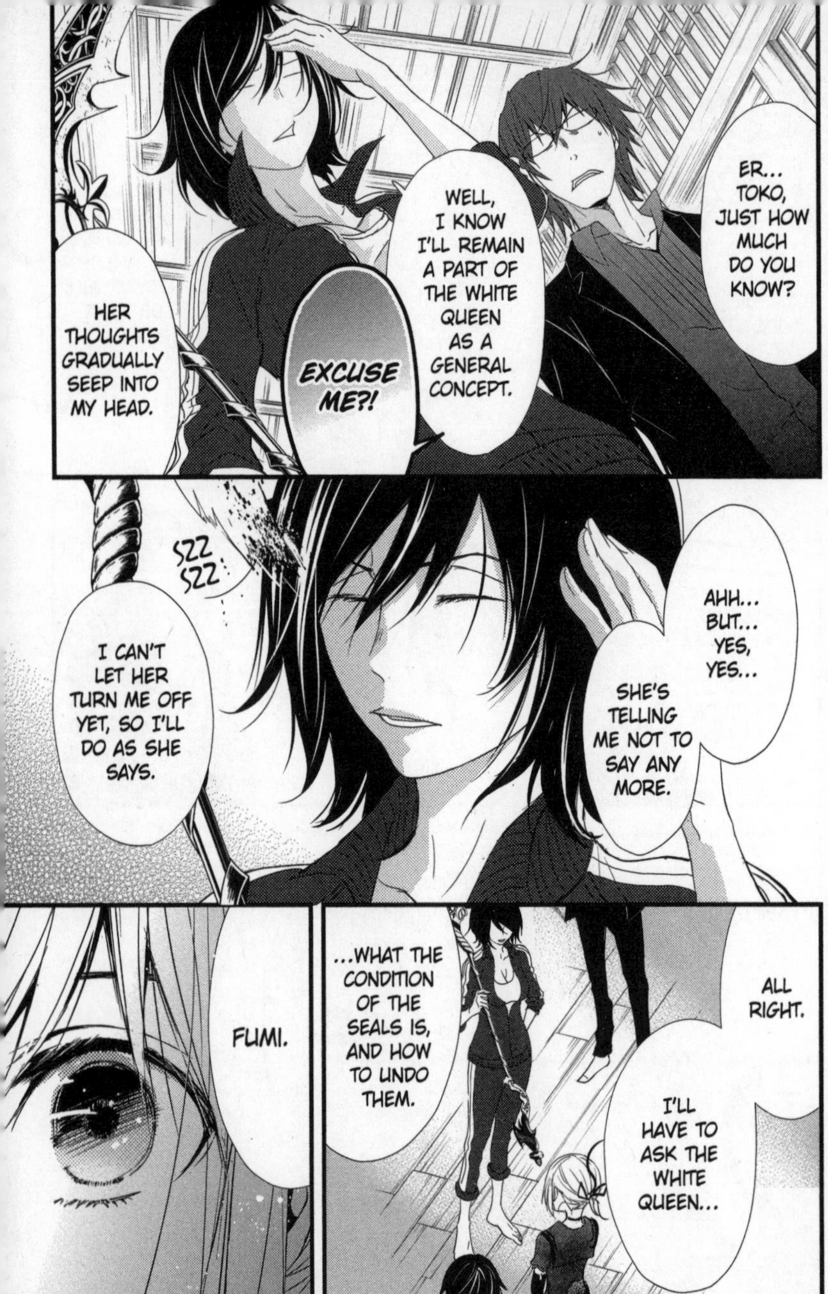
ER... TOKO, JUST HOW MUCH DO YOU KNOW?
WELL, I KNOW I'LL REMAIN A PART OF THE WHITE QUEEN AS A GENERAL CONCEPT.
EXCUSE ME?!
HER THOUGHTS GRADUALLY SEEP INTO MY HEAD.
AHH... BUT... YES, YES...
SHE'S TELLING ME NOT TO SAY ANY MORE.
SZZ SZZ
I CAN'T LET HER TURN ME OFF YET, SO I'LL DO AS SHE SAYS.
ALL RIGHT.
I'LL HAVE TO ASK THE WHITE QUEEN...
...WHAT THE CONDITION OF THE SEALS IS, AND HOW TO UNDO THEM.
FUMI.

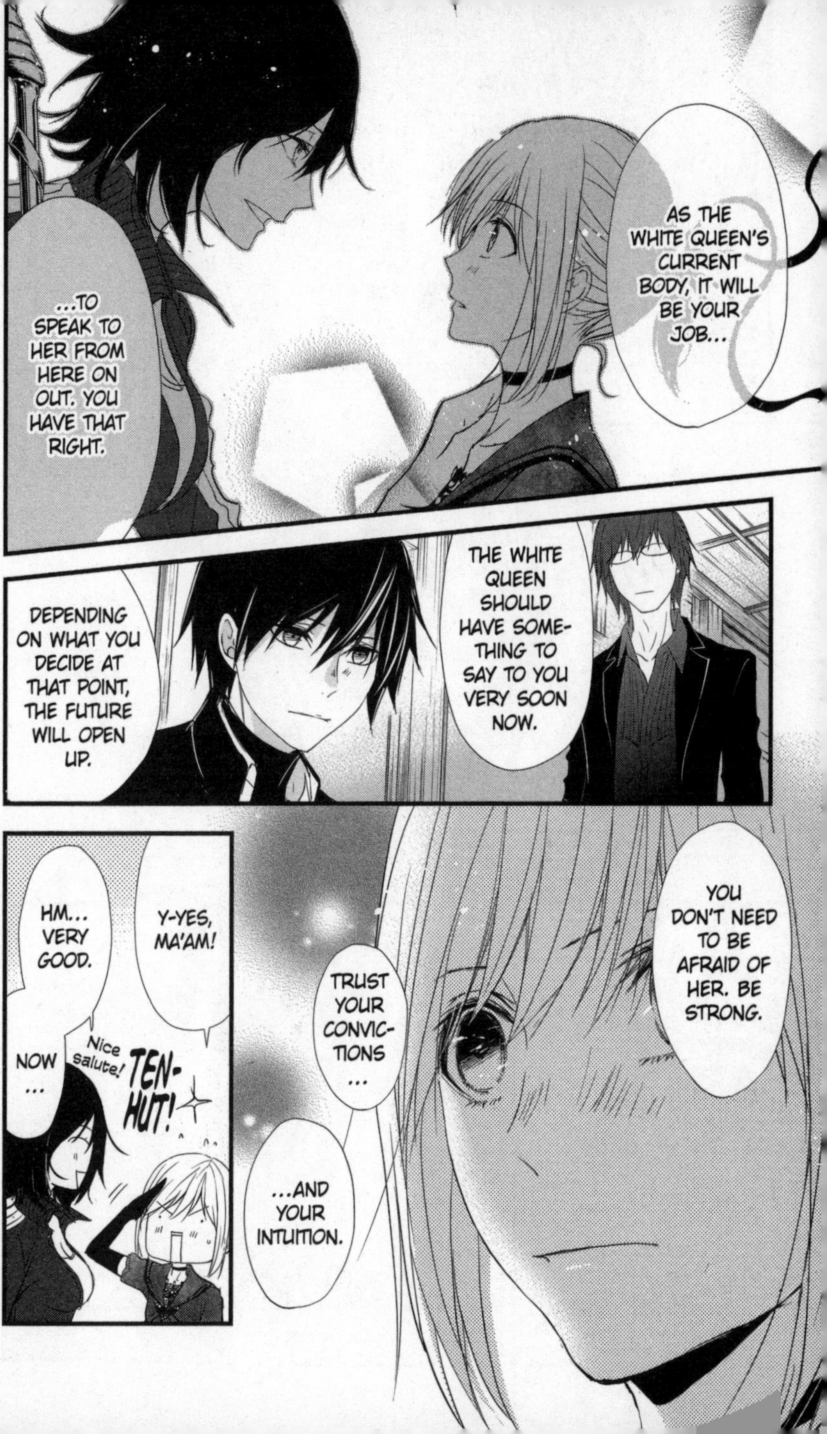
AS THE WHITE QUEEN'S CURRENT BODY, IT WILL BE YOUR JOB...
...TO SPEAK TO HER FROM HERE ON OUT. YOU HAVE THAT RIGHT.
THE WHITE QUEEN SHOULD HAVE SOME-THING TO SAY TO YOU VERY SOON NOW.
DEPENDING ON WHAT YOU DECIDE AT THAT POINT, THE FUTURE WILL OPEN UP.
YOU DON'T NEED TO BE AFRAID OF HER. BE STRONG.
TRUST YOUR CONVIC-TIONS ...
...AND YOUR INTUITION.
Y-YES, MA'AM!
HM... VERY GOOD.
TEN-HUT!
Nice salute!
NOW ...

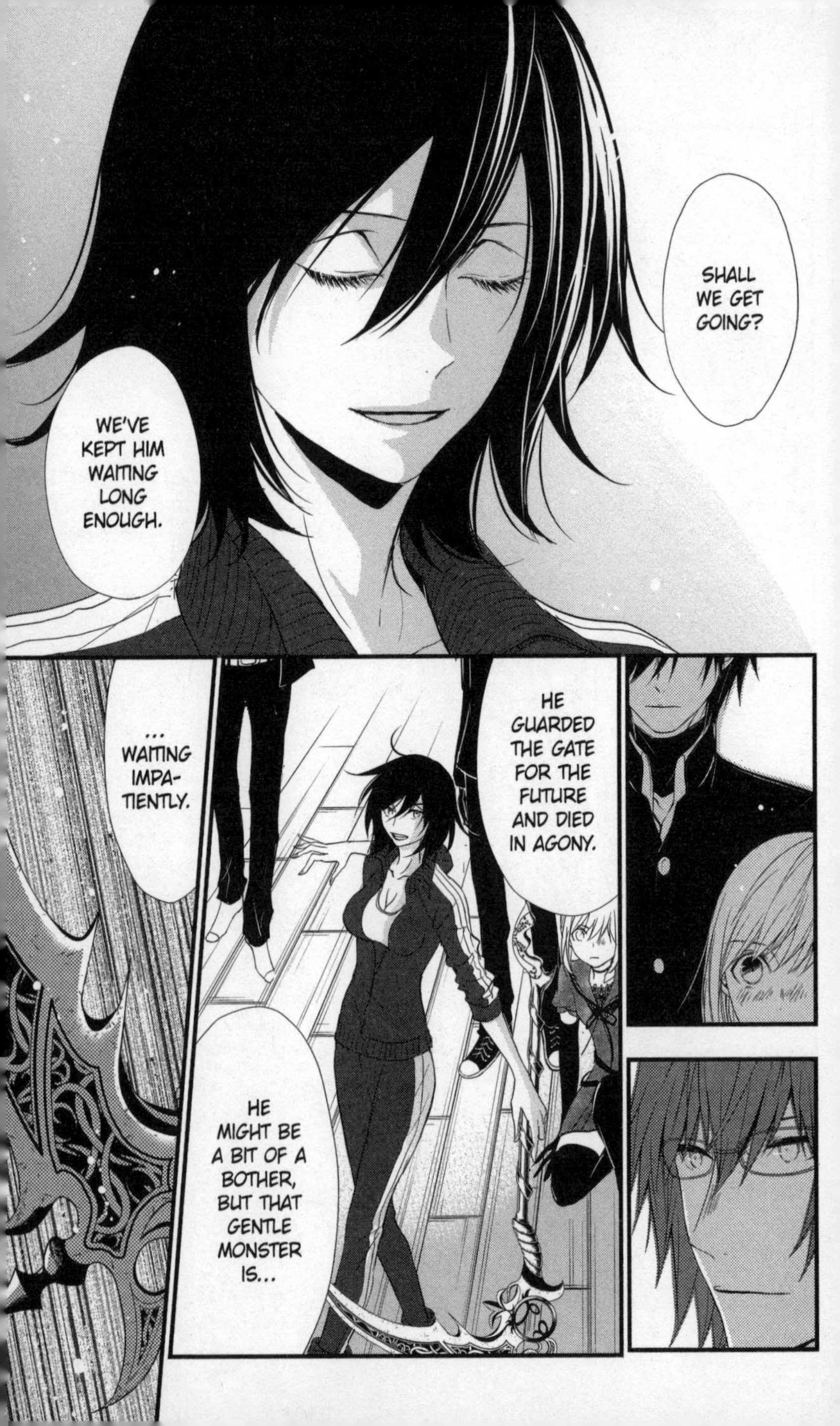
SHALL WE GET GOING?
WE'VE KEPT HIM WAITING LONG ENOUGH.
HE GUARDED THE GATE FOR THE FUTURE AND DIED IN AGONY.
HE MIGHT BE A BIT OF A BOTHER, BUT THAT GENTLE MONSTER IS...
...WAITING IMPA-TIENTLY.

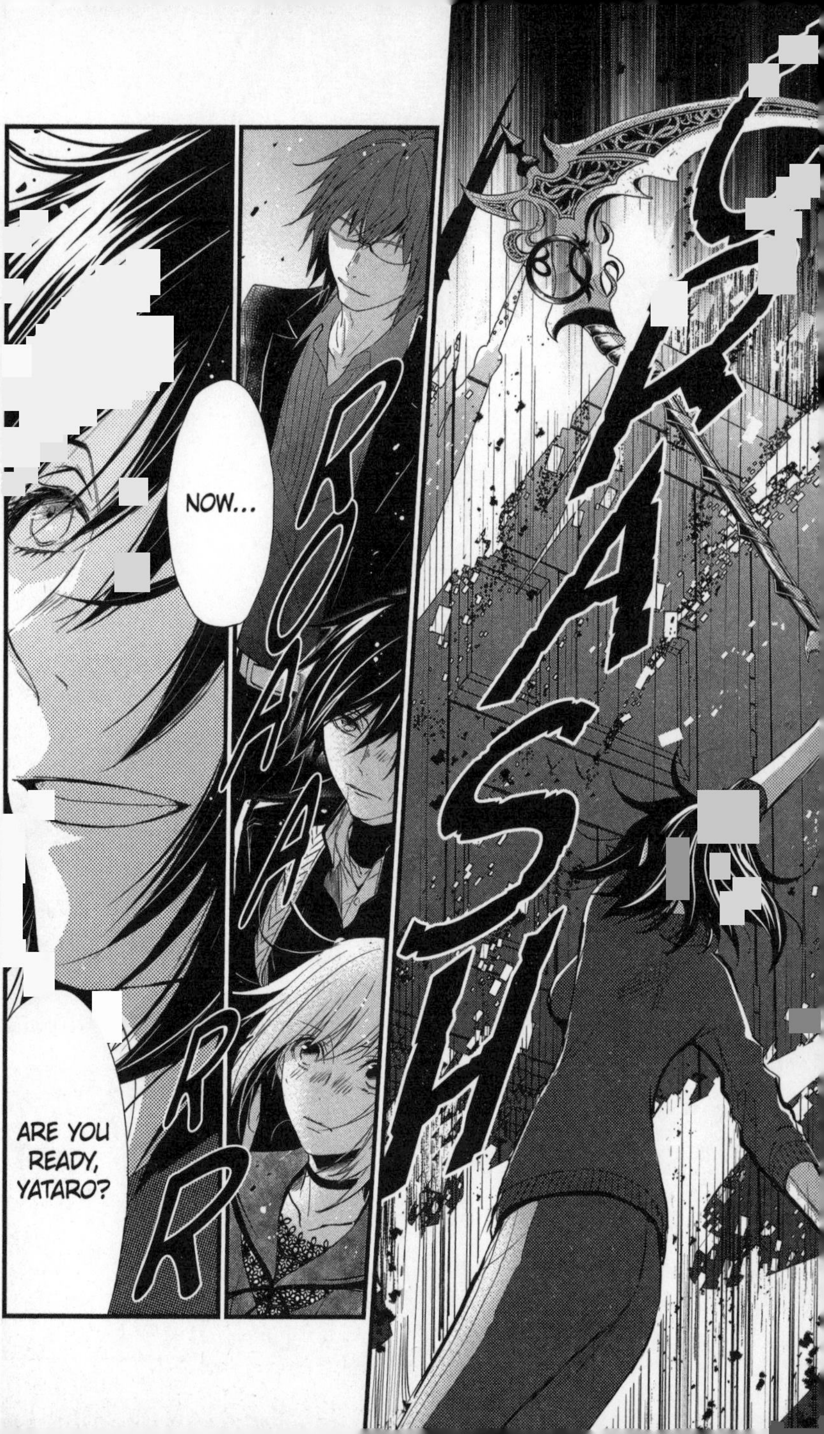
SLASH
NOW...
ROAAARRR
ARE YOU READY, YATARO?

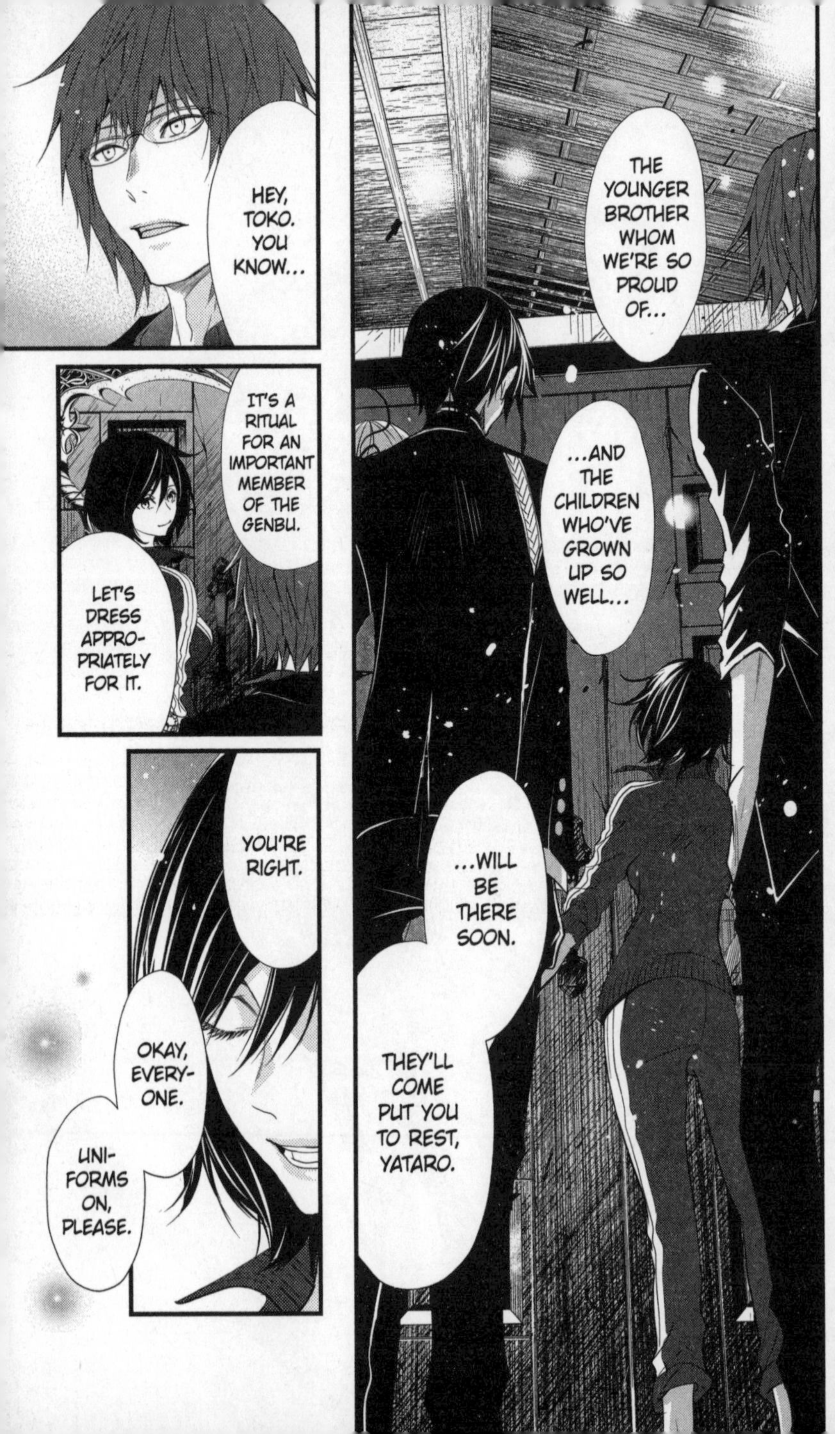
THE YOUNGER BROTHER WHOM WE'RE SO PROUD OF...
...AND THE CHILDREN WHO'VE GROWN UP SO WELL...
...WILL BE THERE SOON.
THEY'LL COME PUT YOU TO REST, YATARO.
HEY, TOKO. YOU KNOW...
IT'S A RITUAL FOR AN IMPORTANT MEMBER OF THE GENBU.
LET'S DRESS APPRO-PRIATELY FOR IT.
YOU'RE RIGHT.
OKAY, EVERY-ONE.
UNI-FORMS ON, PLEASE.

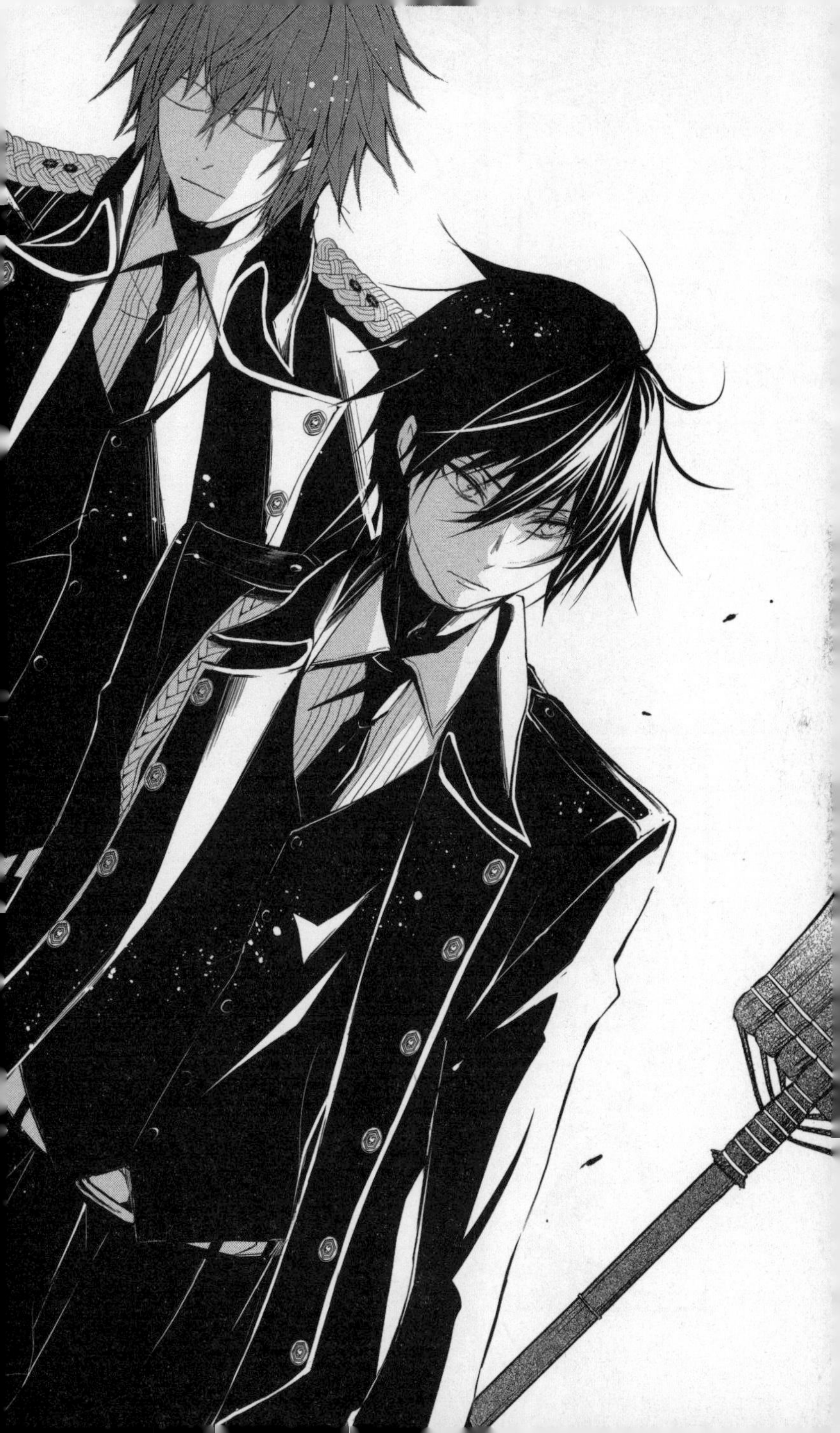

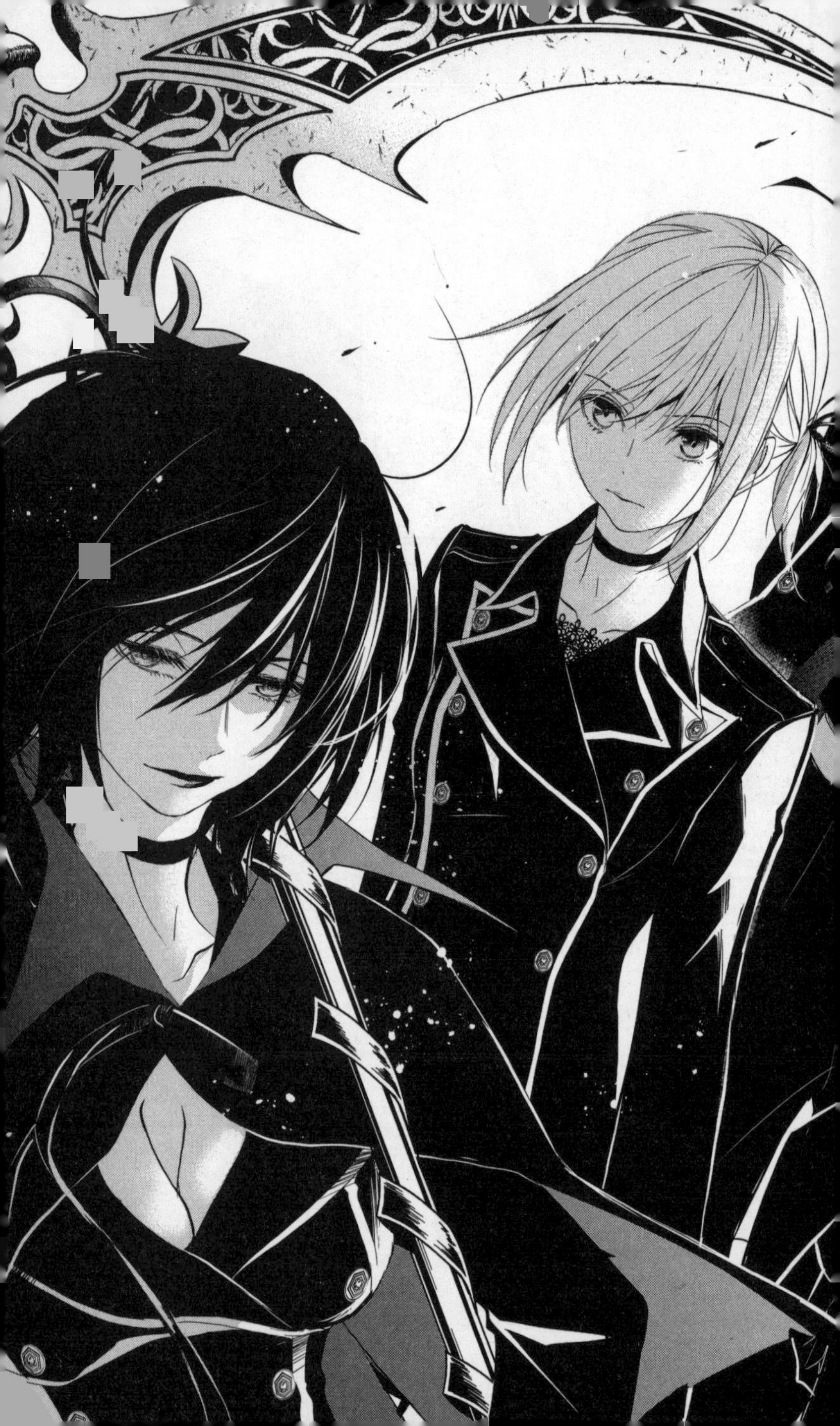

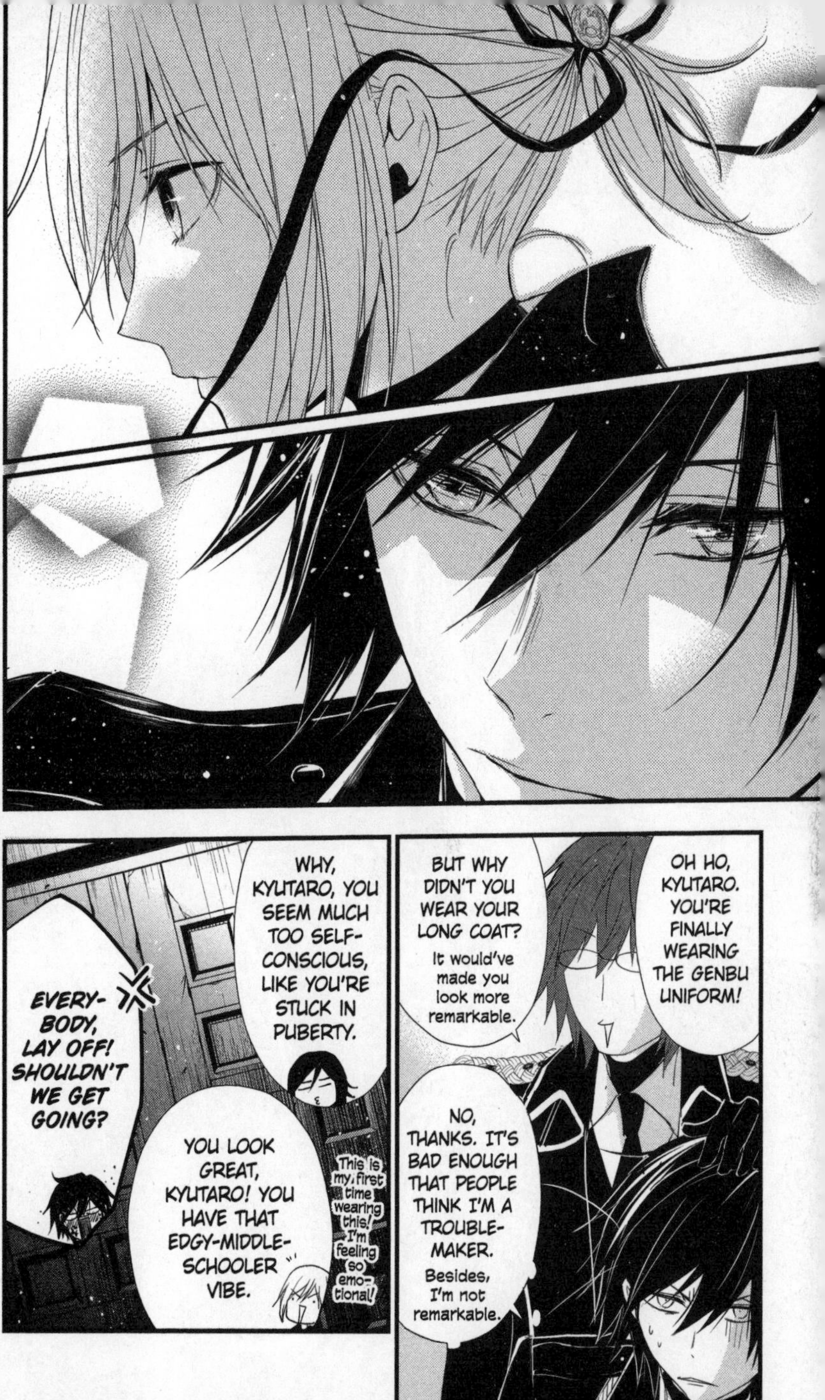
OH HO, KYUTARO. YOU'RE FINALLY WEARING THE GENBU UNIFORM!
BUT WHY DIDN'T YOU WEAR YOUR LONG COAT?
It would've made you look more remarkable.
NO, THANKS. IT'S BAD ENOUGH THAT PEOPLE THINK I'M A TROUBLE-MAKER.
Besides, I'm not remarkable.
WHY, KYUTARO, YOU SEEM MUCH TOO SELF-CONSCIOUS, LIKE YOU'RE STUCK IN PUBERTY.
YOU LOOK GREAT, KYUTARO! YOU HAVE THAT EDGY-MIDDLE-SCHOOLER VIBE.
This is my first time wearing this! I'm feeling so emotional!
EVERYBODY, LAY OFF! SHOULDN'T WE GET GOING?

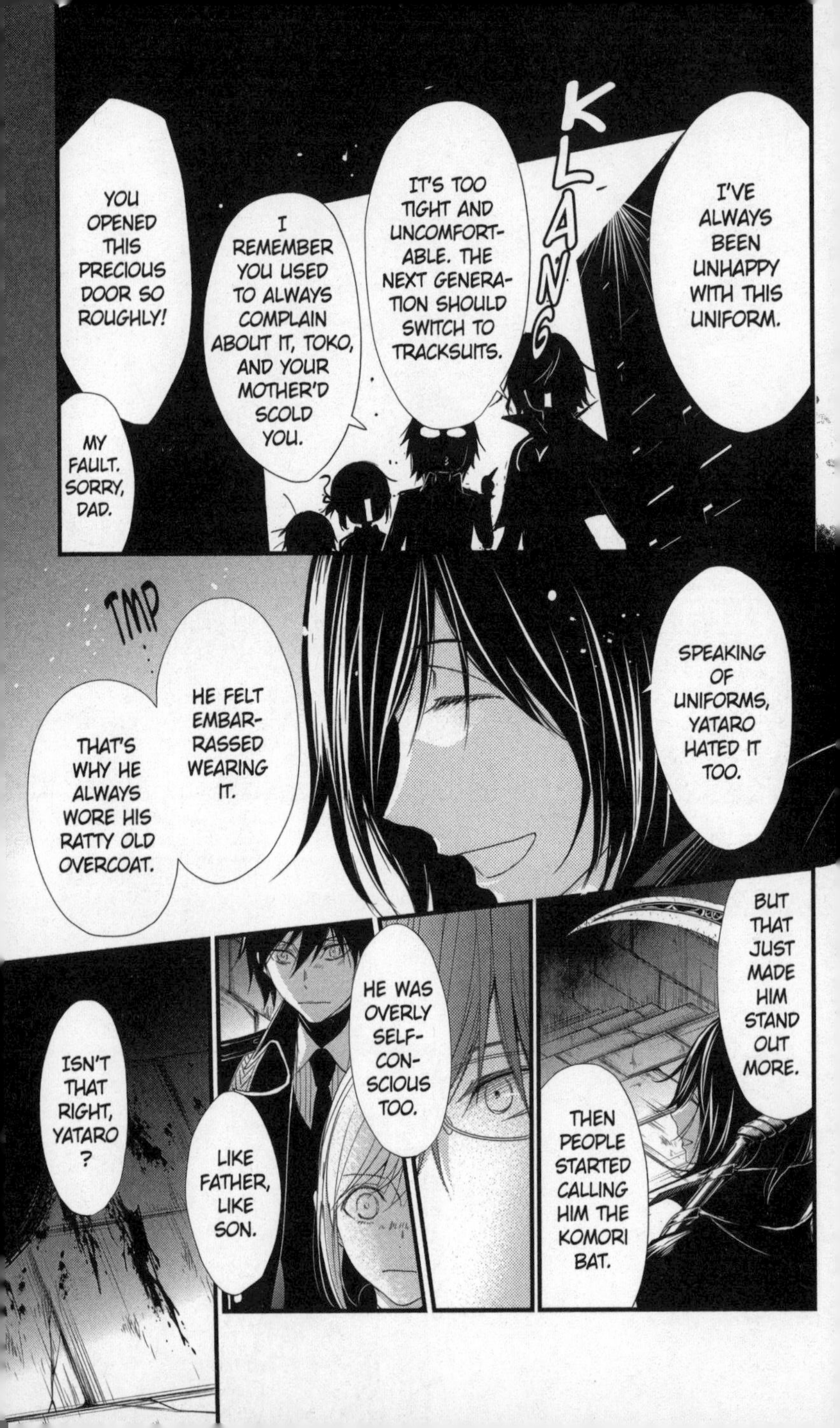
I'VE ALWAYS BEEN UNHAPPY WITH THIS UNIFORM.
KLANG
IT'S TOO TIGHT AND UNCOMFORTABLE. THE NEXT GENERATION SHOULD SWITCH TO TRACKSUITS.
I REMEMBER YOU USED TO ALWAYS COMPLAIN ABOUT IT, TOKO, AND YOUR MOTHER'D SCOLD YOU.
YOU OPENED THIS PRECIOUS DOOR SO ROUGHLY!
MY FAULT. SORRY, DAD.
SPEAKING OF UNIFORMS, YATARO HATED IT TOO.
HE FELT EMBARRASSED WEARING IT.
THAT'S WHY HE ALWAYS WORE HIS RATTY OLD OVERCOAT.
TMP
BUT THAT JUST MADE HIM STAND OUT MORE.
THEN PEOPLE STARTED CALLING HIM THE KOMORI BAT.
HE WAS OVERLY SELF-CONSCIOUS TOO.
LIKE FATHER, LIKE SON.
ISN'T THAT RIGHT, YATARO?

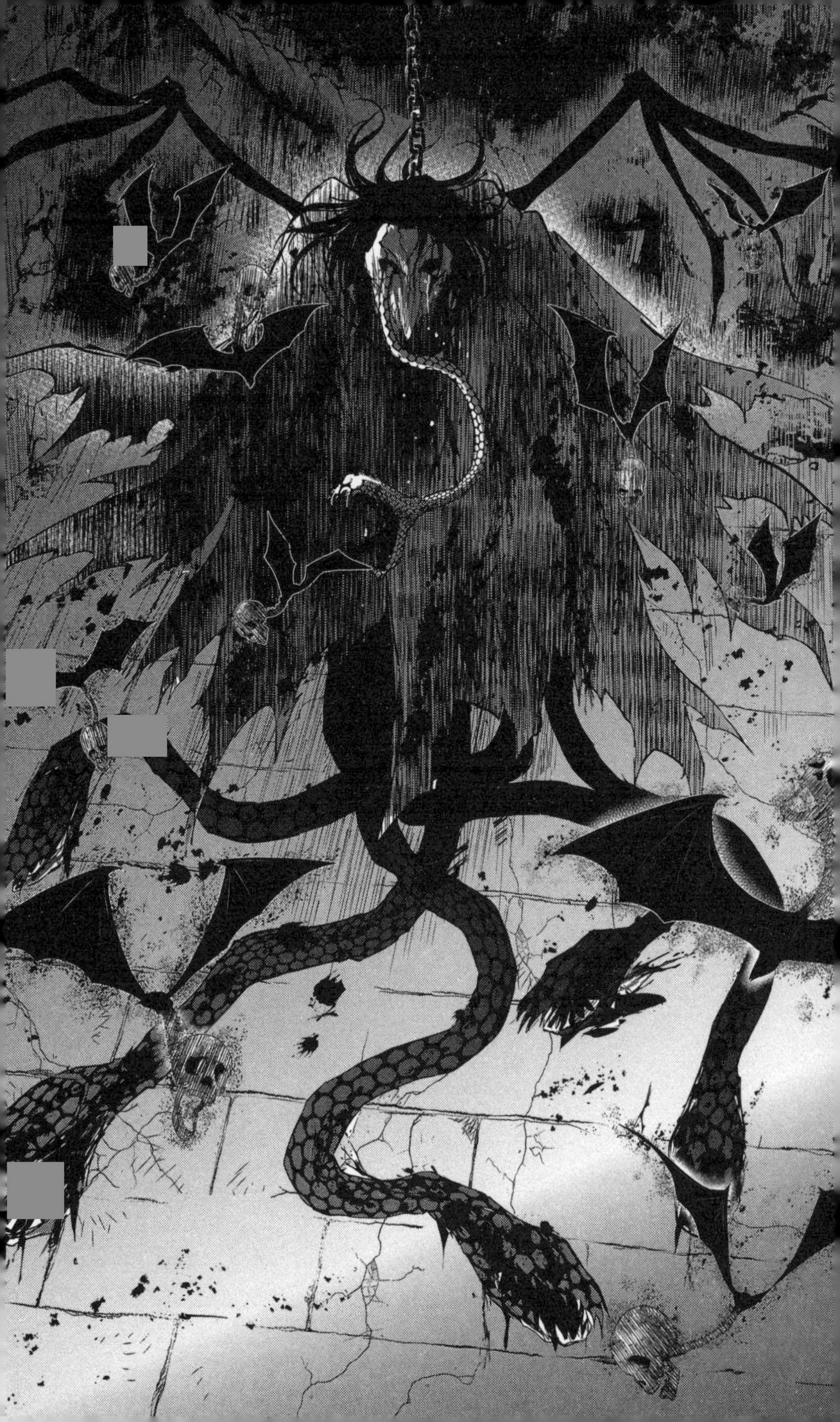

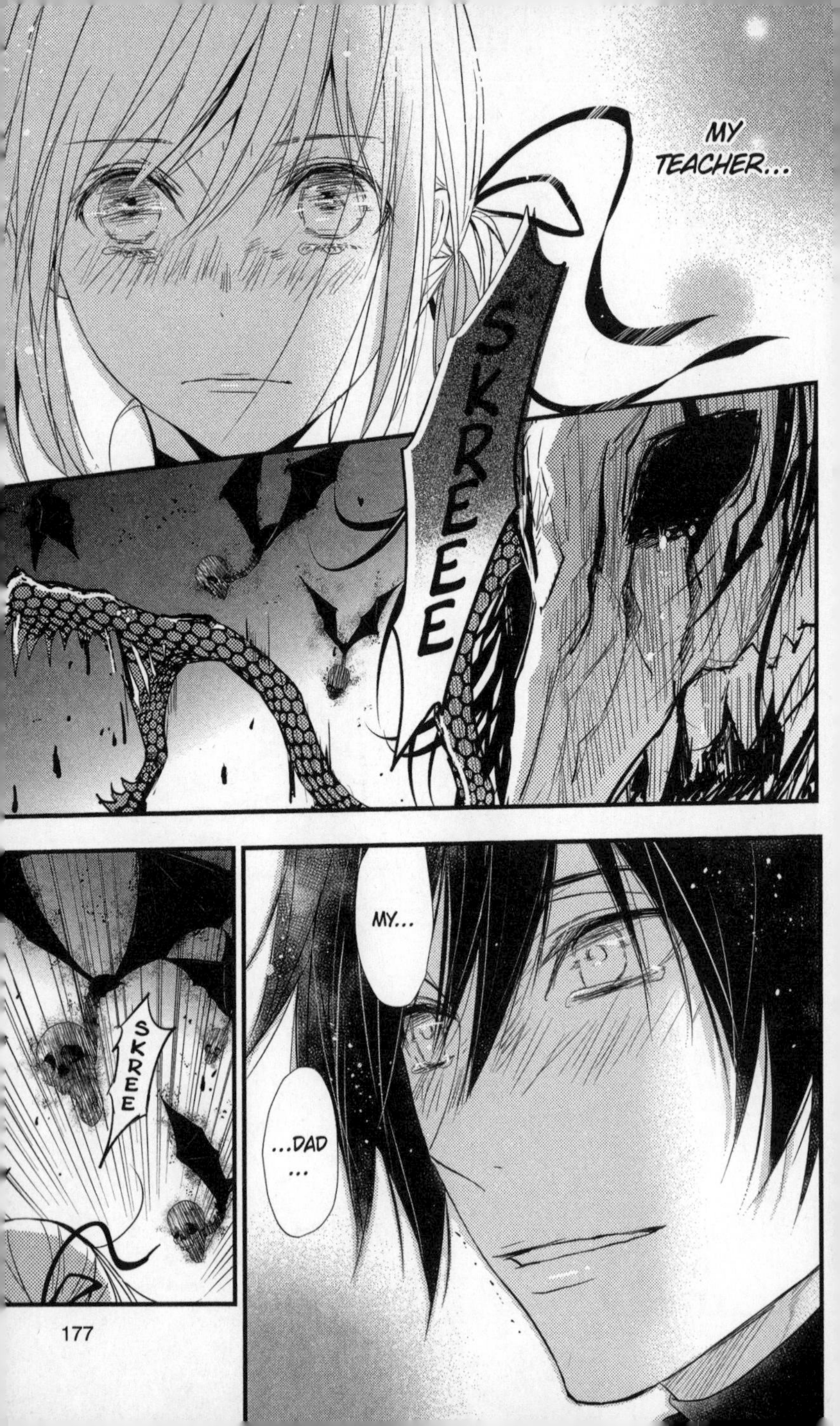
MY TEACHER...
SKREEE
MY...
...DAD ...
SKREE

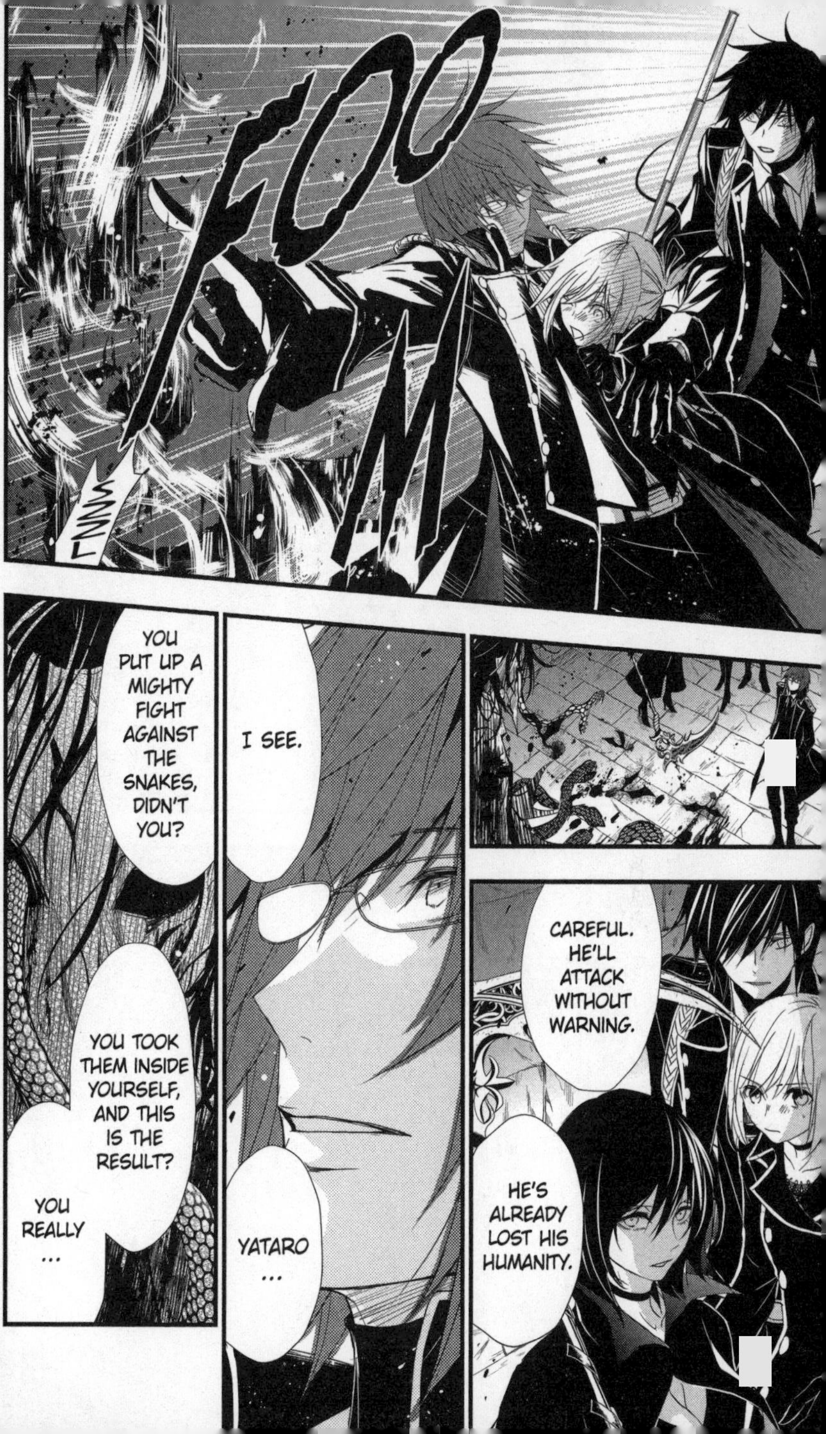
FOOM
SZZL
CAREFUL. HE'LL ATTACK WITHOUT WARNING.
HE'S ALREADY LOST HIS HUMANITY.
I SEE.
YATARO...
YOU PUT UP A MIGHTY FIGHT AGAINST THE SNAKES, DIDN'T YOU?
YOU TOOK THEM INSIDE YOURSELF, AND THIS IS THE RESULT?
YOU REALLY...

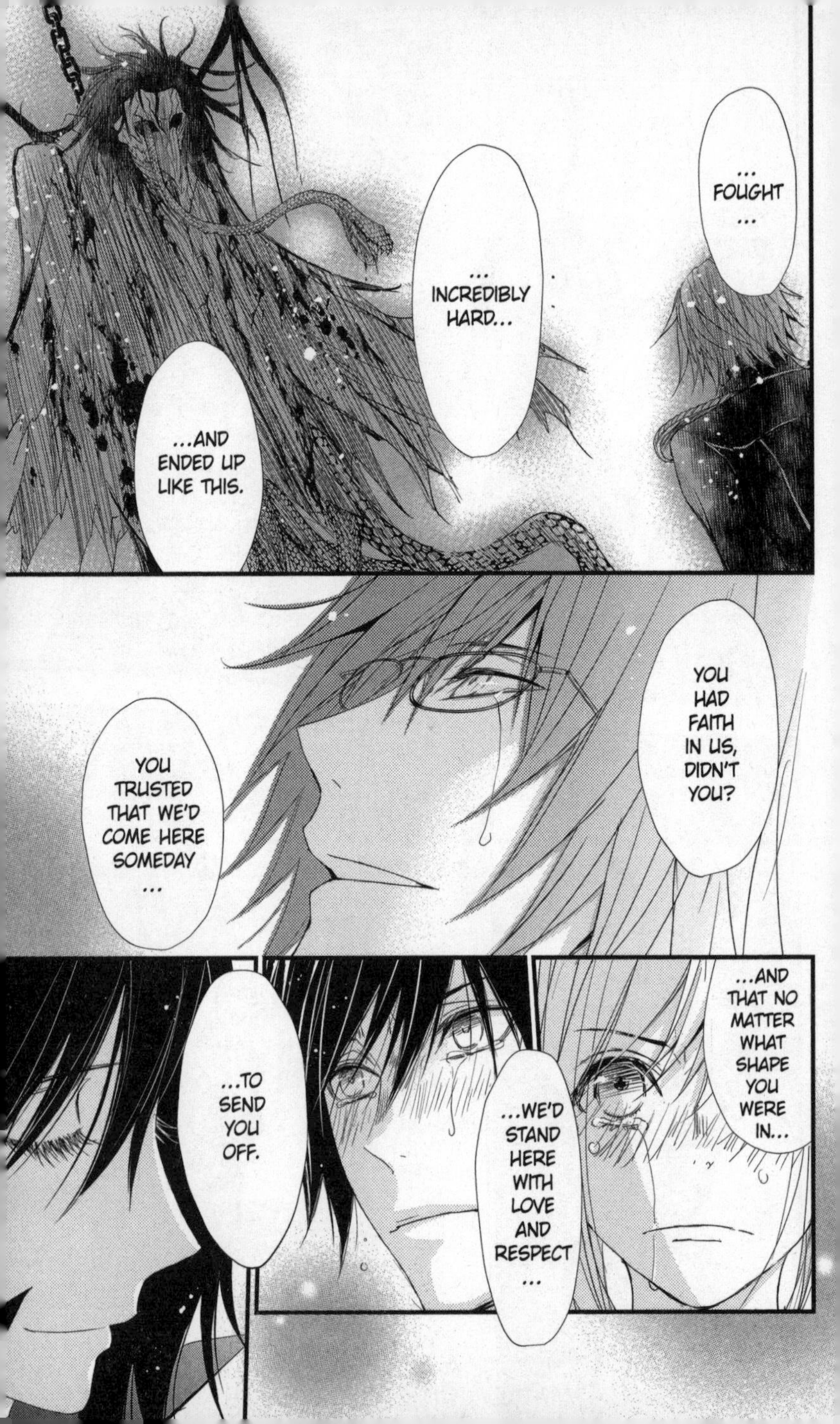
...FOUGHT...
...INCREDIBLY HARD...
...AND ENDED UP LIKE THIS.
YOU HAD FAITH IN US, DIDN'T YOU?
YOU TRUSTED THAT WE'D COME HERE SOMEDAY...
...AND THAT NO MATTER WHAT SHAPE YOU WERE IN...
...WE'D STAND HERE WITH LOVE AND RESPECT...
...TO SEND YOU OFF.

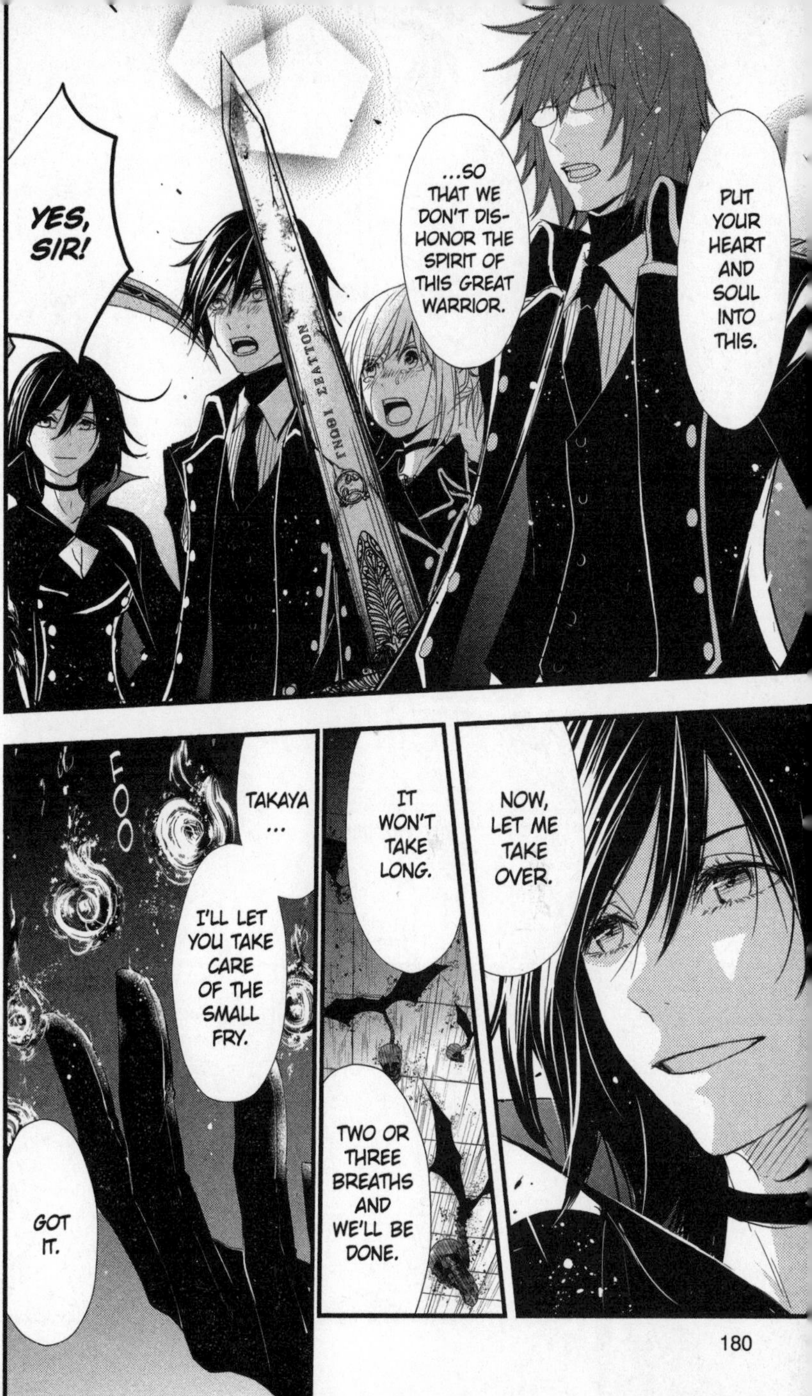
PUT YOUR HEART AND SOUL INTO THIS.
...SO THAT WE DON'T DIS-HONOR THE SPIRIT OF THIS GREAT WARRIOR.
YES, SIR!
NOW, LET ME TAKE OVER.
IT WON'T TAKE LONG.
TWO OR THREE BREATHS AND WE'LL BE DONE.
TAKAYA ...
I'LL LET YOU TAKE CARE OF THE SMALL FRY.
FOO
GOT IT.

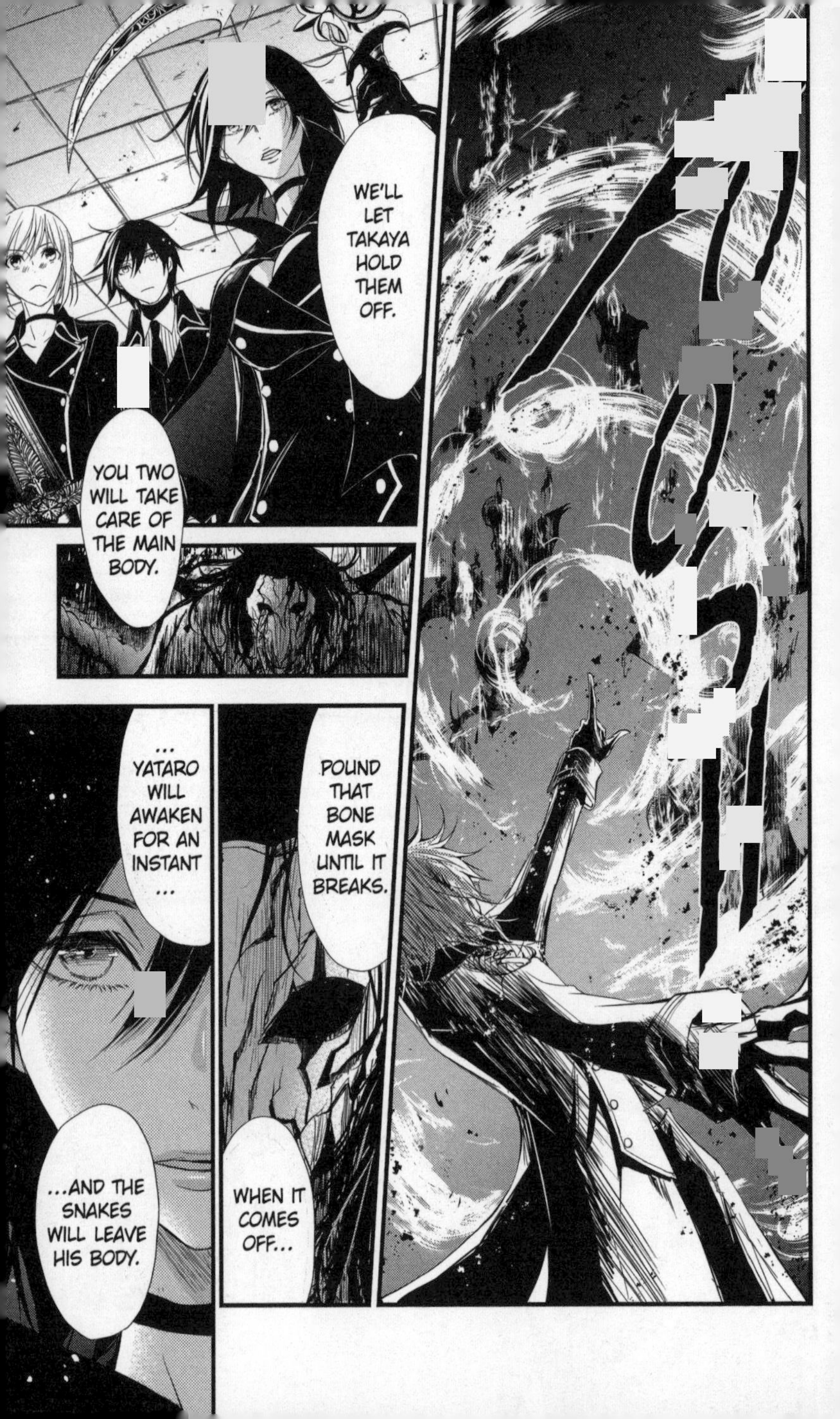
WE'LL LET TAKAYA HOLD THEM OFF.
YOU TWO WILL TAKE CARE OF THE MAIN BODY.
POUND THAT BONE MASK UNTIL IT BREAKS.
WHEN IT COMES OFF...
...YATARO WILL AWAKEN FOR AN INSTANT...
...AND THE SNAKES WILL LEAVE HIS BODY.

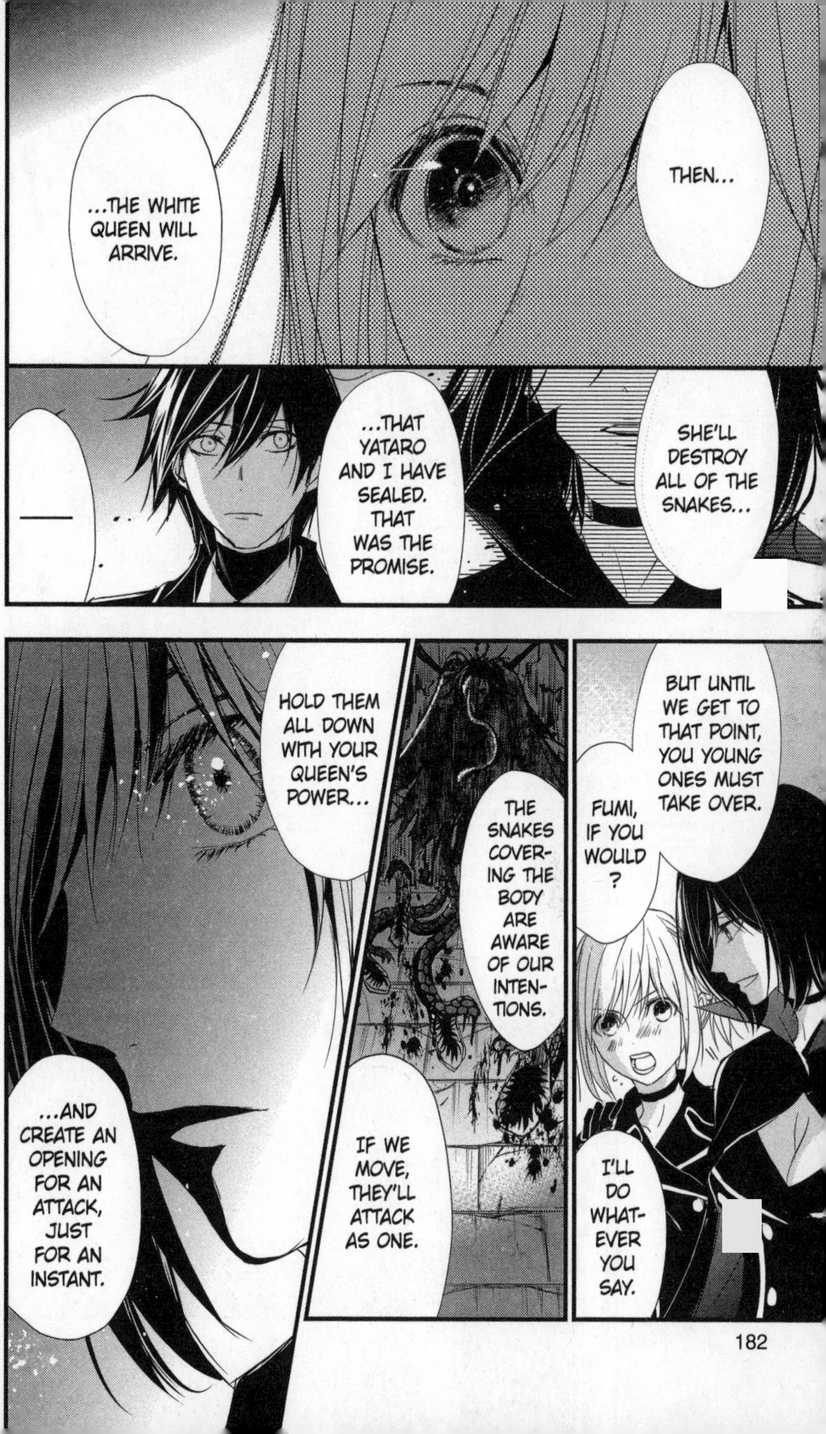
THEN...
...THE WHITE QUEEN WILL ARRIVE.
SHE'LL DESTROY ALL OF THE SNAKES...
...THAT YATARO AND I HAVE SEALED. THAT WAS THE PROMISE.
——
BUT UNTIL WE GET TO THAT POINT, YOU YOUNG ONES MUST TAKE OVER.
FUMI, IF YOU WOULD?
I'LL DO WHATEVER YOU SAY.
THE SNAKES COVERING THE BODY ARE AWARE OF OUR INTENTIONS.
IF WE MOVE, THEY'LL ATTACK AS ONE.
HOLD THEM ALL DOWN WITH YOUR QUEEN'S POWER...
...AND CREATE AN OPENING FOR AN ATTACK, JUST FOR AN INSTANT.

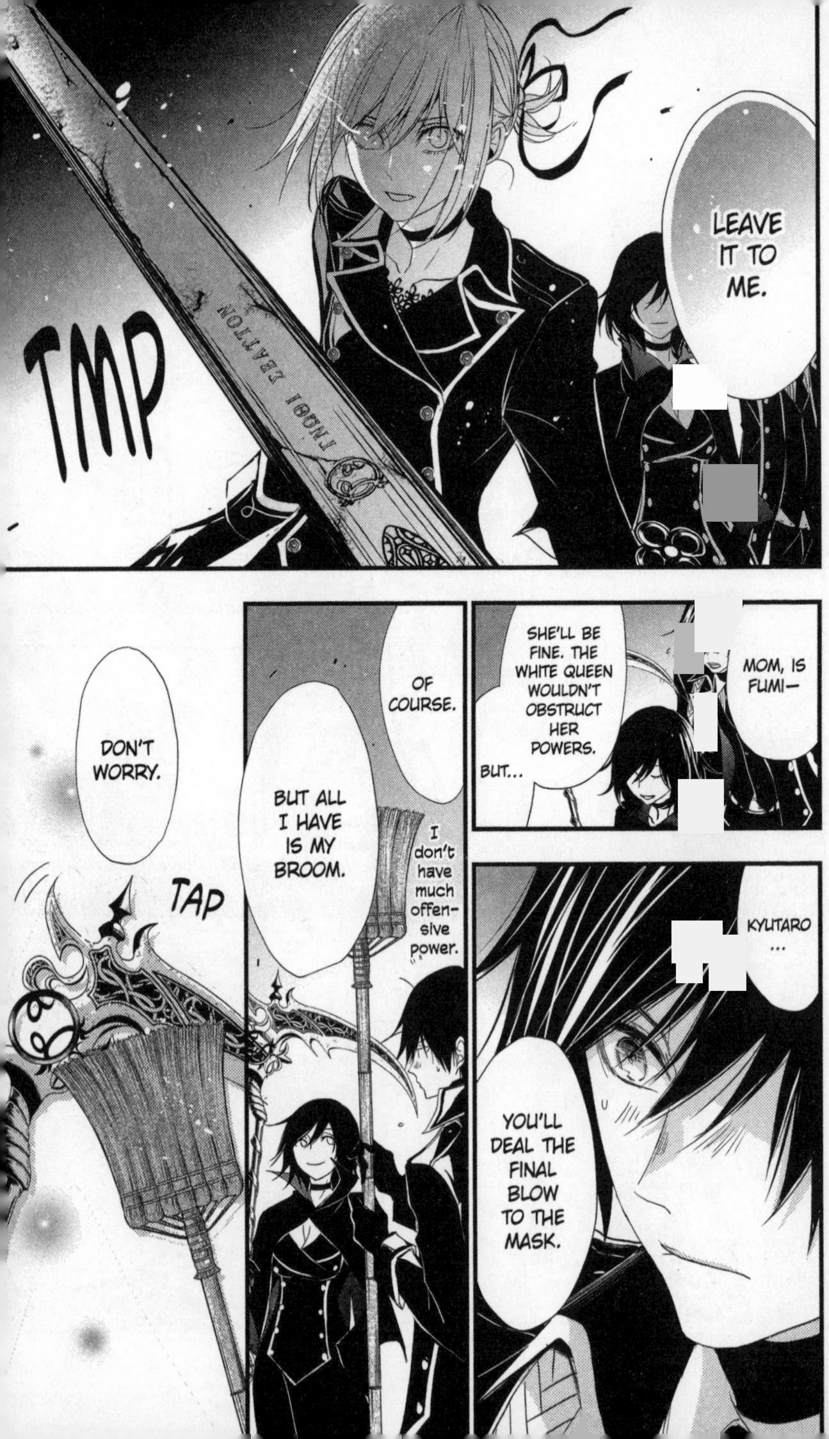

LEAVE IT TO ME.
TMP
MOM, IS FUMI—
SHE'LL BE FINE. THE WHITE QUEEN WOULDN'T OBSTRUCT HER POWERS.
BUT...
KYUTARO...
YOU'LL DEAL THE FINAL BLOW TO THE MASK.
OF COURSE.
BUT ALL I HAVE IS MY BROOM.
I don't have much offen-sive power.
DON'T WORRY.
TAP

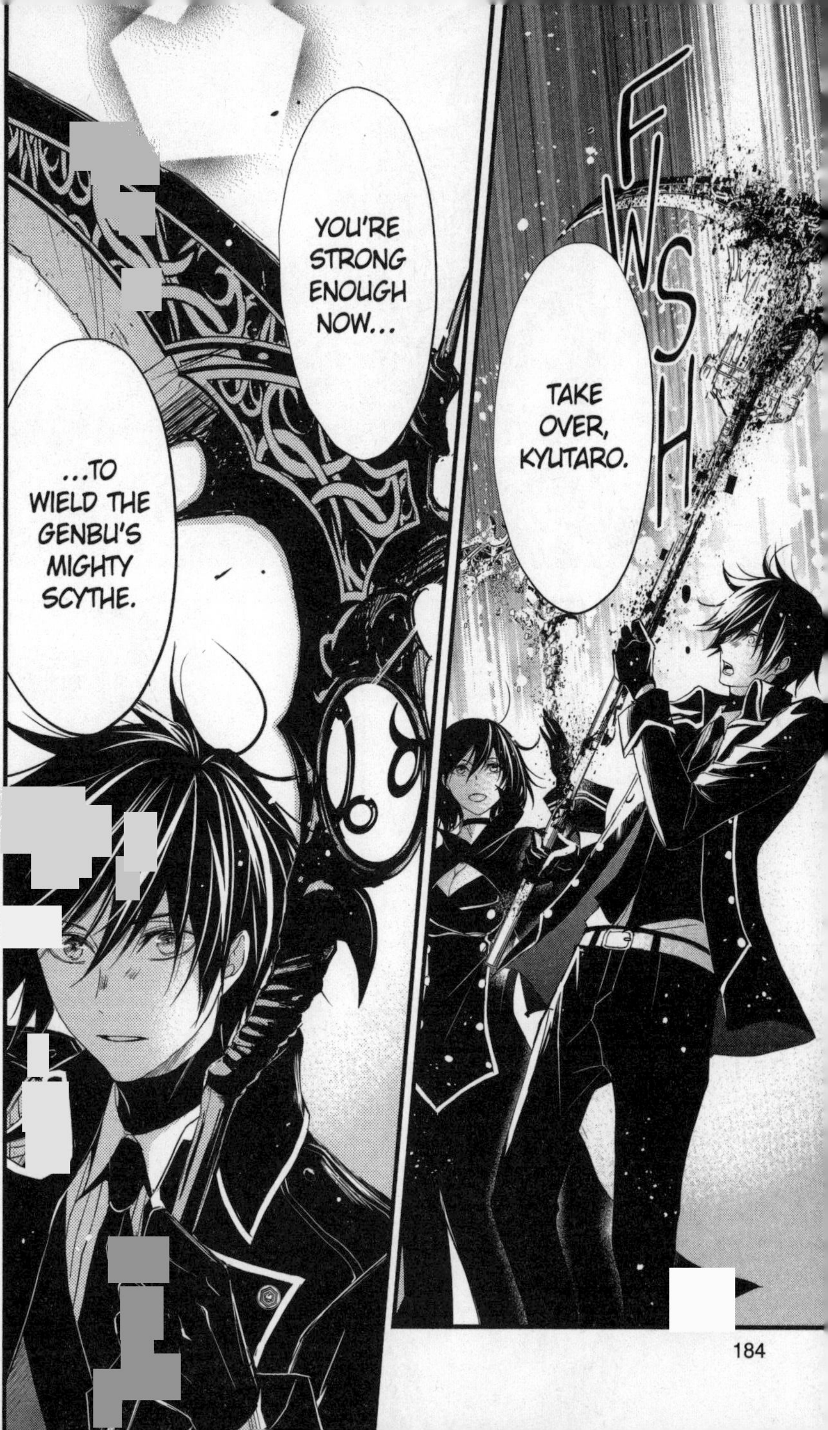
FWSH
TAKE OVER, KYUTARO.
YOU'RE STRONG ENOUGH NOW...
...TO WIELD THE GENBU'S MIGHTY SCYTHE.

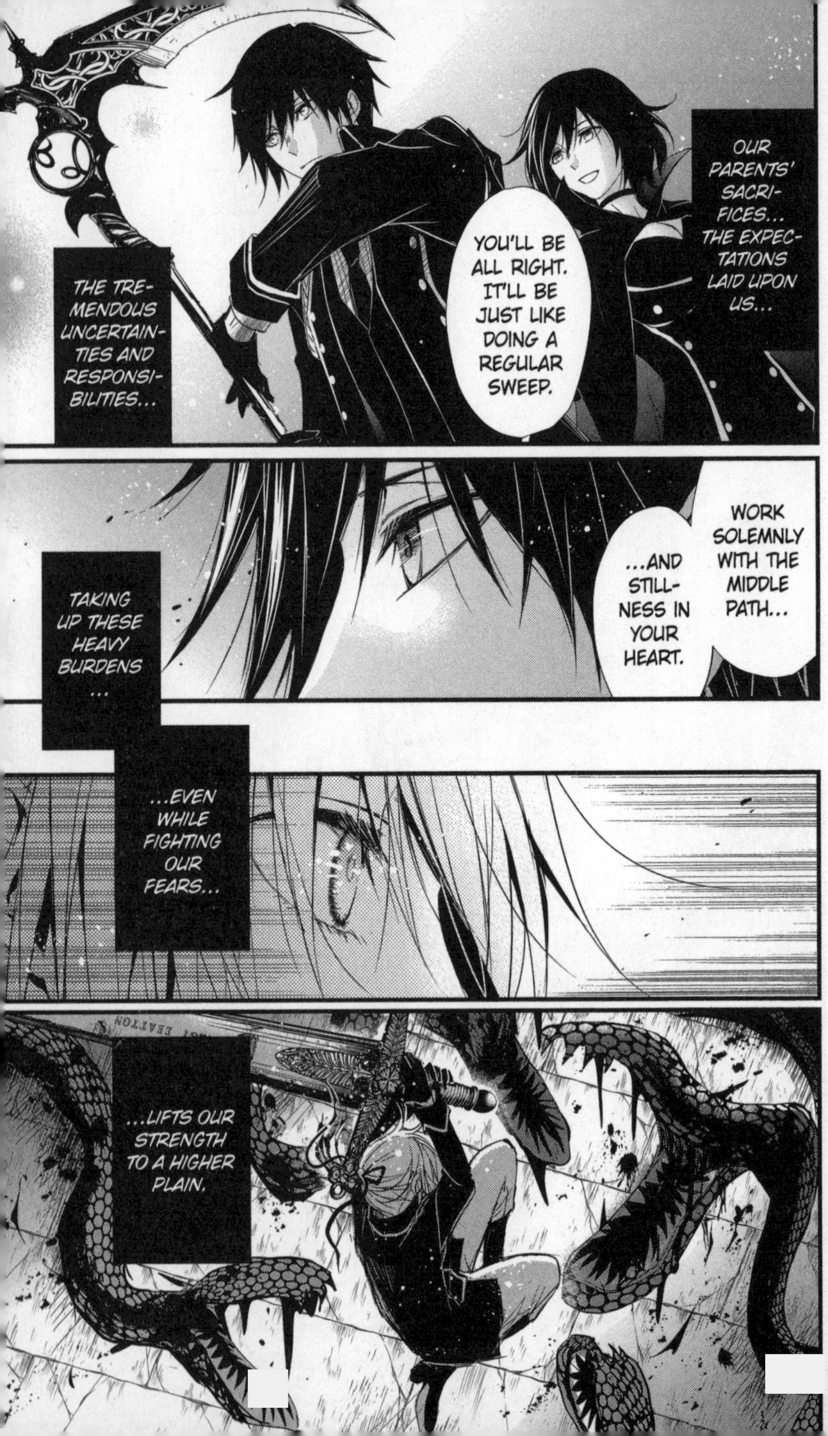
OUR PARENTS' SACRIFICES... THE EXPECTATIONS LAID UPON US...
YOU'LL BE ALL RIGHT. IT'LL BE JUST LIKE DOING A REGULAR SWEEP.
THE TREMENDOUS UNCERTAINTIES AND RESPONSIBILITIES...
WORK SOLEMNLY WITH THE MIDDLE PATH...
...AND STILLNESS IN YOUR HEART.
TAKING UP THESE HEAVY BURDENS...
...EVEN WHILE FIGHTING OUR FEARS...
...LIFTS OUR STRENGTH TO A HIGHER PLAIN.

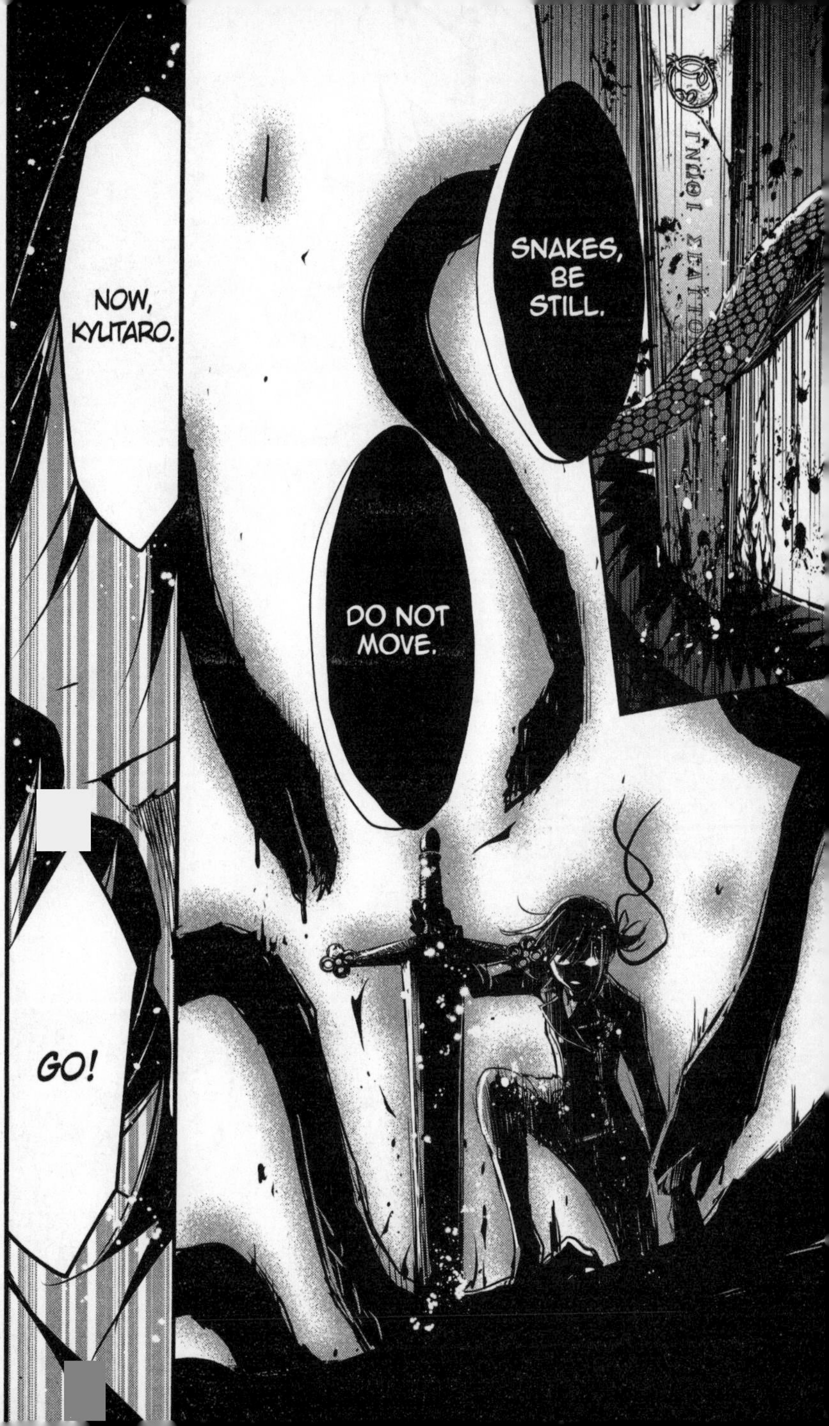
SNAKES, BE STILL.
DO NOT MOVE.
NOW, KYUTARO.
GO!

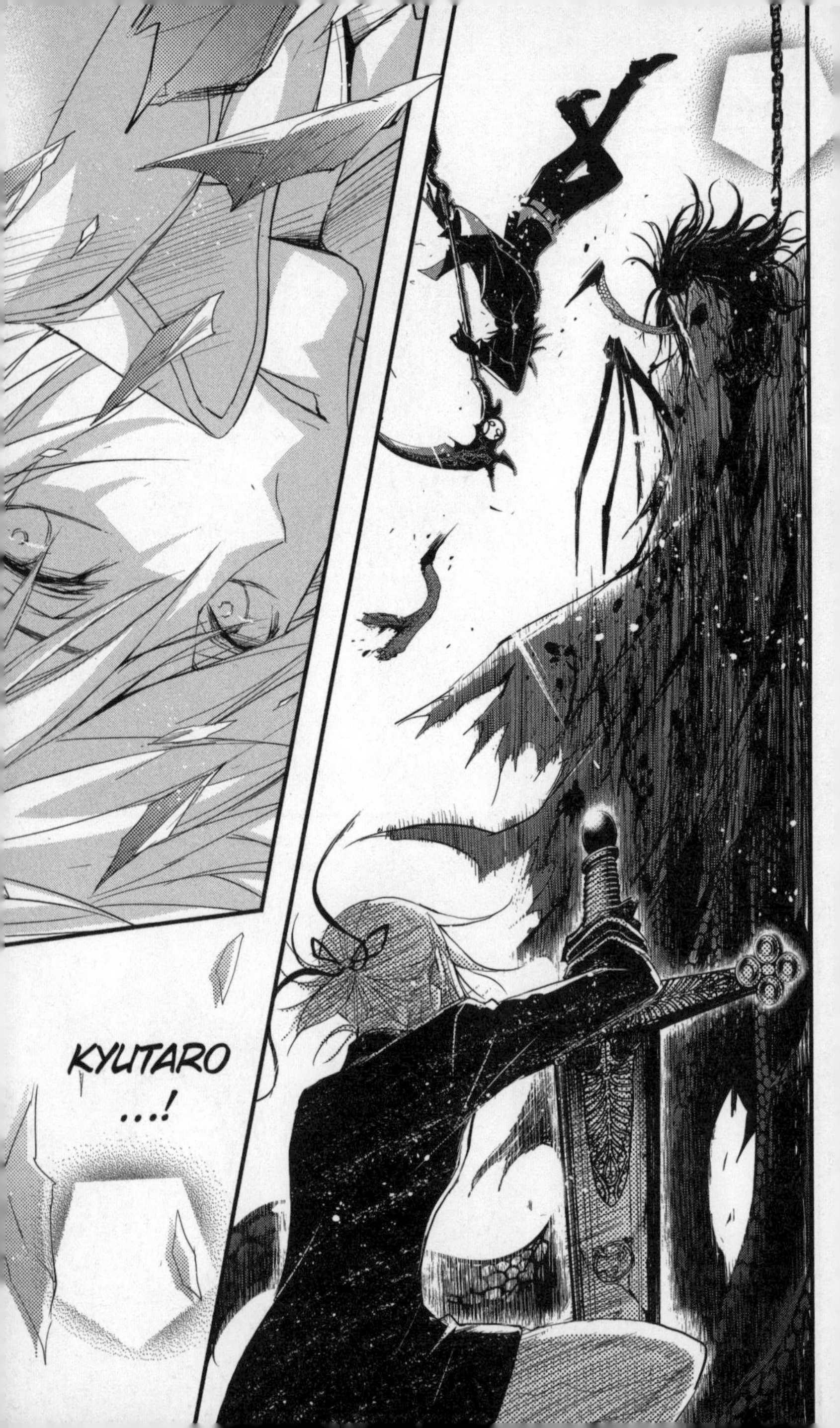
KYUTARO
...!

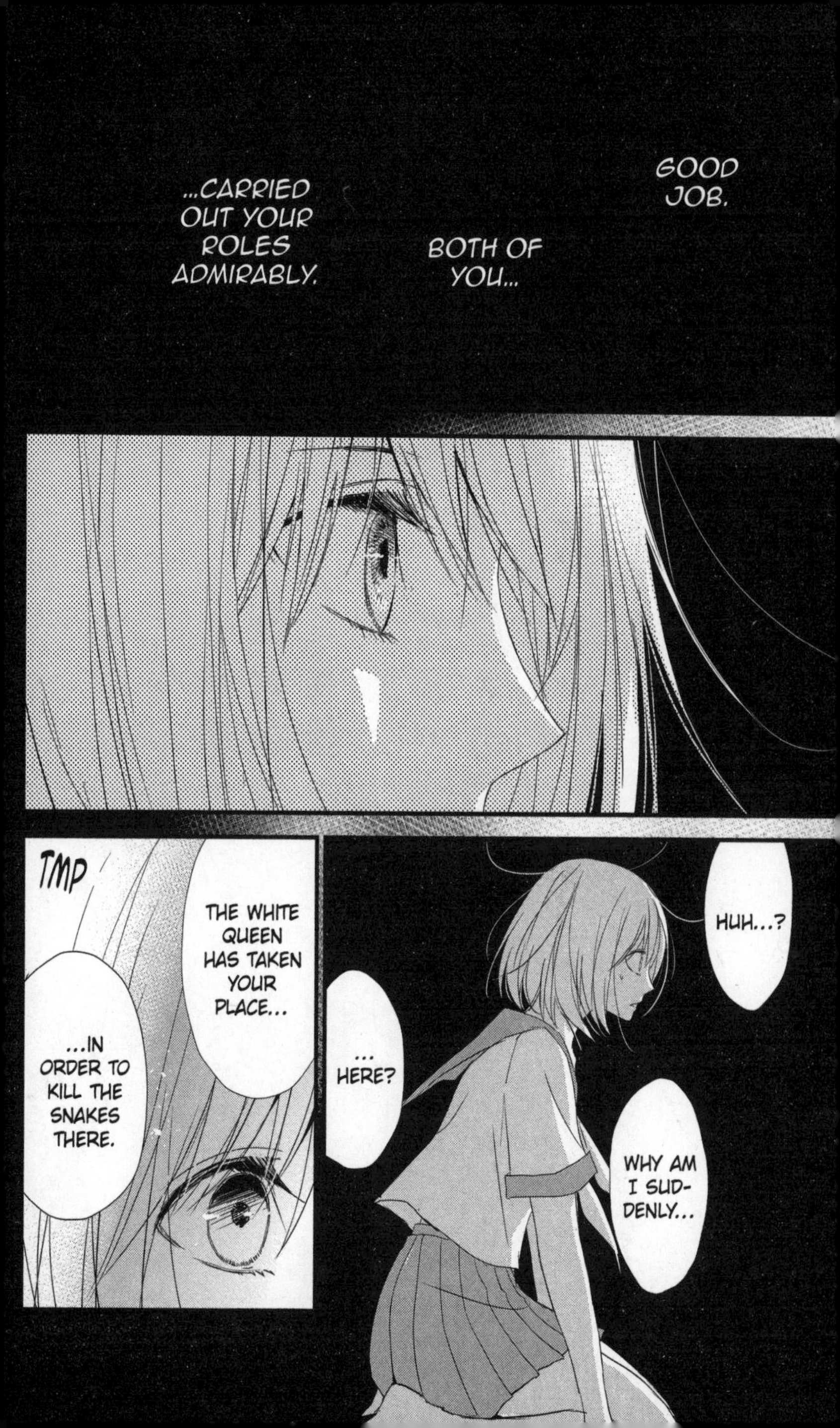
GOOD JOB.
BOTH OF YOU...
...CARRIED OUT YOUR ROLES ADMIRABLY.
HUH...?
WHY AM I SUD-DENLY...
...HERE?
TMP
THE WHITE QUEEN HAS TAKEN YOUR PLACE...
...IN ORDER TO KILL THE SNAKES THERE.

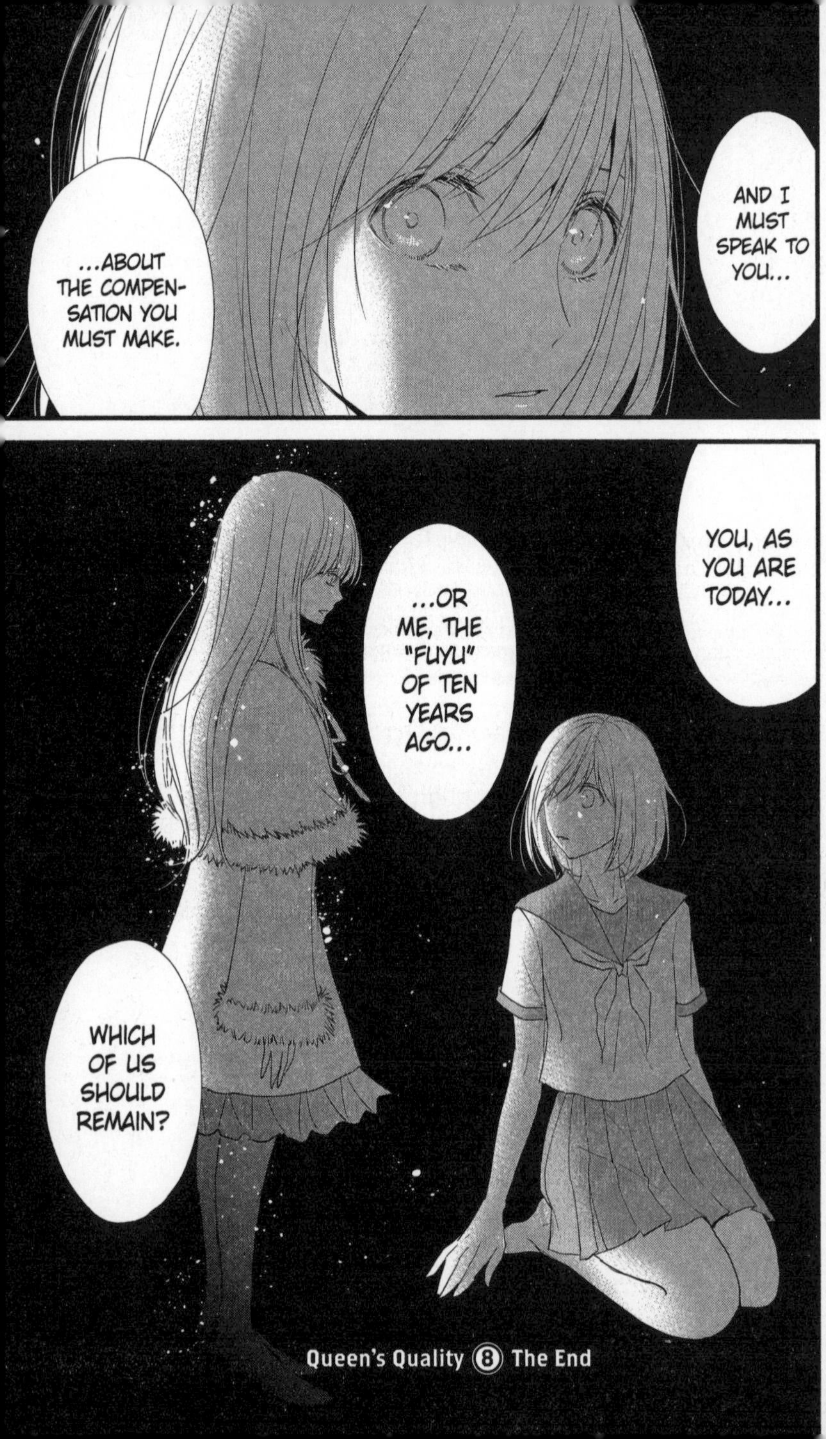
AND I MUST SPEAK TO YOU...
...ABOUT THE COMPEN-SATION YOU MUST MAKE.
YOU, AS YOU ARE TODAY...
...OR ME, THE "FUYU" OF TEN YEARS AGO...
WHICH OF US SHOULD REMAIN?
Queen's Quality 8 The End

This is my silver Java sparrow, Kojiro. He observes my work from his cage, which is right next to my desk. No matter if I'm having a difficult day or not, he sits there looking cute. And he bathes every day, which is more than I can say for this manga artist.

—Kyousuke Motomi

Author Bio

Born on August 1, Kyousuke Motomi debuted in *Deluxe Betsucomi* with *Hetakuso Kyupiddo* (No Good Cupid) in 2002. She is the creator of *Dengeki Daisy*, *Beast Master* and *QQ Sweeper*, all available in North America from VIZ Media. Motomi enjoys sleeping, tea ceremonies and reading Haruki Murakami.